Hoover, Conservation, and Consumerism

Hoover, Conservation, and Consumerism

Engineering the Good Life

Kendrick A. Clements

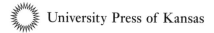 University Press of Kansas

© 2000 by the University Press of Kansas
All rights reserved

Published by the University Press of Kansas (Lawrence, Kansas 66049), which was organized by the Kansas Board of Regents and is operated and funded by Emporia State University, Fort Hays State University, Kansas State University, Pittsburg State University, the University of Kansas, and Wichita State University

Library of Congress Cataloging-in-Publication Data

Clements, Kendrick A., 1939–
    Hoover, conservation, and consumerism : engineering the good life /
    Kendrick A. Clements.
        p.   cm.
    Includes bibliographical references and index.
    ISBN 0-7006-1033-2 (alk. paper)
        1. Consumption (Economics)—United States—Moral and ethical aspects. 2. Conservation of natural resources—United States. 3. Environmental economics—United States. 4. Environmental policy—United States. 5. Hoover, Herbert, 1874–1964.

    HC110.C6 C53 2000
    333.7′0973—dc21   00-028316

British Library Cataloguing in Publication Data is available.

Printed in the United States of America

10 9 8 7 6 5 4 3 2 1

The paper used in this publication meets the minimum requirements of the American National Standard for Permanence of Paper for Printed Library Materials Z39.48-1984.

The Compleat Angler

How to use a dunghill grub,
How to lure a bream or chub,
How to make a rod that whips,
And a hundred other tips—
Here are tales and hints galore
To delight you, piscator.

Long ago, these angles worked,
Creels filled up and spirits perked;
Free from care and trouble, you
Strolled with Izaak W.,
While he rapped with charm and wit
On the bait-and-tackle bit.
Ah, what sport the fish to burke!
Ere pollution did the work.

—Izaak Walton

Contents

Preface

When I began graduate school in the early 1960s, only a few hardy pioneers, such as Roderick Nash and Samuel Hays, were writing environmental history. So, although I was introduced to conservation by my parents and spent a lot of time in the outdoors, it did not occur to me to attempt to make a career as an environmental historian. This book is a belated return to an early love.

But how much richer environmental history has become since the 1960s! Agriculture, economics, business history, resource management, medicine, ecology, and an enormous variety of other subjects have all been shown to be relevant to a full understanding of the history of human relationships with the environment. Even since I last visited the subject of Hoover and conservation in a 1984 article in the *American Historical Review,* the boundaries of the field have expanded. Readers hoping to find a synopsis of this book in that article should be warned that it is now outdated.

I hope and believe that the book is the better for having been postponed for a number of years. Had it been written in the 1980s, one of its central themes, the relationship between Hoover's environmental activities and the development of the consumer economy, would have been largely missing. My colleague Larry Glickman introduced me to this field and has been my reliable guide through it. Larry also gave the manuscript a thorough and perceptive reading, and his helpful comments ranged far beyond consumer issues.

My recognition of the complex relationship between consumerism and the environment was the starting point for a reexamination of what I had envisioned originally to be mainly "gap" history, a book on conservation during a period previously little studied, the 1920s. Aside from the pioneering work of Donald Swain, which was written before the opening of the Hoover Library and therefore focused almost exclusively on the activities of federal bureaucracies responsible for conservation, and later suggestive articles by such historians as Douglas Drake and Carl Krog, most interpreters tended to dismiss Republican administrations as anticonservationist. For most people, Teapot Dome was emblematic of the decade.

But as I dug through the documents in the Hoover Library, the National Archives, and a number of other collections, including those at the Hoover Institution and Stanford University's library, I began to understand that

Hoover envisioned conservation in quite different terms than most people had assumed. He saw it as a foundation for and an integral part of a prosperous economy whose benefits he hoped to extend not just to the wealthy but to all Americans. He believed that prudent, planned use of resources could assure widespread prosperity, and he assumed that a rising standard of living would bring demands for greater opportunities for outdoor recreation and for a healthy, attractive environment. Quality of life thus came to be nearly as as important to him as assuring prosperity. Increasingly, he came to think, as did many other Americans during the years after World War II, that protecting the environment was essential if people were to be able to enjoy fully the benefits of a successful economy.

All of this makes it tempting to suggest that Hoover anticipated the environmental movement that Samuel Hays argued, in *Beauty, Health and Permanence*, began only after World War II, and there was a time when I considered doing just that. In the end, I decided against that interpretation because I realized that while there were strains of environmentalism in Hoover's thought, it also included a preconservation frontier ethic of development, elements of the Progressive idea of utilitarian conservation, and even adumbrations of the envirocapitalist theories of our own day. To stress one theme at the expense of others would distort reality, so although *Beauty, Health and Permanence* was in my mind as I wrote (as it will probably be for many readers), I did not introduce it specifically until the last chapter, which deals with the post-World War II period. Interestingly, it is evident at that point that Hoover was *not* an environmentalist in Hays's terms. He probably never was.

Given Hoover's background and experience, it is hardly surprising that there were contradictory elements in his environmental thought and policy. American prosperity in the 1920s was based on the rapid and frequently careless exploitation of resources by large organizations. As a mining engineer and businessman, Hoover was a part of that process. Conservation and environmentalism, on the other hand, seemed to require less instead of more resource development, simplified and less materialistic lifestyles, and a shift in control over daily life from large organizations to individuals. By background and personal taste, Hoover shared these ideals; but by training and profession, he was a part of the era's trend toward development, organization, and centralization. How the tensions among these approaches to life affected his outlook and policies is one of the main issues that this book attempts to explore. It seems to me an issue relevant to our own times as well.

Acknowledgments

In a project that takes so many years to come to fruition, debts to others become mountainous. I would like to acknowledge a few in particular, though I realize that I am surely overlooking other people who equally deserve my thanks. In addition to my gratitude to Larry Glickman, whom I have already mentioned, I would particularly like to thank George Nash, whom I first met at the Hoover Library in the 1980s, and who has been a never-failing source of wise counsel over the years. As my notes will testify, I have made good use of the prodigious research that went into George's three large volumes and several smaller works on Hoover's life prior to 1918. These beautifully written and carefully argued books well deserve to be called definitive. But my debt to George does not end with what he has published. He read an earlier version of the manuscript of this book with meticulous care and provided me with extensive notes and comments, all of which were expressed with characteristic courtesy and kindness, even when he disagreed with me. I'm sure he won't agree completely with this version either, but I am grateful to him for his many suggestions, and particularly for pushing me to look at Hoover's activities and ideas in their own terms, and for introducing me to the modern field of conservative environmentalism, or envirocapitalism, which I have found helpful in explaining some strengths and weaknesses of Hoover's views.

Others who read the manuscript from many different perspectives include my colleagues Jessica Kross and Robert Weyeneth, and my old friend Richard Rempel. I asked them to read it largely because their own work has been in fields distant from Hoover and environmentalism. Their questions and suggestions were of enormous benefit to me in revising the manuscript to make it more readable and comprehensible to nonspecialists. I probably imposed on them unfairly, but I profited from their advice more than they may realize. I am also grateful to a reader for the University Press of Kansas who gave the manuscript an amazingly quick but perceptive reading and declined to be identified because he felt he had not been as thorough as he would have liked, and to David E. Hamilton, the second reader, whose constructive suggestions and generous comments I'll go back and reread in the future whenever I'm feeling low. At the University Press of Kansas, Fred Woodward, Susan Schott,

Melinda Wirkus, and freelance copyeditor Darlene Bledsoe shepherded the manuscript through the publication process quickly and efficiently.

During the two months I spent at the Hoover Library in the 1980s, and in various subsequent visits, I had the benefit of the wisdom and experience of two generations of skilled archivists. Directors Thomas Thalken and Timothy Walch were both accessible and supportive, while staff members, including Mildred Mather, Dale Mayer, Dwight Miller, Shirley Sondergard, J. Patrick Wildenberg, and Robert Wood, provided information, advice, and informal companionship. If there is a pleasanter place for an historian to work, I don't know what it is.

As a stranger in a small town, I was particularly happy to find Elliot Rosen also working at the Hoover Library. His wit and shrewd judgments brightened many a lunch we shared on the grounds of the library, and he and his wife Carol frequently welcomed me to their apartment in Iowa City, and later to their home in New Jersey. Old friends Kris and Gene Ridings also enlivened my stay with an invitation to their home in Minnesota for a long weekend. And Mrs. George Jensen, who rented me a pleasant room in her home just across the street from the library, was a welcoming and friendly face after many a long day.

Elsewhere, Richard Crawford and Donald Mosholder at the National Archives were cordial and professionally expert despite budget cuts that left them overworked and, I suspect, underpaid. Mrs. Virginia Rust at the Huntington Library, Carol Rudisill at the Stanford Library, Linda Long at the Stanford University Archives, Gene M. Gressley and Emmett D. Chisholm at the University of Wyoming's Special Collections, Hilary Cummings and Brian Lematta at the University of Oregon Library, and Ron Fahl, Mary E. Johnson, and Harold K. ("Pete") Steen at the Forest History Society facilitated my work in many ways. Other scholars who gave me access to unpublished work, answered questions, or provided helpful advice include Patrick Allitt, Hugh Gorman, Barry MacKintosh, Gerald Nash, Steven J. Randall, Elmo Richardson, William Robbins, and Joseph E. Taylor III. I owe a special debt to Northcutt Ely, who not only gave me permission to use his papers at Stanford, but who took time from a busy family weekend to talk to me and answer some questions.

In Berkeley and elsewhere my brother- and sister-in-law, David and Susie Hodges, have offered me generous hospitality and thoughtful comments on my work. Dave, a distinguished engineer, read my chapter on Hoover's engineering work and helped me avoid technical blunders. My cousin and his wife, Tom and Valen Kendrick, welcomed me to their home in Washington while I was doing research, and later Valen made me equally welcome in her apartment there. An old friend, Nancy Welch Barnby gave me a pleasant and convenient place to stay near Stanford. To all these friends and family, including my wife, Linda, and sons, Wilson and James (who salvaged a number of "lost" computer files at a crucial moment), I can only say that I wish I could express adequately how much your love, friendship, and encouragement have meant over the years.

Finally, I am indebted to the University of South Carolina Research and Productive Scholarship Committee and to former dean Chester Bain for grants that forwarded this project. And I am especially grateful for the generous support of the Hoover Presidential Library Association, whose Perrine Fellowship enabled me to take a year's leave from teaching, during which most of the basic research for the book was completed. This book truly demonstrates that all scholarship builds on the work of others.

Hoover, Conservation, and Consumerism

Introduction

During the 1928 presidential campaign, Herbert Hoover famously declared that America was "nearer to the final triumph over poverty than ever before in the history of any land."[1] The remark sounded absurd during the depression, but it did not strike hearers as unreasonable when Hoover said it. After all, Al Smith's campaign manager, Du Pont executive John Raskob, was saying, even more emphatically, that everyone "ought to be rich."[2] The economic boom of the 1920s had not guaranteed universal affluence, but it seemed at least to put widespread prosperity within reach.

America's consumer economy came of age in the 1920s. Wages rose and working hours fell, giving Americans more leisure, and more resources with which to enjoy their free time, than they had ever had before. As a result of this unprecedented situation, two questions increasingly occupied the attention of a number of economists and social theorists: Could prosperity be sustained and expanded without exhausting the resources upon which it depended, and what would Americans do with the affluence and leisure they were acquiring?[3]

Although Hoover had not thought methodically about these questions before becoming secretary of commerce in 1921, his whole career up to that point gave him a perspective that was particularly appropriate for the 1920s. Raised by Quakers in the American West, trained as an engineer, and experienced both as a businessman and as a public official in administering national and international programs, he had enormous practical experience in the efficient use of resources and deep personal convictions about the moral use of leisure. He agreed with prewar conservationists that resources must be husbanded and developed carefully in order to sustain and enhance general prosperity, but unlike Progressive Era leaders, his experience during and prior to the war convinced him that federal control of conservation could be replaced by a decentralized and largely voluntary system, which would take its energy and specific programs from local conditions, but which would still draw guidance from experts at the national level.

In the sense that he thought of himself as a member of a national, even an international, elite of engineers, Hoover was a notable representative of what Robert Wiebe has called the "new national class," made up of people whose primary allegiance was to expertise rather than to local interests.[4] Yet it is also obvious that Hoover's political philosophy was more local and old-fashioned than national; he hoped to enable local governments, companies, and private individuals to make use of the national class's knowledge without being controlled by it. Insulated by his background and his experience around the world in a fiercely individualistic business environment, he was not swept up by the nationalizing trend of the early twentieth century. His political outlook remained that of the frontier West in which he had grown up. He recognized that many conservation problems were national rather than local and could be understood only from a national perspective, but he also believed that individual creativity and local experience needed to be incorporated into the solution of those problems.

Since most conservationists were clearly members of the national class, this sort of thinking was alien to them, as it was to most of the engineers, corporate managers, and political progressives with whom Hoover worked during the 1920s. On the other hand, people with local ties rooted in real estate and commerce found his political opinions congenial but had little enthusiasm for the sort of technical expertise that Hoover also valued. His commitment to the national culture of expertise was thus in tension with the voluntarist/decentralist aspects of his thought. Nowhere was this tension more evident than in his efforts to draw upon the knowledge of the experts to diagnose and prescribe solutions for environmental problems while keeping control of the applications of this knowledge at the local level.[5]

Hoover's unique blend of centralized planning and local initiative could produce remarkably creative and effective collaborations. Such was the case with the Belgian relief program, the Food Administration during World War I, the Mississippi flood relief operation of 1927, and, to a somewhat lesser extent, the negotiation and implementation of the Colorado River compact. He also had considerable success in stimulating a national grassroots discussion of the question of how to occupy the leisure that seemed to be one of the most valuable benefits of the consumer society. The National Conference on Outdoor Recreation, until its work was cut short by the depression, helped to popularize not only a traditional conception of conservation but also new approaches to outdoor recreation and environmental quality. In these instances Hoover combined large-scale planning and organization with personal and local autonomy in a way that had generally eluded the Progressives. Here lies an interesting answer to Arthur Link's old question about what happened to Progressivism in the 1920s.[6]

It would be wrong, however, to conclude that Hoover had found an infallible way to combine Progressive goals with conservative methods. Not all of his attempts at centralized planning and decentralized execution were successful. Economic pressures vitiated his attempts to control overproduction in the oil, timber, and fishing industries, while a complex tangle of individual and local interests, opposition from federal agencies, past practices, and partisanship subverted his plan to transfer federal lands to the states. During the depression, his efforts to stabilize the economy through a combination of federal planning and local initiatives was simply overwhelmed by the scale of the collapse.

It can be argued that a fundamental defect of both the Progressives' centralizing approach to conservation and Hoover's decentralizing one was that they shared a common assumption. The outlook on the natural world for most Americans in the early twentieth century, conservative and Progressive alike, was shaped either directly or indirectly by the frontier experience. From this perspective, which of course was that of both Hoover's childhood and his early adult work experience, it was easy to believe that America had unlimited natural resources and "was a land void of physical limitations and ecological thresholds."[7] Early conservationists had some doubts about the validity of this assumption but were keenly aware that their fears of scarcity were not shared by most people. If they were to win support for a conservation policy, they must create a sense of urgency about resource exhaustion without antagonizing people by challenging the underlying confidence in progress. In his 1908 speech to the Governors Conference on Conservation, Theodore Roosevelt painted a grim picture of approaching scarcity and decline but assured his listeners that wise stewardship of remaining resources would guarantee continued growth. Designed to maximize political support, this formulation of the problem left unquestioned the belief that progress is defined by rising standards of material well-being. Thus Roosevelt's definition of conservation "perpetuated the very attitudes and norms that had given rise to the environmental exigency his policy proposed to solve."[8]

Hoover also accepted Roosevelt's definition of conservation as a policy designed to maintain a steadily rising standard of living for all Americans. He believed, however, that a nationally mandated conservation policy might endanger the very thing it was supposed to promote by stultifying the individual initiative upon which he thought economic progress depended. He was convinced that it was possible to design a conservation program that would achieve Roosevelt's goals even more efficiently and without the danger of smothering economic growth. One element of such a policy would be the local implementation of nationally planned policies. A second would be a program of education that would lead users of natural resources to understand that conservation was a matter of self-interest.[9]

The same conception of government as teacher was also evident in Hoover's approach to outdoor recreation during the 1920s. He was convinced that outdoor recreation opportunities could be made so attractive that Americans would willingly choose to spend their new leisure hours in what he regarded as healthy and moral ways. An ardent fisherman, he had little personal interest in commercial entertainments, and he was convinced that given a choice, others would feel the same. As secretary of commerce, Hoover made the restoration of commercial and sport fisheries and the work of a National Conference on Outdoor Recreation priorities. Fearing the commodification of leisure through commercial recreations, he warned that the moral and physical condition of the nation would decline unless American leaders offered healthful activities to fill the people's free time.

Hoover was also one of the first American leaders to suggest that as Americans had more time and money, the quality of the environment as a whole, not just the conservation of specific resources or the preservation of natural wonders, would become important. While secretary of commerce, he urged the adoption of the nation's first law to control water pollution; he encouraged Americans to find their own slice of outdoor life in suburban, single-family houses surrounded by yards; and he supported programs to benefit Native Americans and children as important to the "conservation of human resources." Far more than most of his predecessors, he defined conservation as a policy to be applied over a very long time period and was willing to consider some resources as having value other than economic. In so thinking, and in his focus on the environment of everyday life, he anticipated, to some extent, the environmental movement of the post–World War II United States.

If there were elements of "social control" or "cultural hegemony" in Hoover's attempts to lead Americans to conservation and to offer them what he regarded as moral activities to fill their leisure hours, such tendencies were contradicted by his deep commitment to individual freedom. Liberty, he wrote, was more than "political 'rights,'" more even than economic freedoms. It was, he declared, the basis of the "material, moral, and spiritual achievements of men."[10] He saw it as the government's opportunity and duty to present Americans with the possibilities of beneficial leisure activities, but it was up to individuals to decide whether to accept—or reject—what was offered. For example, when his efforts to restore fisheries or to find ways to conserve water and oil through voluntary local efforts failed, he did not recommend federal action. The problems must be left to local governments, he declared, and if they chose not to act, there was nothing the federal government could do about it.

When Hoover spoke in 1928 about the prospects for abolishing poverty, he was doubtless thinking of his record as secretary of commerce in populariz- ing standardization and simplification in various industries, his work in pro- moting the development of river systems for power and irrigation, and his efforts at bringing overproduction in the oil and timber industries under con- trol. All of these, he believed, would contribute to increased production and rising standards of living, while at the same time, because production would become so much more efficient, resources would be conserved. Whether this innovative program might have been a viable alternative to federal domination of conservation cannot be determined because the depression intervened, but Hoover had presented a thoughtful and original alternative to the direction that conservation had hitherto followed. Conservation and political conserva- tism could, in his opinion, be not only compatible but effective allies.

Yet Hoover did not share the outlook of the conservative modern economic theorists who call themselves free market environmentalists or envirocapital- ists. If he was skeptical of the efficacy of conservation policy dictated from Washington, Hoover was equally doubtful that the free market, left entirely unfettered, would assure conservation. His goal, as he said in 1917, was to "centralize ideas and decentralize execution."[11] Government, in his opinion, should provide large amounts of accurate information and helpful advice upon which individuals, businesses, and local governments could base rational poli- cies, and he was also ready to offer strong suggestions about what those poli- cies ought to be. He did not accept the Progressives' belief that control of conservation policy should be centered in Washington; but thoroughly im- bued with his generation's confidence in the ability of engineers and other technical experts to diagnose and prescribe for the ills of society, he agreed with the Progressives that Americans could and should consciously manage environmental policy, not leave it to the workings of the market.

The collapse of the stock market in the autumn of 1929 directly chal- lenged Hoover's confidence that prosperity could become nearly universal and undermined the logical basis of his conservation programs. With factories idle and unemployment spreading, the stimulation of production, not the conser- vation of resources, became the first priority. Driven back upon his bedrock values by the crisis, Hoover emphasized frugality and self-reliance, and all his personal reservations about the morality of a consumer society bubbled to the surface. The way to get through tough times, he felt instinctively, was to hun- ker down, work harder, and pare spending. Those principles, applied to the government as to his personal life, led to sharp reductions in spending for conservation as well as for other programs. Even the budget for the construction of Hoover Dam was slashed.

Focused on restoring business confidence as the key to recovery, Hoover was slow during the 1932 campaign either to claim credit for his own achievements in conservation or to see the political appeal of expanded federal conservation programs that might create jobs. His subsequent antipathy to the New Deal and his conviction that it was leading the nation to ruin through a mistaken centralization of power led him to oppose the New Deal conservation policies as he did its other programs.

Long after Franklin Roosevelt's death, Hoover remained convinced that the New Deal had undermined the spirit of individualism that was the mainspring of American progress. As the dominant member of two postwar Hoover Commissions on federal reorganization, he fought to dismantle New Deal agencies and to turn over power to local governments and private individuals. Typical of his outlook was the stress of the second Hoover Commission on private control over hydroelectric development. Believing that the federal government was smothering private enterprise, Hoover now seemed far less interested in conservation than in curtailing federal power. No conservation program, he suggested, could assure the durability of the prosperity of the 1950s unless the power of American individualism was freed from the shackles of Washington's control.

For the most part, the conservation history of the 1920s is terra incognita. Studies of the period have focused on the Teapot Dome scandal, on conditions in specific industries, or on the work of professionals in the federal bureaucracy.[12] Valuable as these approaches are, they need to be placed into a broader political and economic context. The dominant reality of the 1920s was the rise of consumer society within a conservative political milieu. Yet the historians of conservation issues have made little attempt to understand the assumptions and arguments of the conservative political leaders, and those who have focused on consumerism and political events have paid little attention to conservation.

In general, conservation historians have accepted without question the Progressive assumption that conservation was a national issue that ought to be controlled from Washington. It follows, therefore, that the phrase, "a conservative conservation policy," insofar as it means decentralization of control, must be an oxymoron, a euphemism for exploitation.[13] Environmental policies of the 1920s are seen as mistaken, ineffective, or covertly anticonservationist, if they are examined at all. Since Hoover was at the center of virtually every conservation policy of the Republican era, a study focusing on him makes it possible to test these judgments, to see the era's conservation programs from the inside, and to understand much more clearly their goals and methods. There is, it turns out, much to commend in a policy that sought to engage people in conservation through their self-interest on a local, volunteer basis rather than through a national policy designed and implemented from above. If Hoover's approach was sometimes unsuccessful, the same can also be said for that of his predecessors and successors.

In recent years another approach to conservation—one more theoretical, it must be said, than historical—has emerged. The credentials of the free market environmentalists are, to be sure, impeccably conservative, but their approach does not offer a better theoretical understanding of Hoover and his era than do more traditional ones. The argument that the natural mechanisms of a completely free market tend to produce conservation, or may be made to do so as individuals enforce their rights through the courts, is useful insofar as it compels us to move beyond the simplistic economic theory that is implicit in so much environmental history, and to recognize that environmental policies frequently trigger complex economic interactions that may produce results entirely the opposite of what was intended. But the reality is that although Hoover believed in the value of market mechanisms, he never favored a completely free market. Interpreting Hoover, and hence interpreting the environmental policy of the 1920s, requires us to move beyond both the national model of most conservation history and the free market model of contemporary economic theorists. The reality ranges between the two, and the description of that pragmatic midrange is a part of the aim of this book.[14]

Likewise, Hoover can help us better understand some of the paradoxes of consumer culture that have been identified by historians in recent years. Conservation, it turns out, was central to answering both the question of how a rising standard of living could be achieved for Americans, and the even more perplexing problem of how a "simple," moral life could be achieved in a consumer society. Hoover wanted both, and it is only through understanding his conservation policies that it is possible to see how he thought it would be possible to achieve that end.[15] Historians of this period may thus discover that consumerism was a more contested ground than we have previously realized, and that its direction of development was by no means inevitable.

The stunning changes that swept through America in the late nineteenth and early twentieth centuries transformed the ways that Americans lived, worked, and related to one another. They raised, on the one hand, the vision of a golden age that would encompass not just the few at the top, but all of society. That was what Hoover meant when he talked about a possible victory over poverty. But those same changes also raised fears about the exhaustion of resources upon which prosperity depended, and of a descent into materialism and self-indulgence. No problem seemed more urgent to thoughtful Americans of the 1920s than to find a way to have both a rising standard of living and a moral society. Hoover believed that an intelligent conservation policy offered the solution to that problem, the route to an efficient, prosperous, and happy society. Understanding why and how he pursued that goal illuminates many other aspects of the era.

1 | Through a Child's Eyes

As evening fell, the children climbed Cook's Hill. The day had been warm for midwinter, but now in twilight the snow was crusting with the dropping temperature. Their feet crunched and slipped on the hardening surface, their breath making little clouds in the dwindling light. They were laughing and calling excitedly, knowing that the icy crust was perfect for sledding.

They had come from the little town at the foot of the hill where the first lights were beginning to glow. Among the sleds of various ages and conditions, two stood out. Tad Hoover had a wonderful contraption with polished steel runners, bright red and green paint, and an elegant top made by the town's wagon-maker. Bert, Tad's little brother, a chunky boy with a round face, pulled a clumsier and duller contraption, an experiment built in his father's blacksmith shop.

At the top of the hill the children chattered for a moment, but it was too cold to linger, and one after another they threw themselves, belly-down, onto their sleds and tore off down the hill. The Hoover boys were among the last to go. Tad's covered sled, if not among the fastest, was colorful and exotic. Bert's was neither fast nor showy, and when he returned home that night to have his chilled feet thawed in a bucket of ice water, he was silent and withdrawn. A few days later he traded the homemade sled away for a battered, commercially built "coaster" that another child had replaced with a newer one.

Years later, Herbert Hoover had forgotten the disappointment of that snowy evening. His was a vaguer and happier memory of a "great long hill where on winters' nights . . . we slid down at terrific pace with our tummies tight to home-made sleds." Only Tad recalled that Bert's sled "did not have the beauty of outline and the glory of red and green paint to make up for the lack of speed."[1]

Herbert Clark Hoover was born on 10 August 1874 in the Quaker farming settlement of West Branch, Iowa. "Well, we have another General Grant at our house," his father told a neighbor.[2] Jesse Hoover had come to the village with his parents twenty years earlier, married Hulda Minthorn in 1870, and now, at twenty-eight, was well established as the town blacksmith. Their first child, Theodore (Tad), was born early in 1871, and a third child, Mary (May), was born in 1876. By 1878 the family had outgrown the tiny three-room house Jesse had built next to the smithy, and that year he sold the business and the house, moved the family to more spacious quarters, and opened a farm implement business. Hulda Hoover was a dedicated mother, a fastidious homemaker, and an increasingly zealous Quaker minister.[3] The family seemed destined for worldly and spiritual success.

But it was not to be. On 13 December 1880, Jesse Hoover died at the age of thirty-four of "rheumatism of the heart," leaving his widow, three children, and an estate valued at $1,850.31. Hulda told her mother that she had "made up my mind not to leave home. . . . We will raise [a] garden and I will try to do what I can and not neglect the children—I have rented my north room downstairs."[4] She also worked as a seamstress to earn extra money and was frugal with every penny she earned. In the summers the children sometimes stayed with nearby relatives in order to cut costs further. Herbert Hoover later remembered having once spent "eight or nine months" with his uncle Laban Miles, who was the Indian agent with the Osage tribe in what would become Oklahoma. There, he went to school with the Indian children, learning "much aboriginal lore of the woods and streams, and how to make bows and arrows."[5] He also recalled having lived one summer with his uncle Pennington Minthorn, where he stayed "in a sod house and . . . was privileged to ride the lead horse of the team which was opening the virgin soil."[6]

Young Bert suffered severely from croup. One day when he was about two, he had a major attack, choked, and seemed lifeless. When his uncle Dr. Henry John Minthorn returned from visiting a patient in the country, he was met by Grandmother Minthorn, who called, "Bertie is gone." Throwing the horse's reins to the stable boy, the doctor ran first to his own house to get blankets, then raced to the boy's side. Detecting signs of life, he gently pressed the tiny chest, and after a few minutes was "rewarded by the quiet normal breathing of the child."[7] The incident was so extraordinary that family and friends attributed it to divine intervention. "I have always believed that God raised you up for some special work for him," wrote Dr. Minthorn's partner to Hoover many years later.[8]

Hoover himself did not mention the incident either in the "Information for Biographers" he prepared about 1916, or in his published *Memoirs*, nor, apparently, did he tell Will Irwin about it when Irwin was writing a campaign biography full of human interest stories in preparation for the 1928 presidential race. Although Hoover remarked in his memoirs that during his youth "medical science was still almost powerless against the contagious diseases which swept the countryside," he turned his personal crisis into a jokingly vague allusion to a school examination, telling readers that he "successfully passed the requirements of mumps, measles, croup, diphtheria and chicken-pox."[9] Dr. Minthorn appears in Hoover's memoirs not as a hero but in quite a different guise.

West Branch in the 1870s was a small Quaker town of about 400 residents. Other than prayer or the solemn Quaker meetings, there was little to occupy children except outdoor play. The Hoover children and their friends found a shallow swimming hole in the West Branch of the Wapsinonoc Creek, hunted with bows and arrows for pigeons and rabbits in the remnants of the tall-grass prairies along the railroad, caught fish, visited with relatives, went on picnics, or attended local fairs. Bert remembered fondly that his interest in geology was stimulated when he found pieces of agate and fossil coral among the glacial gravel that ballasted the tracks of the Burlington Railroad.

Since Jesse Hoover died when his second son was just over six years old, Bert's memory of him was "of necessity dim indeed." Unlike Tad, who spoke later of "a void unfillable and unfilled forever" from their father's death, Bert seems not to have had much conscious awareness of sadness or deprivation from this period, and he always believed that his love of outdoor life, as well as his generally robust health, were legacies of his first nine years in West Branch.[10]

Hoover's mother, Hulda Minthorn Hoover, was well educated for her time, with two years in the Preparatory Department of the University of Iowa before she married. Raised and taught by zealous Quakers, she and Jesse took the children with them to First Day meetings in the plain white meeting-house where men and women, separated by a low partition, waited in silence for the Spirit to move someone to prayer or speech. The "long hours of meeting" were "strong training in patience" for a child "who might not even count his toes." Hulda Hoover "was in demand as a speaker at Quaker meetings" and, following Jesse's death, began traveling around eastern Iowa preaching.[11] Although Quakers did not find it strange that a woman should preach, her fondness for singing hymns during meetings shocked some conservatives, and others might have been offended had they known of her private support for women's suffrage.[12]

In the children's minds, the poverty of their fatherless situation was inevitably linked with their mother's frequent absences on evangelical missions. Bert recalled that she had to take in sewing "to add to the family resources," and that only years later did he learn that what at the time had seemed poverty was partly because she had "hoarded" his father's estate to support the family and assure that the boys could even go to college. At her death in 1884, it appeared that she had managed to increase Jesse's legacy to about $2,500. But her scrimping and missionary activities were incomprehensible to the children. When Bert was "parked" with relatives and friends while Hulda was off preaching, it must have seemed that he had lost both father and mother. That his mother contracted typhoid complicated by pneumonia during one of her preaching trips and died on 24 February 1884, made the sense of desertion permanent.[13] Wrote Tad many years later, "A lad of that age feels under those circumstances a helplessness and despair and a sort of dumb animal terror." It would have been better, he believed, if their parents' deaths had been followed "by frequent mention and discussion of pleasant memories and happy days" within the family, but they were not. "Hugging these griefs too close in silence made them sink too deeply into the hearts of the children."[14]

Herbert Hoover's account of his parents' deaths in his *Memoirs* seems baldly factual, devoid of the deep emotion his brother expressed. But was it? Upon closer inspection, his factual presentation proves inaccurate: His father's death date is given in a scholarly looking footnote as 10 December 1880, three days early; his mother's is listed as 24 February 1883, a year early.[15] In a typescript of "Information for Biographers" he prepared somewhere around 1916, he wrote that his mother's death came eighteen months after that of his father, instead of more than three years later.[16] The deaths *felt* close together to the child; even years later, unresolved emotions made it difficult for him to remember details accurately.

Nor do friends and relatives seem to have been very helpful in consoling the children. Perhaps, as Tad suggested, they were merely shy about speaking of the tragedy, but to Bert they seemed cold and unfeeling. "Councils of kindly relatives and others" discussed what should be done with the orphans but refused to allow Bert to be adopted by the only person who really wanted him, his schoolteacher Mollie Brown, who was then unmarried. Instead, he "spent the next two years in the possession of an uncle, Allan [actually Allen] Hoover," and was then "traded off to" another uncle and "another distant relative" in Oregon.[17] Tad and May were sent separately to other relatives. In later years Hoover praised his Aunt Millie's cooking and named a son for Uncle Allen, but his memoirs stressed farm chores and "the mortgage . . .

which was a constant source of anxiety and a dreadful damper on youthful hopes for things that could not be bought."[18] Sometimes at night, Bert lay awake wishing desperately for his mother.[19]

The "distant relative" in Oregon to whom Bert was "traded off" and to whose home in Newberg he "was moved" in November 1885 (not 1884 as Hoover reported in his memoirs) was his mother's brother, Henry John Minthorn, the doctor who had saved his life years earlier—a story missing from the memoirs. The Minthorns, Hoover remembered, had recently lost their only son, and the ten-year-old seems to have suspected that he had been taken in not out of love but to replace the son's labor. He was "at once put to school and the chores," feeding the doctor's team, milking the cow, and splitting wood. One night he forgot to fill the water barrel kept in the barnyard for the horses. Uncle John got him out of bed and made him fill the barrel to overflowing; Bert did not forget again.[20] As time went on, he was introduced to harder tasks. When the doctor cut down one of the primeval fir trees on land he was clearing, Bert was to burn out the stump by boring two intersecting holes, filling one with charcoal, and blowing into the other to keep the fire going. "It was sport the first few times," he wrote.[21]

Bert also remembered lots of real fun. Baseball, dam building, swimming, fishing, and exploring the surrounding woods with other boys filled happy outdoor hours. His distant and forbidding uncle sometimes took the boy with him on visits to patients. On these trips the normally "silent, taciturn man" unbent a little, talking about "medicine, physiology, health and sickness," exclaiming in annoyance at the foolishness that often made people sick, and recounting his experiences in the Civil War, during which he had enlisted in the Union army in defiance of his fellow Quakers.[22]

Bert came to have a great admiration for his uncle's character, intelligence, and charity to the poor, but he found little warmth in the Minthorn family, and his niece regretted later that the family had not taught him more social graces. He never learned how to have "inconsequential social relationships," she believed.[23] Others remembered him as small for his age, dressed in worn clothes, and rather untidy.[24] "I do not think he was very happy," Dr. Minthorn reflected in 1920; "our home was not like the one he left with his own parents in it (indulgent) and with very little of responsibility and almost no work."[25] Many years later, Hoover told a friend "that he was twelve years old in this strict Quaker family before he realized . . . that if you did anything for your own personal happiness and satisfaction, God wouldn't strike you dead."[26]

During the summer of 1887, when Bert turned thirteen, he began to win some independence by getting his first paying jobs, weeding onions on a farm near Sherwood, Oregon, and working in a brickyard in Newberg. By the end of the summer, he had earned $30. "It was a great sum and I kept it or part of it for a long time," he recalled in his memoirs.[27]

That summer also brought another great joy—Tad arrived to enroll with Bert at the Friends Pacific Academy. Wonderful as the reunion was, however, living conditions were difficult. The two boys shared a flea-infested room on the lower floor of the school. Also, although Bert's croup had disappeared with advancing age and the change of climate in Oregon, he was afflicted almost every night with earache.[28] The boys earned their board by doing chores for Benjamin Miles, the father of Uncle John's wife, Laura. Tad remembered Miles as "the best hand I ever met at planning work so that a boy would not have a minute to watch the antics of a terrified beetle or shy rocks at a squirrel."[29]

In his three years at Friends Pacific Academy, Bert studied basic subjects —arithmetic, geography, grammar, spelling, writing, drawing, physiology, American history, algebra, bookkeeping, and rhetoric—and was given abundant doses of religion.[30] He was the smallest child in the school, and often the youngest in a class, but he did well academically, especially in mathematics.[31]

Many years later, his uncle declared proudly that Bert's education at the Friends Academy was "about the same as a good High School," noting that Bert only had to study geometry before being admitted to Stanford.[32] But when Bert and the Minthorns moved to Salem, Oregon, in 1888, Bert clearly felt that his education had been incomplete. He took more mathematics at the Capital Business College and, through the guidance of a teacher he met, Miss Jennie Gray, was introduced for the first time to Sir Walter Scott and Charles Dickens. Even so, when he took the entrance examinations for admission to the new Leland Stanford Junior University in 1891, he would have failed had his dogged determination to succeed not won the admiration of the examiner, Professor Joseph Swain. Swain arranged to have Hoover admitted to Stanford's first class despite the gaps in his training.[33]

Considering that Hoover had graduated from the Friends Academy in 1888 at the age of fourteen and did not resume organized schooling until he entered Stanford three years later, it is difficult to accept Dr. Minthorn's claim that Bert had the equivalent of a good high school education. Hoover himself reported in his memoirs that he was sadly deficient in everything but mathematics at the time of his admission to Stanford.[34] His schooling had been disrupted by family crises and frequent moves, and although he was lucky to have drawn the attention of several dedicated and loving teachers, none of them was able to give him more than a bare introduction to the sort of education that would have been available in bigger schools and larger cities. It was his determination to succeed despite all obstacles, rather than the quality of his education, that carried Hoover forward.

During these years, he did acquire a large measure of practical education, especially after 1888 when the Minthorn family moved from Newberg to Salem so that Uncle John could devote full time to a new venture, the Oregon Land Company. Its object was to buy up wheat farms in the Willamette Valley, plant fruit orchards, build houses, and resell the land in smaller parcels at a profit. The company was a roaring success for several years, increasing its stock value from $20,000 in 1888 to $200,000 two years later. Rather than go back to school, young Bert joined the company as an office boy at $20 a month. By 1890 he was receiving $35 a month and had become valuable to the company as an accountant, filing clerk, typist, and salesman, in addition to his more mundane tasks.[35] In his spare time he pursued education informally, but it was obvious that he relished the independence that earning a salary brought him for the first time.

When not working, Hoover often spent time fishing in Oregon's wild rivers. Back in Iowa, he had begun fishing with "willow poles with a butcher-string line and hooks ten for a dime," but now in Oregon he was introduced to fly-fishing through the generosity of a stranger who gave him three artificial lures. Even with only a bamboo pole and the increasingly tattered flies tied directly to the line, the trout were so plentiful that success was assured.[36] Thus was born a lifelong passion.

As an adult, Hoover became an outspoken advocate of fishing and fishermen. "Fishing," he wrote in 1927, "is not so much getting fish as it is a state of mind and a lure of the human soul into refreshment." "The joyous rush of the brook, the contemplation of the eternal flow of the stream, the stretch of forest and mountain," he added, "all reduce our egotism, soothe our troubles, and shame our wickedness."[37] Years later, after finding the rivers of his youth dirty and depleted of fish, Hoover made control of water pollution, fisheries protection, and restocking of rivers priorities of the Commerce Department and the presidency.[38]

Yet much as Hoover loved fishing, its pleasures were mixed with other feelings. Even seventy years later, as he thought back nostalgically on willow poles, butcher-string lines, and hooks ten for a dime, he could not forget that "the dime was hard to come by." Nor could he refrain from listing in detail all the wonderful tackle "assembled from the steel of Damascus, the bamboos of Siam, the tin of Bangkok, the lacquer of China, or silver of Colorado" that he did not have as a child. With the willow pole and even "a properly spat upon worm," he admitted, it could be "a long time between bites." For Hoover, fishing was at least a little shadowed by poverty and tainted with resentment at relatives who begrudged an orphan a few cents for better lures. Lurking somewhere behind his adult paeans to fishing as an escape from the cares of daily life was the child who knew that hunger was always a neighbor and even play must have a practical value: "we ate the fish."[39]

Hoover's relatives, both in Iowa and in Oregon, were a serious-minded group, made so partly by the necessities of frontier life and partly by their sober Quaker religion. On both sides of his family, Hoover came from several generations of dedicated and often prominent Quakers, and if his father seems to have been somewhat more relaxed than other relatives about the demands of the "inner light," his mother more than made up for it. There were few non-Quakers in West Branch when Hoover lived there, and daily prayers and Bible reading, silent grace before meals, and Fifth Day (Thursday) and First Day (Sunday) meetings of silent worship were normal parts of everyone's life. At home, furnishings were simple, literature other than the Bible was frowned upon, and cards and alcohol were banned. In meetings, which might last two hours, there was no minister, and Quakers sat in silence until someone was moved to speak. Children, even babies, were taken with their mothers to the meetings, "since obviously there was no other place to park them. Their cries and the hushings thereof were often the only relief from the long silences" in which a young boy dared "not even count his toes."[40] Uncle John Minthorn's later comment that Hoover's parents had been indulgent hardly seems to be borne out by what is known about them.

Although Quakers believed deeply that individuals must seek guidance directly from God through the inner light, they also sought order and harmony in society. The reconciliation of individualism and order was achieved through the reading of "Queries" at the monthly Friends meeting. As biographer Martin Fausold points out, the "Queries," little altered since the founding of the movement by George Fox in the seventeenth century, asked Quakers to search their souls to see whether "they conscientiously opposed war, capital punishment, legal oaths, intemperance, gambling, secret societies, extravagance, discrimination, paid ministry, the double standard; and if they favored rights for laborers, education, social relief, temperance, proper treatment of Indians and Negroes, prison reform, the loving care of the insane, foreign missions, equality of the sexes, simplicity, religious tolerance, free ministry, civil liberty, and ecumenical cooperation." By constantly redirecting believers' attention to these common concerns, a degree of conformity was subtly inculcated within the Quaker community. Quakers, Hoover would later say, believed in liberty, but in "ordered liberty."[41]

If Hoover found meetings strong training in patience when he was young, in later years he came to appreciate the secular applications of Quaker religious precepts. Tolerance and religious individualism led, he believed, to economic individualism, and emphasis upon plain living fostered a commitment to education, thrift, and individual enterprise. "In consequence of plain living and hard work poverty has never been [the Quakers'] lot," he declared enthusiastically. "So far as I know, no member has ever been in jail or on public relief."[42] The experience of his youth did not make it easy for Hoover to sympathize with Americans who turned to the government for assistance during the economic crisis of the 1930s, nor did it lead him to favor government relief programs to relieve individual suffering.

Quaker principles became a deep part of Hoover, but it should not surprise us that so much emphasis upon individualism made it difficult for him to submit to the external discipline enforced by his elders. This tension between individualism and order was exacerbated by the death of his parents and the transfer of the boy into "the possession of" relatives. What had earlier found an outlet in harmless rebellion—stolen moments reading the forbidden magazine *Youth's Companion*—now became resentment of an authority that seemed to dictate to him in the name of his best interests. "He felt there was a difference in the way he was treated when his father and mother were alive and the way he was treated as an orphan—he was bound to," said an old friend from Hoover's Oregon years.[43] Thus did Uncle John's heroic role in saving his life slip from Hoover's memory to be replaced by a picture of a stern, forbidding taskmaster driven more by duty than by love.

One Sunday in Oregon, Bert talked a group of his cousins into skipping Sunday school to go fishing. They were gone all day, tipped their boat over, and returned home covered with mud. Greeted with silent reproaches and sent to bed without supper, Bert worried all night what would be done to them. The next day, in a special meeting a cousin remembered as having lasted twelve hours, the Quakers prayed over the sinners, painting "all the horrors of hell" and warning them "over and over again what would happen to us if we did not obey." When they were finally released, the cousin asked Bert what he thought. "He was very angry. He twisted his cap in his strong hands and said, bitterly: 'They can believe in a terrible God if they want to; my God is a good, kind God.'"[44] In later years, although he maintained a membership in the Salem meeting that he joined as a teenager, Hoover seems almost never to have attended Quaker services. His sons received no religious instruction, and they recalled no discussion of religion at home.[45]

After the great crash of 1929 and the onset of the depression, a number of observers commented on Hoover's "incessant compulsion to work and his inability to relax."[46] Perhaps in the end, the Quakers who had prayed so hard over Hoover and his cousins that day had succeeded better than they knew. Fishing may have been his greatest joy, but it was a guilty pleasure. If real work called, he must heed the summons, even if his friends told him during the depression that he would be more efficient after a little relaxation. Somewhere in his subconscious, there was always the voice of one of his Quaker relatives telling him that work must come before pleasure. Even in his old age, he sometimes postponed fishing trips in order to work, and when he did go, he always brought along a pad and pencil so that he could make notes of things that needed to be done.[47]

By studying the models offered by the adults around him, young Herbert Hoover learned to escape their control. But emotional escape was more difficult. His Quaker relatives sustained his body but offered him little emotional support after his parents' deaths. Feeling unloved as a child, the adult Hoover shielded himself from rejection by stressing rationality, hiding his emotions in public, and seeming cold and detached. He became, in short, very much like those relatives who had taken in the young orphan, and, like them, he practiced charity, albeit on a vastly expanded and somehow impersonal scale. Those who knew him testified often to his obsession with feeding the hungry, especially children, yet he rarely had personal contact with those he assisted and often concealed his gifts, even to family members, behind anonymity or channeled them through others.[48] He had little of what a later generation would call charisma but inspired almost fanatic admiration from his family and his professional colleagues. He had a remarkable gift for attracting men and women who shared his "honesty and integrity, and interest in the work to be done rather than in their own careers as such," and he returned their loyalty generously; but he was exceptionally touchy about criticism.[49] He was, thought one keen observer, "abnormally sensitive, filled with an impassioned pride in his personal integrity, and ever apprehensive that he may be made to appear ridiculous."[50]

Although Hoover's justifiable self-confidence in his ability to accomplish great tasks drew others to his leadership, he had an underlying insecurity that seems to have come from his childhood. Those who knew him well testified to a deep strain of pessimism that dominated his view of the world; his childhood had not led him to expect that things would generally come out right.[51] To a considerable extent, there was a conflict between the rationalistic persona Hoover presented to the outer world and the insecure inner man deeply in need of love and uncritical approval. If Quaker values contributed to his worldly success, they were also constant reminders of unhappiness during a childhood in which he could never find more than a moment's respite from the duties imposed on him by others who seemed to care more about his labor than his happiness.

Hoover's happiest times as a child were during the days and nights he spent outdoors—swimming, hunting, camping, fishing. For the most part, the outdoors was for Hoover throughout his youth a place of genuine pleasure and, better yet, of escape from the unhappiness that seemed to come too often from other people. As in the sledding story with which this chapter opened, however, Hoover found throughout his life that even moments of escape were wrapped subtly with webs of poverty and Quaker plainness. Nonetheless, the outdoors always beckoned with the possibility that through experience and knowledge, he could exercise the control over his destiny that had eluded him in his daily life as a child. Wading alone in a trout stream, he relived the fleeting pleasures of childhood, but never without also reexperiencing a sense of uneasiness at having evaded the call of duty. "If you had enough work to do," he told a friend, "you could overcome any kind of disappointment," and thus work became "sort of a panacea" for every uncertainty, failure, or unhappiness.[52] The stern tenets of frontier Quakerism blocked the rebel child's hope of escape, but the struggle never ended. Hoover internalized Quaker values and they served him well, bringing him material success and a generally happy and productive life, but at some level he always resented that those values had been forced upon him, not freely chosen.

The importance of the outdoors for Hoover can scarcely be overstated. In a difficult childhood it was his solace, his refuge. His mastery of outdoor lore brought him friendship and admiration from other children and approbation from adults ("we ate the fish"). And eventually the outdoors offered him an opportunity to choose a career that provided escape at last from his well-meaning relatives in Oregon. Remembering those colorful stones he had picked up along the Burlington right-of-way, and influenced by scientists he met in Salem, he decided to become a geologist. Here was a career that could unite his love of outdoor life with his skills in science and business, offering an escape from poverty and a chance to apply the Quaker values of his childhood in a field where success depended not on winning the favor of other people but on hard work and applied intelligence.

The Progressive Era conservation movement that was flourishing when Hoover entered political life is often described as having two distinct wings: a utilitarian approach that stressed the importance of saving resources for future use, and an esthetic outlook that emphasized the permanent preservation of natural beauty for its own sake. Hoover was unable to separate these two views; for him, the beautiful must also be useful. His childhood seems to have led him to intertwine these two approaches inseparably and sometimes painfully, and what is equally important, to have ingrained in him a belief that people must come to a recognition of conservation policies not through external coercion but through the personal guidance of an inner light. It is of course impossible to say with certainty what inclines a person toward a particular course, but it is difficult to escape the conclusion that both the content of Hoover's conservation beliefs and the distinctive and politically conservative methods through which he proposed to convert belief into policy were molded by his childhood.

2 | The Engineer and the Gentleman

During one of Hoover's many pre–World War I transatlantic crossings, he took his meals at a table with "an English lady of great cultivation and a happy mind, who contributed much to the evanescent conversation on government, national customs, literature, art, industry, and whatnot." Steamship etiquette dictated that while the passengers must strive to entertain one another, personal questions were out of bounds. As the ship neared New York harbor, however, the lady could no longer contain her interest in her sophisticated tablemate, and turning to Hoover she asked, "I hope you will forgive my dreadful curiosity, but I should like awfully to know—what is your profession?" He replied that he was an engineer. Obviously astonished, she blurted out, "Why, I thought you were a gentleman!"[1]

The years of experience that would make Hoover into the engineer and gentleman who so intrigued the English lady began in Salem, Oregon, in the autumn of 1888 when he took a job as an office boy in his uncle's company. The people who met Hoover during the three years he worked for the Oregon Land Company were struck by his energy and ambition. He did his job well, constantly sought new ways to make himself valuable to the company, and delighted in the independence his salary brought. He also realized, even at this early stage of his career, that success in a larger world would require more education. In the fall of 1889 he took mathematics classes at the Capital Business College in Salem, and whenever he could find the time, he read and studied both technical works and literature. When Tad, partially supported by Uncle John, left for William Penn College in Iowa in the fall of 1890, new possibilities opened to Bert as well. The question was what field he ought to pursue, but that was not a problem for long. His native bent for mathematics was reinforced by a chance visitor to the office, an engineer who extolled the opportunities open to men in that profession. Captivated, Hoover gathered catalogs and information about colleges he might attend.[2]

The Minthorns preferred that he attend a Quaker institution, and Earlham College in Indiana proffered a scholarship, but the college had no engineering program. Attracted by a promise that a new institution, Leland Stanford Junior University, in Palo Alto, California, would concentrate on practical education, and that because of the generosity of its wealthy founder, it would charge no tuition, Hoover decided to apply. A mathematician from Stanford, Professor Joseph Swain, was to conduct entrance examinations for the first class at Stanford in the summer of 1891 in Portland, and Hoover signed up to take them.[3]

Although Hoover had not had enough geometry to solve all the problems in Swain's examination, the professor was impressed by his determination and believed that he "would make a success" as a student.[4] He not only admitted the young man but allayed the Minthorns' doubts when they learned that Swain was a prominent Quaker. Hoover boarded a train for Stanford University a few weeks after his seventeenth birthday.[5]

Enrolled initially in mechanical engineering, Hoover was very much impressed by a geology professor, Dr. John Caspar Branner; and after his first year, he switched his major to geology. During Hoover's four years at Stanford, he concentrated heavily in science, taking only a handful of courses in such other subjects as languages, philosophy, and history. The university, with its focus on practical education, did not require a broad liberal arts curriculum, and Hoover was too poor to delay his graduation by taking courses that were not essential. Even without tuition, books and living costs soon would have exhausted his meager inheritance from his mother's estate if he had not worked throughout his university years. He found jobs in university offices, delivered newspapers, served as campus agent for a local laundry, and held a number of other odd jobs that brought a small income. Desperately shy at first, he gradually made friends and became an important figure on campus as manager of the baseball and football teams, treasurer of the junior class, and treasurer of the student association. If his course work was in some ways narrow, the campus atmosphere was generous and humane. From the faculty and students alike, Hoover imbibed a "sense of community and [an] ethos of useful service" that reinforced his Quaker training.[6]

Hoover also met his future wife at Stanford. Lou Henry, who enrolled as a geology student in the autumn of 1894, was an adventurous young Californian who shared Hoover's enthusiasm for the outdoors, travel, and public service, and who had a gift for foreign languages. She and Bert were married at her family's home in Monterey, California, on 10 February 1899 and immediately set sail for China, the first of many trips to exotic places they were to take together. More socially adept than her shy husband, over the years Lou often eased his way in gatherings.[7]

During the summers of his college years, Hoover happily combined outdoor life with practical applications of his studies. The first summer, Dr. Branner secured for Hoover a position with the Geological Survey of Arkansas at a salary of $40 a month, and he spent the summer in the Ozarks, walking and riding horseback through rugged, wild country peopled largely by "mountaineers and moonshiners whose cabins were the only available shelter at night."[8] He returned to Stanford that fall toughened and more self-assured. The next summer, he worked first with Dr. Branner collecting fossils in Oregon, and then made maps and terrain models for the Geology Department, for which he received both academic credit and modest pay.

During the summers of his junior and senior years, he secured a job as assistant to Dr. Waldemar Lindgren, a prominent geologist with the United States Geological Survey in the Sierra Nevada. Dr. Lindgren was so pleased with the young man's work that he gave him a series of raises and in 1895 offered him a permanent position with the service at $1,200 a year, which must have seemed a great deal of money to a new college graduate with $40 left of his inheritance and no other job in sight. Before Hoover could accept, however, a cutback in government spending eliminated the job, and he instead tried to find a position in the California mining industry.[9] A serious depression gripped the country, but Hoover had no doubt he would succeed. "I had lived all my life in hard times," he wrote later, "but I had never heard of depressions . . . , nor did I have to worry about what the government was going to do about it. No one was crying over 'helpless youth.'"[10]

Unable to find work as an engineer, Hoover took a $2-a-day job as a laborer in a gold mine. A shift was ten hours, and the work was hard and dirty, but it was practical training in mining. He stuck it out for a few months and then moved to Berkeley to join his brother and sister. There he drew upon his Stanford contacts to arrange an interview with Louis Janin, who was perhaps the most eminent mining engineer then working on the West Coast. Although Janin had no mining jobs to offer, he mentioned that his office needed a typist, and Hoover leaped at the opportunity. He believed that "something might turn up if I kept near the throne," and so it proved. Soon afterward, Janin was employed as an expert witness in a lawsuit between two California gold-mining companies. Hoover, having worked in the area under dispute, both as a miner and as a surveyor with Waldemar Lindgren, was able to provide expert assistance in preparing the maps and exhibits that helped to win the case for Janin's client. On 17 March 1896, the day after the verdict, Hoover became a member of Janin's firm. He quickly showed his extraordinary skill in evaluating mines and prospects throughout the Southwest, and his future in the profession was assured.[11]

There was little if anything in Hoover's reactions to his experiences in this early stage of his career that would have led an observer to anticipate that he would become a conservationist in his later life. Few of his letters from this period survive, but those that do, as well as his memoirs, are filled with amusing stories of encounters with suspicious mountaineers in the Ozarks and rattlesnakes and insects in the Sierras. Forced to spend much of his time on horseback, he became convinced that the horse was "one of the original mistakes of creation . . . , too high off the ground for convenience and safety on mountain trails," with too few legs for riding comfort, a hide too thin to resist fly bites, and too much need for water in the desert.[12] Only occasionally did a letter mention in passing the spectacular scenery amid which Hoover was working, and only in few cases did he say more than that the country was "exceptionally fine" or "grand."[13]

One of very few indications that Hoover was not entirely indifferent to his surroundings may be found in a letter to his sister, written during a week's enforced idleness on the shore of Lake Tahoe in August 1895. The beauty of the still, blue lake, surrounded on all sides by the ice-scoured, silvery Sierras, whose peaks flew long white banners of storm clouds, moved him as it does visitors today:

> No prosaic description can portray the grandeur of forty miles of rugged mountains rising beyond a placid lake in which each shadowy precipice and each purple gorge is reflected with a vividness that rivals the original. Along their western summits gaunt peaks of similar strength and nobility, vast proportions combined with simplicity and grace, stand out like buttresses and turrets from a great wall, their sides splashed with snow, their passes and lateral ridges covered with a wealth of vegetation which gives the whole an air of solidity and affords a restful contrast from their rugged summits.
>
> Gradually from the south end of the lake the range takes a more gentle outline, the timber line approaches nearer the summit and, as you turn from the southwest, your nerves tingle with awe at the giant palisades whose sharp Gothic pinnacles and deep precipitous rock faces are broken only by deep glacial gorges to find relief in the forest clad slopes whose gentle contours are sombre and indeed more monotonous but suggestive of richness and depth of color, and whose spirit is serene and restful.
>
> We do not here have the sharp contrasts of the desert, the dark gray precipices fade gently into the darker vegetation below and the white snow above, the whole veiled by a flood of blue air bathing the rock faces and blending distance with the greatest charm.
>
> The mountains descend so abruptly to the lake that not even a trail is possible, and here on the west side we are compelled to often return to the desert at the foot of the Great Sierra wall in order to make our way southward, so that the

constant relief from the searching sun and burning sands of Nevada to the cool breezes and grand views of California is almost intoxicating.

I saw the snow banners last Thursday for the first time. They are known in Europe as the Aperglow and are seen only in very high mountains and under peculiar conditions.

Southeast of Lake Tahoe there is a sharp ridge of jagged granite peaks, each rising to over 11,000 [feet], their bare sides cut by deep gorges into pinnacled precipices and saw-toothed crags until in the distance the whole seems a cathedral more abundantly spired than Milan. The snow trails down the deep gashes in their sides or collects in immense folds just above the timber line and here and there a group of gnarled old tamaracks relieve the utter nakedness of their ice-worn slopes.

There had been a storm gathering from the west and the heavy clouds of mist mingled with snow rolled up against their battlements spreading their fleeces over turret and crest, sending long streamers of mist down the gorges like the limbs of some great dragon. As the clouds blew against this great barrier, the eastward currents turned upward by the mountainside tore the vapory mass into great whorls, wrapping them about the peaks and pinnacles, scattering the fleecy shreds among the rock faces and gradually the desert dried currents from the east gained the mastery, and from each icy peak like a streamer from the masthead waved a snowy banner, a half-mile in length, widening toward its outward end and fading away in bits of detached clouds until it was gone entirely.[14]

If his metaphors were conventional—"buttresses and turrets from a great wall," "sharp Gothic pinnacles," "pinnacled precipices and saw-toothed crags"—the letter is nevertheless moving and dramatic. His work forced him to look down at terminal moraines and lava dikes, but it could not extinguish a deep joy like that of John Muir in the mountain contrasts of light and shadow, barren rock and shaded forests, snow and desert, peaks and canyons. Hoover seldom took the time to set down his feelings and perhaps felt a little embarrassed to have done so in this letter—the passages quoted above were quickly followed by humorous remarks about the small servings in his hotel dining room—but he was not insensitive.[15] Engineer and romantic coexisted in Hoover as in so many Americans of his generation who could not imagine that the enterprises they were founding would alter beyond recognition the magnificent places they loved. Raised on the frontiers of Iowa and Oregon, and even enrolled in the "pioneer" class at Stanford, Hoover shared the attitude of the frontiersmen who saw the wilderness as an enemy to be subdued or as a reservoir of raw materials with which self-reliant, determined men could build prosperous lives. But just as he had sought education to escape the frontier, so his vision was beginning to encompass more than the commercial possibilities of the lands in which he worked.

Hoover went to the mountains in the 1890s not for pleasure but for business, and most of the time his concentration on professional issues precluded much concern with other matters. So it would be for the next twenty-five years as he built his career in mining engineering and finance, but if he was not often sensitive to the esthetic, social, and cultural importance of the environment, the practical realities of his chosen profession tended to force a sort of conservationist outlook on him. To make gold mining pay, methods must be efficient enough to make a profit from a ton of ore that contained as little as an ounce of gold, but no matter how well a mine was run, sooner or later the ore body would be exhausted. At some level, maybe not entirely conscious, he and other engineers of his generation were thus beginning to sense that modern technology might create problems as well as blessings.[16]

Success with Janin was followed in March 1897 by an offer to work for the London firm of Bewick, Moreing and Company as a mine surveyor and locator of new prospects in the mining region of western Australia. Two years later, after a spectacularly successful stay in Australia, Hoover moved with his new wife, Lou Henry, to China, where he was to serve as Bewick, Moreing's technical adviser to the Chinese official responsible for administering a major mining district and as the representative of foreign bondholders who were financing a large project in the region. In 1901, after further successes, he returned to London at the age of twenty-eight to become a full partner in Bewick, Moreing.[17]

A successful self-made man, Hoover's political and social values during the decade after his graduation from Stanford were very much what one would expect. In 1896 his political sympathies were Republican, and although he was away from home and could not vote that autumn, he commented that William Jennings Bryan's campaign calling for the federal government to use its influence on behalf of farmers and workers against big business was his "first shock at intellectual dishonesty as a foundation for economics." While in Australia and China as "both . . . engineer and administrator," as he put it, he identified with management, not with labor.[18] Although he favored paying reasonable wages to skilled men, he expected miners to work hard for their pay and to accept technical innovations that would increase production without higher pay. He also extended working hours when he could, resisted unionization of the workers, brought in Italian miners when Australians proved difficult, and frequently expressed his contempt for the pro-labor government of western Australia and for the corruption that riddled China.[19] "If a man has not made a fortune by 40 he is not worth much," he once told an Australian friend, and it frequently seemed to workers or rivals who came up against the aggressive American that profits were all Hoover cared about. As a brilliant technical expert and a "tireless, cost-cutting, hard-driving, ever-striving manager of mines and of men," writes his best biographer, he was perfectly suited for the harsh, competitive mining business.[20]

Yet if Hoover had a keen eye for maximizing profits, he was well aware that he could not succeed single-handedly. He admired expertise and rewarded competent salaried employees handsomely. "Our operations were a demonstration," he wrote later, of "an industrial fundamental—greater technical service, more labor-saving devices, lower costs, and larger production and higher wages."[21] Hoover believed that the goal of management should be modest profits over an extended period rather than immediate windfalls. He thus stressed long-range planning, heavy capital investment, and the reinvestment of a substantial share of profits, and he was willing to pay reasonable wages and to count on rising production by workers making maximum use of technical innovations.[22] These opinions distinguished Hoover from many of his contemporaries among mine managers and businessmen and offer a key to understanding his later approach to the Commerce Department and the presidency. Hoover's business and technical experience in these years confirmed for him a belief common among American engineers—that technical advances and efficiency could benefit everybody without deleterious side effects. He saw himself not as a conservative defending the interests of capital against labor, but as a progressive offering an advancing standard of living to everyone. Efficiency was the road to universal prosperity and happiness.

By 1901, when Hoover left China to become a partner in Bewick, Moreing, he was shifting increasingly from the technical to the managerial and financial side of the business. For the next thirteen years, his principal concerns were the buying, selling, promotion, and financing of mining properties, and he spent almost as little time in the United States as he had while in Australia and China.[23] Although he traveled widely to visit possible investment sites, his activities were increasingly those of the corporate businessman far from the world of the miners in the shafts under the ground. He became, in the words of a friend, "a coordinator, an executive, an administrator of industrial enterprises, an eliminator of waste and folly" and, although the friend did not mention it, a considerable speculator as well.[24] Nothing in this period challenged Hoover's belief that rational planning, efficiency, and the prudent development of human and material resources could assure widespread prosperity. Indeed, the opening of successful mines in places as exotic as China, Burma, and Russia suggested that a rising standard of living and happiness could be universal. The progressive engineer's view of the world was reinforced.

Along with a remarkable ability to evaluate the worth of a mining property after only a brief inspection, Hoover revealed in these years a sensitive understanding of men and an ability to draw out their best work. Blunt, taciturn, and seemingly humorless, he drove others as hard as he pushed himself and ruthlessly fired those he thought incompetent, but he won the undying loyalty of the able men who worked for or with him because he gave them responsibility and left them alone to carry it out. They knew he would give them full credit for what they achieved, would not second-guess them, and would back them up in times of crisis, just as he would quietly, often anonymously, extend loans or gifts to relieve personal problems. He was, moreover, a genius at organizational improvisation who knew, as an admirer said, "when to take organization and when to leave it alone."[25] No devotee of chains of command or organizational charts, he was willing to work with any structure that would get the job done.

These qualities would be precisely the ones needed for Hoover to cope with an enormous new responsibility that befell him with the beginning of World War I in 1914. By that time Hoover was no longer finding business fulfilling. He believed that he had made enough money "to live on comfortably and to be certain that the family is secure," and he wanted to return to the United States to spend time with his wife and his two young sons. In the decade before 1914 he liquidated investments and gradually withdrew from personal management of Bewick, Moreing's enterprises. It was time, he thought, to move beyond mere moneymaking to take on "some job of public service—at home, of course."[26] Before he could do that, however, he was faced with an enormous challenge of public service in Europe.

When World War I began in August 1914, Hoover was in London attempting to wind up his business affairs in preparation for a return to the United States, where he was considering buying a newspaper in Sacramento.[27] The sudden outbreak of war, little anticipated by most people, disrupted international finance, paralyzed steamship companies, and left thousands of Americans stranded on the Continent or in Britain without money and with no way to return home. Hoover and other wealthy Americans living in London responded quickly to the crisis, organizing the Committee of American Residents in London for Assistance of American Travellers (more commonly, the American Committee), with Hoover as chairman and Lou Henry Hoover chairing a similar committee to assist women in particular. Although there was some squabbling between the American Committee and other volunteer organizations attempting to help the stranded travelers, Hoover's committee ultimately won sole charge of the task. In October, with most Americans who wanted to leave Europe back in America, the American Committee quietly went out of existence. All told, it had disbursed about $400,000, mostly in the form of loans that were nearly all subsequently repaid, and aided nearly 120,000 Americans. It was an impressive example of rapid, efficient, volunteer organization, and it gave Herbert Hoover a new reputation for public service.[28]

His reputation was soon to be put to the test in Belgium. That small country became an early victim of the war when German armies swept through it to attack France. Conquered, heavily damaged, occupied, and cut off from outside supplies by the British blockade, Belgium faced starvation as the winter of 1914–15 approached. First efforts at seeking foreign relief came from a committee of prominent Belgians, but it soon became clear that they hadn't the money to buy huge amounts of food and that the British were unwilling to open their blockade for food shipments unless they could be sure the supplies would not fall into German hands. Early in October 1914, Hoover stepped into the crisis, proposing to create an American relief committee that, operating under the semiofficial sanction of the State Department, would attempt to feed the Belgians until their next harvest came in. Thus began the Commission for the Relief of Belgium, the CRB.[29]

For the next two and a half years, until the United States entered the war and Hoover turned over day-to-day administration of the CRB to others, his organization fed nearly 9 million people in Belgium and German-occupied northern France. It acquired and transported across the United States, across the ocean, and through Belgium and northern France approximately 2.5 million tons of food, and distributed the food to 4,700 communes in those countries. The CRB, averaging a membership of 55, many of them volunteers, arranged the purchase, shipment, and distribution of the food, and coordinated the efforts of nearly 130,000 other volunteers who raised money, acquired food, and actually distributed it to families and individuals. At the top, Hoover supervised it all and made his own invaluable contribution by negotiating with the British, French, German, and Belgian governments to secure the funding and to clear away military and diplomatic obstacles to the enterprise. It was an unprecedented achievement in international relief, made the more remarkable because it was all accomplished without the slightest scandal or corruption, and at an administrative cost of under 1 percent.[30]

Hoover's CRB experience confirmed for him the value of having engineers with business backgrounds in charge of decentralized operations, with himself as the final authority in all cases.[31] He ran the relief operation very much the same way he had functioned as a mining consultant and manager: seeking out the best men he could get and trusting their judgment and integrity. To his men, who responded to his trust with fanatical loyalty, he became The Chief, a title with which they would honor him for the rest of their lives. For Hoover, on the other hand, the CRB confirmed his belief "that business could be applied to philanthropy in our hands with an efficiency and an integrity which should be a creditable mark on our national history."[32]

The Belgian experience also gave Hoover a very high opinion of the value of voluntary organization as a mode of attacking large public projects. He early recognized that it would be impossible to raise enough money through public appeals to finance the immense costs of Belgian relief and thus turned to subsidies from the Belgian, British, and French governments to cover most costs. But the commission's staff were largely volunteers, as were the French and Belgians who actually distributed the food and the hundreds of thousands of Americans who gathered and shipped it.[33] Hoover even persuaded the railroads to ship relief supplies free of charge. The voluntary aspect of the relief program was especially valuable in securing the publicity for the organization that Hoover realized was essential to gaining the cooperation of belligerents and the support of neutrals. But it was also more than that; to Hoover, the voluntary service of commission members in particular was proof that they were "gentlemen . . . willing to devote their entire time, at their own expense," to the task, a validation of his own status as an engineer and a gentleman.[34]

By the spring of 1917 the CRB was functioning smoothly enough so that Hoover was free to think about going back to the United States to seek new challenges. With the nation on the verge of entering the war, he was eager to make use of his experience with the CRB to help the United States move to a war footing. Through friends, he lobbied to secure an appointment as coordinator for the mobilization of industries and resources. He told Will Irwin, who was writing an article for the *Saturday Evening Post*, that war mobilization must not be handled by bureaucrats who "tend toward mediocrity," but by "the best brains of the country—which means its industrial brains," for "promotion, [in industry], is not by seniority, but by the hard law of merit."[35] On April 8, just two days after Congress voted to declare war on Germany, the Council of National Defense (made up of the secretaries of war, agriculture, commerce, labor, the interior, and the navy) invited Hoover to become chairman of an advisory committee on food supply and prices. Three days later, he accepted the appointment.[36]

What Hoover really wanted, and believed was necessary to victory in the war, was not an advisory committee but the individual authority over food comparable to that he had held as head of the CRB. He received that power when President Wilson signed into law the Lever Food Control Act on 10 August 1917, Hoover's forty-third birthday. The act created the U.S. Food Administration under Hoover's sole leadership and gave it broad power to control the production, sales, consumption, storage, export and import, and shipment of food and fuel. Although the Agriculture Department, as well as the various military services, would have liked to control food and fuel themselves, Hoover persuaded Wilson that a separate organization, staffed by volunteers drawn from industry, would be easier to disband after the war.[37]

From the outset the Food Administration embodied curiously contradictory ideas. Its major members served without pay, and the organization touted voluntary cooperation by producers, processors, and consumers as the way to increase the amount of food produced and shipped; yet the Lever Act gave the administration, and particularly Hoover as administrator, virtually dictatorial powers over the whole field if he chose to use them. The seeming contradiction was no accident: Hoover meant to rely upon mobilizing a national volunteer effort to produce and save food, but he was realistic enough to know that the threat of his extensive powers would help businesses and private citizens alike see that self-interest dictated cooperation.[38]

Hoover believed that voluntarism would work only if the war were short and, paradoxically, if the sacrifices asked of citizens were substantial. "Democracy," he pointed out, "is a form of government born of peace, constructed for peace and maintainable only in peace. To carry on war successfully requires a dictatorship of some kind or other. . . . No other way has ever been found." But, he contended, "if we lean to the side of rigorous control while the emergency lasts," if we adopt "full measures, strong enough to hurt," then as soon as "the war is over the people [will] insist on abolishing them entirely."[39] He believed that Americans would make great voluntary sacrifices over the short term, and he hoped that the very severity of those sacrifices would assure a return to limited government after the emergency was over. The authority granted to the Food Administration would thus be self-limiting.

Hoover did not, however, trust only to this complex and optimistic assessment of what would happen in the future. He also saw to it that producers and processors were encouraged to cooperate by assuring them solid profits. Antitrust regulations were suspended, and large firms and trade associations were permitted, under Food Administration supervision, to pool information and set prices based on prewar profits plus the cost of the delivered products. The price of wheat, the most essential food staple, was fixed at $2.20 a bushel, which assured farmers a good profit and encouraged production increases, but which kept the price of bread from rising excessively. In addition, processors, middlemen, and even retailers were coerced into keeping prices reasonable because the Food Administration could withhold licenses to do business from those who refused to cooperate.[40] Profits, along with indirect controls, helped farmers, processors, and other businessmen see the virtues of voluntary cooperation with the Food Administration's exhortations to produce and conserve.

Hoover also promoted voluntarism through controlled decentralization. The Food Administration appointed state and even county food directors, mostly volunteers, who carried on local campaigns to encourage people to save food, to utilize substitutes for some items, and to boost production. Editors, business groups, and fraternal organizations were also recruited to encourage cooperation with the national campaign and to focus publicity on those companies and individuals who did not join the crusade.[41] Although real power remained in Washington at the Food Administration, these local activities gave individuals a sense of participation and power.

Like the CRB, the Food Administration was a remarkable success. When the organization was terminated in June 1919, it was able to return all of the $150 million working capital that had been appropriated by Congress and hand over to the Treasury about $60 million in profits. Total administrative expenditures for the organization, which had continued after the war as a relief agency for Europe, were just under $8 million. Hoover estimated that the organization had succeeded in increasing by about 28 million acres the land under cultivation in the United States.[42] As he noted proudly, the agency succeeded in providing a very large percentage of the food for the American people and for the civilian and military populations of the Allies as well, and it achieved all that with no scandal. The Food Administration was never investigated by Congress.

On 7 November 1918 President Wilson asked Hoover to turn the Food Administration into an agency for the relief of the shattered nations of Europe. Ten days later, Hoover sailed for Europe, where he would become head of the American Relief Administration (ARA), a new organization created by Congress, as well as a member of a half-dozen other interallied commissions and councils designed to promote the reconstruction of Europe. Hoover and Wilson believed that a rapid restoration of the European economy would reduce suffering, foster political stability, weaken the threat of Bolshevism, and promote the growth of markets for American products. Under his direction, the ARA functioned very much as the CRB and Food Administration had, but on a much larger economic and geographic scale. By June 1919, when the congressional authorization for the organization expired (it continued as a private agency), it had delivered approximately $5 billion in food to Europe, from the Atlantic to the Urals.[43] Hoover's work as a volunteer executive with the private relief program continued into 1921, after he became secretary of commerce.

Hoover's years of experience as a miner, engineer, businessman, and executive of vast relief projects reinforced and supplemented the patterns implanted by his childhood training. Beginning with the values and skills he learned as a child, he successfully molded himself into the type of man who was emerging at the forefront of American society in the early twentieth century—the technical expert and shrewd businessman whose domination was made acceptable to others because it was veneered with the polish of a gentleman. Perhaps Hoover was fortunate that he acquired his business experience in London, where the custom had been to have mining companies fronted by some titled person. He had no use for that practice; he wanted real experts at the head of any company with which he was associated—but he also recognized that to succeed in the British business world, he must acquire at least a modicum of the manners of those with whom he associated. The English lady who was so surprised that Hoover could be both an engineer and a gentleman was confronted with a man who was polished by British society, but who was at the same time a characteristic American figure of the era.[44]

Hoover told the story of his English tablemate as a humorous episode of upper-class British snobbery, yet he had not forgotten it forty years later when he wrote his memoirs. Engineers, he admitted, "must for years abandon their white collars except for Sunday," but, he insisted, engineering had within his lifetime been transformed from a trade into a profession. It should be accorded, he believed, "the dignity of a profession on a par with the law, medicine, and science." Indeed, it demanded "of its members equally high mental attainments" as those other professions, and it also required "a more rigorous training and experience."[45] In addition to all the technical skill and knowledge required of an engineer, he must increasingly "devise the finance, construct and manage the works which he advises."[46]

In this opinion, although his ideas were based upon experience acquired outside the United States, he reflected an outlook increasingly prevalent among Americans, who were not only accepting engineers as gentlemen but thrusting upon them governmental as well as technical authority. Seeking to reconcile expert, efficient government with democracy, reformers concluded that politics should be separated from administration and professional, apolitical, administrators given dominion over a very large share of what had traditionally been reserved to politicians. To these reformers, "the scientific expert became the prototype of all administrators," for such a person united scientific knowledge with practical experience. "He brought scientific wisdom down from the ivory tower and set it to work for the man in the street," as one historian has put it.[47]

The point being made by advocates of the sort of technocracy that Hoover espoused was more than that technical experts could make the state more efficient. They were claiming "that they could scientifically predict and control the direction, pace, and effects of social change."[48] Hoover took the assertion even further, contending that the engineer's training in "the exact sciences . . . makes for truth and conscience."[49] Laconic as usual, he did not explain what he meant by this seeming claim for the moral superiority of engineers, but it echoes an argument advanced by Thorstein Veblen.

David Burner suggests that Hoover may have read Veblen's 1914 book, *The Instinct of Workmanship*, and been influenced by his contention that "technicians, schooled in the impersonal precisions of a mechanical matter-of-fact world, fulfill themselves in exacting workmanship; and their task compels them to seek a smoothly performing economy." Like Veblen, writes Burner, Hoover believed that "a community of professionals and consumers" based on "a right allocation and use of resources" would be guided by a morality growing out of an instinct of "devoted and serviceable workmanship" and united by social bonds of "self-interest and altruistic working cooperation." The exigencies of modern society would, in short, compel the adoption of efficiency, fairness, and morality (Hoover's "truth and conscience").[50]

Although we cannot know whether Hoover read Veblen, his Quaker background and his technical and business experiences around the world led him to very much the same conclusions—that an efficient, prosperous society that would bring workers and capitalists together could be attained under the rational guidance of technical experts.[51] Because Hoover spent most of his professional career outside the United States, he did not participate in the early phases of the American engineering profession's effort to develop socially responsible professional organizations.[52] Nevertheless, he benefitted from the breakdown of old distinctions of class and from the growing popular admiration for technically trained experts whose knowledge seemed essential to the smooth functioning of an urban-industrial society.[53]

But if Hoover's claim to authority rested largely upon expertise, he also clearly understood, as he demonstrated to his fellow traveler, that the expert's status could be enhanced if he consciously acquired the behavior of a gentleman. Gentility's claim to authority arose from sources that long antedated engineering, and engineers seeking political influence quickly realized that combining the "character, integrity, social consciousness and proud individualism" of the nineteenth-century gentleman "with the efficiency and technical virtuosity of the modern manager" would unite both the old and the new bases of power. The gentleman expert could not only claim to bring his knowledge to bear on public problems but could also declare that in so doing he would "rise above private interests to serve the commonweal."[54]

Although neither Hoover nor his transoceanic traveling companion may have been aware of them, a number of novels and films of the early twentieth century celebrated "cultured but rugged" engineers who were "destined to advance civilization."[55] Hoover aspired to be just such a new type of man, citizen, and statesman who would combine the virtues of a disappearing elite with the skills of a new technocracy. "From the point of view of accuracy and intellectual honesty," he said, "the more men of engineering background who become public officials, the better for representative government."[56]

By 1908 Hoover had concluded that he needed to put this philosophy into practical application. Just making money was not enough; he must bring his skills to some sort of public service.[57] That of course was a conclusion derived not only from his conception of the obligations of his profession, but from his Quaker training and Stanford's atmosphere of communal service. Yet if his background and training pushed him toward a public role, in some ways Hoover's experience gave him an unrealistically inflated conception of what he could expect to achieve. Like other engineers of his era, he assumed that technical experts could find ideal solutions to society's problems that would eliminate the unsatisfactory side effects of economic growth and technology. In so thinking, he underestimated the difficulty of bringing voters in a democratic society to accept the long-term planning and short-term sacrifices that the intellectual and economic elite believed were necessary to maximize the benefits and minimize the costs of economic and technical development. He was also overoptimistic about finding perfect solutions to technological problems; growth and development, it turned out, brought societal and environmental costs. Nor was Hoover able to harmonize his belief in the individual creativity and individual responsibility of the engineer with the reality of modern society in which engineers even more than others are inextricably dependent on large corporations and governmental bureaus. The centralization and bureaucratization of modern society against which Hoover would later inveigh were, "in good part, consequences of the technological changes that [engineers] championed."[58]

Engineers were central to the rise of what Robert Wiebe has described as a new "national class" of technical experts whose authority derived from their specialized knowledge and whose loyalty was more to professional standards than to local interests and allegiances.[59] Hoover was certainly part of this new class, but he also retained both ideological and emotional ties to an older world of individualism and localism. These divided instincts contributed to his predilection for paradoxical combinations of national authority and local autonomy, central control and voluntarism, collective action and individualism.

"The world is Hoover's engine," said an admirer, "and he is always moving about in his overalls, tinkering to make it better."[60] That certainly was Hoover's image of his own role, although he put it somewhat more grandly. The "only interest" of a professional engineering organization, he declared, was "to give voice to the thought of the engineers" in "public service. . . . Their calling in life is to offer expert advice in constructive solutions to . . . group problems."[61] The "selective processes" of engineering training, he added, produced men of "the most high intellect and of stable character," trained in "precise and efficient thought," and "in their collective sense independent of any economic or political interest." They "comprise a force in the community absolutely unique in the solution of national problems."[62] Whether or not Hoover was right that professional expertise represented a panacea for the world's problems, America was fortunate that he and other active, intelligent men believed that duty called them to the service of their country.

If Hoover's convictions about the moral and intellectual authority of engineers seemed to imply the desirability of centralized authority, planning, and organization, he also drew upon experience from his frontier youth and his engineering years. In particular, when called on to deal with problems, he tended to set up organizations that paralleled those with which he had worked as an entrepreneurial engineer. These were structures that defied efforts to chart the flow of authority and decisions. Instead, they emphasized the delegation of authority to individuals on the basis of expertise and permitted great latitude and initiative to those working on various parts of the problem. Although Hoover invariably retained final authority in his own hands, his goal, as he told a Senate committee in 1917, was to "centralize ideas and decentralize execution."[63]

The epitome of such decentralization was, of course, the voluntarism that was the hallmark of the Belgian relief program and Hoover's Food Administration. On the surface, he seemed to assume that those who volunteered their services to these agencies were disinterested gentlemen, but it is worth noting that he kept final authority in his own hands and ruthlessly forced out those volunteers who failed to live up to his expectations. In running the Food Administration, he kept voluntarism in the forefront but backed it both by the stick of punitive authority granted by the Lever Act and by the carrot of assured profits for those who cooperated with the agency. A realist with a rather pessimistic view of human nature, Hoover believed in managed voluntarism and controlled decentralization, not so much because he regarded these organizational methods as panaceas, but because his experience suggested that the alternatives were even more unsatisfactory.

Closely related to Hoover's rather paradoxical approaches to voluntarism and decentralization was his attitude toward publicity. Intensely shy and self-effacing in public, he found speech-making painful and was seldom able to meet the eyes of visitors. Yet he recognized that publicity was essential to the success of his wartime undertakings and learned to use "the press and public relations to a degree extraordinary for his times . . . to win support for and implement the diverse programs and policies with which he was associated."[64] Inevitably, of course, publicity about the organizations that Hoover dominated aroused public interest in him, which he professed not to want, although we may wonder whether the little Quaker boy who received so little overt love and approbation in his childhood did not secretly relish this belated recognition. Certainly, he was extremely sensitive to any hint of criticism and lashed out in response to attacks with every means at his command; such behavior seems at odds with Hoover's claim that he sought no personal recognition.[65] Equally striking is Hoover's drive to control and direct the flow of publicity from behind the scenes, just as he kept ultimate authority in his own hands even as he encouraged voluntarism and decentralization. One senses here a tremendous drive for control not surprising in a man who had so little control over anything as a child, but a drive for control that was, to a considerable extent, at war with what Hoover had been taught as a Quaker about personal freedom and responsibility, and with what his years of engineering experience had demonstrated was an efficient form of organization. The constant tension between Hoover's need for control and his intellectual commitment to voluntarism and decentralization offers a key to understanding apparent contradictions in his personality and behavior that are otherwise baffling.

As the war came to an end and Hoover began to consider what he would do next, few people—even those who knew him well—would have predicted that he would emerge as a major figure in the conservation movement. Perhaps still lurking down inside was the romantic young man who had waxed lyrical over the beauties of the Sierras, but there had been little time or occasion during his engineering or humanitarian careers to cultivate that sensibility. In most of the remote places where Hoover had worked, nature was clearly the enemy, and a dangerous, unromantic enemy at that. All his skills as an engineer and businessman were focused on wresting minerals from the earth or on compelling the earth to bear more abundantly in order to keep peoples and armies alive and fighting. His view of the world was that of an engineer who thought in terms of organizations and systems, and who seemed to believe "the illusion that human social systems could be understood and manipulated with the same efficiency as mechanical systems."[66]

The handful of stories about Hoover's leisure activities that have come down to us from this period do not suggest a budding conservationist. Rather, they indicate the engineer at play. At least half a dozen accounts exist, for example, of outings taken by Hoover, his children, and various friends during World War I. On these expeditions into the countryside around Washington, Hoover's passion was to build rock dams to divert streams or to create small ponds. Whole days were spent in these activities, with men, women, and children all pressed into service carrying rocks and digging new channels under Hoover's direction.[67]

Equally suggestive is a story of a picnic organized by Hoover during his residence in England. On this occasion he rented a boat and invited some English friends to join his family in watching the famous regatta at Henley. They had a splendid day, picnicking as they enjoyed the races, and when the time came to go home, Hoover gathered up the trash and started to throw it overboard. His guests protesting at this littering, he said that the river would soon carry it away, but since they objected, he had another idea. Suiting the action to the word, he filled a couple of empty bottles with water, tied the other trash to them, and sank the whole works in the river! He seemed unmoved when his friends pointed out that if everyone did that, there would soon be no river.[68] Nothing suggested that preserving the beauty of the area he had chosen for the party was important to him, or that the sensitivity to the natural world he had occasionally displayed in earlier years had not withered away. He seemed the archetypal mining engineer, indifferent to the impact of his activities on the environment.

Yet if Hoover showed little of the esthetic conservationist's concern with protecting and preserving the beauties of the outdoors, it was possible that as an engineer concerned with efficiency, he might be interested in the other great strain of the progressive conservation movement: utilitarian conservation. The essence of that movement was "rational planning to promote efficient development and use of all natural resources," and of course that was precisely what Hoover had dedicated most of his career to.[69] He was instinctively a utilitarian conservationist long before he ever encountered the concept directly, but his experience as an engineer and a businessman led him to look for elimination of waste and greater efficiency in the use of resources *after* raw materials were extracted as well as in the mining process. As president of the Federated American Engineering Societies in the autumn of 1920, Hoover took his first significant steps toward becoming an active conservationist by appointing a committee to study ways to eliminate waste in industry. From that modest beginning he would gradually enlarge his approach to environmental issues.

The stress of the progressive conservation movement on planned use of resources would undoubtedly have attracted Hoover's interest at some point, but he was drawn to it for more than the obvious reason. Samuel Hays has pointed out that the Progressive Era conservationists epitomized the tension in American life between centralization and decentralization. The growth of science and technology fostered the development of large-scale organization, planning, and centralization, a shift from personal and local autonomy "to larger patterns of human interaction, to ties of occupation and profession over wide areas, to corporate systems which extended into a far-flung network, to impersonal media of communication and impersonal—statistical—forms of understanding, to the reliance upon expertise and to centralized manipulation and control."[70] All of this Hoover sensed, understood, and willingly participated in, yet at the same time he was drafting a passionate defense of American individualism. Like many others of his generation, he shared in the rise of corporate, professional, and governmental structures that shifted power away from individuals, but at the same time he resented this loss of private freedom and personal authority. A central theme of his political, economic, and conservation thought would be the quest for a way to unite the benefits of centralization with the renewed local and individual power and satisfaction.[71] The tensions and ambiguities so evident in his engineering, business, and philanthropic careers before 1920 would shape his approach to governing thereafter, and his development as a conservationist and environmentalist reveals these contradictions.

3 | Consumption and Conservation

On 21 August 1928, two months after receiving the Republican presidential nomination, Hoover paid a visit to West Branch, his Iowa birthplace. In his speech he reminisced nostalgically about growing up among family farms, where "we ground our wheat and corn on toll at the mill; we slaughtered our hogs for meat; we wove at least a part of our own clothing; we repaired our own machinery; we got our own fuel from the woods; we erected our own buildings; we made our own soap; we preserved our own fruit and grew our own vegetables." In this self-sufficient world, "only a small part of the family living came by purchases from the outside," and the rise and fall of distant markets and exchanges had no power over daily life.

As the 1920s drew to a close, however, agriculture had become commercial, and uncontrollable price fluctuations could "make the difference between comfort and freedom from anxiety or, on the other hand, debts and discouragements." Yet despite that terrible risk, Hoover declared that he did "not suggest a return to the greater security which agriculture enjoyed in its earlier days, because with that security were lower standards of living, greater toil, less opportunity for leisure and recreation, less of the comforts of home, less of the joy of living." He felt only "sentimental regret for the passing of those old-time conditions."[1]

Of all of Hoover's speeches and writings, this West Branch speech may be the one that most clearly exposes a fundamental contradiction in his thought. On the one hand, it extols self-reliance, frugality, simplicity, and freedom from the market; on the other, it urges listeners to embrace market economics, consumerism, and interdependence. Had Hoover been able to admit that his childhood was less happy than he proclaimed it to have been in the speech, the contradiction might have been less glaring, but it would still have existed. As a socially responsible engineer and as a political leader, Hoover sought during the 1920s to provide for Americans both the rising standard of living dependent on growth and development, and the moral values and control of one's own destiny that seemed inextricably linked to a preindustrial world.[2]

Hoover returned from Europe to the United States in September 1919. As soon as he could, he headed west, where Lou and the two boys—and the mountains—awaited him. For nearly six years he had seen his children only for fleeting moments, and now he announced that he would not speak in public, would not read letters longer than a page, and would not even answer the telephone until he had reacquainted himself with the family. With rods and reels in hand, the Hoovers set off for the Sierras, where the peaks still flew their snowy banners of cloud, the ice-worn slopes shown like snow in the sun, and the streams in the deep glacial gorges were home to fish and the water ouzel, that stubby gray bird whose strolls on the bottoms of racing streams had so fascinated John Muir many years before.[3]

Although, as in his youth, the outdoor interlude bought him a temporary respite from the pressure of duty, he could not escape the claims of public life for long. A number of his friends and admirers, especially in California, wanted him to run for president in 1920, and he was certainly interested, primarily to promote American ratification of the Treaty of Versailles. The period was one of inflation, labor unrest, fear of radicalism, race riots, uncertainty about how the economy would be reconverted to peacetime functions, bitter but fruitless debate about the League of Nations, and a leadership void because of Woodrow Wilson's illness. Almost overnight optimism about the progress of the economy toward higher productivity, better management, and greater stability was replaced with horror at wild cyclical swings, postwar depression, and industrial warfare.[4] Hoover captured the public's imagination in these troubled times less as a great humanitarian than as an "heroic administrator," a man capable of making the existing political machinery work to resolve domestic problems and of cooperating with other nations without sacrificing American independence. Engineers admired him because he embodied their dream of achieving respectability and public influence, but his appeal transcended any group or party. Eschewing radicalism of the left or the right, Hoover drew the attention of the press as a progressive who could overcome the postwar economic and social crisis because he was, in the words of one editorial, "a practical man who will do the business of the nation."[5]

Some Democrats, including Franklin Roosevelt and Edward M. House, hoped Hoover would seek their party's nomination, and for a time the New York *World* boomed him, only to lose enthusiasm when he declared himself a Republican. In a Michigan primary, in which he was entered in both the Republican and the Democratic races (without his permission), he ran first in the Democratic primary and well among Republicans.[6] But if Hoover ever considered trying for the Democratic nomination, which was plausible given his close association with the administration during the war and his admiration for Wilson, he moved back to the Republicans when Wilson flirted with a third term despite being desperately ill.[7] Hoover allowed his name to be entered in the California Republican primary in opposition to isolationist Hiram Johnson, but he did not campaign actively and was defeated by two to one in the 4 May vote. That ended his candidacy, although he had a momentary fantasy that his fourth-place delegate count might enable him to emerge as a compromise nominee at the Republican convention if the front-runners deadlocked.[8]

In the absence of any organized campaign, the strength of Hoover's appeal to Republicans in 1920 was remarkable. By his own account he had never voted in a presidential election, and neither his contribution of $1,000 to Theodore Roosevelt's campaign in 1912 nor his staunch support of the Treaty of Versailles put him in the conservative mainstream in 1920. As Food Administrator he had alienated some midwestern Republicans through his price policies, while a 5 November 1918 public letter calling for "united support of the President" on the eve of congressional elections earned him the anger or suspicion of most Republican leaders, particularly those opposed to the League of Nations. Opponents seized on the fact that he had lived outside the country for more than twenty years to impugn his patriotism and fitness for the presidency.[9]

Despite the collapse of his presidential bid, Hoover's wartime administrative triumphs made Americans eager to hear his advice about how to solve the postwar recession. When a presidentially called Industrial Conference composed of representatives of business, labor, and the public divided along class lines about what should be done to restore economic peace, Wilson asked Hoover to convoke a second conference made up only of representatives of the public, who turned out to be mostly public-spirited, retired businessmen like Hoover, Owen Young, and Julius Rosenwald. Hoover presided over many of the conference sessions, which began on 1 December 1919, and had a large hand in drafting the meeting's report, which reflected his confidence in a prosperous future instead of others' pessimism about the current crisis.[10] Among the most important of the group's recommendations were a forty-eight-hour workweek, a minimum wage, equal pay for equal work for men and women, abolition of child labor, and the creation of regional arbitration boards to promote the settlement of industrial disputes. Drawing upon the so-called Rockefeller Plan drafted by Canadian W. L. Mackenzie King, the report urged the creation of "shop committees" that would enable representatives of labor and management to meet continuously in each industry to work out disagreements. Hoover and others who had been leaders of the Wilson administration's wartime mobilization program hoped that this approach to industrial relations would create an "organic" relationship between workers and bosses that would enable both sides to see their common interest in avoiding conflict, increasing production, and maximizing prosperity for all. Reducing strikes and lockouts, he suggested to Samuel Gompers of the American Federation of Labor (AFL), would boost production by from 5 to 30 percent, and the money saved might be used to fund a national program of unemployment and sickness insurance. Neither labor nor business welcomed the proposals, however. Organized labor feared that shop committees would undermine unions, and businessmen disliked the idea of giving workers an increased role in management decisions and a larger share of profits. The conference report had little immediate effect, but the hope that class conflict could be replaced by labor-management cooperation would become one of the popular goals of the 1920s.[11] In a period of major strikes and political radicalism, Hoover's confidence that a community of interests could be built enhanced his reputation as a model administrator with a positive vision of a better future for the American people. His vision of a high wage–low price consumer economy would win increasing acceptance among both workers and businessmen as the 1920s went on.[12]

At the same time that Hoover was urging the Second Industrial Conference to find ways to end labor-management conflict, he was pursuing the same goal through the Federated American Engineering Societies (FAES), a new umbrella organization representing more than thirty engineering societies, of which he had been unanimously elected president in November 1920.[13] In his inaugural address to the new organization, he called upon engineers "to offer expert service in constructing solutions of problems" for employers, labor, farmers, merchants, and bankers on the basis of a "wider vision" of the common interest that was possible for them because they did not belong to any of these groups. "There is," he contended, "a great area of common interest between the employer and employee through the reduction of the great waste of voluntary and involuntary unemployment and the increase of production. . . . If we could secure this co-operation throughout all our economic groups we should have provided a new economic system, based neither upon the capitalism of Adam Smith nor upon the socialism of Karl Marx." It was, he concluded, up to the engineers, with their "training in quantitative thought" and their disinterested position, to lead in finding "those safe steps that make for real progress."[14]

A part of the engineers' contribution to progress, Hoover thought, would come from recommending ways to eliminate waste. In this he was following the path blazed by the prewar Taylorite Movement, which proclaimed that engineers would resolve American social conflicts through more efficient production. Howard Coffin, vice president of the Hudson Motor Car Company and president of the Society of Automotive Engineers (SAE), had offered a demonstration of the potential of this approach in 1910 when the SAE achieved widespread standardization of specifications and materials in the automobile industry.[15] Soon after Hoover was elected president of the FAES, he proposed to extend engineering leadership through an "exhaustive inquiry into elimination of industrial waste as a basis for increased national efficiency, productivity, and thus for both reconstruction and progress." For that purpose, he and his principal lieutenant, Edward Eyre Hunt, named seventeen prominent engineers to a Committee on Elimination of Waste in Industry and raised $50,000 in private donations to finance its work.[16]

Operating under considerable pressure from Hoover and Hunt, the committee completed its study in June 1921. In Hoover's foreword to the committee's published report, he listed eight kinds of waste that the committee had identified and that he believed might be eliminated to increase "efficiency in the operation of our industries": "the wastes of unemployment during depressions; from speculation and over-production in booms; from labor-turnover; from labor conflicts; from intermittent failure of transportation of supplies of fuel and power; from excessive seasonal operations; from lack of standardization; from loss in our processes and materials." Taken together, he concluded, these wastes "combine to represent a huge deduction from the goods and services that we might all enjoy if we could do a better job of it."[17]

The "primary question," Hoover told a group of engineers in September 1919, "is the better division of the products of industry and the steady development of higher productivity." Farmers, industrial workers, professionals, and employers must all recognize that they were "absolutely interdependent" and must work together for "the reduction of waste both nationally and individually."[18] That could be achieved, he insisted, without government control, but with government support through "research, intellectual leadership, and prohibitions upon the abuse of power."[19] "While I am no believer in extending the bureaucratic functions of the Government," he declared, "I am a strong believer in the Government intervening to induce active cooperation in the community itself."[20]

Hoover's insistence upon voluntarism and decentralization in this process was somewhat surprising, given the fact that as an engineer he was a leading member of the "new national class" whose claim to authority was scientific knowledge.[21] These technical professionals were drawn to standardized, national solutions of problems, and in the Progressive Era they had established conservation as the preserve of the federal government. Like other engineers, Hoover was beginning to see the benefits of conservation, but he viewed it as a means to an end, not as an end in itself. His goal was to make the economic system more efficient, and conservation seemed likely to do that. But unlike many engineers, he was also a businessman concerned about economic motivation as well as efficiency. As he explained a number of years later, the American system of free individual enterprise had produced an economy of plenty, within which it had become possible to talk about diffusion of income, economic security, and the abolition of poverty, but "national regimentation" would nullify the very freedom and initiative that had made such discussion possible.[22] Engineers could suggest ways of making the economy work even better, but to impose those proposals from above would destroy the freedom that made the system work. Thus Hoover found himself in the paradoxical position of advocating a national program that he was willing to see implemented only through local, voluntary initiatives.

His campaign for the reduction of waste and for the fair distribution of the higher profits to be realized from more efficient production represented a distillation of the lessons he had learned as a mining engineer and as a business executive. It also built upon arguments for the planned development of resources that had been advanced by prewar progressives. Whereas earlier conservationists had emphasized planned exploitation of resources in their natural state, however, Hoover took the logic a step further. If it was sensible to mine only minerals that were actually needed, or to reforest cutover areas, it was equally sensible to make sure that once raw materials entered the manufacturing process, they were used with the greatest possible efficiency. That was the principal thrust of the FAES report on industrial waste.

The report concluded that greater efficiency could extend resources in such a way that prosperity would be accessible to everyone. Neither the Progressive Era utilitarian conservationists nor Hoover made a distinction between renewable and nonrenewable resources. Everyone assumed, as an FAES fund-raising letter put it, that all sorts of resources were "apparently unlimited," and that "industrial democracy" could assure the equitable distribution of prosperity.[23] Hoover's own habits were frugal, and he was raised in a society of scarcity where more production was an unquestioned goal and trained as a mining engineer whose primary duty was to find and exploit new mineral resources. His campaign against waste was a creative attempt to extend prosperity to more people. He did not ask whether there were enough resources of all sorts in the world to assure universally high living standards.

Hoover was confident that if conservation could make production more efficient, cut costs, and raise profits, not even the most conservative business-man was likely to object. And if his argument had stopped there, he would probably have been right. He went on to contend, however, that the advent of a consumer society "preoccupied with . . . comfort and bodily well-being, with luxury, spending, and acquisition, with more goods this year than last, more next year than this," made cooperation essential between managers and workers, and that such cooperation could assure happiness for both. Many representatives of both labor and capital doubted that such cooperation was possible or desirable. The FAES report was thus more about something that might be called welfare capitalism than conservation.[24]

Even before the war, Hoover's claims that engineers would find innovative ways to use resources for the benefit of all had attracted attention. In December 1916, at the urging of a number of engineers who argued that much of the work of the Interior Department had to do with engineering, Secretary Franklin K. Lane had offered Hoover an appointment as assistant secretary in charge of the Bureau of Mines, the Bureau of Indian Affairs, the Reclamation Service, and the Alaskan Railroad. Hoover was tempted, but decided in the end that he could not leave the Belgian relief program.[25]

Lane's offer reflected the main thrust of the progressive conservation movement. "Its essence," as Samuel Hays has pointed out, "was rational planning to promote efficient development and use of all natural resources." They "envisaged, even though they did not realize their aims, a political system guided by the ideal of efficiency and dominated by the technicians who could best determine how to achieve it."[26]

Other, less dominant, strains in the early conservation movement also appealed to Hoover. As a westerner who had grown up among farmers and small businessmen, he shared the attitude of William Howard Taft's secretary of the interior, Richard Ballinger, that federal conservation policies must not block the rise of small entrepreneurs.[27] Unlike some of the easterners who dominated the early conservation movement, Ballinger, Franklin K. Lane, and Hoover stressed development more than restriction and also favored local rather than central control. They did not see themselves as populists attacking private corporations and expected business to recognize that conservation was very much in its own interest.[28]

Hoover believed that programs should be designed by experts but administered as much as possible by the people most affected by them. This was a principle he developed as an engineer and refined during the war. When applied to federal resource policies, it delighted westerners frustrated with the centralized programs of the pre–World War I era.

The original progressive conservation policies, developed by Theodore Roosevelt and Gifford Pinchot, had assumed that control over resources would be closely held in Washington, in large part because most of the remaining public lands of the United States were under federal authority. By the end of the Roosevelt administration in 1909, what were seen as high-handed, insensitive, antigrowth policies emanating from Washington had aroused growing hostility in the West. In the 1908 presidential election the only two western states carried by Democrat William Jennings Bryan were Colorado and Nevada, both centers of opposition to federal conservation policy. In Oregon Governor Jay Bowerman denounced "officious and unwarranted" interference with the livestock industry by federal authorities, while in Congress western representatives proposed various schemes to turn authority and revenues from western forests, minerals, and grazing lands over to the states within which they were located.[29]

By the beginning of the Wilson administration in 1913, the struggle over conservation had lost some of its bitterness. Gifford Pinchot had been fired by President Taft, and many state leaders had come to the reluctant conclusion that the states had neither the money nor the organization to take full control over resources. Moreover, federal reclamation and forestry programs were bringing benefits to many western states at minimal cost. Voters, Congress, and the federal courts had all endorsed the federal control of major conservation programs, making a large-scale transfer of authority from Washington to the states unlikely. Under the circumstances, western state leaders softened their position, asking to share in making decisions and setting priorities rather than seeking full control. The Wilson administration was receptive to this new western attitude, with Californian Franklin K. Lane as secretary of the interior more interested in pleasing westerners than in dramatic innovations or enlarging conservation programs.[30]

Secretary Lane proved ingenious in finding conservation programs such as reclamation and the development of Alaska that won goodwill in the West. His support of a professional National Park Service that had as its goal both the protection of the parks' natural features and the attraction of tourists pleased not only western advocates of development but those Americans who saw the protection of natural beauty as the principal objective of conservation. On the other hand, Lane's support of San Francisco's application to convert the Hetch Hetchy Valley of Yosemite National Park into a reservoir drew the applause both of westerners and of Pinchot's followers who emphasized the planned development of resources. Esthetic conservationists were outraged by the Hetch Hetchy decision and concerned about Lane's bias toward development, even in the national parks, but the secretary's ambiguous policies quieted the criticism of conservation that had been growing in the West.[31]

Much of Lane's success was attributable to his genial, open, honest personality. He was able to smooth over disputes and soothe prickly personalities much more successfully than his predecessors; but beneath the surface, major disagreements remained. Many westerners were still suspicious and skeptical about federal control over so many of the resources in their states. Increasingly professionalized federal agencies, such as the Park Service, believed that use decisions should be made on scientific rather than political grounds. Esthetic preservationists saw utilitarian conservationists as exploiters in disguise, while utilitarians suspected the preservationists of opposing all development. Small businesses frequently favored rapid, unregulated, resource exploitation, whereas large corporations saw benefits in controlled development. At bottom, the main issue was a profound disagreement about America's future, which had, among other things, significant class implications: Was the goal to be rapid growth and a rising standard of living, even at the cost of environmental degradation, or was it to be protection of the quality of life (measured, depending on the observer, either in nonmaterial terms or as the prerogative of the privileged), even if that meant retarding economic growth? Hoover assumed that the problem could be solved in ways that would benefit everyone.

Before the 1920s, probably few Americans, even those most active in the conservation movement, believed that progress and preservation were incompatible. The movement had its origins in the mid–nineteenth century, with small groups of citizens concerned about preserving wildlife or protecting watersheds, and with scientists worried about dwindling forest reserves. In the frontier era their ideas seemed eccentric to most Americans, but as settlement moved into the arid regions of the West, water became a resource so vital and scarce that conserving it and planning its exploitation emerged as essential to continued development. What was more, the costs involved with damming rivers and diverting water for power and irrigation were so great that private individuals, groups, or even local governments could not afford them. Only the federal government had the resources necessary to plan and manage the development of whole river basins.[32]

In the late nineteenth century, conservationists won federal support for setting aside forest reserves in the West in an effort to bring the wasteful exploitation of timber under control, but the high point of this first period of governmental action was the passage of the Reclamation Act of 1902. The act epitomized the guiding principles of the early conservationists: planned development (of watersheds, in this case); freedom from political influence by putting independent experts in charge of projects; multiple uses of resources; and the creation of a self-sustaining development program through user fees. In combination with President Roosevelt's aggressive practice of withdrawing many public lands from private entry, the reclamation policy seemed to commit the government to wide-ranging management of natural resources and public lands.[33]

One result of this approach was to arouse opposition from westerners who, although the main beneficiaries of the conservation policy, resented its limitations on state and private control over resources. A second result, somewhat less obvious, was the rapid growth of a scientifically trained federal bureaucracy of resource managers. In the Forest Service, the Biological Survey, the Bureau of Fisheries, the Bureau of Mines, the Bureau of Soils, the Geological Survey, the Reclamation Service, and later, the National Park Service, scientific bureaucracies pressed forward the agenda of planned development.[34] From these experts came policies to maintain and improve renewable resources and plans for the development of nonrenewable ones, as well as powerful arguments for federal management of resources in opposition to the claims of local politicians and businessmen. In the 1920s these activities continued and expanded, but dissenting voices would also rise among government scientists as they began to understand the science of ecology and to see some of its implications for resource policy.[35]

Outside the government, the older conservation organizations like the National Audubon Society (founded 1905) and the Sierra Club (1892) focused on esthetic issues; or, like the Boone and Crockett Club (1887) and the American Game Protective Association (1905), on sport hunting; or, like Gifford Pinchot's National Conservation Association (1909) and the American Forestry Association (1875), on the promotion of a philosophy of managed development. None of these organizations could claim more than seven thousand members, and although they might influence public debate from time to time, none had broad and sustained political power. In 1922, however, an enthusiastic Chicago advertising man, Will H. Dilg, opened a new era when he founded the Izaak Walton League. Named after the seventeenth-century author of *The Compleat Angler* and guided by Dilg's unlimited optimism, the Waltonians acquired a membership of one hundred thousand by 1925 and became the dominant extragovernmental conservation force of the 1920s.[36]

A boundlessly energetic booster, Dilg created "a clubhouse atmosphere of masculine fellowship" that drew thousands of urban men like Herbert Hoover who longed for the clean, unpolluted fishing streams of their youth and enjoyed an opportunity to "rough it" in the woods with friends. But Dilg was more sophisticated than he seemed on the surface. The Walton League's magazine, *Outdoor America,* featured some of the finest writers in America, and its articles ranged over many environmental and conservation issues. There were plenty of articles on fishing, of course, but there were also essays on water pollution, the draining of wetlands, forest fires, reforestation, camping, guns, and even a short-lived woman's section. Behind Dilg was a nineman executive committee made up mostly of wealthy executives.[37] Dilg was no radical. He spoke for those American leaders who believed that a consumer society needed a clean, wholesome environment, and that progress could coexist with a healthy natural world. Although Dilg, a better promoter than manager, ran the Izaak Walton League into debt and eventually lost control of the organization, his conception of conservation and environmentalism as vital elements of the consumer society became a major focus of the movement in the 1920s.

A significant reason for the lasting importance of Dilg's ideas was that one of the Izaak Walton League's early and enthusiastic members was Herbert Hoover. Hoover contributed a two-paragraph note extolling fishing and the "scientific conservation and . . . replenishment" of fisheries to the first issue of the organization's magazine in the summer of 1922. The league gave enthusiastic support to his efforts as secretary of commerce to protect the Alaskan salmon fisheries and to control oil pollution in coastal waters, and he responded warmly, accepting the organization's honorary presidency from 1926 to 1932. Like Dilg, whose work Hoover applauded, he believed that there was a wider issue than merely the protection of fisheries. "As we are improving our economic life," he wrote to Dilg, "we are steadily decreasing our hours of labor and extending periods of vacation, and one of our problems now is to find healthful and sound recreation for our people in this increased leisure time. The work of your association is a direct and great contribution to this end."[38]

The source of this new leisure, whose fruitful employment was the focus of Dilg's and Hoover's concern, was the advance of the consumer economy in America. Many people had been startled by the performance of the economy during World War I, when, despite a heavy commitment to the military and the support of the Allies, there was scarcely any disruption of production for the civilian market. Apparently, the economy was capable of levels of production scarcely imagined before the war; and during the 1920s, this promise was realized. Per capita income rose about 30 percent, productivity per factory man-hour increased by 75 percent, real earnings of wage workers went up about 22 percent, and the work week was reduced by 4 percent.[39] Even before the war, the conviction that people achieved fulfillment only by making things of lasting value had been weakened by a rosy vision of rising incomes and unlimited consumption, and the wartime boom put affluence within reach. Although Hoover could not accept the idea of measuring his own happiness in terms of consumption—the engineer's achievements, he bragged, are all embodied "in hard substance"—he believed that affluence was the inevitable result of the success of modern capitalism, and that Americans must learn to live with it. "He is never sympathetic to the old-fashioned political economy which lays emphasis on thrift," said a friend in 1923. "He believes in the maximum of consumption so long as that consumption is in proportion to the earning capacity of the consumer. He thinks this is what makes for the higher stage of civilization."[40] Society's leaders must show how Americans could achieve meaningful lives in the consumer society. The problem, as Hoover saw it, was that "in the specialization of industry we have dulled the worker by intense production, without giving him any other interest."[41]

Hoover probably did not know it, but this was a problem that by 1920 had occupied one of America's leading economists, Simon Patten, for more than thirty years. Between 1886, when Patten first took a position at the Wharton School of Economics in Philadelphia, and his death in 1922, he "developed a theory of consumption that fused his rejection of the past with a dream of a better future."[42] He argued that industrial America was capable of creating a society free of hunger, contagious diseases, and unemployment. Modern capitalist businesses, he believed, would find it in their interest to cooperate rather than compete with each other and to advance the public welfare through full employment, high wages, and the promotion of the general condition of society and the economy. As a result of this change from an economy of scarcity to one of abundance, "men would no longer be forced to struggle for the basic necessities and comforts of life" and "must develop new social, aesthetic, moral, and religious values and new restraints against destructive desires."[43]

Professional economists of Patten's day praised his originality but largely ignored his central thesis—that an economy of abundance would require the development of new standards of behavior. Leaders of the pre–World War I Progressive movement, however, had seized upon the idea that a society of surplus offered the possibility of eliminating all poverty and injustice in America. Social workers and sociologists such as Lester F. Ward, Edward A.

Ross, and Edward Devine found in Patten's ideas a justification for new programs to lift the poor into the ranks of consumers, and Patten's student Walter Weyl popularized some of Patten's ideas in the influential 1912 book *The New Democracy*. Put in somewhat exaggerated terms, their message was that "real 'happiness' could be had largely through money incomes and consumption, not through satisfying labor or a stake in the community. Like other Americans who feared the social results of the industrial revolution, they believed Americans should forget about work and turn instead to leisure, entertainment, play, and consumption."[44]

The key point in Patten's theory was his application of the law of marginal utility to morality. According to the principle of marginal utility, as a person consumes more and more of a commodity, each additional portion becomes less and less appealing, and the consumer turns to other goods. When an essentially unlimited supply of goods is available, desire is satiated more and more quickly, and the level of desire is thus kept low. "To have a high standard of life," wrote Patten, "means to enjoy a pleasure intensely and to tire of it quickly. Any pleasure soon becomes stale unless it can be dropped to make place for something new." Surplus energies left over when desires are so easily satiated could, Patten contended, be rechanneled into helping other people, into promoting the public welfare. To create the perfect society, then, it was essential to do away with "all traditional restraints on consumption, all taboos against luxury," although Patten's prediction about how people would choose to use their new affluence perhaps reflects the innocence of a man who cared little for material things. Country holidays, boat excursions, and Sunday picnics were the activities he believed would fill Americans' free time. Small wonder he could conclude that "economic activity exercises the faculties which, at a later period, become moral."[45]

Patten was inconsistent in his treatment of the marginal utility idea, sometimes arguing that it would exercise a natural restraint on consumption and automatically divert people's energies into socially beneficial channels, and at others indicating that guidance would be necessary to achieve that end. Nor did he, as an individual, live according to his own principles. An ascetic rather than a hedonist, Patten showed no interest in recreation or consumption, owned little, and was more likely to give away money than to spend it on himself. Unmarried and with few friends, he spent his years in work instead of play.[46]

Like Patten, Herbert Hoover was incapable of abandoning himself to a life of leisure and consumption, but he too recognized that industrial work was providing affluence but not satisfaction. He believed that socially responsible corporate managers should promote the welfare of society as well as raise profits, and he hoped to find leisure activities for workers that would give them personal pleasure and strengthen the community. We have no way of knowing whether Hoover had ever heard of Patten, but both were grappling with a widely expressed concern in postwar America: a sense that old injunctions to frugality and hard work no longer seemed urgent enough to give life purpose, but uncertainty about what should take their place. As a study commissioned by the President's Research Committee on Social Trends concluded in 1933, "The traditional amusements of a rural people [had become] pitifully inadequate and unsatisfying for factory workers and for the large numbers of people caught in the meshes of the business and industrial world."[47]

Even if Hoover did not read Patten's work, many of the professional economists with whom he consulted during the 1920s were concerned about similar problems. Representative of those with whom he worked closely were Edwin Gay, first dean of the Harvard Business School, first chairman of the National Bureau of Economic Research founded in 1919, and one of Hoover's principal advisers in the reorganization of the Commerce Department; Julius Klein, head of the Bureau of Foreign and Domestic Commerce in the Commerce Department; Leo Wolman, an adviser to the Amalgamated Clothing Workers of America, an early member of the National Bureau, and a member of the Economic Advisory Committee appointed by Secretary Hoover in September 1921; Wesley Clair Mitchell, research director of the National Bureau, a member of the Economic Advisory Council, and a student of Veblen's, whose work in the 1920s focused on trying to understand and control business cycles; George E. Barnett, a Johns Hopkins University professor who specialized in the study of the impact of technology on consumption and unemployment; and Allyn Abbott Young, who taught that increased production led to increased demand which, in turn, stimulated production in an endless cycle. All of these men (and many other economists of the era) "shared with Hoover," writes Guy Alchon, "a basic faith in the social virtues of technocratic analysis and prescription."[48]

These economists agreed with Patten and Hoover that distribution and consumption had become more central to the economy than production, they generally favored the payment of high wages to maintain that situation, and they groped for new psychic rewards to replace pride of craftsmanship among workers in the consumer economy.[49] One of the most striking features of the 1920s, declared Leo Wolman in a report by a committee of professional economists chaired by Hoover in 1928–29, was "the rapidly increasing number of families in the United States having a considerable margin of earnings available for 'optional consumption'—optional in the sense that this portion of the income may be saved or spent, and if spent the manner of its spending may be determined by the tastes of the consumer or the nature of the appeals made to him by the industries competing for his patronage." Moreover, the decade saw a marked trend toward increased leisure as the result of better planning and modern machinery in factories and the adoption of time-and-labor-saving appliances and services in the home. For these affluent Americans, leisure began to be seen as "consumable," and businesses increasingly realized "that people can not 'consume' leisure without consuming goods and services."[50]

A prominent sociologist, commissioned by the President's Research Committee on Social Trends (created by Hoover in 1929) to study leisure and recreation, concluded that recreation "was no longer stigmatized as a form of idleness" but had "gained recognition as a means to healthful living." Governments at all levels had found it profitable to provide public recreational facilities, and "recreation [had] become so securely entrenched in the habits and folkways of the people that it is now a dominating force wielding strong influence in many directions." Its power to shape the futures of governments, industries, and culture made it, declared this scholar, a subject deserving of the most serious study.[51]

Like these scholars, Hoover had come to see the triumph of the consumer economy as inevitable, the creation of leisure as an important byproduct of that situation, and the management of the consumption of leisure as one of the most important challenges facing modern society.[52] Hoover was, however, even less willing than Simon Patten to leave the development of socially beneficial leisure activities to the natural workings of the law of marginal utility, nor was he willing to empower the state to dictate, through taxation for example, what would be acceptable uses of leisure, as Walter Weyl seemingly advocated.[53] Since Hoover did not believe in a coercive state, his dilemma was how to persuade affluent Americans that they should voluntarily invest their leisure in activities he regarded as constructive.

Complicating Hoover's thought about how to manage the benefits of affluence was his lingering concern that the prosperity of the present was not a permanent change in mankind's status.[54] He agreed that science and technology had given a huge boost to productivity, which offered the opportunity for alleviating poverty and dramatically raising living standards, but he saw affluence as no more than the foam upon the wave of production. What mattered was the maintenance of the productive capacities that satisfied basic needs, and nothing must be allowed to threaten that base. Raised in a culture of scarcity in which production rather than consumption was the goal, he believed that the amelioration of society's problems must come from the surplus of production that went beyond the satisfaction of absolute needs. If, for any reason, that surplus shrank or disappeared, then social programs dependent on redistribution of the surplus, such as the promotion of recreation, would become irrelevant.[55]

It did not require the collapse of the stock market in 1929 to bring out the doubts of Hoover and others about the consumer society. Many Americans felt ambivalent about what was happening to their society during the 1920s. Hoover's discomfort with unlimited consumerism was shared by many businessmen, who believed that giving workers too much money to spend and too much leisure time would lead to sloth and moral decline. And if businessmen's doubts can be dismissed as self-interested, it should be noted that similarly pejorative judgments about the use workers were making of leisure also ran through the study of "Middletown" by the social scientists Helen and Robert Lynd, and through a book on leisure activities published by a committee appointed by President Hoover to study "recent social trends." Whether from the Right or the Left, the critics were not opposed to having affluence and leisure more widespread, but they "shared a hostility to commercial recreation and hoped that with affluence people would pursue 'higher' goals."[56] "'Bad' use of leisure . . . ," declared a 1928 study of the subject, "usually involves the more widespread and specious forms of commercial recreation."[57] The problem was how to get Americans to agree with these critics about what constituted desirable leisure activities, and then to prefer those activities over others.

Hoover had been thinking since before the war about setting down his ideas on business, politics, and values, and in 1922 he published his most systematic analysis of these subjects, a pamphlet entitled *American Individualism*.[58] The individualism he celebrated in this essay was not selfish or egocentric. To Hoover, individualism meant personal opportunity like that which had allowed him to rise from poverty to success. It was essential, he wrote, to "safeguard to every individual an equality of opportunity to take that position in the community to which his intelligence, character, ability, and ambition entitle him."[59] This did not mean that those who rose to the top through competition would then be free to indulge themselves selfishly. "The problem of the world," he declared, "is to restrain the destructive instincts while strengthening and enlarging those of altruistic character and constructive impulse." Although he was somewhat vague as to how these altruistic ideals were to be promoted and the selfish instincts held in check, Hoover was confident that education and "a rising vision of service" would assure that "liberty, justice, intellectual welfare, equality of opportunity, and stimulation to service" would come more and more to characterize American society. Socialism would fail because it demanded too much altruism; the "frozen strata of classes" in European society would preclude progress because the class system prevented the rise of able individuals.[60]

Hoover's vision of the earthly paradise that would spring forth when individual energies were liberated was worthy of Simon Patten in his most optimistic moments. "We have long since realized," wrote Hoover, "that the basis of an advancing civilization must be a high and growing standard of living for all the people, not for a single class; that education, food, clothing, housing, and the spreading use of what we so often term nonessentials, are the real fertilizers of the soil from which spring the finer flowers of life." To assure "further advance in the standard of living," it was only necessary to have "greater invention, greater elimination of waste, greater production and better distribution of commodities and services." And paradoxical as it might seem, the cooperative movement among industries that was reducing "many of the great wastes of over-reckless competition in production and distribution" did not threaten opportunity for individuals, for "cooperation in its current economic sense represents the initiative of self-interest blended with a sense of service . . . ," although Hoover also admitted that there were "forces in business which would destroy equality of opportunity." It was up to government to curb those forces without interfering with the production and distribution of commodities and services. Progress, he concluded, "requires only a guardianship of the vital principles of our individualism with its safeguard of true equality of opportunity in them."[61]

Hoover's environmental program grew out of the arguments expressed in *American Individualism.* If industry could be made more efficient, one of the benefits of the process would be opportunities for greater individual leisure. It seemed important to him that Americans enjoying the leisure created by affluence should be steered away from the destructive, synthetic, or mass-produced pleasures of commercial play and toward the "constructive rejuvenating joy" of the out-of-doors.[62] Like his contemporaries, Hoover was a materialist who believed that progress in the physical conditions of life was within reach, and that experts—particularly those like engineers trained in rational calculation—could shape and direct that progress to the benefit of all. But he was unable to escape his childhood religious training and accept the ultimate materialist conviction that affluence was the highest value of human life.[63]

Nevertheless, Hoover recognized that, as Andrew Ross puts it, "in the age of environmental accounting, nature enters the market not just as source of property or mineral value, nor just for its capacity to sustain its soil, water, and air, but also for its own sake, as a desirable signifier with inherent worth and value to consumer markets."[64] Hoover was one of the first American leaders to recognize that nature's commodity value included its recreational as well as its extractive uses. He believed, perhaps naively, that policies could combine conservation and consumption. If Americans learned to use leisure well, they would reaffirm the spiritual and cultural values that were, he feared, in danger of being subverted by affluence.

4 | Conservation in Commerce

On 5 November 1920 president-elect Warren Harding invited Herbert Hoover to visit him in Marion, Ohio. Although Hoover aroused the suspicions of some Republicans because of his reputation for liberalism, of others for his support of the Treaty of Versailles, and of still others who feared he would try to dominate any administration of which he was part, his reputation as a brilliant administrator and as a rising figure in the Republican Party made him an almost inevitable candidate for a cabinet position. At their meeting on 12 December, the two men discussed whether Hoover would enter the cabinet, and if so, in which department. His skills and experience seemed appropriate for either Interior or Commerce, but Hoover saw greater opportunities in Commerce, even though Interior was traditionally more important.[1]

Reports that Hoover would be in the cabinet released a flood of criticisms and complaints from Republicans opposed to the Treaty of Versailles, and on 22 December Hoover drafted a letter to Harding asking that his name be dropped from consideration to spare the administration any embarrassment.[2] With interesting business opportunities in view, he had no taste for a political brawl over a relatively minor cabinet position. Whether or not the letter was actually sent, Hoover's doubts disappeared after Harding engineered a series of deals that reduced opposition to him among Senate Republicans and assured him that the secretary of commerce would have more influence in the new administration than ever before.[3]

In a long telegram to Harding on 23 February 1921, Hoover spelled out his understanding of the powers that had induced him to accept the Commerce post. These included the rebuilding and strengthening of the department through transfer to it of "such bureaus as properly belong in its field" and the cooperation of the department of state in undertaking an aggressive program of promoting foreign trade. Hoover would also be authorized to initiate "a vigorous policy of leadership in stimulation of industries to cooperation among themselves in the direction of reduction of waste in our manufacturing and distribution methods, in the direction of greater standardization in the production of certain essentials and in the direction of stimulating and organizing our foreign markets." He would be empowered to work with the Labor Department to find ways to reduce labor-management conflict, and he would be free to solicit information about "social and industrial currents" from individuals and organizations.[4] The full implications of these terms were not clear from the telegram, but it was obvious that Harding was giving Hoover unprecedented authority to make the Commerce Department a dominant force in administration policy.

What was most novel about Hoover's approach to the Commerce Department was not spelled out in his telegram to Harding. Unlike his more conservative Republican colleagues, Hoover believed that the federal government should take an active role not only in combating the postwar recession that was then gripping the country, but in promoting long-term economic growth and moderating business cycles. He intended, through the voluntary cooperation of business, agriculture, and labor, to reduce waste, expand markets, promote countercyclical investment, and raise living standards for all Americans. These plans, said the new secretary, rested on "three legs": the implementation of the waste reduction study then being conducted by the Federated American Engineering Societies (FAES), the provision by the government of new statistical information about business and trade that would promote rational planning of production, and the expansion of markets at home and overseas.[5] In all of these areas Hoover envisioned the Commerce Department providing large amounts of precise information and expert advice to business, but not dictating or controlling business practices beyond what was necessary to prevent unscrupulous men from taking advantage of the public.

The ideas that Hoover thus sketched out at the start of his career in the Commerce Department implied a distinct vision of what a consumer society ought to be. Whereas some members of the new administration wished to free business from all government control, Hoover assumed a continuing, positive role for federal authority, in providing information, offering vision and advice, and, if necessary, stepping in to prevent selfish and unfair practices. His goal was less the accumulation of wealth by those at the top of the economy than the diffusion of prosperity throughout the society. Nor did he measure economic success solely in terms of wealth; a society that provided its members large measures of leisure and the opportunities to fill it with personally enriching and socially beneficial activities might present a very different definition of a culture of consumption.

His plans also implied, in one degree or another, the development of a conservation program. Waste reduction was of course very much at the center of Progressive Era conservation, as was the idea of rationalizing production on the basis of statistical information provided by experts. But there was another side to conservation in Hoover's new era. Domestic market expansion (and to some extent the same was true of foreign markets) depended in large part on the high wages and increasing leisure of the consumer economy. Hoover was one of the first to realize that this new generation of affluent consumers was likely to regard outdoor recreation, environmental quality, and the purchase and use of recreational products as essential amenities of their increased leisure. The more Hoover argued that the government should promote the growth and stability of an economy based largely on consumer spending, the more he was led toward adopting the conservation and environmental policies that could both sustain and potentially fulfill the consumer society.

The FAES report, completed in June 1921, was the starting point for Hoover's attack on industrial waste. It recommended measures to rationalize production, to minimize labor conflicts, and to economize through standardization, but it did not apply these recommendations to individual industries.[6] Secretary Hoover was eager to make the specific implementation of the committee's principles an early priority of a reorganized and revitalized Department of Commerce.[7]

When Hoover became secretary, the department had about ten thousand full-time employees in eight bureaus. Their offices were scattered around Washington, and they had little connection with one another and no sense of a common mission. Thus the Bureau of the Census was concerned almost exclusively with its decennial count of the population. The Bureau of Standards was the depository for official standards of measurement and carried on testing in relation to government purchases. The Bureau of Fisheries conducted rather academic research about fish and fisheries, raised fish to stock depleted waters, and attempted some primitive regulation of the seal and salmon fisheries of Alaska. The Bureau of Foreign and Domestic Commerce, despite its name, was concerned almost exclusively with collecting statistics about foreign trade. Other small divisions included the Bureau of Lighthouses, the Coast and Geodetic Survey, the Bureau of Navigation, and the Steamboat Inspection Service.[8]

The Bureau of Standards was Hoover's choice to promote the implementation of the FAES recommendations regarding standardization and elimination of waste in manufacturing. First established in 1901, the bureau had been employed primarily in testing materials purchased by the government, but during the war it had demonstrated its potential by recommending the standardization of ordnance, airplanes, and other military supplies. It seemed to Hoover that the bureau's scientists and laboratories, if made available to industry, could develop standardized specifications for many individual products and simplified techniques for manufacturing them. He believed strongly that standardization and simplification would result in savings in manufacturing costs that would be passed along to consumers. To promote these developments, he created within the bureau a new Division of Simplified Practice.[9]

In a January 1922 letter, Hoover spelled out in detail how he wanted the simplification and standardization process to be promoted by the Division of Simplified Practice. The division was to "locate fields in which simplification is desired by producer, distributor or user," and then form a small committee made up of representatives of the affected interests to draft a preliminary proposal. On the basis of the preliminary report, the division was to call a conference, "at the Department or at some more convenient central point, of representatives from all associations interested to discuss the [preliminary report] as a basis for simplification or more complete standardization," and to "secure from the conference action" leading to the adoption, implementation, and constant oversight of a formal Simplified Practice Recommendation.[10] From start to finish, the approach was characteristic of Hoover's philosophy of guided voluntarism—a program initiated and supervised by government experts but implemented voluntarily by the interests affected. As he explained to one of the groups called to Washington to draft a Simplified Practice Recommendation, "There is no question of governmental interference in business involved. Such help as we can offer in experience and experts and in getting interested groups—of producers and consumers both—together is given only upon the expressed wish of the trades themselves." The principal object of the whole process, Hoover stressed, was to reduce the price paid by consumers or users.[11] In short, the secretary contended that simplification and standardization would make production more efficient, thus permitting price reductions for consumers without reducing profits for producers. Both producer and consumer would win, living standards would rise, and the growth of the consumer economy would be stimulated. By 1928 the Commerce Department estimated optimistically that standardization and simplification were already saving as much as $600 million a year.[12]

Whether simplification and standardization would result in conservation over the long term was by no means clear. The point of reducing production costs, after all, was to cut prices consumers paid, thus stimulating demand and consumption, which seemed likely to result eventually in greater exploitation of resources. The problem was explicit in a discussion Hoover had with representatives of the bituminous coal industry in March 1924. "If," he told them, "we are to have continuation of large employment . . . , we must have reduction in the price of coal as well as other basic industrial commodities. . . .

The only way to constructively secure an assurance of lower prices necessary for assured production is by the elimination of wastes both in production and distribution."[13] Hoover's assumption was that conservation would result in more efficient production and lower prices, thus encouraging greater consumption, which would seem to negate any conservation benefits. But was that the end of the story? Although Hoover did not say it and may have been unaware of the possibility, over the longer term, rising consumption would presumably drive prices up, thus curtailing demand. Whether the new balance between demand and price would ultimately promote conservation remained to be seen.

Hoover's belief that raising the American standard of living by assuring high wages to producers and low prices to consumers would also promote the nationwide conservation of natural resources is well exemplified in the Commerce Department's campaign to secure a standardization and simplification program in the lumber industry.[14] Beginning in the 1880s, a small group of lumbermen began to try to reduce overproduction and to control cycles of boom and bust through cooperative action. Whatever modest successes they achieved in good times, however, were lost in bad periods when many companies increased production to compensate for falling prices, thus intensifying competition and overproduction. Moreover, industry efforts to restrict production frequently drew the hostile attention of the Justice Department. In 1917 Wilson Compton, secretary-manager of the National Lumber Manufacturers Association, declared that the effort to reduce production had been "discouraged from within and repressed from without."[15]

The lumber industry was given a brief glimpse of what might be when lumber shortages during World War I led to a temporary relaxation of antitrust laws. The opportunity for cooperation did not long outlast the war, however, being declared illegal by the Supreme Court in the Hardwood Case of December 1921. Hoover deplored the court's decision, but there was no doubt the Hardwood Case dealt a blow to his efforts to assist the industry through cooperative action.[16]

There might, however, be indirect routes to the same goal that the court could accept. Standardization, waste elimination, and sustained-yield forestry all required cooperative activity among producers that would have as an indirect effect cuts in production but did not directly involve price fixing and might thus be legal. Although Hoover was very interested in ideas proposed by forester David T. Mason for sustained-yield forestry and reductions in timber sales from government-owned lands, these approaches to the problem fell within the purview of the Agriculture Department's Forest Service rather than the Commerce Department, so his emphasis in the 1920s was on standardization and waste elimination.[17]

The industry itself had begun to consider standardization during the war. The first American Lumber Congress, meeting in 1919, had called for standardization of sizes of finished lumber, and the proposal was renewed at the second meeting of the group in April 1920.[18] Early in 1922, the Forest Service took up the idea, proposing a national conference on "the question of simplification and grading of wood products." Hoover was instantly on his guard. These issues, he declared, were "specifically" under "the authorities of the Department of Commerce." Secretary of Agriculture Wallace, faced with Hoover's feisty defense of his turf, beat a retreat, agreeing that Commerce was responsible for promoting standardization.[19] When the National Lumber Manufacturers' Association opened a special four-day conference in May 1922 to discuss standardizing "trade nomenclature and grades and to eliminate unnecessary varieties," Secretary Hoover was on hand to greet the delegates. He emphasized, as he had all along, the potential of standardization for simultaneously reducing costs to consumers and increasing profits to producers.[20]

There the matter remained for the next year as the producers struggled to agree on a system of standardized lumber sizes and grades. In January 1924, however, in a message to the Southern Forestry Congress meeting in Savannah, Hoover raised a new issue. Not only would standardization "and better adaptation of lumber products to the needs of various consumers" increase profits, he declared, but such changes "are also a great field for conservation of forest products."[21] That autumn, Agriculture Secretary Wallace called a national conference on utilization of forest products to discuss ways "to cut down our enormous forest drain and lessen the severity of the timber shortage" and invited Hoover to address the meeting. Although Hoover said initially that he could not attend the conference, he changed his mind, became a dominant force at it, and was selected as the chair of a new National Committee on Wood Utilization, whose charge stressed the importance of finding ways to reduce the rate at which timber was being cut. Now thoroughly aroused to the need for conservation, Hoover argued that "two-thirds of the original primeval forests of the country have been cut," and that "timber is now being cut at a rate four times faster than the replacement through new growth." He also sounded his old theme that "between the cutting of the forest and the final use of the wood nearly sixty-five per cent of the total volume was previously lost."[22] He had now joined conservation to waste reduction as a fundamental objective of his policy. "The elimination of waste is all assets," declared Hoover enthusiastically. "It is an asset to the manufacturer, to the dealer, to the consumer. Waste in wood is a waste of our diminishing forests; it is a national waste."[23] Or, as a song published by the Pine Institute of America put it, "De wolf am a coming right in de door, When de old Piney Wood ain't here no more."[24]

Hoover praised the National Committee on Wood Utilization as "Exhibit A of government by cooperation," but its work did not by any means represent the only approach to conservation during his tenure in Commerce.[25] A second major area of concentration was on fishing and fisheries, where Hoover also tried, with mixed results, to find ways for government and industry to work together to conserve resources without sacrificing producers' profits.

Hoover was determined from the beginning of his term as Secretary of Commerce that the Bureau of Fisheries would pursue an active conservation policy in cooperation with the fisheries industry. Fisheries Commissioner Hugh M. Smith, a Wilson administration appointee who had developed an extensive program of scientific research, was regarded by his new boss as having "outlived his usefulness." Hoover gave him "the opportunity to resign" and appointed in his place a twenty-five-year veteran of the bureau, Henry O'Malley.[26] Described by one of his subordinates as a "dedicated, bullheaded, warm-hearted Irishman," O'Malley was not a technical expert, but he could claim practical scientific credentials because of his work as superintendent of a number of Pacific salmon hatcheries. Above all, he was a terrific promoter who met Hoover's insistence that the chief must be focused on "developing the commercial side of our fisheries." Popular with both canners and congressmen, he pleased the industry and squeezed increased appropriations out of Congress.[27]

For all of O'Malley's assets, however, it was clear that basic policy for the bureau was set by the Secretary of Commerce. Hoover's objectives were stated with characteristic clarity and bluntness. The first was to promote conservation through cooperation between the fishing industry and the government. As he told a convention of commercial fishermen, "We can no more overfish and expect to have seafood than we can outcut the growth of our forests and expect to have timber." But if the situation was ominous, Hoover did not think drastic actions were necessary. It would be enough, he assured a Seattle audience, to practice "moderate restraint and scientific propagation." For the salmon and halibut fisheries of the West Coast, this meant building more hatcheries, adopting modest restrictions on catches in the Northwest and Alaska, and negotiating a treaty to coordinate fisheries policy with Canada. For the already severely depleted littoral species of the East Coast—the sturgeon, salmon, shad, lobster, crab, oyster, and clam—it meant a vigorous attempt to restore diminished populations, and for the deepwater species, it meant international controls like those proposed for the West Coast. His second goal was enactment of a bill to prevent water pollution of coastal waters by oil-burning and oil-carrying ships, and "the prevention of pollution from sources other than ships both in coastal and inland waters." His third objective was "to undertake the reinforcement of stocks of game fish throughout the United States."[28]

Hoover's concerns about fish were not new to fishermen. As early as the 1860s sport and commercial fishermen had begun to be alarmed about declines of fish populations along the east coast, and by the end of the decade twenty-five states had created fish commissions to study local species and experiment with restocking. They also began to draw attention to pollution from silt, sawdust, garbage, sewage, and, by the 1880s, to chemical pollutants. For reasons that are unclear, however, initial concerns about pollution abated in the early twentieth century.[29] A few scientists were alarmed about oil pollution and declines in fish populations, but the general public usually seemed oblivious to the problems until the price of fish rose in the 1920s, floating oil in several harbors actually caught fire, and bathers at the seashore began to complain that they frequently found themselves coated with sticky, floating tar.[30]

In May 1921 Hoover called a conference of fish commissioners from Atlantic and Gulf states, who met in Washington on 16 June and decided to call local conferences and to seek pollution-control legislation from Congress. "I have no doubt," Hoover told the group, "that the ideal arrangement would be for every state to heartily enforce pollution laws in regard to its own coast and streams, [and] the Federal Government could confine itself to acts of pollution outside of state waters."[31] Eight days later, Representative William Appleby of New York introduced H.R. 7369, which prohibited oil pollution of navigable waters by ships and land sources. In October the House Rivers and Harbors Committee opened hearings on Appleby's and related bills.[32]

At the hearings the American Petroleum Institute strongly opposed any law that singled out oil pollution. Their opposition made immediate passage of any law unlikely, and a series of other issues further complicated the matter. For example, there were disagreements about whether the power to control pollution should be given to one of the Commerce Department's bureaus or to the War Department's Corps of Engineers; sport and commercial fishermen each suspected the other of seeking some advantage; southern states' rights advocates feared any federal regulation of fisheries; American shipowners worried that legislation would bear particularly on them, crippling their already shaky industry; and many supporters of industrial development wanted to regulate only the pollution from ships, not from shore-based sources. Moreover, since no feasible method had been found to separate oil from ballast water, no one was sure how the purposes of the proposed legislation were to be achieved. Above all, however, it was the opposition of oil companies, especially Standard Oil, that doomed legislation in the congressional session ending in March 1923.[33]

Hoover was disappointed, but he pressed ahead with another aspect of the issue, the promotion of an international conference to seek methods of controlling pollution outside of national waters. A preliminary conference of representatives of the State, War, Navy, Interior, Agriculture, and Commerce Departments, and the United States Shipping Board was held in January 1923 to attempt to coordinate policy for the international meeting. This avenue also proved to be a dead end, however, when the meeting concluded that calling an international conference was pointless until an efficient, economical shipboard separator had been devised to remove oil from bilge or ballast water. As it turned out, no such separator came into use until 1926, and by the beginning of the 1930s only a minority of ships had installed them.[34]

Despite these discouraging developments, Hoover continued to press for the adoption of a pollution-control law. But action was further delayed by squabbles over which agency would enforce the law and whether it would cover both ships and on-shore sources. Eventually, Representative Walter Lineberger of California introduced, with Hoover's support, a compromise bill that omitted any controls on shore-based pollution sources but instructed the Secretary of Commerce to investigate the matter further in the next two years and recommend additional legislation if necessary. New Jersey Senator Joseph Frelinghuysen and other pollution-control advocates were convinced that Lineberger and Hoover had sold out to the oil companies. Hoover was furious at the accusation. "I resent the idea that because I am willing to support a [compromise on a] major issue that I am supposed to be allied with the refiners," he said. "It seems to me that this is the old case of people unwilling to proceed step by step insisting on the whole loaf or none."[35]

Neither Frelinghuysen nor Hoover really addressed an underlying assumption shared by both conservationists and industry that largely accounted for the inadequacies of the attack on oil pollution—the assumption that pollution was to be measured only in economic terms. The benefits of pollution abatement—in terms of tourism, improved fisheries, and the elimination of harbor fires—was to be balanced against its costs in reduced economic growth.

As long as this cost-benefit analysis determined the value of pollution control, it made sense to have abatement essentially a matter of industrial self-regulation based on economic incentives. As with so much else in his conservation program, Hoover was convinced that if producers were given adequate information about how to use resources more efficiently, they would choose conservation. Both he and congressional sponsors of antipollution legislation readily accepted the industry's argument that regulation of shore-based pollution sources would stifle economic growth.[36]

Hoover's willingness to accept compromise was further tested when the Lineberger bill, which vested enforcement in the War Department instead of Commerce, passed Congress. If Hoover was disappointed at this minor defeat, he did not say so, and President Coolidge (who had succeeded to the presidency in August 1923, following Harding's sudden death) signed the bill on 7 June 1924.[37] As Hoover said in a speech that autumn, passage of the bill was "only a beginning at solution of the pollution problem," but it was an important step, and the secretary followed it up by pressing research on devices to separate oil from water aboard ships, and by urging that an international conference be called to deal with pollution outside territorial waters. Early in April 1926, President Coolidge issued invitations to ten nations to attend a meeting on the subject. The American delegation to the sessions, which ran from 8 to 16 June, reflected Hoover's influence, but he could not control the other participants at the meeting. The conferees agreed that more than five-hundredths of one percent of oil in dumped water would constitute pollution, but they could not agree on how far ships must be from land before they could dump polluted water, on whether separators would be required or voluntary, or on how the agreement would be enforced. The meeting eventually produced a draft convention making a weak effort at controlling oil pollution on the seas, but Germany, Italy, and Japan—all major maritime powers—refused to sign. Whether the 1926 convention had any effect on pollution is unclear, but it seems to have been the most the international community was willing to accept at the time. Further action did not come until the 1953 International Conference on Pollution of the Sea by Oil.[38]

In the spring of 1926 an Interdepartmental Committee on Oil Pollution of Navigable Waters reported, in preparation for the coming international conference, that the 1924 act had been effective in relieving oil pollution in most American harbors, but that pollution of rivers and lakes from ships and land-based sources was a serious problem, as was pollution of the open seas.[39] Hoover had no answers for these problems. Although he admitted they were serious and offered the services of the Bureau of Fisheries to study the effects of pollution on Mississippi River fisheries, he believed that control of river, lake, and shore-based pollution must be the responsibility of the states, not the federal government. He was not, as some antipollution zealots believed, in collusion with the oil companies and other polluters, but both his insistence on local autonomy and voluntarism and his conviction that regulations must not impede economic growth certainly played into their hands. The best he could suggest was that each state should survey its streams, dividing them into three categories: those that were clean and could be protected; those that were hopelessly polluted and could not be saved without excessive cost and economic disruption; and those that were polluted but could and should be restored. It was thus clear that although Hoover was more aware of environmental problems than most of his contemporaries, and more eager to attack them, his definition of the issue in solely economic terms, plus his philosophy of voluntarism and local autonomy, seriously limited what he was willing to propose in the way of solutions.[40]

Nowhere was that limitation more evident than in Hoover's attempts to restore the commercial fisheries on the east and west coasts. As a fisherman himself, Hoover gave special attention to the efforts of the Bureau of Fisheries to halt and reverse "the steady degeneration in American commercial fisheries in the Northwest and Alaska."[41] In a speech to the United States Fisheries Association in September 1924, he laid out what sounded like an ambitious program: "to cultivate a sense of national responsibility toward the fisheries and their maintenance . . . ; to make a vigorous attempt to restore the . . . littoral fisheries on the Atlantic Coast; to secure the prevention of pollution from sources other than ships both in coastal and inland waters; to undertake the reinforcement of stocks of game fish throughout the United States."[42] Upon closer inspection, however, there is less to these proposals than at first appears. The crucial limitation was that, in his opinion, "except in Alaska the fisheries are under state and not Federal control." Aside from seeking to protect fisheries by treaty, improving the "propagation of fish, [the] scientific study of fisheries and general education," and promoting the adoption of "interstate compacts designed to correct some of the worst evils in our fisheries depletion," Hoover believed that the department had "practically come to the end of our conservation activities through Federal legislation."[43] Substantive fisheries conservation actions would have to come from the states.

In Alaska, which was still a territory, Hoover could and did act vigorously. By 1921 Alaskan salmon catches had been declining for several years, and even commercial fishermen favored controls. Hoover sent Dr. Charles Gilbert, a Stanford expert, to study the situation, and Gilbert concluded that over-fishing was the problem. The secretary tried at first to secure voluntary restrictions of fishing by working through packer associations, but they proved uncooperative. In December 1921 Hoover recommended that President Harding issue an executive order setting aside a large area of Alaskan coastal waters as a reserve under the control of the Bureau of Fisheries. Harding issued the order on 17 February 1922 and expanded the protected area to include almost 40 percent of Alaskan fisheries with a second order on 3 November 1922. By the time Congress passed the Alaskan Fisheries Act in 1924, the region had been under government regulation for two years. In 1926 an increase in the catch seemed to show that the approach was working, although subsequent declines undermined early optimism.[44]

Not everyone in Alaska welcomed Hoover's efforts to protect the fisheries. The announcement of the creation of the fishery reserves claimed that the policy was supported by "representative canners," but some fishermen, canners, and native groups attacked the reserves as benefitting only the larger canners and fishing companies.[45] Never one to ignore opposition, Hoover lashed out at what he described as scurrilous and demagogic attacks on department policy and spent a great deal of time over the next two years assuring members of Congress that fishing regulations were necessary and fair. When President Harding planned a trip to Alaska in the summer of 1923, Hoover prepared a lengthy briefing paper explaining and defending the necessity of limiting fishing.[46]

During Harding's Alaskan trip, Hoover held hearings on the fishing regulations at Seward, Anchorage, Cordova, Fairbanks, and Nenana, at which criticism of administration policy was generally muted, although a hostile reporter accompanying the group proclaimed that the secret purpose of the new regulations was to provide patronage jobs for Republicans.[47] By the time Hoover returned to Washington, he was convinced that the controversy would not die until the executive orders were replaced with legislation. In late 1923 and early 1924 he urged Congress to replace the stop-gap executive orders with a permanent method of conservation.[48]

Despite the support of the administration and influential Alaskans for the fisheries bill, opposition by small canners, fishermen, native groups, and the Hearst press delayed its passage. Hoover himself campaigned vigorously for the bill and enlisted the support of President Coolidge as well as friends in the Izaak Walton League. When it finally passed, he declared that he could "stand any amount of personal abuse with all the amiability of the winner," but even three and a half years later he was still smarting and anxious to strike back at those who had attacked him.[49] Nevertheless, he was delighted at the passage of the bill and proud of his leadership in restoring the fisheries. He rejected the charge that his policy favored large fishing companies and packers, insisting that his only concern had been "to preserve the future livelihood of the fishermen and this great food supply to the American people."[50]

Yet for at least two reasons, Hoover's western fisheries policy proved to be a failure. One reason was hardly his fault—the scientists were overoptimistic about the efficacy of catch limits, restocking, irrigation screens, and fish ladders as solutions to declining salmon runs. In an effort to find other solutions, Hoover supported increased funding for scientific research within the Fisheries Bureau, but answers were elusive and catches continued to decline during the late 1920s. At the same time, Hoover's policy was also something of a social and political failure. Many Alaskans, feeling that their needs had been ignored in policy development, simply violated the new law, while large canners pulled political strings to have Congress set catch limits at unrealistically high levels. At least one historian argues that Hoover's policy neither achieved effective conservation nor transferred control of policy to local officials. It was "chimeric conservation" which "reinforc[ed] Alaska's colonial status," a particularly cutting charge, given Hoover's commitment to local autonomy in other conservation issues.[51]

If the adoption of an Alaskan fisheries policy was not easy, the fact that the federal government had undoubted authority made action easier than in other cases. Hoover was as eager to restore the East Coast fisheries as he was those in Alaska, and he wanted to see sport fishing on interior waterways improved as well—but he did not believe the federal government had the power to dictate policy in these cases.[52] Four years after entering office, he admitted to President Coolidge that his efforts to secure protection of the coastal fisheries by cooperative action among state fisheries authorities had accomplished little. He would still promote the adoption of interstate agreements, he reported, but beyond that, there seemed to be little that could be done except to cultivate public opinion.[53]

Hoover's continued active role in the Izaak Walton League, including a major address to the organization's meeting in 1924 and the acceptance of its honorary presidency for several years in the late 1920s, was partly intended to mobilize this important organization on behalf of his policies. In addition to lobbying for conservation of commercial species and the creation of "fish reservations," Hoover suggested that the Waltonians could take a direct role in improving sport fishing by purchasing small parcels of swampland, diking it to create ponds, and using the ponds to grow fish born in government hatcheries to a size where they would be more likely to survive when released in streams.[54] Considering the magnitude of the problems in both commercial and sport fishing, the solutions Hoover proposed, restricted as they were by an ideology of voluntarism and limited government, were sadly inadequate.

Similar problems attended Hoover's attempts to promote the adoption of conservation and rational development policies in the oil industry during the 1920s.[55] During the two decades prior to 1920, oil rapidly supplanted coal as the industrialized world's main energy source. Railroads, ships, and increasing numbers of automobiles used oil directly, and new household appliances expanded demand for the electricity that oil could be burned to generate. But the outbreak of World War I in 1914 quickly showed that civilian needs for oil were miniscule beside the military's appetite during this first petroleum-powered war. Even before the United States entered the war in 1917, leaders of the American petroleum industry were becoming alarmed by the rapid depletion of known resources. A number of states had adopted regulations that sought to reduce the prodigious waste that characterized oil drilling, and the Taft and Wilson administrations began to create federal oil reserves on public lands to safeguard supplies for the military. Under the Council of National Defense, its successor the War Industries Board, and the United States Fuel Administration (with its subsidiary Oil Division), the Wilson administration sought to promote the conservation and prudent allocation of oil resources for military and civilian uses.[56]

Mark Requa, the head of the Oil Division, was a friend and admirer of Hoover. As a prominent California petroleum engineer, he had long been an advocate of cooperative production control among oil companies in order to conserve what he estimated in 1916 to be American oil reserves sufficient for no more than ten to twenty-five years.[57] Under Requa's guidance, the Oil Division used the war emergency to justify encouraging the oil industry to enter into voluntary production agreements, pool fuel oil supplies and sell the oil at a single price, adopt more efficient production and distribution methods, and in general to substitute cooperation for competition. Delighted by his wartime achievements, in 1919 Requa supported the creation of a trade association, the American Petroleum Institute, to extend the cooperation of the war years and to meet what he and many other oilmen believed was an impending oil shortage. Amid alarmist reports about the imminent exhaustion of oil reserves, scientists, military leaders, and oilmen also urged the adoption of a militant foreign policy to explore, develop, and protect overseas oil concessions if that should prove necessary.[58] In December 1920 Hoover introduced Requa to president-elect Harding in a letter filled with warnings about the "manifest approaching exhaustion of American oil reserves and the militant policy of the British Government in attempting to corner the whole of the oil territory in the world outside of the United States." Over the next several months, he continued to press the urgency of the situation on the president and anyone else who would listen.[59]

As a result of the alarms raised by Hoover and others, the United States pursued throughout the 1920s an aggressive policy designed to secure access by American companies to foreign oil on the most favorable possible terms.[60] But American oilmen also insisted that a more positive domestic oil policy must be adopted. In December 1924 President Coolidge responded to this pressure by creating a Federal Oil Conservation Board (FOCB) made up of the secretaries of interior, war, navy, and commerce, with Interior Secretary Hubert Work as chairman.[61]

By the time the FOCB came into being, however, the nature of the problem had changed dramatically. Prospective shortage had become present glut. As early as the summer of 1922, new strikes in California had produced a local surplus, and by the end of 1924, discoveries in Oklahoma, Texas, and other areas were expanding the problem.[62] The challenge faced by the board thus became much more complicated than merely developing a conservation program for a scarce commodity. What was needed, industry analysts argued, was an interstate agreement that would "force consolidation of producing acreage into large units and regulation of this production to meet the requirements of the market." Without some such arrangement, prices would crash, waste and overproduction would increase, companies would collapse, and exploration would cease. The situation might bring short-term benefits to consumers, but in the long run it meant shortages, rising prices, and huge waste of an irreplaceable resource.[63]

The Teapot Dome scandal of 1924, however, made it difficult for the administration even to consider any government-industry arrangement that might lead to higher prices for consumers. In that famous scandal Secretary of the Interior Albert Fall, with the collusion of Secretary of the Navy Edwin Denby, had arranged to have naval oil reserves at Elk Hills in California and Teapot Dome in Wyoming leased to the Doheny and Sinclair oil companies. An investigation by Senator Thomas Walsh of Montana revealed that all the government got from this deal was the use of some oil tanks at Pearl Harbor, while Fall received at least $400,000. Although Fall and Denby were forced to resign from the cabinet, and Fall eventually went to prison, the episode fatally tainted all subsequent proposals for cooperation between the government and the oil industry.[64]

As if Teapot Dome was not in itself a major problem, the oil industry also reacted with growing hostility to what it saw as FOCB "snooping" into corporate secrets.[65] Amid these conflicting interests, the FOCB struggled to find a policy that would win broad support. In a series of reports the board assessed industry production methods, estimated national petroleum reserves, analyzed possible alternatives such as oil shales, and discussed oil imports and their relationship to domestic production. The reports provided essential information for the development of a national petroleum policy, but they did not assure agreement on what that policy would be.[66]

Two problems—one practical and one legal—made the development of a national oil policy difficult. The practical problem arose from the fact that drilling companies normally acquired rights to only a small parcel of land located, they hoped, above a large, subterranean lake of oil. But other companies, on neighboring small parcels, had access to the same pool, which put a premium on each company pumping at top speed in order to acquire as much of the pool as possible (the "law of capture"). An obvious solution to this problem—to have all companies pumping from the same reservoir agree to a common policy of restraint (a unit plan)—raised the specter of corporate collusion in violation of the antitrust laws and thus posed a serious legal obstacle to a conservation program.

Most oil companies opposed the unit operations idea initially, but the oil glut of the mid-1920s brought the larger companies around, and the idea of industry self-regulation fitted Hoover's theory that voluntary cooperation among businesses and between businesses and government was the best approach to almost every problem. In 1926 and 1927 Hoover several times suggested to industry organizations that they lobby Congress for modifications to the antitrust laws that would legalize unit operations.[67]

Hoover was not successful in persuading Secretary Work or President Coolidge of the desirability of relaxing the antitrust laws to legalize unit plans for the oil industry. They believed that the industry needed help, but they were unwilling to endorse a plan that seemed certain to produce higher prices for consumers.[68] Discouraged by the administration's coolness to antitrust modification, Mark Requa and some oil industry leaders began to talk about direct federal regulation of the industry as the only alternative.[69] Another segment of the industry, including many smaller concerns, proposed state regulation as the best solution of the problem. By the time Hoover was elected president in 1928, there was widespread agreement in the oil industry that comprehensive conservation policies needed to be adopted, but there was as yet no consensus on which plan would be best.[70] Perhaps President Hoover, with his strong support for cooperation among producers and his advocacy of changes in the antitrust laws, would provide the leadership necessary for the adoption of a national plan.

Prior to Hoover's appointment, the Commerce Department had been a backwater of the federal government. It was not even particularly important to business, and it certainly was not a center of the growing conservation movement. Hoover's ambition and energy galvanized the department and made it an active servant of the business community. The war had fostered a cooperative spirit in America. This, he said, "offered the Department a special opportunity through cooperation with business, labor, and agriculture to help secure stability in production and employment, together with increased efficiency through elimination of industrial waste, and by means of such joint activities to help change the attitude of government relations with business from that of interference to that of cooperation."[71]

An immediate practical result of this philosophy was the expansion of the size of the Commerce Department by 50 percent, from about 10,000 to 15,000 employees, while total expenditures nearly tripled. The Bureau of Mines was transferred to Commerce from Interior, and existing bureaus, especially the Bureau of Standards and the Bureau of Foreign and Domestic Commerce, were given new responsibilities to promote Hoover's goals. The Bureau of Fisheries received new powers to protect and restore fisheries. All of the bureaus held frequent conferences with producers and manufacturers that were intended to promote the harmonious and efficient growth of the economy, with "high wages to producers and low prices to consumers."[72] The department's successes excited admiration even from political rivals.[73]

What was unique about Hoover's Commerce Department was that it made waste reduction central to its efforts to assure Americans a rising standard of living, and that it brought the principle into the daily operations of American business in ways that were entirely new. Planned use of resources was of course a major theme of the prewar conservation movement, but its advocates had envisioned conservation as applying primarily to raw materials and undeveloped natural resources. They did not generally see it as a direct part of manufacturing and production. Under Hoover's leadership, the conviction that engineers could find ways to make production more efficient at all stages and thereby conserve resources became a mainspring of departmental policy. The "one and only way" to maintain a rising standard of living for all Americans, said Hoover, was "to improve methods and processes and to eliminate waste."[74] In addition to the Bureau of Fisheries campaigns to stop commercial overfishing, to improve sport fishing, and to promote cooperative conservation practices by states and fishermen, Hoover's Bureaus of Standards and of Foreign and Domestic Commerce conducted vigorous programs to standardize products, find uses for byproducts previously discarded, and to develop new and more efficient methods of production. Conservation was to be integrated with production at every step.

Hoover also differed with his predecessors in believing that the goals of conservation could be achieved through local initiatives and voluntary programs of cooperation between federal authorities and private interests. In lumber, fishing, and oil, the Commerce Department generally assumed that big companies and industry associations spoke for whole industries, but critics who accused Hoover of being a tool of big business were in error. He shared the progressives' desire to open opportunity for everyone and believed that workers must share in the benefits of prosperity, but he did not realize that those goals were to some extent negated by the methods he employed in dealing with business. He shared and sometimes exceeded the conservation goals of the most advanced progressives, but his determination to decentralize and voluntarize the implementation of conservation programs was a radical departure from prewar practices of the Roosevelt-Pinchot school. It reflected both the bias of westerners in favor of development and local control, and Hoover's personal philosophy.

Hoover's central objective, he said frankly, was "a widening range of consumption" and "increasing standards of living" for Americans.[75] A tension that had always been implicit in the conservation movement between the preservation and the planned development of resources was thus sharpened and increased in Hoover's policies. He was oblivious to the problem because his primary goal was never conservation per se, but rising standards of living for Americans.

On the other hand, Hoover drew upon some of the most advanced economic thought of his day to consider what would happen if, in fact, the nation was "finally upon the golden stairs to the industrial millennium."[76] He was one of the first American leaders to understand that affluence would greatly expand the number and power of consumers, and that rising living standards could be accompanied by greater leisure for most people. He quickly realized that new industries would arise to fill this new market, but his Quaker principles made him uncomfortable with commercialized leisure. Finding socially desirable activities for people with time and money on their hands was a major reason for his emphasis upon the restoration of sport fishing and the abatement of pollution while he was secretary of commerce. His concern with the quality of life in the consumer society also led him to undertake activities that went well beyond the responsibilities of the Commerce Department.

5 | Engineering the Good Life

In an interview published in 1924, Hoover explained, only half-jokingly, how a public-spirited engineer could remake the world for greater efficiency and beauty:

> Some waterfalls are in the wrong place, where few people can see them. Moreover, in many waterfalls the same effect could be secured by a smaller expenditure of water. Waterfalls could be constructed with a view to their better public availability as scenery; and the sheet of water used to produce the scenic effect could be much thinner. We could save water and we could also have waterfalls in better locations if we handled the subject of waterfalls with the aid of human intelligence added to the resources of nature. Scenically as well as industrially we can be better off through the civilizing of our rivers.[1]

Hoover's colleagues in the cabinet admired his energy and intelligence, but from the beginning, many of them resented his tendency, backed by the authority of his original agreement with Harding, to meddle in matters outside his own department. In resource issues, his interests, based on his confident assumption that he knew how to maximize the efficiency of the economy and the happiness of the American people, carried him far and wide. It was indicative of how much he came to dominate the cabinet that President Harding considered him for secretary of the interior in 1922, and that in 1924 Coolidge asked him to become secretary of agriculture.[2] In the course of the 1920s Hoover came more and more to define the Republican vision of conservation in the consumer society.

Conservation was a relatively new concept to Hoover in 1921 when he entered the cabinet, and he had not progressed beyond the belief that it meant the efficient use of resources already extracted. The shallowness of his ideas was manifest in his 1921 suggestion that all "functions relating in the main to the Public Domain" and all "functions relating in the main to Public Works Construction" be consolidated under an assistant secretary in the Interior Department. His idea was endorsed in 1923 by the Congressional Joint Committee on the Reorganization of Government Departments and embodied in a bill introduced in the House by Carl E. Mapes of Michigan and in the Senate by Reed Smoot of Utah. The bill quickly drew the opposition of the affected agencies, including the Forest Service and the National Park Service, and did not pass.[3] One prominent conservationist declared flatly that uniting the Forest and National Park Services would mean that "every decision by the Secretary will always mean victory for one side and defeat to the other."[4] Stephen Mather, head of the Park Service, dismissed the idea of moving his agency to the Agriculture Department as "a part of the poison gas that is floating around the country."[5]

Hoover, oblivious to disagreements about their mission among conservation agencies, continued throughout the 1920s to support the creation of "a conservation division" under the Department of Interior that would unite the Bureau of Fisheries, the Geological Survey, the National Park Service, the "Public Lands," the Reclamation Service, the "Alaskan Reindeer," the "water power" division of the Federal Power Commission, the Forest Service, the Biological Survey, the naval oil reserves, and other subunits scattered through the government. His goal, he said, was to promote "the conservation of our natural resources and our recreational opportunities."[6] What he was thinking about, obviously, was the traditional definition of conservation: the planned development of resources for human use. He showed no awareness of differing conceptions of conservation that created tension among various agencies.[7]

Nowhere was Hoover's conviction that conservation did not mean "prevention of use" more evident than in his vigorous advocacy of the development of river systems. "Every drop of water that runs to the sea without yielding its full commercial returns to the nation is an economic waste," he said at Seattle in 1926.[8] Time after time he urged the drafting of comprehensive plans for "the coordinated long-view development of each river system to its maximum utilization." Such plans should be implemented for all the great river systems, he believed, including the Columbia, the Colorado, the Great Lakes, the Mississippi, and even for smaller streams.[9]

The issue was of particular urgency in the early 1920s in regard to the Colorado River. Interest in development of the river arose in Southern California in the early twentieth century, where the city of Los Angeles was beginning to look longingly at it as a source of water. A syndicate of owners of irrigated land in the Imperial Valley wanted a dam on the lower Colorado that would stop disastrous floods like those of 1905, 1906, and 1907, and that would permit the construction of a new canal entirely within U.S. boundaries to carry water to the valley, in place of the existing canal that ran partially through Mexican territory.[10] Phil Swing, a Republican congressman from Southern California, organized the Imperial Valley Irrigation District in 1911 and served as its counsel, and Harry Chandler, publisher of the Los Angeles

Times, was one of the largest landowners in the Imperial Valley. Chandler later bragged that it was he who interested Hoover personally in the Colorado River question. That may have been true, but by the 1920s the issue was becoming so urgent for a variety of reasons that the federal government could not ignore it.[11]

In March 1917 a board of engineers appointed by Secretary of the Interior Franklin K. Lane recommended the construction of an "All American Canal" to carry irrigation water from the Colorado to the Imperial Valley, and in February 1918 the Interior Department agreed to pay one-third of the cost of an engineering survey of the proposed route. The engineers located a feasible route for the canal and recommended that the federal government build a large storage reservoir on the Colorado River. Legislation to launch the project never cleared Congress, however. It was blocked in large part by the opposition of Arthur Powell Davis, director of the Reclamation Service, who believed that relatively small-scale projects like the All American Canal would fail unless they were incorporated within an overall plan for the control and development of the whole river. In 1922 the Reclamation Service published the Fall-Davis Report, which methodically surveyed the Colorado River system and concluded that the key to successfully harnessing it would be the construction of a giant dam "at or near Boulder Canyon."[12]

The idea of a great dam on the river thrilled everyone interested in the development of the Colorado—except those in the states of the river basin above the dam site. The problem was the western doctrine of "prior appropriation," which held that the first user of water from a stream acquired permanent rights to it. If California diverted a large part of the Colorado's flow, the upper basin states (Colorado, New Mexico, Utah, and Wyoming), which had not yet begun to draw upon the river heavily, would be forever prevented from expanding their uses. In June 1922, four months after the publication of the Fall-Davis Report, the Supreme Court reaffirmed the right of prior appropriation in *Wyoming v. Colorado.* And adding to the complications was the fact that among the three lower basin states (Arizona, California, and Nevada), only California had definite plans for using Colorado water. Arizona in particular was as distrustful of California as were the upper basin states.[13]

Implementing any plan for the development of the whole Colorado River obviously required the consent of all or nearly all of the seven states through which it flowed. Representatives of the seven failed to agree at San Diego and Tucson in 1918, at Salt Lake City in 1919, and at Los Angeles and Denver in 1920. Finally, at the Denver meeting in August 1920, someone suggested solving the problem through an interstate compact that would permit the

Boulder Canyon and All American Canal projects to go forward while reserving a share of the river's flow for the future use of the upper basin states and Arizona.[14] During early 1921, the legislatures of the affected states approved this concept, and in August Congress approved the principle of a compact and authorized the president to appoint the chairman of what was to be called the Colorado River Commission.

The chairmanship would be a delicate task. It was essential that the person have both the technical knowledge to understand data on geology, stream flows, dam construction, and other specialized issues likely to come before the commission, and the political and diplomatic facility to guide representatives of seven states to agreement. Secretary Fall believed that Director Davis of the Reclamation Service, although technically qualified, was too closely associated with California's interests. Because the chairman would "practically control the decision of the joint States and the United States Commission," Fall argued, it was essential that he be "a man of nation wide reputation . . . whose advice would be respected by the Congress and by the people of the different States interested." Someone "of the Elihu Root type" would be ideal, Fall thought.[15]

By early November Harding had settled on Hoover as the chairman—a nationally respected expert whose official position as secretary of commerce seemed to give him no reason to favor one interest over another.[16] On 17 December 1921 Harding officially appointed Hoover chairman of the Colorado River Commission, and Hoover summoned the representatives of the seven states to meet with him in Washington in late January 1922. Subcommittees were set up to investigate the amount of water available, the water needs of the various states, and the legal issues involved in a possible compact. The commission also decided to hold public hearings throughout the region. Beginning in March at Phoenix and thereafter at Los Angeles, Salt Lake City, Grand Junction, Denver, and Cheyenne, with a final hearing at Santa Fe in the autumn, the commissioners listened patiently to a variety of concerns. What came out in the hearings was of relatively little importance, however, compared to the impact of the Supreme Court's decision in *Wyoming v. Colorado* in June, and the results of the elections in November, in which six of the seven incumbent governors were unseated. The court's decision made reaching agreement on an interstate apportionment of water imperative, while the elections made the task vastly more difficult.[17]

Hoover proved to be an excellent chairman, adept at keeping discussions on track and at summarizing arguments briefly and fairly. By November a consensus was emerging on a plan proposed by Colorado commissioner Delph

Carpenter for a fifty-fifty division of the use of the river's water between the upper and lower basins.[18] On the assumption that a part of the water used for irrigation in the upper basin would return to the river, this meant that in practice the lower basin, with its larger urban population, would have available slightly more than the half of the flow it was officially assigned. The fact that the agreement said nothing about apportionment of water among the states *within* each basin was an effort to avoid raising a dispute between Arizona and California. A promise that the whole issue could be reopened in forty years allayed fears that inequities would be permanent.[19]

At a farewell meeting of the commission at The Bishop's Lodge near Santa Fe on 24 November 1922, the commissioners paid Hoover enthusiastic and richly deserved compliments for his part in securing agreement. Two weeks earlier, Hoover had arrived in Santa Fe to discover that all but one of the commissioners were lame ducks, appointees of now-defeated governors. He immediately telephoned the governors-elect, flattering and cajoling them, and got them all to extend the credentials of their commissioners, and even, in several cases, to come to Santa Fe for the celebration of success. He failed only with the new Democratic governor of Arizona, George W. P. Hunt, who reappointed W. S. Norviel as the state's commissioner but, in an ominous gesture for the future of the compact, refused to come to Santa Fe himself. Privately, Hoover denounced Hunt as a Bolshevik (because the governor insisted on a separate agreement to apportion water among the lower basin states before Arizona would ratify the Colorado compact) and admitted that his temper had been "sorely tried" in the last two weeks of negotiations, but publicly he could not say enough nice things about the commissioners. They were, he declared fulsomely, "honest men" of "veracity and character" who had been "honest and straight throughout." But the talk was now over, he concluded, and it was time for "western men" to turn to the "practical" job "of construction."[20]

If Hoover really believed that negotiations were finished and construction could begin, he was soon disillusioned. Six of the seven states ratified the Colorado compact within the next five months, but Arizona refused to do so, and Hoover failed to change Governor Hunt's mind during a face-to-face meeting in December 1923. Arizona's main concern was that it receive enough water, but state leaders also feared that California would take the lion's share of power generated by dams on the system. Neither Hoover nor others were able to budge the Arizonans from this position, and the upper basin states blocked passage of the Swing-Johnson bill authorizing construction of the dam at Boulder Canyon until all of the signatories had ratified the agreement.

In hopes of breaking the logjam, Hoover proposed that the compact go into effect when it was approved by six of the seven original signatories.[21]

By 1925 five of the signatory states were ready to proceed even without Arizona, but California now raised a new issue, demanding an assurance that the dam at Boulder Canyon would be high enough to generate power and create a reservoir for irrigation as well as provide flood control.[22] Hoover, believing that any delay would invite the other members of the compact, as well as Arizona, to make additional demands, urged the Californians to withdraw their objection. In Sacramento, however, a coalition of interests pressed the reservation to passage in the legislature. These included representatives of Southern California cities desperate for water and the growers of the Imperial Valley, who wanted the high dam to assure their irrigation supply. Nothing Hoover or others could do seemed to crack this alliance, and the legislature approved the six-state proposal in early April, with the reservation that the compact would not be binding upon California until Congress adopted legislation assuring the construction of a high dam.[23]

What the Californians wanted was the passage of a bill sponsored by California Representative Phil Swing and Senator Hiram Johnson, which had been introduced in Congress in slightly differing forms in 1922, 1923, and 1925. They hoped to use their reservation to compel passage of this bill that provided funds for the construction of a high dam at Boulder Canyon. Led by Delph Carpenter, the upper basin states refused to give in to this pressure. At a conference in Denver in August 1925, they declared their opposition to all development on the river until the compact had been ratified fully. Upper basin leaders were fearful that a high dam would give the lower basin states a preemptive right to more than their share of the water unless the apportionment agreed to in the compact was legally binding on all of them, including Arizona.[24]

Hoover continued to work on behalf of the compact during late 1925 and 1926, but by 1927 the upper basin states were losing patience. In January Utah repealed its ratification of the six-state compact. A conference of the governors of the seven states at Denver in August 1927 made one last attempt to secure unanimous acceptance of the compact but could not get California and Arizona to agree on a division of the lower basin's allotment. By the end of the year it was obvious that the only hope for a settlement would come from passage of a federal law that would impose compromises on all concerned. Unless local squabbles could be suppressed, Hoover advised the president, there would be no "reason to expend further time and [federal] money in connection with the project."[25]

The real threat to Arizona and the upper basin states was not the loss of federal funding. It was that if the other six states of the Colorado basin did not find some way to agree, California was in a position to establish a dominant claim to the river's water. Only the absence of a suitable dam site within California had prevented this from happening already, and the threat that the federal government might build a dam at Boulder Canyon gave the other states little choice but to come to some agreement. If Congressman Swing and Senator Johnson could assemble a majority in support of their perennial bill, it was highly probable that the other states in the Colorado watershed would accept it.

The fourth Swing-Johnson bill, introduced in December 1927, drew national support in part because of the huge losses that had resulted from the great Mississippi River flood earlier that year—1.5 million people flooded out of their homes, 2 million acres of crops inundated, and hundreds of millions of dollars in property damage. With images of widespread suffering and destruction spread across countless magazines and newspapers, Americans were sympathetic to the argument that a similar catastrophe from the Colorado must be averted.

The administration also supported new efforts to get around some of the objections to previous Swing-Johnson bills. Of these, the most important was a change in the Interior Department's position on the financing of the dam at Boulder Canyon. The first Swing-Johnson bills had proposed to pay for it through a direct appropriation; in early 1926, however, Secretary Work suggested that it be financed by a bond issue, with the interest and principal on the bonds to be paid by the sale of power and water.[26] Although Secretary of the Treasury Andrew Mellon objected to a bond issue for the project, and private power companies on the West Coast howled in protest at the prospect of publicly generated power, the idea that the project would pay for itself made it more palatable in the rest of the country. The fourth bill also sweetened the proposal for Nevada and Arizona by providing that 37.5 percent of power profits over and above the amount needed to cover construction costs would go to those states in place of the taxes they would have collected if the generation of power had been handled by private companies. The bill pleased the states in both basins, but especially Arizona, by putting a 4.4-million-acre-feet limit on the amount of water California could take from the lower basin's allotment until Arizona approved the compact and the two states agreed on a formal division of their share.[27]

Changes in the bill, the administration's steady support for it, and Swing and Johnson's determined pressure to get it passed succeeded in winning over a majority. The House passed it in May 1928, and the Senate, by a 64 to 11 vote, on 14 December 1928, despite the continuing opposition of the power industry and a disturbing new report by a committee of engineers who concluded that the calculations of stream flows upon which the original apportionment of water between the two basins had been based were too optimistic.[28]

Passage of the Swing-Johnson bill at last broke the impasse among the states with claims to the Colorado, and by early March 1929 all except Arizona had approved or reapproved the interstate compact that was necessary to put the bill into effect. On 25 June 1929, after waiting the six months required by Swing-Johnson if Arizona did not ratify, President Hoover proclaimed the law in effect. The way was now cleared to begin construction of the dam at Boulder Canyon, although the issue of the division of water in the lower basin between Arizona and California remained entirely unresolved.[29]

Hoover played a crucial part in the Colorado story. His firm and vigorously stated conviction that river systems should be developed to serve those who lived near them informed the whole process; his leadership was vital to the success of the conferences that negotiated the Colorado compact; when Arizona's opposition threatened to wreck the whole project, he suggested that the pact go into effect when six of the seven states approved it. In the end, his support for paying for the dam and other parts of the project through the sale of publicly generated power helped to win wide support for the Swing-Johnson bill.

The Colorado agreement was a reaffirmation of the Progressive Era belief that conservation meant the planned development of resources, but Hoover claimed to see in it proof of another important principle as well. He cited it as evidence that state and local governments could, through voluntary cooperation, take on major roles in conservation projects that had previously been exclusively or primarily federal responsibilities. He was, however, mistaken. The Colorado compact did not show that unforced cooperation was likely to produce major conservation achievements. Hoover's subsequent claim that the Swing-Johnson Act was unnecessary because "the construction of the dam was inevitable once the Compact was ratified" was inaccurate.[30] Without Hoover's personal guidance and constant pressure, and without Swing-Johnson's threat to the recalcitrant states, there would have been no agreement at all.

In other water projects of the 1920s, Hoover's hope that "State, Municipal, Federal governments and private agencies" could pool information and become partners in planned development was also disappointed. Fourteen interstate compacts to apportion water resources were attempted after the initial negotiation of the Colorado River Compact in 1922, but only three were actually implemented by 1929.[31] Hoover's proposal that authority over reclamation projects already in operation should be transferred from the federal Bureau of Reclamation to the states was ignored by Interior Secretary Hubert Work.[32]

Although Hoover favored the principle of shared authority over conservation projects between federal and state governments, in practice he realized that the federal government alone had the resources to fund and organize really large projects. Only the federal government could finance the construction of a high dam on the Colorado, or sponsor flood control measures and navigational improvements on the Mississippi. In the case of one of his favorite projects, the construction of a waterway capable of carrying oceangoing ships from the Great Lakes to the Atlantic, he believed that the federal government must not only undertake part of the massive construction necessary, but must arrange with the Canadian government for international sponsorship of the project, and must also restrain New York State's ambition to make the Erie Canal the principal waterway in place of opening up the St. Lawrence River.

Appointed chairman of the St. Lawrence Commission of the United States by President Coolidge in March 1924, Hoover pressed forward a joint Canadian-American engineering survey of the feasibility of a St. Lawrence waterway that strongly endorsed the project on the grounds of opening the Great Lakes to shipping and of the waterway's power generation potential. Although the report declared tactfully that New York had "a special interest in the power developments . . . and the coordination of these improvements with the state should be undertaken," it was clear that the commission did not favor giving the state a veto over the project. The federal government, declared the report, "must necessarily assent to and negotiate power development questions from the American side." The report concluded optimistically that the state would gain from cheap power and indirectly benefit from the increasing prosperity of the Midwest.[33]

Nevertheless, Hoover did not willingly give up his ideal of decentralizing and privatizing conservation projects, and occasionally he achieved success. One such case was in his concern with saving Niagara Falls, where he was able to find a plan that promised to protect the falls from erosion, improve their scenic effect, permit the diversion of more water for power generation, and achieve all of these benefits at no public cost.

Hoover first became interested in Niagara Falls in 1925 when, as chairman of the St. Lawrence River Commission, he learned that the Canadian (Horseshoe) side of the falls seemed to be eroding at an accelerating rate, while the American side of the falls was carrying less and less water. At his initiative, the State Department brought the problems to the attention of the Canadian government, and the two nations agreed to instruct the bilateral Niagara Falls Commission to investigate and report on what could be done to improve the situation. The Americans were at first discouraged that the Canadians insisted on discussing additional diversions of water from the river for power generation along with ideas for preserving the scenic aspects of the falls, but in the end the Canadian proposals offered a solution to both problems. The international board's report, released early in 1928, recommended building underwater channels and weirs to spread the river's flow more evenly across its whole channel, thus reducing erosion of the Canadian falls and increasing the flow over the American side. The best part of the plan was that relatively modest construction promised to improve the appearance of the falls while permitting further diversion of water for power generation. The Canadian and American power companies, delighted by this finding, offered to build the conservation works at their own expense. As Hoover had remarked on another occasion, "Waterfalls could be constructed with a view to their better public availability as scenery; and the sheet of water used to produce the scenic effect could be much thinner."[34] In this instance, his belief in the ability of engineers to find solutions to problems that would serve the interests of the whole public seemed to be notably borne out.

Hoover's role in the Niagara and St. Lawrence projects was as much a recognition of his prominence as an engineer as secretary of commerce. His technical qualifications also led to his appointment in October 1920 to the advisory board of the "superpower" project sponsored by the Interior Department's Geological Survey, and he was reappointed to the post by Secretary Fall after he became secretary of commerce. Superpower advocates wanted to create an interconnected power network covering the East Coast. They argued that such a grid would "conserve the fuel and water resources of the country" because of its "high economy."[35]

The distance Hoover was willing to go to promote the coordination between public authorities and industries that would be necessary if the superpower project was to become a reality was indicated by his willingness to consider a plan introduced by board member E. G. Buckland for the creation of a federally chartered corporation to own, build, and maintain "a plant for the development, purchase and sale of electrical energy in the Boston-Washington zone."[36] The corporation thus created would, moreover, have the power of eminent domain enforceable in federal courts to secure the rights of way needed for its transmission lines.[37]

Subsequently, Hoover backed away from this proposal and instead endorsed the creation of a Northeastern States Superpower Committee to be made up of representatives of appropriate federal agencies and state utilities commissions. This commission would work closely with separate committees of public utilities executives, chambers of commerce and manufacturers' associations, and public utility engineers to plan interconnections among independent utility companies and to work toward resolving legal and technical obstacles to the creation of the superpower grid.[38] Such a vast engineering project, Hoover argued, could "only be compassed with the permission and aid of the federal government or by its direct action," but he much preferred that the interested parties work together voluntarily as partners. Federal legislation, he thought, should be avoided if possible.[39]

By early 1924 the Northeastern States Superpower Committee had agreed on three major recommendations: the rapid extension of interconnections among various systems; the building of large, centralized steam generating plants; and the immediate development of large hydroelectric projects. Expected benefits from the creation of such an integrated system included large-scale conservation of coal and other resources, savings in human effort as electrification spread, and protection against power interruptions.[40]

Hoover's confidence that practical men could clear away all obstacles to the Superpower project now ran into a major obstacle. As the idea assumed its final shape, a fundamental conflict arose between supporters of public power and supporters of private power, and a related but separate disagreement between advocates of federal regulation and those who believed control could be maintained through "coordinated state regulation."[41] Hoover tried to escape these disputes by dropping the term superpower in favor of "central generation and interconnection," which he claimed meant only "that large central generation plants at advantageous points serve large districts and that such neighboring districts shall be connected with each other in order to secure the maximum load factors, etc." Since the object of such interconnection was purely practical, he insisted, it would bear "no more relation to monopoly or financial relations than does the interchange of cars between railways."[42]

Critics of the superpower idea were unwilling to accept Hoover's attempts to refocus the debate on practical issues of conservation and waste elimination. Amos Pinchot charged that Hoover, now a presidential candidate, had sold out to the "industro-financial interest" of the power companies. Pinchot declared that claims of the need for a wider interconnection of regional power systems were an outrageous exaggeration intended merely to fatten the profits of the public utility interests.[43] Although there is no evidence that Hoover's preference for private ownership and local control was influenced by anything other than a genuine belief that this method of organization was the most efficient, he was naive to think that arguments for efficiency would avoid fundamental disputes over public and private ownership, or over federal versus state regulation. The northeastern grid proposal was the first casualty of these disagreements, but by the end of the 1920s, even efforts to merge the generating and transmission systems of two or three states proved out of reach.[44] The failure of the superpower project was ultimately the result of the fact that Hoover was still thinking like an engineer rather than a politician; long-term efficiency was not necessarily the major goal of politics.

The political ambiguities into which Hoover's interest in efficiency could lead him were also evident in the Muscle Shoals issue. During World War I, the federal government had built a plant on the Tennessee River at Muscle Shoals, Alabama, to produce nitrates for gunpowder. Hoover and his colleagues in the Harding administration assumed that since the government no longer needed nitrates for munitions, the installation would be leased to a private company (Henry Ford was interested) for conversion to the manufacture of nitrate fertilizer. Difficulties in agreeing on terms for a lease were compounded, however, when Senator George Norris proposed that Muscle Shoals be made the centerpiece of a huge public project for fertilizer production, flood control, and power generation. Although these were all conservation objectives, Hoover was unwilling to have the federal government undertake the project. He suggested that the issue of public or private operation of the facility could be resolved by the appointment of an independent investigatory group of engineers and representatives of "agricultural interests," who would, presumably, conclude that private development would be more efficient. The members of the Muscle Shoals Inquiry, who were appointed by Coolidge in March 1925, preferred not to enter this minefield; they reported that the issue was political, not technical.[45] Hoover continued to try to work out terms for a private lease of the Muscle Shoals facilities, but by the time he assumed the presidency, it was evident that Senator Norris could and would block any lease proposal.

During the 1928 campaign, Hoover suggested that "there are local instances where the government must enter the business field as a by-product of some great major purpose, such as improvement in navigation, flood control, scientific research, or national defense," but he also said that he did "not favor any general extension of the Federal Government into the operation of business in competition with its citizens."[46] In a public statement after Congress passed Norris's Muscle Shoals bill in early 1931, Hoover contended again that the bill must be judged solely by "the cold examination of engineering facts," and in his veto message of 3 March 1931, he expressed his strong doubts that the government could run the project efficiently and profitably. But in the end his main objection came down to the political principle that the government should not operate any enterprise where the generation of power or manufacturing were "not . . . a minor by-product but . . . a major purpose."[47] Thus Hoover, like Norris, ultimately acted on the assumption that there were higher issues involved in the Muscle Shoals controversy than merely the efficient use of resources. Conservation, it appeared, was not such a simple issue as it had seemed to Hoover a decade earlier.

Hoover's prominence as the main advocate of waste elimination and the planned development of resources during the Harding and Coolidge administrations drew the interest of various private conservation organizations. California's Save the Redwoods League solicited his support in their efforts to purchase several large groves to save them from logging, but he declined to become an active fund-raiser for the group. However, his membership in San Francisco's Bohemian Club, which held annual encampments at the Bohemian Grove of redwoods, contributed to his willingness to support the preservationists' efforts whenever he could.[48] The nature author Ernest Thompson Seton asked that he become honorary president of the Woodcraft League of America, and Hoover declined that also.[49] He did become a member of the Izaak Walton League in 1922 and served as its honorary president from 1926 to 1932, frequently finding the time to address the group's annual meetings.

In 1924 Hoover agreed to become not the honorary but the actual president of the National Parks Association (NPA) in addition to his many other duties. Aside from the fact that his old friend Ray Lyman Wilbur was a member, Hoover's main reason for this unusual decision seems to have been his belief that he could use the NPA to forward one of his major projects, the promotion of a national program of outdoor recreation. In his letter accepting the presidency of the organization, he wrote, "Recreation grounds and natural museums are as necessary to our advancing civilization as are wheat fields and factories. Indeed, I should like to see the Association not alone devote itself to defense of the areas that have been set aside by our Government for perpetual use in these purposes, but to expand its activities in the promotion of other forms of recreational areas."[50]

Hoover's emphasis on recreation must have sent cold chills down the spine of Robert Sterling Yard, executive secretary and principal sparkplug of the NPA. Yard had organized the NPA in 1919 with money given to him privately by Stephen Mather, the wealthy director of the National Park Service, primarily to establish a lobbying group that would work to keep the parks pristine and free of all commercial development. Beginning in 1920, Yard had fought tooth and nail to block the construction of an irrigation dam in Yellowstone Park, and to prevent Interior Secretary Albert Fall from creating a Mescalero Park made up of unspectacular recreational lands in Fall's home state of New Mexico.[51] Nevertheless, shocked as he may have been by Hoover's stress on recreation, Yard made the best of the situation. "Our National Parks System . . . ," he wrote, "cannot remain a museum system of undisturbed nature and meet also the demands of this budding age of out-door recreation. . . . We believe that a National System of Recreational Reservations, open when needful to industrial utilization [that is, mining or dams] and clearly distinguished by title from our National Parks System if established in the public lands and handled in cooperation with existing National and State park systems, will work out a mission of beneficence to the nation." A recreational reservation system, he concluded optimistically, would actually protect the national park system by providing a "dignified alternative classification for areas which lack National Park requisites."[52]

How much attention Hoover paid to Yard's lengthy letters and memoranda is difficult to determine, but it gradually became clear that the organization's president and its executive secretary did not agree on much. Hoover liked the parks well enough, but his real interest was in the development of a national outdoor recreation program that would productively fill the leisure hours of American workers. In December 1924, Chauncey Hamlin, chairman of the National Conference on Outdoor Recreation, which had been created by President Coolidge (with Hoover as a dominant member) earlier in the year, proposed that the National Parks Association affiliate with the American Civic Association, the American Park Society, the Park Executives Institute, the State Parks Conference, and possibly other organizations to form the American Federation of Parks and Planning. Advocates of unification claimed that it would promote fund-raising; and Hoover, who may have originated the unification proposal, argued that reducing the number of similar organizations would increase their effectiveness and public usefulness, thus making the issue seem merely one of efficiency.[53]

Yard was not deceived. In his opinion, the effect of the merger would be to change the organization's purpose from the protection of what he called the National Museum Parks to the promotion of recreation. By the end of January 1925 he had made it clear that he would not allow that to happen.[54] Hoover attempted to ram through approval of the creation of a Public Parks Council to coordinate "activities of various associations interested in national, state, municipal, and county parks and playgrounds," but when only two of the thirty-one trustees of the NPA supported him, he admitted defeat. On 21 May 1925 he resigned as president of the organization.[55]

Hoover had made a mistake in agreeing to become president of the NPA. Very likely, he had no idea when he agreed to take the position that there was such a fundamental difference between the passion for preservation of wilderness among the purists of the association like Yard, and his own ideas about outdoor recreation. Clearly angry at having failed to achieve what he wanted in the NPA, he turned his energies to the new National Conference on Outdoor Recreation.

The conference was the result of an initiative by Theodore Roosevelt Jr., assistant secretary of the navy, who spoke for a group of influential conservationists and sportsmen in the Explorers Club and the Boone and Crockett Club. Roosevelt pointed out that there was a rapidly growing interest in outdoor recreation among the American people, resulting in part from the mobility provided by automobiles. He argued that "the physical vigor, moral strength, and clear simplicity of mind of the American people can be immeasurably furthered by the properly developed opportunities for life in the open." From life in the open, he contended, "much of the American spirit of freedom springs." He suggested that President Coolidge call a conference of the organizations interested in various aspects of outdoor recreation, with the hope of developing "a general plan of development [and] all working toward a common objective and mutually supporting each other."[56]

Coolidge, although initially skeptical of the idea, was eventually won over. He decided, said Leon Kneipp, the first executive secretary of the new organization, that "it would be a good thing to let people know he was human, that he was a nature lover."[57] Coolidge appointed the secretaries of war, interior, agriculture, commerce, and labor, with Roosevelt as executive chairman, to a Committee on Outdoor Recreation, and in May 1924 the committee convened 309 delegates representing 128 different organizations for a three-day National Conference on Outdoor Recreation (NCOR).[58] The program for the meeting declared that outdoor recreation was a means of promoting higher standards of citizenship; general conditions of health; military preparedness; vocational, patriotic, and social and moral development; and "appreciation of the attractions of rural life." It promised that the conference would seek ways to promote the protection of wildlife, enhance the preservation and enjoyment of the "scenic resources of the United States," and encourage cooperation among the participating organizations in developing outdoor recreation.[59] Although the conference was organized by a committee of cabinet secretaries appointed by the president, and its first meeting was opened with a speech by Coolidge, the new organization was funded entirely by modest private donations, and it had no power to enforce any of its recommendations.[60]

Neither the Commerce Department nor Secretary Hoover were principals in the organization of the NCOR, but Hoover delivered a major address to the group's advisory council meeting in Washington in December 1924 that made clear the importance he assigned to outdoor recreation. In his remarks he stressed the importance of coordinating the policies and purposes of the many federal and other governmental agencies that exercised some control over aspects of outdoor recreation (consolidation of such federal agencies having been one of his longstanding goals). At very least, he remarked, the diverse organizations involved in such programs needed simplification and a little standardization, but "above all they need a definition of the social objective to which they are directed."[61]

The social objective to which Hoover referred was the development of "constructive recreation" to fill the increasing hours of leisure available to Americans:

> Now it seems that one of the by-products of our increasing production and standardization of living is greater leisure. Every decade shows that through the development of science and invention, of elimination of waste, and of improved organization in commerce and industry, we increase our production per capita and consequently our standards of living, and parallel with this increase every decade shows a decrease in the average hours of work by the American people. Consequently they have a larger and increasing period of leisure. This leisure must be provided for by increased facilities of recreation and of education. It will be of no avail to us to show increased leisure without constructive occupation during that period, for leisure, which is idleness, will generate a disastrous train of degeneration. So that constructive recreation which improves physical strength, which creates stimulation of mind and strengthens the moral fiber of our people is just as important as their efforts in labor.[62]

Agreeing wholeheartedly with these sentiments, the delegates adopted as Section 3 of Article I of their bylaws a statement declaring that the organization sought to "make available to the people of the Nation the fullest opportunity for wholesome outdoor recreation essential to their happiness, morale and physical and moral welfare."[63]

At the second meeting of the conference a year later, Hoover returned to the same theme. "Never in history," he said, "have general standards of comfort been higher and work hours been shorter and some kind of holidays more universal than they are today in the United States. . . . Our main trouble is, however, that we have been thinking a whole lot less about what we are going to do with this leisure than we have about trying to get it. And it is no use going on making more leisure if we are going to use it for moral and physical degeneration—destructive joy." "We are an industrial people . . . ," Hoover declared, but "the spiritual uplift, the good will, cheerfulness and optimism that accompanies every expedition to the outdoors is the peculiar spirit that our people need in times of suspicion and doubt. They ought to be sent fishing or camping periodically, and if they are to be sent fishing we must build up the opportunities for them to fish and camp."[64] In a speech to the Izaak Walton League, he explained further: "We go to chain theatres and movies; we watch somebody else knock a ball over the fence or kick it over the goal post. I do that and I believe in it. I do, however, insist that no other organized joy has values comparable to the outdoor experience."[65]

The conference's final report, published in 1928, drew an explicit parallel between the alleged regenerative function of the frontier of the nineteenth century and outdoor recreation in the twentieth. Chairman Chauncey Hamlin wrote in the introduction:

> For nearly 300 years . . . there has been a frontier to beckon the adventurer, a wilderness to conquer, and free soil to subdue. Each generation bred of the pioneer stock and with common social ideals found its opportunity for the fullest expression of the pioneer spirit. . . . The 25 years following the final close of the era of free soil has witnessed a remarkable transformation in the structure of American society. The individualism of the pioneer has been submerged in collective enterprise. . . . Population has become concentrated and heterogeneous. . . . The homogeneity of the original stock has crumbled steadily since 1890 through the influx of great migrations from southern and eastern Europe. . . .
>
> The exploitation of natural resources by a young and vigorous people has brought a level of unsurpassed well-being. Moreover, the development of science and improved organization in industry have made possible an unprecedented distribution of physical comforts and increasing periods of leisure to all classes. . . . The general level of prosperity has been made possible by the exploitation of natural resources of unparalleled variety and abundance, but manifestly this natural capital can not continue to be consumed without husbandry or replacement if accepted standards of living are to be sustained. And the present drain upon natural resources must take into account not only legitimate if extravagant consumption but insensate waste.[66]

The NCOR report suggested surprisingly simple solutions for this alarming situation: immigration restriction and a national land use planning program that would complement similar state and local planning. Through such measures, Hamlin concluded optimistically, opportunities for outdoor recreation, the "necessary complement of material well-being," and "the most wholesome expression of leisure," could be assured for all Americans.[67]

By 1928 the NCOR was losing its focus. Hoover hoped that it could be used to promote the merging of all federal land and conservation organizations into a single subcabinet agency, but the conference merely endorsed the creation of a federal land planning committee made up of the secretaries of agriculture, commerce, and interior. Early in 1929, Hoover, now president-elect, consulted with former NCOR Executive Secretary Arthur Ringland about setting up a major study of leisure, but in the end the study amounted only to a single slim volume by sociologist Jesse Frederick Steiner, which was published as part of a series sponsored by the President's Research Committee on Social Trends.[68] Although Steiner declared that recreation had become increasingly important to an industrial society "on the grounds of health and efficiency as well as relief from the routine of daily toil," his book was mainly a study of what recreational opportunities existed in America rather than an analysis of the alleged relationship between recreation and social health.[69]

A more tangible demonstration of Hoover's belief in the connection between outdoor life and social health (aside from his promotion of fishing) was his enthusiastic support of the suburban home ideal. The lack of suitable homes for Americans, Hoover declared in 1924, was a "thriving food for Bolshevism." As to what might constitute a suitable home, Hoover suggested the use of standardized plans to eliminate building waste and to lower costs for the construction of modern, single-family houses located on suburban lots. The Commerce Department endorsed four private organizations that promoted this ideal: the commercial "Own Your Own Home Campaign"; the nonprofit Better Homes in America Movement; the Architects' Small House Service Bureau; and the commercial Home Modernizing Bureau.[70] The ideal of home ownership as an incentive to social order thus combined with a vision of the suburban home as a locus for the affirmation of the value of outdoor (albeit a controlled outdoors) life.

As Hoover's term in the Department of Commerce drew to a close, he had expanded his concept of conservation. No longer did he think of it merely as an adjunct to economic growth. He now regarded it as a means of making the benefits of the consumer society universally accessible, as a way of turning the leisure created by modern industrialism into an opportunity for growth and development for average Americans, and as an essential method for making the urban and suburban environment healthful and attractive.

Still unresolved, however, was a tension between the vision of the world

Hoover held as part of the new national elite of technical experts, and his political and economic philosophy of decentralization, voluntarism, and localism. As an engineer, he was confident that he had a unique preparation to "understand a problem, to visualize the objective and to press without diversion toward that end," which seemed to imply a preference for national planning and national control.[71] During the Commerce years he had searched energetically and creatively, but not often successfully, for ways to reconcile the engineer's approach with that of the local politician or businessman. In the White House he would have an opportunity to see whether those two seemingly incompatible ideals could somehow be combined.

Horace Albright (left) and Herbert Hoover in Yellowstone Park in 1927. Albright, then superintendent of Yellowstone, became director of the National Park Service during the Hoover administration. A friend of both Herbert and Lou Henry Hoover, Albright strongly influenced conservation policy. (C. F. Culler)

Former President Hoover fishing in 1936. Although Hoover loved all kinds of fishing, his favorite was always fly-fishing. (King Features Syndicate)

Hoover's uncle, Dr. Henry John Minthorn, saved Bert's life during a childhood illness, then adopted him after Bert's parents died. Hoover's youth with the Quaker Minthorn family in frontier Oregon helped to shape his personality and values. (Unknown)

Hoover asked the Weyerhauser Company to ship a sample of a "standardized" plank to the Commerce Department to be used as an example in promoting his simplification and standardization program. Some joker in the company sent the board by first class mail. (Unknown)

ne of Hoover's many interests during his years as secretary of commerce was the restora-
on of sport and commercial fisheries. In this 1925 photo Hoover (center) observes while the
hief of the Fisheries Bureau, Dr. Henry O'Malley (light suit), pretends to measure a fish at
hatchery. (Unknown)

Secretary of Commerce Herbert Hoover on his fifty-second birthday, 10 August 1926, working as usual. The maps on the walls behind him suggest his interest in world trade. (Unknown)

Lou Henry Hoover, like her husband, loved the outdoors. She was also a linguist and a serious scientist. For many years, she was head of the Girl Scouts. (Harris and Ewing)

The President's Research Committee on Social Trends published a multivolume study of American life in 1933. The study was typical of Hoover's belief that thorough, scientific study of issues was the first step toward dealing with them. Members of the committee pictured are (from left) Wesley C. Mitchell, Howard W. Odum, Shelby M. Harrison, Alice Hamilton, Charles E. Merriam, Edward Eyre Hunt, and William F. Ogburn. (Unknown)

he Colorado River Compact, which apportioned the river's waters among bordering states
d permitted the construction of Hoover Dam, was one of Hoover's proudest achievements.
was a bitter blow when FDR's secretary of the interior renamed the structure Boulder
m, and Hoover was deeply appreciative when Harry Truman restored the original name.
nited Airlines)

Hoover with John D. Rockefeller Jr. at a New York State Chamber of Commerce banquet in 1949. At least partly because of his friendship with Hoover, Rockefeller made generous contributions of land and money that played an important part in nearly doubling the size of the national parks. (New York *Herald Tribune*)

President Dwight Eisenhower with Hoover at the Byers Peak Ranch near Fraser, Colorado, in 1954. Hoover and Eisenhower did not always agree on conservation issues, but Ike's charm helped to smooth over differences. (Unknown)

Since the early 1920s, Hoover had dreamed of a waterway that would permit ocean-going ships to enter the Great Lakes. When the St. Lawrence Seaway project finally began in the 1950s, he was pleased to be recognized as a pioneer of the idea. He is shown here in 1957 at a seaway construction site with Robert Moses (left), chairman of the New York State Power Authority, and James Duncan, chairman of Ontario Hydro. (International News [U.P.I.])

Next to fly-fishing, Hoover most loved bonefishing in the Florida Keys. Even in his old age, however, he seldom went fishing without taking along a pad and pencil to record ideas or work on problems. Calvin Albury (at the rear of the boat) was his longtime guide on these fishing trips. (Unknown)

Secretary of the Interior Ray Lyman Wilbur (center) at a 17 September 1930 cere-
mony celebrating the opening of the Union Pacific branch line that would supply
the construction site for Hoover Dam. Wilbur was one of Hoover's oldest and
closest friends. Pictured with him (from left) are Senator Key Pittman (Nevada),
Governor Fred B. Balzar (Nevada), President C. R. Gray of the Union Pacific, and
Senator Tasker L. Oddie (Nevada). (Unknown)

6 | "Specialist in Public Calamities"

"Will Coolidge Shatter the Third-Term Tradition?" asked the headline of the lead story about possible candidates for the 1928 presidential election in a May 1927 issue of the *Literary Digest*. A dozen or more cartoons culled from newspapers across the country raised the same question in the June issue of the *American Review of Reviews*. Everyone agreed that if the dour Vermonter wanted the nomination, it was his for the taking. Those who muttered that this would amount to a third term because Coolidge had served a year of Harding's term before being elected in his own right were more likely to be Democrats than Republicans. With the country, except for farmers, generally prosperous and happy, the president's reelection seemed a certainty if he chose to run.[1]

Other candidates did not flourish in the president's shade. Governor Frank Lowden of Illinois was the most often mentioned, but always with the proviso that he would become a serious candidate only if Coolidge withdrew and if Charles Evans Hughes did not seek the nomination. Regarded as longer shots were Nicholas Murray Butler, Charles G. Dawes, and Nicholas Longworth. Hoover was sometimes mentioned as a possibility, but some pundits, such as the author of an article on possible candidates published in *Survey* magazine early in 1927, ignored him completely.[2]

By September, however, after Coolidge announced on 2 August that he did not "choose to run for President in nineteen twenty-eight," Hoover suddenly emerged as the most likely candidate. His nomination, he told reporter Will Irwin, was "nearly inevitable."[3] Of course, as a highly visible secretary of commerce in a prosperous era, he had always been a possible choice, but what really catapulted him to the forefront among Republicans in the spring and summer of 1927 was his role as director of relief during the great Mississippi River flood. All of the old images of the "great humanitarian" who had organized a successful international relief operation in Belgium during the war and in much of Europe after the armistice, now reemerged. As the Mississippi's waters inundated the Midwest and the South, the architect of Republican prosperity became again the "specialist in public calamities," whose engineering expertise combined with humanitarianism to convey special authority in this "greatest peace-time calamity," as Hoover described the flood.[4]

After the flood was over, Hoover remembered the relief effort and the postflood reconstruction program as triumphs of private voluntarism in which he had served mainly as a catalyst, though he did take credit for having "pointed out the major directions" of the river-control system that was begun as the flood waters receded. The reality is that his memory understated the importance and creativity of the vast public-private collaboration he organized and directed in dealing with flood relief, but that it overstated the success of postflood private reconstruction programs and exaggerated his role in the engineering aspects of the flood control system built after 1927 while minimizing his political importance in securing governmental support of it. In emphasizing the purely private and voluntary aspects of the 1927 relief and reconstruction projects, Hoover diminished his own achievement in mobilizing a successful and innovative cooperative effort among federal agencies, private volunteers, and state and local governments.[5]

The great flood that swept Hoover into the White House in 1928 began with heavier than normal rains in the Mississippi River valley and the upper Midwest in the late summer and fall of 1926. Although it was the dry season, floods drowned crops and even inundated cities in Nebraska, Kansas, Iowa, Illinois, and Indiana. In October the river gauge on the Mississippi at Vicksburg exceeded forty feet—nine feet higher than ever before recorded at that location. By New Year's Day 1927, the Mississippi reached flood stage at Cairo, Illinois, the earliest for any year on record. During the late autumn and early winter, the saturated lands of the river's valley were drenched again with rain and then, in the North, buried under huge snowfalls. Localized flooding was now widespread throughout the Midwest, and, with heavy winter rains sweeping the South, rivers overflowed their banks in Arkansas, West Virginia, Kentucky, Tennessee, and Mississippi as well as in the upper Midwest.[6]

Floods on the Mississippi were of course nothing new. As early as 1717 an engineer built a small levee at New Orleans to protect the new city. In 1849 and 1850 serious floods on the river focused the federal government's attention on the problem, and in 1861 Captain A. A. Humphreys, Chief of the Army Corps of Engineers, completed a major study of flooding and recommended the construction of a levee system to keep the river within its banks. After the Civil War, a joint civil-military commission restudied the problem and confirmed Humphreys's conclusion—that levees alone, without artificial reservoirs to store overflows, cutoffs of bends to speed flood crests downstream, or emergency outlets, could control flooding. In 1879 Congress created a Mississippi River Commission to oversee flood control and the improvement of navigation. Between 1879 and 1926, the commission spent almost $229 million building ever higher levees (reaching forty feet or more in some places), yet despite their best efforts, destructive floods hit the Mississippi valley in 1882, 1884, 1890, 1897, 1903, 1912, 1913, and 1922.[7] Indeed, as a number of people pointed out, the levees actually increased the potential for serious flooding by so constricting the river that there simply was nowhere for an exceptional flood to go. The imperfect success of the levee-building program might have suggested the need for humility, but in 1926 Major General Edwin Jadwin, Chief of Engineers, declared in his annual report that the levee system was "now in condition to prevent the destructive effects of floods."[8]

Jadwin's calculations did not include the floods that struck in the spring of 1927. Beginning in January, rainfalls as great as four or five inches in twenty-four hours were recorded in a number of places throughout the lower Mississippi valley and its tributaries. In March, high winds whipped flood-waters into large waves that pounded at levees. All along the lower river, alarm rose with the water level. Cities, states, and local levee boards recruited or forced poor men, mostly black, into gangs to reinforce and raise the levees. Throughout the area, roads, railroads, and bridges washed out, and newspapers carried more and more stories of storm-related deaths. By the beginning of April more than a million acres of land were already underwater as the result of floods on tributaries of the Mississippi, downtown Pittsburgh and Cincinnati had been flooded, and more than fifty thousand refugees were living in railroad cars or tents in the Midwest. But the levees on the Mississippi were still holding.[9]

The federal levees along the river were enormous structures, often thirty feet high, as wide as a football field, and filled with more than four hundred thousand cubic yards of dirt per mile, all carefully shaped and planted to minimize damage from floods. When the water began to rise, they were regularly inspected and patrolled, and if any weakness appeared, gangs of workers were summoned to pile sandbags or build walls. The engineers were still confident—until the rains got worse. On Good Friday, 15 April, more than a foot of rain fell on Cairo, Illinois, Little Rock, Arkansas, and Jackson, Mississippi, within eighteen hours; fifteen inches fell in New Orleans.[10] Every tributary of the Mississippi was now far above flood stage, and the main river was carrying more water than ever before, perhaps as much as three times more than in some earlier floods.

The first levee break in the federal system occurred on 15 April at Walnut Bend, Missouri, 278 miles below Cairo. The next day, at Dorena, Missouri, thirty miles below Cairo, a more serious break occurred when twelve hundred feet of levee collapsed, and 175,000 acres were flooded. On 19 April a mile-wide hole opened at New Madrid, Missouri, inundating a million more acres. Two days later, the levee collapsed at Mounds Landing, Mississippi, and a huge wall of water, nearly a mile wide and at least a hundred feet high, roared out into the Delta. Within ten days, the break flooded 1 million acres more than ten feet deep and scoured a channel a hundred feet deep for a mile and a half from the main river. Twenty-five miles from the Mississippi, the spreading waters were still running in great waves five or six feet high. Buildings, animals, and people vanished in seconds, never to be seen again. Eventually, this single break flooded an area a hundred miles long and fifty miles wide with water up to twenty feet deep, and in succeeding days other crevasses in the levees opened, creating a vast, yellow-brown inland lake more than a thousand miles long, sometimes more than fifty miles wide, and covering large parts of seven states. Before the flood was over, the Red Cross would house 325,554 people and feed 311,922 others whose homes, farms, or businesses were only partially inundated.[11]

Up to mid-April, federal and state officials had agreed that relief was a local responsibility, but the Mounds Landing levee break made the disaster so enormous that the federal government had to act. On 22 April President Coolidge named the secretaries of the treasury, war, navy, agriculture, and commerce to assist the Red Cross and local relief organizations in relieving the victims of the flood. Because of Hoover's previous experience with relief and with the Food Administration during the war, Coolidge asked him to chair the committee, though the president was no great admirer of the energetic secretary of commerce.[12]

Hoover was in his element in flood relief. Establishing a staff headquarters at Memphis, he mobilized federal and private resources. Often working from a radio-equipped private railroad car, he circled the flood area, popping up everywhere to inspect refugee camps, commiserate with survivors, and inspire volunteers. Recognizing that publicity was essential to raising the money needed for relief and reconstruction—and perhaps to his own political ambitions—he saw to it that a special car for reporters was attached to his train. His goal, he announced, was "to coordinate the activities of the War, Navy, Treasury and Commerce Departments into support of the Red Cross, which it was determined must continue the primary responsibility for the organization and administration of the relief measures to be taken."[13]

Although Hoover proclaimed that volunteers would be the core of the relief effort, he did not ignore the possibilities of federal assistance. The mere idea that the federal government should exercise primary responsibility in a disaster of this magnitude was an important precedent. Hoover called upon a variety of government agencies to secure some six hundred boats, sixty airplanes, virtually all tents, cots, blankets, and field kitchens used by the Red Cross camps, radio and telegraph facilities within the flood area, doctors and nurses from the Public Health Service, experts from the Agriculture Department, and thousands of National Guardsmen, all at federal expense. He also arranged for reconstruction loans through a federal agency. His own authority within the flood area was essentially dictatorial, though masked in the language of voluntarism. At his orders, various public and private groups undertook rescue work, set up refugee camps, and then began rehabilitation.[14]

Exactly who paid for all of this is difficult to determine accurately. The Red Cross estimated that it collected about $17.5 million in private donations and dispersed about $17 million of that in direct aid; other reliable sources put Red Cross expenditures either somewhat higher or significantly lower.[15] The *Congressional Digest* stated that the federal government had spent $7.5 million for relief, but it is impossible to tell whether that included such things as the $2.5 million that the Red Cross estimated was the value of services and supplies provided by the government to the organization. The published estimate obviously did not include the $10 million in reconstruction loans provided by the Federal Intermediate Credit Corporation, an adjunct of the Federal Farm Loan Board.[16] Hoover himself estimated that the relief phase of the operation alone expended some $27 million, but he did not say where the money came from.[17] State and local government spending is even more difficult to pinpoint. The *Congressional Digest* put it at $10 million, but that evidently did not include what David Burner labels "emergency state credit corporation funds of $12 million," and it is not clear whether it included the $500,000 worth of supplies and services that the Red Cross identified as state government contributions to its work.[18] In addition, the Flood Credits Corporation, an organization created by the Chamber of Commerce of the United States, may have provided some $10 million in private loans to businesses and state credit corporations.[19]

No matter how one adds up the relief figures, they come nowhere near covering the total damage done by the flood, variously estimated at from $300 million to $1 billion. Nevertheless, this was an unprecedented relief effort by private charity and by local, state, and federal governments. Hoover was correct that voluntarism played an important role in the overall relief program (in addition to money and supplies donated, most workers were volunteers), but his version of the story omits the fact that federal and state governments provided roughly two-thirds of the money expended as well as leadership, critical equipment, and personnel. As Bruce Lohof has pointed out, Hoover's ideologically shaped recollections of the relief program actually understate the importance of his achievement, which was to create an effective "bureaucratic machine" that nourished and supported grassroots voluntary activity. Hoover's flood relief plan, writes Lohof, illustrated the concept that "properly administered, a bureaucracy would not replace or stifle individual effort or community enterprise; rather, it would vitalize these activities by coordinating and rationalizing the resources upon which they draw."[20]

Hoover, through his efficient federal bureaucracy, was able to help the Red Cross establish 154 refugee camps from Illinois to Louisiana. The first camp had been set up in Mississippi a week before he took over, and with his support, others quickly followed, eventually providing housing for more than 325,000 people. Living quarters may have been in tents, but the camps provided modern sanitation, running water, electricity, and medical care that many rural families had never seen before. Hoover also saw to it that residents of the camps were given plenty of opportunity for recreational, spiritual, and educational uplift, calling on social workers and state universities to make their services available to the residents. All able-bodied men were expected to work to keep the camps clean and orderly, though the main responsibility for maintaining law and order rested with the military and with local authorities. The whole operation was so successful, the Red Cross bragged later, that "after the families had been in camp for two or three days, a spirit of contentment developed which frequently led to expressions of sincere regret when the time came for them to leave."[21] As a longer-term benefit, Hoover arranged for a Rockefeller Foundation grant to provide, on a fifty-fifty cost-sharing basis with local governments, a health unit composed of a doctor, a nurse, and a sanitary engineer for each of the flooded counties. Where health units were established, he said later, disease statistics were cut below preflood levels.[22]

In addition to assisting the people actually housed in camps, the Red Cross also provided supplies, food, and medical assistance to almost as many others who were not actually forced out of their homes—almost 312,000. Nor, in these rural areas, could the welfare of animals be ignored. Although hundreds of thousands of animals were drowned, the Red Cross estimated that it spent almost $2.5 million dollars in housing and feeding over 270,000 animals rescued from the flood.[23]

Hoover's role in all of this was primarily in planning, organizing, and coordinating. His office provided plans for camps, technical information, funds, materials, and the initiative for organization. A Central Purchasing Department at his headquarters bought supplies in bulk, provided for their storage until they were needed, and oversaw their distribution.[24]

This emphasis on Hoover as the supporter of local volunteers manning the front lines did not mean that he disappeared from sight. Traveling incessantly with his entourage of reporters, he visited everywhere and appeared nearly as often in news photographs as did the images of drowned landscapes. Admiring reporters might declare that he was "the most unassuming official within a thousand counties," but they were never allowed to overlook the fact that he had "stitched together one of those rapid organizations at which he is so adept—sound yet fluid, economical yet supremely efficient." Nor was Hoover depicted as a distant, uninvolved administrator. "Two or three times," wrote a reporter, "I saw Hoover enter a town which expected a rush of water or of refugees, burned with zeal to do something, and did not know exactly how to proceed. A few quiet words of order and advice from the ever-serene Hoover, and things began to move."[25] Another recorded that "Secretary Hoover is always at the point along the river where the danger to life is the greatest. . . . He may be found in the refugee camps at the embarkation piers—and at the worst of the flood breaks he was on the threatened levees giving council and courage."[26]

Hoover's own role as orchestrator of this favorable publicity was suggested by the fact that he proposed to George Horace Lorimer, publisher of the *Saturday Evening Post*, that he himself write an article about the flood because of his "intimate knowledge of this river . . . that might enable me to say something that would be entertaining to your readers."[27] Although Hoover never got around to writing the article, by the time the waters began gradually to recede, he was firmly identified in Americans' minds as a hero of the disaster.

Hoover's desire to be seen as the virtually omnipotent rescuer of the flooded region led him to make at least one totally impossible claim—that "only three lives . . . were lost after [he] took charge."[28] To read reporters' accounts of levee breaks where huge crevasses suddenly opened at the feet of large gangs of men—usually black laborers who were sometimes forced to work at gunpoint—who had been frantically trying to shore up the levee, is to know that far more than three people were killed in the more than a dozen major crevasses that opened after Hoover took over. In addition, the homes of African Americans were often crowded into undesirable areas near the levees, and as one student of the disaster found, perhaps as many as a third of the African-American farmworkers and sharecroppers of the Mississippi Delta "never returned to their former homes" after the flood.[29] These findings assume a dreadful meaning when coupled to the number of laborers likely lost in levee collapses. Official estimates of flood deaths, which ranged from the Red Cross's 246 to the Weather Bureau's 313, were tragically low, and Hoover's claim that no more than three died after he began work was appalling.[30] His insistence upon it over the years conflicts with his humanitarian image and cheapens and diminishes his monumental achievement as director of relief.

The second phase of Hoover's role in the flood began well before relief ended. Indeed, in many places it was months before the water receded, and often long after that until the land dried out enough for people to return.[31] But Hoover was unwilling to wait. To an audience in New Orleans on 23 May, he declared that the flood offered an opportunity to give a new meaning to the word "reconstruction." "I believe we may give it a new significance in the relations of North and South," he said.[32]

Hoover's immediate goals included returning people to their homes and lands with supplies for rebuilding and replanting, and on 12 May Hoover and Red Cross flood relief director James Fieser announced that the Red Cross would provide for each family leaving a refugee camp seeds, a temporary supply of food and feed for livestock, farm implements, some livestock and poultry, basic furniture, and assistance and supplies to provide modest shelter.[33] Although this rehabilitation aid amounted to only a few dollars for each family (one estimate was less than $20 per family), it added up to a considerable sum when multiplied by the nearly 121,000 families who received it. The Red Cross continued its drives to raise money for relief long after the rivers had returned to their banks.

More important, Hoover realized that short-term assistance would be useless unless credit was made available on a massive scale to sustain recovery. He left initial assistance to the Red Cross and devoted himself to securing the large-scale credit needed to provide a viable economy over the long term. At his urging, bankers and business leaders in Louisiana, Mississippi, and Arkansas established state Agricultural Finance Corporations to make loans to farmers. The loans would then be sold at a discount to the Federal Intermediate Credit Corporation, and the money from the sales would be used to make more loans. And when it became apparent that this self-help system could not generate sufficient capital, he summoned a meeting of leaders of the U.S. Chamber of Commerce and browbeat them into creating a nonprofit corporation called the Flood Credits Corporation, with a capital of $1.75 million that could be loaned to state reconstruction corporations. All told, Hoover thus managed to raise some $13 million in capital for reconstruction without asking Congress for direct relief appropriations.[34]

The federal government had never before gone so far toward offering relief—even indirectly—in a disaster, but the amounts Hoover raised were scarcely more effective than the sandbags desperate workers threw into the yawning crevasses in the levees. Aside from the fact that his $13 million worked out to just over $20 for each flood victim, it was not distributed equally. Whole groups of people—tenants on large plantations, for example—received little or no assistance, while substantial amounts were given to planters, mill owners, and manufacturers. "The cooperative spirit of Main Street is what is putting the Mississippi Valley back on its feet after the flood," said Hoover. "The people of the valley are settling their own problems of rehabilitation without a great deal of outside help."[35] From an economic point of view his argument may have been sound, but the most impoverished victims of the flood needed direct assistance as well as the restoration of companies and plantations. If, as a reporter claimed in July, "the South itself feels that its salvation today is in the hands of Herbert Hoover," by autumn the glow was wearing off.[36] As would be the case in the Great Depression a few years later, Hoover's rejection of direct federal aid to victims of catastrophe eroded his popular reputation as a great humanitarian.

To be fair, the fault was not entirely Hoover's. Although the Treasury collected a surplus of $635 million in 1927, there was no overwhelming sentiment in Congress or the country to undertake a federally financed program of direct relief, or even to offer a program of federal reconstruction loans. Senators and congressmen from the flood area urged the president to call a special session of Congress to meet in November to consider relief, and Hoover, although he did not agree with those who favored a federal relief program, supported the idea of a special session in hopes of obtaining an appropriation to finance immediate repairs to the flood control system. Coolidge refused to call a special session, ignored the need for an appropriation for levee repair, and exceeded his legal authority by ordering the Mississippi River Commission to begin rebuilding.[37] Hoover certainly did not intend it that way, but his enthusiastic support for private reconstruction enabled the president—and much of the country—to avoid responsibility for all but the most immediate needs of flood victims.

Hoover certainly shared Coolidge's reservations about the propriety of federal aid to individuals affected by the Mississippi disaster, but he was well ahead of the president in insisting that the federal government assume responsibility for building a better system of flood control for the river. Even before the flood began, he had strongly supported substantially increased federal expenditures for development of the Mississippi River system and for the development of other river systems as well.[38]

He took the flood as proof of his longstanding belief that river systems must be considered as units, not separated under various jurisdictions, which meant that only the federal government was capable of developing a flood control program for the Mississippi drainage basin. In this case, he told a reporter from the St. Louis *Post-Dispatch* in late April or early May, the thing to do was to "build higher levees and more of them." Storage reservoirs on tributaries might help a little in preventing local floods, he thought, but would be useful mostly for "power development." Reforestation of watersheds, a pet proposal of many conservationists, he dismissed as "impracticable in the present situation, and in any event, a dubious solution."[39]

By midsummer Hoover had modified his apparent initial commitment to a levees-only plan. In a report to the president on 20 July and an interview with the New York *Evening Post,* he talked about "higher and consequently wider levees and the extension of Federal responsibility for levees on some of the tributaries," but he also proposed "a spillway, more properly called a 'by-pass' to the Gulf to protect New Orleans and southern Louisiana." And he made clear his belief that while the federal government could not foot the entire bill for building a better flood control system, it must contribute much more generously than ever before. After all, he argued, "we must remember that the whole country between the Rocky Mountains and the Appalachians is drained by the Mississippi River, and it isn't fair, is it, to ask the man who lives at the end of the sewer to pay for the whole sewer?"[40]

In the eyes of the admiring reporters who followed Hoover around, his engineering background and position as head of flood relief made him seem an authority on everything relating to the Mississippi. But he was by no means the principal author of the postflood plan eventually adopted by the federal government, as he implied in his *Memoirs.*[41] The old policy of levees-only flood control had been shown to be totally inadequate when it became necessary to dynamite the levees below New Orleans in order to save the city. Thereafter, a consensus was formed among federal and state engineers, the Army Corps of Engineers, the Mississippi River Commission, and most politicians that levees would have to be supplemented with some sort of relief system, probably at the Atchafalaya River above New Orleans.[42] Hoover partook of this consensus but did not shape it.

Agreement on the broad outlines of a plan did not, of course, assure agreement on its details. Early in May 1927, President Coolidge had asked the Mississippi River Commission for a comprehensive flood control plan, and at the same time he also requested a similar plan from the Chief of the Army Corps of Engineers. In November the House Flood Control Committee began extensive hearings on the two plans.

The Mississippi River Commission's report took as its starting point an assumption of the need to provide protection for a flood 25 percent greater than that of 1927. It envisioned massive new levees 5 feet higher than the highest estimated flood level, two major diversion channels, and "safety-valve spillways" designed to relieve pressure before levees collapsed. Given the enormous amount of construction the plan would require, and the high costs of acquiring rights of way for diversion channels and spillways, the commission estimated the basic cost of its plan at more than $407 million, and the total if all features were implemented at $775 million. The plan assumed that most of the money would come from the federal government.[43]

The Army Corps of Engineers' plan (more commonly known as the Jadwin Plan, after Major General Edgar Jadwin, Chief of Engineers) started from the same assumptions and incorporated many of the same features as did the commission's. It differed from the commission plan mainly in that it proposed slightly lower levees; it anticipated sending greater volumes of water through diversions; it proposed to create in some areas a system of secondary levees about five miles back from the river that would, in effect, serve to establish a huge reservoir to contain floodwaters; and it recommended creating a number of "fuse-plug sections" in levees above major cities so that water could be diverted in large quantities before the cities were inundated. The plan's cost was estimated at only about $296 million, a huge savings over the Mississippi Commission's proposal, which appealed greatly to President Coolidge. The expected savings were largely the result of excluding from the plan any payments to the owners of lands that lay in the path of floodwaters diverted from the main river. Jadwin argued that such channels were natural outlets for the river and that the owners of lands in the channels must bear the risk and cost if their lands were flooded. In the president's annual message to Congress on 8 December 1927, he recommended the adoption of the Jadwin Plan.[44]

Because the administration was backing the Jadwin Plan, the House Committee on Flood Control had no choice but to consider it, but committee chairman Frank R. Reid (R, Ill.) openly favored the Mississippi River Commission's approach. Reid saw to it that witnesses before the committee's extensive hearings brought out every weakness in the Jadwin Plan. By one estimate, "perhaps ninety-five per cent of the witnesses had some criticism of the Jadwin plan as an engineering project."[45] Some of those objections were politically motivated, coming from people who saw in the larger expenditures proposed by the commission report opportunities to fund local pork-barrel projects, but there were also serious concerns about engineering aspects of the Jadwin Plan, particularly about the uncontrolled floodways that would lie behind the fuse-plug sections of levees. Not only was the plan vague on what the effects would be of floodwaters suddenly rushing into these areas, but the residents of such regions were understandably alarmed that their lands might be repeatedly inundated without the federal government having any obligation to compensate or help them.[46]

All of these issues were, however, mere shadows beside the question of who would pay for any new program. Traditionally, states and local governments had been required to match federal expenditures with cash, lands, or rights-of-way, but the cost of the proposed new construction was so great, and local governments so impoverished by the 1927 flood, that representatives of the affected areas insisted that cost-sharing was impossible. Hoover had agreed publicly with this point of view, and in a meeting with local leaders at Hot Springs, Arkansas, on 12 September 1927, he helped to work out a formula designed to get around the problem. Money already spent by the affected states on flood prevention would be counted as their contributions toward the new program. In addition, the bill would be drawn as narrowly as possible, excluding federal responsibility for flood control on tributaries and focusing only on the Mississippi itself. Since the War Department would be the author of the narrow bill, it would draw the anger of those whose pet projects were excluded. If it later proved necessary to add projects on tributaries in order to win political backing for the bill, the conferees agreed, the bill's sponsors could seem generous by bowing to necessity.[47]

The strategy was brilliant, but getting it implemented was difficult. President Coolidge was unwilling to give up full cost-sharing and insisted on the less expensive Jadwin Plan. Congressman Reid hated the Jadwin Plan and introduced a bill embodying the Mississippi River Commission plan. In the end, it was left to the Senate to come up with a compromise. There Wesley L. Jones (R, Wash.), chairman of the Commerce Committee, proposed a bill that although ostensibly based on the Jadwin Plan, authorized $325 million (as opposed to the Jadwin Plan's $296 million) for immediate construction, and most important of all, provided for surveys that opened the possibility of large additional expenditures. While the Jones bill's moderate initial cost and rejection of federal payments for damages caused by floodwaters released through the floodways appealed to the president, its open-endedness drew support from people who preferred a much larger program.[48]

Hoover's position in all of this was delicate. He had already said in July that he believed the federal government must pay for flood control, and in September he had agreed with the proposal to count flood expenditures by the affected states as contributions toward new construction. But the president insisted adamantly on local cost-sharing. In a speech before the Mississippi Valley Association in St. Louis in November 1927, Hoover declared that "the destruction of property [from the 1927 flood] is the loss of the entire nation—it is not solely the loss of the individual sufferers," and he expressed his confidence that some national policy would be adopted that would "give assurance of safety to the whole of our fellow citizens in the flood territory . . . [and] guarantee the continued development of this great region," but he offered no specifics.[49] And he was equally cautious in testimony on the Jones bill before the Senate Commerce Committee. He endorsed the idea that "the amount of money which the people in the South have already expended in construction of the existing works needs to be taken into account" in assessing their contribution to the new program, but he did not venture to suggest how that should be done, or what proportion of local obligations should be written off in this way.[50] To suggest, therefore, that Hoover took a leading part in the passage of flood control legislation is to exaggerate. His opinion that the federal government should pay for the project was reasonably well known, but he was unable to take a lead in the debate as long as the president remained opposed to federal responsibility.

If Hoover was constrained because of his position in the cabinet, others were not. Up and down the Mississippi valley, local interests mobilized, drumming on the theme that the whole country's economy would be affected if the region did not recover quickly and completely. The message got through. The Investment Bankers Association of America and the American Bankers Association both urged passage of the Jones bill, and a special committee of the U.S. Chamber of Commerce concluded that "*the federal government should hereafter pay the entire cost of constructing and maintaining works necessary to control floods of the lower Mississippi River.*"[51] Faced with this heavy pressure from the business community, Coolidge, who in April had described the proposed bill as "the most extortionate piece of attempted legislation" he had seen in all his public experience, backed down.[52] He accepted the principle that in view of previous contributions by local governments, their obligations had been fulfilled, and the federal government would fund future works. On 15 May 1928 the president signed what was now referred to as the Jones-Reid bill into law.

Passage of the bill evoked rejoicing in the lower Mississippi valley because it proclaimed clearly and for the first time the responsibility of the federal government for the control of the river. Engineers were less enthusiastic about the technical aspects of the plan, and many people in the valley were angry about the lack of compensation for use of private lands. Hoover was reported to have muttered privately that the plan demonstrated "the viciousness of Army engineers."[53]

Despite criticisms, the plan adopted in 1928 has generally been successful, controlling major floods in 1937, 1945, 1950, 1973, 1975, 1979, and 1983. With the significant exception of the construction of a series of cutoffs designed to remove the so-called Greenville Bends and thus move crests downstream more quickly, and the building of the Old River Control Structure to prevent the Atchafalaya from becoming the new main channel of the river, Project Flood, as the control system is called, is very much as it was envisioned in 1928.[54]

Project Flood is certainly one of the greatest engineering projects in North America, and perhaps in the world. Hoover and the other creators of the system envisioned the problem from the outset as one of engineering, not one of conservation or environmentalism. The suggestion that the federal government should purchase floodways outright, which might have allowed those areas to become natural wetlands and flood absorbers, was rejected because of its cost, and the idea of reforestation as a natural method of flood control was dismissed as irrelevant. When the Forest Service recommended the acquisition and reforestation of 8.5 million acres of land in the Mississippi valley, General Jadwin replied contemptuously that all of that "would reduce flood stages in the Mississippi River by only one-half an inch." Other engineers, including Hoover, were of the same opinion.[55]

The cavalier dismissal of the reforestation argument by Hoover and the engineers overlooked an important point. The problem of the Mississippi was not only one of too much water; it was also a problem of too much soil—soil, that is, carried by the river in the form of silt. Although the power of the river in flood would carry immense amounts of silt, eventually the whole level of the channel would be raised, as had already happened at New Orleans, and the levees would have to be pushed higher and higher to contain it. A number of exotic inventions to deal with this problem were proposed to Hoover by people all over the world, but none of them seemed as likely to work as did the simple idea of reducing siltation at the source by reforestation. Proponents freely admitted that reforestation would not reduce the amount of water in a flood very much, but they believed it would greatly prolong the useful life of any works built to contain and control floods. An engineering solution alone was inadequate, declared Gifford Pinchot. What was needed was a comprehensive approach that would include every aspect of conservation, water and land management, power development, and social reformation, as well as brilliant engineering.[56] That was an argument that seemed very much in harmony with what Hoover himself had been saying prior to the flood, but even if he had been sympathetic to it in 1928, there was little he could do to convince the president that spending even more hundreds of millions on a comprehensive plan for the Mississippi valley was worthwhile. The truth seems to be, however, that for all his talk about planning the development of whole river systems, Hoover saw the role of the federal government in that process mainly as a catalyst and coordinator of local initiatives, as in the case of the Colorado River pact. His willingness to have the federal government fund flood control along the Mississippi was an exception to that general rule, not a fundamental change of philosophy.

Hoover enjoyed an enormous boost in public visibility as a result of his work during the Mississippi flood. His image, as a brilliant administrator and an internationally recognized humanitarian, and as an engineer capable of wisely deciding virtually every technical issue before the country, was immensely enhanced. Starting as only one of a number of possible Republican candidates for the 1928 presidential nomination in early 1927, by autumn he had become the front-runner.

Observers sometimes stressed only one of the three aspects of Hoover's image to the exclusion of the others. Thus one shrewd but not very friendly observer described him as "the perfect human machine, destitute of error, with a vision beyond cosmic bounds, who resolves every problem in its mathematical elements."[57] If in this case the author's intent was unfriendly, Hoover's admirers did not reject the superhuman Hoover entirely. Republicans were aware that in 1928 many voters were more interested in progress and efficiency and profits than in the candidate's humanity. Hoover deserved support, the New York *Herald-Tribune* editorialized, because he represented a "precise fusion of engineering and business ability."[58]

A second interpretation of Hoover that derived from his role during the flood also focused on only one aspect of his popularity—his administrative skills, which admirers depicted as radically novel. "As only an engineer, as only an administrator," wrote William Hard, "Mr. Hoover might have rescued the Mississippi flood-sufferers with the Army. He in fact rescued them with an infinitely complicated network of local committees of leading local citizens." Hoover was thus revealed as something new in American politics, "an unprecedented organizer of private citizens for public purposes" who made "a drastic discrimination between organized society that is private and voluntary, and organized society that is public and coercive." For Hoover, Hard concluded, "the State is only a means by which private citizens can be more statesmanlike."[59] Although not explicitly stated, the implication of such language was that Hoover's ability to evoke and organize voluntarism was a panacea for every problem facing the United States. Perhaps that was what he himself believed.

Some supporters worried that the picture of Hoover as a superhuman engineer and organizer had been so reinforced by his role during the flood that it might have gotten out of hand. "Is Hoover Human?" was the title of an article that, on the eve of the 1928 election, tried to assure the voters that he would really prefer to be "a rollicking Roosevelt . . . rather than a chubbier Coolidge."[60] Hoover's 1928 campaign biographer, Will Irwin, insisted that the country did not have to deny itself the humane man in order to have the visionary engineer. Hoover's sympathy for the unfortunate, Irwin wrote, "translates itself not into tears but into action. 'What can I do?' he asks himself; and the mind once more takes control. Henceforth while others weep, he works!" He was, Irwin wrote after sketching a grand panoramic view of Hoover's flood relief efforts, "the transmuter of altruistic emotion into benevolent action."[61]

In the end, it was this blending of the "great engineer" with the "great humanitarian" that came to dominate the image of Hoover presented to voters in 1928. He became the "spokesman of humane efficiency," as Bruce Lohof has described him.[62] He embodied, his supporters claimed, a dramatically new approach to American government and public administration, under which guided voluntarism would solve every future problem just as it was claimed that Hoover had mobilized volunteers to deal with Belgian relief, the Food Administration, the Commerce Department, and, most recently and perhaps most dramatically, the Mississippi flood. For Americans old enough to remember the Great War, Hoover's role in flood relief was a reminder of his past accomplishments; for those younger, it was a striking example of the sort of leadership they believed was necessary for a booming consumer economy.

Hoover himself became a prisoner of his own mythology. In memory he enhanced aspects of his own role, overlooked ugly aspects of the relief effort such as its massive racial discrimination and its failure to provide adequately for the individual needs of victims, and glossed over the limitations of the rehabilitation program, but he also largely ignored his very real success in uniting governmental action with voluntarism and his central role in developing a politically viable program for flood control in the Mississippi valley. In his account of the flood in his *Memoirs,* virtually everything dropped away but his own role in relief and, somewhat paradoxically, a claim of a volunteer spirit so pure that "the merest suggestion sparked efficient and devoted organization."[63] His memory of the period thus seems to caricature the complex and sophisticated organization he actually built. If his later account really reflects the way he understood what had happened in 1927, it becomes easier to understand why he was unable to cope successfully with the Great Depression.

Not everyone, of course, accepted uncritically Hoover's claims about voluntarism as a panacea. There were cases, wrote Oswald Garrison Villard presciently, where Hoover's approach might not be adequate. In the economic collapse of Europe after World War I, Villard recalled, "socialism took hold of a dozen countries when they were utterly wrecked, and no one else was there to take charge."[64] Whether Hoover could deal with a national crisis on that scale remained to be seen, but most Americans in 1928 assumed, based on newspaper and magazine accounts of the 1927 flood story, that there was no challenge he could not surmount. Hoover, proclaimed Will Irwin, had "shown a new way," "engineering our material civilization" by "inspir[ing] volunteers."[65] It was all wonderfully evocative of the optimistic, confident mood of America in 1928—perfect campaign rhetoric for a new era.

7 | "Long Run" Conservation

Conservation was not a major theme of Hoover's 1928 presidential campaign, and the index to a collection of his campaign speeches includes only two references to the subject.[1] The Republican platform also said little on the topic, merely enjoining "the avoidance of waste so that future generations may share in this natural wealth." In one of the seven major speeches Hoover gave during the campaign, at St. Louis on 2 November, the candidate expanded on the platform to reiterate his well-known support of federal responsibility for inland waterways, flood control, reclamation, and parks. In another speech at Stanford on 11 August, he proclaimed, "We in America today are nearer to the final triumph over poverty than ever before in the history of any land," and he added that the near universality of prosperity meant the increase of leisure for all Americans. "We have so increased the number of sportsmen fishing in our streams and lakes," he declared facetiously, "that the longer time between bites is becoming a political issue."[2] Just as he had in the past, Hoover thus urged conservation as a way to expand prosperity and depicted outdoor recreation as an amenity of affluence. A member of the Forest Service concluded, not surprisingly, that the new president was more interested in the economic benefits of conservation than its esthetic or "spiritual" aspects.[3]

As with so many other aspects of Hoover's thought, his ideas about conservation are not easily pigeonholed. Was he "the last Progressive president, combining many of the best ideas of both Theodore Roosevelt and Woodrow Wilson," or was he an enlightened conservative dedicated primarily to raising material living standards and interested in the protection of nature only as a means to that end?[4] Insofar as American conservatism is usually associated with ideas of libertarianism, small government, voluntarism, and the encouragement of private business, Hoover was certainly a conservative, but in his concern for equality of opportunity, prevention of business excesses, the long-term calculation of national interests, and the moral value of outdoor recreation, he was a progressive. As George Nash points out, Hoover's political ideas defy easy categorization because he favored an active government that would "stimulate the private sector to *organize and govern itself.*" He was, Nash concludes, a "political orphan."[5]

From the beginning of the conservation movement at the turn of the century, most of its leaders had seen the protection of natural resources as primarily a federal responsibility. The progressive conservation movement was an important element in the growth of the power of the federal government (especially the presidency), which was a major feature of American political life in the early twentieth century. Hoover believed, however, that "voluntarism stimulated by publicity from Washington and organized on a vast scale" could be applied to conservation as to other societal commitments.[6] Conservationists, habituated to federal authority in this area, regarded his ideas with suspicion. Some of the administration's conservation experiments drew the opposition of professionals and private organizations; others, incompletely thought through, backfired, ending by reinforcing federal authority. Still others, launched on the eve of the depression, seemed to confront Hoover with a stark choice between conservation and production. In those circumstances, he almost always chose the more conservative course, preferring production over preservation, decentralization over federal responsibility, private over public control, and the utilitarian over the esthetic. But where he was not forced to make an absolute choice, he followed policies that demonstrated how unclear is the line in America between exploiters and conservationists, or in this case, between conservatives and progressives.[7]

Hoover chose a friend of forty years, Dr. Ray Lyman Wilbur, then president of Stanford, for secretary of interior. The president-elect wanted a westerner he could trust in Interior, and in Wilbur he also got a physician with long experience in public health questions who was sympathetic with Hoover's desire to study and assist the poor, sick, aged, and other outcasts of American society such as the Indians.[8] Hoover and Wilbur were also old fishing friends, and some of the conservation professionals in the Interior Department were pleased with their first impressions of the new secretary. He "is the world's best," gushed the National Park Service's Arno Cammerer, "the most approachable and human I've yet encountered." Cammerer believed that the new secretary would "form one of the strongest helps we have got in the adjustment of things, as they should be adjusted." Others found the secretary's rapid-fire decision making and habit of doing two or three things at the same time disconcerting.[9]

Wilbur shared with Hoover the belief that conservation meant primarily "use without waste," but he went beyond some of his predecessors who had mouthed that easy slogan. Americans, he declared, must put "the prosperity of the commonwealth . . . before the individual" and must recognize that "in the long run, individual success is promoted by serving the public interest."[10]

Wilbur expanded the definition of conservation well beyond what most people then understood by the term. "I saw conservation as the important link throughout the [Interior] Department," he said later, "the conservation of human resources, particularly through the activities of the Office of Education, the Office of Indian Affairs, the Territories, the Eleemosynary Institutions, and the National Parks in their recreational and informational aspects, and the conservation of our natural resources—of water through the activities of the Geological Survey and the Bureau of Reclamation—of watersheds and the public domain, of oil and minerals."[11] Yet Wilbur's sweeping rhetoric translated into less action than might have been expected; he took a conservative view of the federal government's powers and was eager to devolve responsibilities onto the states or private volunteers. He was also a conservative in the sense that his central goal was always the use and development of resources, differing from those who might be labeled exploiters only in the fact that he viewed issues in a longer timescale than they did, not in a fundamental difference of purpose.

For the other cabinet member whose responsibility for conservation was significant, Hoover made what seemed an odd choice. Secretary of Agriculture Arthur M. Hyde was an automobile dealer from Kansas City who had been governor of Missouri, and whose only "connection with agriculture was the fact that his rich wife owned a large number of farms."[12] He had no record as a conservationist, nor was he Hoover's first choice for Agriculture. As secretary, Hyde turned out to be the strongest voice in the administration for traditional, federal control over conservation. He opposed Hoover's main conservation initiative, a plan to transfer the public domain to the states, speaking out against the proposal in private and organizing a National Conference on Land Utilization in November 1931 that ignored a presidential commission's recommendation to transfer the lands to the states and instead called for improved federal administration of public lands.

Despite these differences, the president came to value Hyde for his vigorous defenses of the administration and his endless fund of jokes. "I have known no Secretary of Agriculture before or since who was his equal," wrote Hoover in his memoirs.[13] Since Hoover intended to consolidate conservation functions in the Interior Department, perhaps he felt that Hyde's views on the subject were unimportant.[14]

Along with the secretary of interior and a dozen others, Hyde was a member of the "Medicine Ball Cabinet," which met every morning at 7:30 to throw an eight-pound medicine ball back and forth over a ten-foot net set up on the White House lawn. Hoover contended that the group never discussed policy, but its members certainly enjoyed a personal relationship with the president that others less privileged must have envied.[15]

The agenda of the new administration in regard to resource conservation was shaped by Hoover's interests during the cabinet years. Reorganization of agencies responsible for conservation, the completion of the Colorado River project and the inauguration of similar projects for other river systems as well as expansion of reclamation, the adoption of a system to rationalize the production of oil and gas, the development of a national program to promote outdoor recreation, and the planned development of Alaskan resources were all carryovers from projects in which Hoover had previously taken an interest. The expansion and consolidation of the national parks and national forests, and the consideration of a radically new approach to the administration of the public domain were ideas that had been a little outside even Hoover's ambitions before 1928. So were the "conservation of the Indian" and the "conservation of the child," which became major concerns of the Interior Department, although in both cases the administration's policies were based on Hoover's long-standing interests and convictions.[16]

Soon after taking office, Secretary Wilbur asked an executive assistant, William Atherton Du Puy, to review the activities of the department and make recommendations. Du Puy concluded that the department did "not have as much to do as it should." Many of the department's bureaus—Land, Pension, Indian, and Geological Survey—were "of declining importance" and "should tend to disappear" or be merged with others. Only the National Park Service and the Reclamation Service seemed to him to be "going along as [they] should go." Du Puy suggested that the historical parks (mainly battlefields) should be transferred from the War Department to the Park Service, and that the Forest Service and the Bureau of Public Roads be brought under Interior.[17] Two weeks later, the Reclamation Bureau warned the secretary that the Army Corps of Engineers was encroaching on bureau reclamation projects.[18] Wilbur used the two reports as arguments for reorganizing the conservation functions of the government under the Interior Department.

The secretary's support of reorganization did not produce any more result than Hoover's had previously. A Joint Committee on Cooperation between the Departments of the Interior and Agriculture, established in the spring of 1929, was not only unable to agree on consolidating the conservation functions of the two departments, but it seemed to heighten tensions between them.[19] Leading the opposition were Interior's National Park Service and Agriculture's Forest Service, each of which was willing to absorb the other but unwilling to be absorbed.[20] Hoover tried to smooth over the conflict in his

1929 Annual Message by suggesting that "the particular department or cabinet officer under which [conservation functions] should be placed is of secondary importance to the need of concentration," but neither he nor Wilbur was able to secure congressional authorization of the changes they wanted.[21] And as was the case with so many other plans, the onset of the depression in the autumn of 1929 disrupted the administration's hopes for reorganization. When they returned to the issue three years later, their arguments and purposes would be quite different.

More happily resolved, from Hoover's point of view, was the long and difficult task of determining the future of the Colorado River. On 25 June 1929 Hoover had the pleasure of signing an official proclamation making effective the compact among six of the seven states of the Colorado basin for the apportionment of water and power.[22] Almost a year of difficult negotiations then followed, during which one of Secretary Wilbur's executive assistants, Northcutt ("Mike") Ely, worked out the details of the contracts allocating power to be generated by the new dam among the states of the basin and providing for the sale of waterpower to generate that electricity to municipalities and private companies. On 26 April 1930 Wilbur signed the final contracts.[23] Three months later, with the passage of the final appropriation bill on 7 July, the Boulder Canyon project officially commenced. That September, when work began on the railroad leading to the dam site, Secretary Wilbur christened the new structure Hoover Dam. In characteristically restrained but nonetheless passionate words, Hoover recorded his pride at this conversion of a hitherto "wasted" resource to human use: "The waters of this great river, instead of being wasted in the sea, will now be brought into use by man.... The whole of this will translate itself ... into millions of happy homes ... out under the blue sky of the West. It will ... assure livelihood to a new population nearly as great as that of the state of Maryland."[24] Secretary of the Interior Harold Ickes's decision in May 1933 to rechristen the dam "Boulder Dam" led to a bitter conflict between Hoover's friends and the Democrats that was only resolved in 1947 when Congress changed the name back to Hoover Dam.[25]

From 1928 onward, Hoover consistently supported the policy that power from Hoover Dam would be distributed through public agencies. Although his personal preference for private power was well known, he played a key role in getting the Coolidge administration to accept the public power provisions of the Swing-Johnson bill, and according to Northcutt Ely, the Hoover administration arranged that 93 percent of power generated by the new dam would be allocated to public agencies. It was unfair that the president was accused by some opponents of intending to keep Colorado power development in private hands; but given his continuing and well-publicized opposition to making the Muscle Shoals installation in Alabama the centerpiece of a massive public power project, perhaps confusion about his attitude was predictable.[26] It may have been clear to him, as he said at Elizabethton, Tennessee, on 6 October 1928, that the federal government had a particular responsibility to "assure the conservation of our governmentally controlled natural resources in the interest of the people" and an equal obligation to avoid "any general extension of the Federal Government into the operation of business in competition with its citizens," but the Colorado and Muscle Shoals cases showed that applying principles to projects was difficult.[27]

Hoover regarded the Colorado River project as a triumph for his conviction that conservation need not mean the growth of the federal government's power. He pointed to the interstate compact that cleared the way for the construction of Hoover Dam as an example of decentralization, but the reality was not so simple. The states may have agreed among themselves (under federal pressure) how to divide the river's water, but their compact was ratified by Congress, and only the federal government, through the Bureau of Reclamation, could build the huge dam and apportion power rights. For all of Hoover's talk about millions of happy homes, the people in those homes did not control the river. Their happiness was dependent on federal policy as surely as it had been when earlier conservationists proclaimed the control of western resources exclusively a federal responsibility. The completion of Hoover Dam, writes Norris Hundley, marked "the emergence of the government in Washington as the most powerful authority over the Colorado River and, by extension, over other interstate and navigable streams as well."[28] In seeking an ingenious way to reduce federal responsibility for conservation, Hoover had ended up centralizing it even more than had been the case in the past.[29]

Other problems also faced the administration in its reclamation policy. With agriculture in a chronic recession even before the crash of 1929, Secretary Hyde suggested that new reclamation projects be postponed and the Bureau of Reclamation be moved to Agriculture. Reclamation chief Elwood Mead and western interests who profited from reclamation were quick to denounce this idea, but Hoover and Wilbur were concerned about the fact that so few reclamation projects seemed to be paying for themselves through user fees, as they were supposed to do.[30] Perhaps, the president suggested, it might be better for the federal government simply to build dams and hand "them over free of charge to the states as a Federal contribution," presumably leaving the states to run the projects and charge water users appropriately.[31]

Hoover's suggestion was later repeated in a broad review of administration conservation policies published by the Interior Department in 1932, but it never became official policy.[32] Instead, in May 1929 Commissioner Mead announced that a group of private consultants would review existing and proposed reclamation projects and offer recommendations about "the economic principles and policies which should govern our conclusions as to the feasibility or final development of projects . . . , the qualifications of settlers, the kind of agriculture which should be followed, and in general, those factors which determine earning power and well-being and contentment of the people of the communities created."[33]

The consultants took their charge broadly, and in March 1930 they reported their conclusion that reclamation policy, for all its merit, needed serious reevaluation. Some proposed projects, they argued, could not be justified on any terms, while others needed to be evaluated not only for their local irrigation benefits, but for the flood control and power they would provide to larger regions. Still other projects were feasible, but only if the period during which farmers were expected to pay off the cost of works was much longer than the twenty or forty years normally allowed. It was no longer enough, the group argued, to take for granted that successful settlement would be automatic once water was available. Unless Congress became willing to subsidize construction without requiring repayment, the experts concluded, much tougher economic standards should be applied to new projects than had been used previously. Also, if states demanded the construction of doubtful projects, they should guarantee to share costs "on a dollar for dollar basis" over and above the amount that could be recouped from farmers.[34] This conservative evaluation of the future of reclamation seems to have fitted very well with the president's growing conviction that all federal spending must be curtailed in the face of a worsening economic situation.

Somewhat less affected by the onset of the depression were the administration's attempts to secure a rational production policy for the oil industry, which was already in economic trouble. When Hoover was inaugurated in March 1929, many people in the oil industry were optimistic that he would find a way to curtail chronic overproduction and raise depressed prices. As a member of the Federal Oil Conservation Board (FOCB) since 1924, Hoover had repeatedly endorsed modification of the antitrust laws to permit agreements to restrict production among competing companies, and industry leaders hoped he would quickly secure legislation from Congress. Alternatively, some influential members of the American Petroleum Institute (API), which represented the larger producers, were seriously considering proposals for direct federal regulation of production. Unfortunately for their hopes, by 1929 Hoover had concluded that loosening the antitrust laws would be a mistake, and he was also opposed to federal controls.[35]

Nevertheless, Hoover, Wilbur, and their advisers, particularly Mike Ely and Hoover's old friend Mark Requa, the former director of the oil division of the World War I Fuel Administration, believed the situation necessitated action. Ely argued that less than ten years' worth of proven reserves were available to power the over 80 percent of the nation's fixed and mobile horsepower that had become dependent on petroleum, that overproduction and waste were rife, and that prices were so depressed that oil companies were close to losing money.[36] "The record of all time for the waste of a national resource has been broken in the past decade in the oil fields of the United States," declared Secretary Wilbur.[37]

Hoover took the first steps toward a new policy by announcing, at a press conference on 12 March 1929, that the government would issue no new permits for drilling on the public domain; and three days later, by declaring that outstanding leases would be reviewed and canceled if the holders had not actively exploited their concessions.[38] These dramatic announcements brought praise from some oilmen but were bitterly denounced by the governors of Colorado, Utah, and Wyoming, who foresaw a complete loss of royalties from drilling on their large areas of public land. Some small producers also criticized the administration's policy as preferential to big companies. Largely lost in the hubbub was the fact that only about 10 percent of domestically produced oil came from public lands.[39] Thus Hoover's first steps accomplished little in the way of reducing production and antagonized both small producers and some western political leaders.

In the meantime, the executive committee of the API took matters into its own hands, proposing a voluntary agreement among producers that would hold 1929 production at the same level as 1928. Secretary Wilbur asked Attorney General William Mitchell whether such an agreement would be legal under the antitrust laws. Mitchell replied that the FOCB had no "power to grant to any persons immunity from the operation of Acts of Congress prohibiting agreements in restraint of interstate commerce." The president, who had earlier told the attorney general that he was anxious that the oil companies' "activities should be closely scrutinized to see if they are being kept within the law," accepted the opinion. At a press conference on 2 April, he said flatly that any production restriction agreement would be a violation of

the Sherman Antitrust Act and declared that "the drilling of oil wells is entirely an intrastate question." The federal government, said Hoover, had absolutely "no authority" in the matter.[40]

Having ruled out the method that had seemed to oil industry leaders the
most likely to curtail overproduction, the administration turned instead to
the approach Hoover had taken on water—state action and interstate agreement. At the suggestion of Mark Requa and Geological Survey Director
George Otis Smith, the Interior Department began to consider a meeting of
representatives of the oil-producing states to discuss these courses of action.[41]
In the meantime, the department urged restraint in drilling and the prevention of waste as partial solutions to the oil companies' economic woes.[42] Ely
even suggested that the Interior Department keep a "blacklist" of wasteful or
careless drillers who could be denied future permits and leases, although
doubts about such a policy's legality prevented it from being adopted.[43]

Requa won the reluctant approval of the API for the interstate compact
plan in late April, and he and George O. Smith then began sounding out the
governors of the oil states about a meeting. In Washington, Ely was hard at
work on a draft compact to be presented to state leaders.[44] By mid-May Requa
had agreed to chair a meeting of representatives of the major oil-producing
states at the Broadmoor Hotel in Colorado Springs, with other states to be
invited to participate if they wished. On 10 June 1929 Secretary Wilbur
opened the meeting, which included the governors of Wyoming, Colorado,
Kansas, and Montana, as well as numerous oilmen and members of the FOCB,
with a speech broadcast coast to coast on the radio. He urged the adoption of
uniform state laws on drilling and an interstate compact to assure that those
laws were enforced.[45]

When the conference adjourned on 12 June, Requa telegraphed the White
House that although no specific agreement had been reached on a compact,
he believed that the conference had been worthwhile and had made progress.[46]
Privately, he was much less optimistic. Too many state delegates were political
appointees, he thought, and there were too many "unattached enthusiasts,
cranks, etc.," for the meeting to take definite action. What was more, many
of the representatives of the mountain states were still bitter about the withdrawal of permits for drilling on public lands, although it turned out that
Texas, Oklahoma, and California were the principal opponents of the compact
idea. All Requa could do, in the end, was to let everybody talk to "get it out
of their systems."[47] Secretaries Wilbur and Hyde later argued that what the
oilmen had hoped to secure at Colorado Springs was price controls, and what
the administration had offered was "a conservation measure, not a production

control and price-fixing measure."[48] There was truth in that, but it oversimplified the situation.

The depth of western anger against the withdrawal of federal lands from drilling came as a surprise to members of the administration who attended the conference. Ely suggested that a promise to permit limited drilling might be used to elicit from the states agreement on effective conservation laws and might even save the compact idea, but no one in the administration seemed interested in his proposal. Hoover and Wilbur preferred to await the report of an "Oil States Advisory Committee" set up by the governors of the oil states. In the meantime, the FOCB created a "Voluntary Committee on Petroleum Economics" to report on conditions in the oil industry and to make recommendations. Disgusted by what seemed to him meaningless activity, Requa resigned on 23 July as chairman of the Federal and States Petroleum Conservation Conference (the official name of the Colorado Springs meeting), with the observation that he did not see how anything effective could be accomplished without modification of the antitrust laws.[49]

Some oilmen urged raising the tariff as a solution to the oil glut in the United States. Requa pointed out, however, that the United States exported more oil than it imported, and warned that a tariff hike would lead to the construction of refineries overseas and the loss of American jobs. His argument was endorsed by others in the administration, but by October the situation had become so desperate that Requa reversed himself and came out in favor of a higher tariff.[50]

In the meantime, the Interior Department was pressing its last solution to the overproduction problem—unit operation. The idea of unit operation was simple—that all drillers on a field would agree to delay drilling until oil prices went up—but the application of the principle was difficult. The FOCB had endorsed the idea as early as 1926, but in most fields ownership of wells was so dispersed that unit operation was impossible to achieve. A new strike at Kettleman Hills in Southern California in 1928, however, offered an opportunity to provide a demonstration of the value of unit operation. Because more than half of the Kettleman Hills field was government owned, and much of the rest was leased from the government by Standard Oil of California, there was a better than usual chance of reaching a unit agreement. George Otis Smith of the Geological Survey succeeded in winning the assent of the main leaseholders to a unit operation plan in July 1929, but a handful of small producers in the area were unwilling to join. If they started pumping oil from the common pool, everyone else would have to do the same or lose out completely. Not until January 1931 was a unit contract finally completed, and even then, as Secretary Wilbur admitted, "certain land and lease holders about the fringe of the field remained obdurate, insisted on independent production, and caused the results to be less than complete." Wilbur touted the agreement as "an impressive object lesson" of the value of unit operation, but the difficulties of securing it even under unusually favorable conditions made it the only such success achieved by the administration.[51]

At the end of 1929, with the specter of depression growing, the FOCB issued a puzzling report. Tacitly rejecting the demands of the industry for federal assistance, it reviewed the events of the year and proposed no new initiatives. Instead, the report reiterated the old argument that continued importation of oil was desirable to reduce the drain on American reserves—a seemingly contradictory conclusion, unless the board believed that the ultimate solution to the crisis lay in reducing the number of producers, an event that would surely be hastened by expanded imports.[52] Given the administration's consistent refusal to support federal measures to rescue the industry, such a conclusion does not seem unwarranted, although there is no direct evidence to support it.

The overproduction that plagued the oil industry also afflicted the timber industry in only slightly less urgent forms. During the 1920s, Hoover had chaired the National Committee on Wood Utilization, which urged cooperation between government and industry to further the efficient use of wood, but the committee found no way to curtail overproduction, which became worse with the onset of the depression.[53] In the spring of 1930 Wilson Compton, president of the National Lumber Manufacturers Association, urged the creation of a new body to study overproduction, and in May Hoover announced the creation of the National Timber Conservation Board.[54] He charged it to develop "sound and workable programs of private and public effort, with a view to securing and maintaining an economic balance between production and consumption of forest products and to formulate and advance a deliberate plan of forest conservation."[55] The administration was slow to appoint members of the new board, however, and it did not begin work until January 1931. That spring, the administration sharply curtailed cutting in the national forests. The condition of the timber and lumber industries, declared Wilson Compton, had become "perilous, in fact ominous."[56]

In some ways the problems of the timber industry were more obvious than those of the oilmen. Whereas new discoveries kept increasing the oil glut, timber industry leaders expressed fears that overproduction, forced by falling retail prices on a highly competitive industry that included far more small producers than found in oil, would lead to timber shortages. A half-baked proposal to reduce production costs by lowering stumpage charges for cutting on Indian reservations would only worsen the situation, and even sustained yield forestry, which might offer a long-term solution, was no cure for the industry's immediate crisis. The Forest Service estimated that only about 60 percent of the original American forests remained, and they were being cut at rates that would soon exhaust them.[57]

Although the producers and the Forest Service depicted the situation as a conservation crisis, it is equally plausible to see it as an economic one in which overproduction resulted from too many companies cutting and finishing lumber. Reducing the number of lumber companies would solve both overproduction and conservation problems, albeit at a cost to the industry and its workers. The industry, of course, did not like that possibility, preferring to have the federal government somehow stabilize prices. The Timber Conservation Board (TCB) was initially unsympathetic, recommending voluntary restraint on the part of producers, and state and regional agreements as solutions. But when these methods failed to stem the price collapse, in October 1932 the TCB bowed to political pressure and recommended the implementation of a controlled production system under competent federal supervision. That, of course, was the plan that would be implemented during the New Deal under the National Recovery Administration.[58]

In the cases of both oil and timber, it is possible to argue that a determined policy of governmental inaction would have resulted in a reduction in the number of producers, the curtailment of overproduction, and the conservation of the resources. There is little direct evidence to support a contention that the Hoover administration diagnosed the situation in those terms, however, and in any event, the worsening of the depression made such a course politically impossible.[59]

Outdoor recreation was another area in which the administration promised much but found its hopes blighted by the beginning of the depression. Hoover had long believed that healthful outdoor recreation was essential to a successful industrial society, and he had been an active supporter of the National Conference on Outdoor Recreation since that organization's founding in 1924. The conference's formal authority expired with the end of Coolidge's term in March 1929, and although Rockefeller funding kept it going until summer, Hoover had to decide whether to propose a renewal of its official mandate. At the recommendation of the conference's executive secretary, Arthur Ringland, the executive committee voted in May to disband, but

Ringland and the conference's chairman, Chauncey Hamlin, urged the president to appoint a new committee drawn from the Commerce, Interior, and Agriculture Departments to undertake recreational planning for federal lands.[60]

The possibility that Ringland, a former Forest Service employee, would head the new committee was enough to damn it in the eyes of Park Service leaders, and the idea was allowed to die.[61] Nevertheless, Hoover remained interested in outdoor recreation, and when professional recreation workers organized a National Recreation Congress to meet at Louisville in October 1929, he issued a statement endorsing the meeting. From this meeting came yet another proposal for the revival of the National Conference on Outdoor Recreation. The central goal of the new organization, according to a mimeographed letter circulated among potential supporters, was to be the study of "the social problems involved in the increasing measure of leisure time made available through the shortening hours of labor."[62]

By the late autumn of 1929, as the crash precipitated the nation into depression, increasing leisure was something that for most workers was acquiring a distinctly ominous tone. In December Hoover decided that it "would seem . . . ill-advised to bring forward such a proposal at the present time." Instead, he asked economist Wesley C. Mitchell to head a President's Research Committee on Social Trends in the United States that was charged with studying social change "in order to throw light on the emerging problems which now confront or which may be expected later to confront the people of the United States." Sociologist Jesse Frederick Steiner undertook the committee's study of recreation and leisure and produced a volume, published in 1933, which surveyed the growth of public recreation during the 1920s. Only at the end of the book did Steiner note that "the curve of recreational expenditures" had been going downward since 1929, but he concluded guardedly that in a period of slower development there would be an opportunity to build "a well-balanced recreational program more carefully planned in the interests of the general welfare."[63] Hoover's own ambivalent outlook—that recreation was important enough to merit a major study, but that in a time of economic crisis the government should cut every nonessential expenditure— was exemplified in the fact that he arranged for the social trends study to be financed entirely with private donations.[64]

In a statement announcing the publication of the social trends series in January 1933, Hoover made clear how much his outlook had darkened. The studies, he said, would serve as "correctives to [an] undiscriminating emotional approach and to [an] insecure factual basis in seeking for constructive remedies of great social problems." Now faced with the collapse of the economic system in which he had so deeply believed, Hoover was seeking "scientific" solutions to structural failures, not thinking of ways to spread the benefits of affluence.[65]

The idea that recreation was to be associated only with good times seemed to touch some deep personal strain in Hoover. Soon after his inauguration, he had purchased 164 acres on the Rapidan River about three hours' drive west of Washington, and during the spring and summer of 1929, he paid to have a rustic camp erected there. Its isolation, noted Senator Hiram Johnson, "had a very great charm for one with Hoover's peculiar disposition."[66] That summer, the president often drove up to the camp on a Saturday, sometimes taking a guest or two, spending a quiet afternoon fishing or talking, and returning refreshed to Washington on Sunday evening. When the depression hit, however, the lessons of his Quaker childhood returned, and although his friends and staff urged him to take an occasional holiday, he refused. Sleeping only a few hours at night, he absorbed himself totally in work and, even during visits to Camp Rapidan, seldom relaxed. He canceled an announced trip to visit the national parks of the West that his advisers believed would have been a valuable reassurance to the country that he was confident of recovery.[67] Hoover's fundamental conviction was thus made clear: production, not consumption, was America's economic engine.

If Hoover would not take time away from work to visit the national parks during the depression, other Americans did. The number of park visitors actually increased from about 3.4 million in 1929 to 3.8 million in 1932, although the number who stayed in hotels, as opposed to camping, dropped.[68] To meet the demand, the administration formally opened two parks (Carlsbad Caverns and Grand Teton), took initial steps to create other new parks in the East (including Great Smoky, Shenandoah, Mammoth Cave, the Everglades, and Isle Royale), and also enlarged twenty parks and national monuments. In keeping with Hoover's goal of encouraging voluntarism in conservation as in other areas, a large part of the money to purchase new parks, enlarge existing ones, and eliminate private lands within parks or monuments came from state and private donations—in the case of Great Smoky Mountains National Park, 50 percent from states and 50 percent from the Rockefellers, who also contributed generously to other Park Service projects.[69] The administration did its part for the parks by increasing appropriations for the Park Service's operating budget from $2.2 million in 1929 to $3.7 million in 1932; cutbacks thereafter reduced the 1934 budget to $2.5 million, still larger than that of 1929. In addition, the administration sharply increased the service's road and trail construction budget as a relief measure, expanding it from $3 million in 1928 to over $7 million in 1931, and to $7.5 million in 1932 and 1933.[70] Horace Albright, appointed director of the National Park Service after Stephen Mather's resignation in January 1929, had known Hoover since World War I, had taken the Secretary of Commerce fishing in Yellowstone Park, was one of four men who helped to select the site for the Hoovers' Rapidan Camp, and enjoyed the full support of the president.[71]

The breadth of the administration's definition of conservation was suggested not only by its willingness to use conservation projects for relief, but also by its inclusion of relations with American Indians as a part of conservation. As Ray Lyman Wilbur explained, "the purpose of conserving our natural resources is for the benefit or protection of the human beings who are living or who will live on this earth."[72] Wilbur himself had for many years been associated with the missionary-led Indian Rights Association and also had supported the more militant American Indian Defense Association.[73] In order to raise the Indians' living standards (the same objective Hoover set for other conservation activities), the Interior Department increased its spending on Indians from $16.7 million in 1929 to $25.6 million in 1932, putting much of the new money into improving schools and hospitals that served Indians. Better health and education, Wilbur believed, "will doubtless lead to [the Indian's] final transformation and assimilation," so that the Indian Bureau could "work itself out of a job in 25 years."[74]

Yet paradoxically, while the administration aimed at assimilating Indians into white society, it also actively promoted the revival of Indian arts and crafts. Wilbur wrote many years later that his goal was "to preserve a native Indian people and their culture wherever it was possible or promising enough to survive." Administration leaders did not think there was a contradiction between helping natives to fit into white society on the one hand and the preservation and cultivation of Indian culture on the other.[75] Perhaps in some measure this ambiguity of purpose reflected Hoover's own experience as a boy visiting his Indian agent uncles, Laban Miles and Dr. John Minthorn, knowing of the Quakers' commitment to the welfare of the Indians, and playing with Indian children and learning woodcraft from them. It was certainly no coincidence that Hoover named Quakers Charles J. Rhoads and J. Henry Scattergood as commissioner and assistant commissioner of the Bureau of Indian Affairs.[76]

The contradictions and uncertainties of the Hoover administration Indian policy resulted in part from the fact that reformers themselves were in the midst of a radical reevaluation of the Indians' situation. Until the 1920s the Indian Rights Association had endorsed the 1887 Dawes Act, which provided for the allotment of tribal lands to individual Indians, only to recognize belatedly that the act had not helped the Indians but had resulted in the transfer of almost two-thirds of tribal lands to whites.[77]

In 1922–23 Indians, anthropologists, and the powerful General Federation of Women's Clubs came together for the first time to fight a particularly egregious grab of Indian lands in New Mexico and in the process launched a major muckraking attack on Indian policy in general. Coolidge's secretary of the interior, Hubert Work, responded to the popular uproar by asking the Institute for Government Research to make a thorough survey of Indian affairs. The report, coordinated by Lewis Meriam, was published in early 1928 and documented in detail its findings that the "overwhelming majority of the Indians are poor, even extremely poor, and they are not adjusted to the economic and social system of the dominant white civilization." Government efforts to rectify this situation, the report concluded, had been largely ineffective. Somewhat ambiguously, it concluded that the Indian Service should be reformed and given as its primary mission the training of Indians "so that they may be absorbed into the prevailing civilization *or be fitted to live in the presence of that civilization* at least in accord with a minimum standard of health and decency."[78] Although the report treated Indian cultures largely in economic terms as a possible source of income from native crafts, its recognition of the persistence of those cultures and of their continuing conflicts with white culture implied a rejection of the assimilation policy by Indians that neither the authors of the report nor conservative reformers like Hoover and Wilbur were willing to accept.[79]

If it was difficult even for reformers to imagine a policy that did not have assimilation as its major objective, the administration nevertheless quickly adopted some of the practical reforms recommended by the Meriam Report. In 1929 Interior Department officials, working closely with the Indian Defense Association (IDA), authorized new expenditures for Indian education, health, and administration. They also endorsed IDA proposals to provide a federal trademark for genuine Indian crafts, to propose federal legislation to protect Indian civil rights, to begin eliminating boarding schools, and to transfer some responsibility for Indian health and welfare to the states. But moving beyond these first steps proved difficult. Commissioner Rhoads sent four letters to Senator Lynn Frazier, chairman of the Indian Investigating Subcommittee, asking somewhat vaguely for revision of the Dawes Act to protect tribal properties and for legislation to improve the financing of public works and irrigation projects on tribal lands.

Unfortunately, specific proposals to implement these ideas, which were submitted to Congress by Secretary Wilbur in the late spring of 1930, were blocked by administration and House leaders determined to cut government spending in response to the depression.[80] Considering the state of the economy and the uncertainty among reformers about what should be done, the congressional reluctance to act was understandable. Wilbur and Rhoads deserve credit for what they achieved under difficult circumstances, including improvements in education and health services, better administration of Indian affairs, and the cancellation of several million dollars of tribal debts for various public works projects.[81]

Perhaps most important of all, the Hoover administration began to inch away from the traditional assumption that Indian cultures must be ruthlessly eradicated. While attempting to provide Indians with an education that would enable them to assimilate into white society and encouraging them to do so, they nevertheless left open the possibility that in making the Indians "self-supporting and self-respecting," they would enable them to maintain their cultures as "artificial islands in our civilization" if they chose to do so.[82] As David Burner points out, this goal was conservationist in the sense that the administration sought to preserve Indian culture as "one more element of the national inheritance."[83]

A similar spirit lay behind the administration's efforts to implement reforms affecting women, children, and families. "Of all national assets in the conservation of which the [Interior] department is concerned," wrote Secretary Wilbur, "the children of the country are by far the most important."[84] Hoover, whose own childhood had been difficult, had always showed a special concern for the problems of children. His relief work during and after World War I focused particularly on children, and he was determined to make child welfare a priority in his administration. Soon after his inauguration, he called a White House conference on child health and protection that met in the autumn of 1930. The conference, financed by a $500,000 grant from surplus funds from the World War I American Relief Administration, published a monumental thirty-five-volume report, which provided a wealth of information for educators and social workers for many years. But with the onset of the depression, Hoover sadly noted that the national mood did not permit much federal action to follow up on the report. He did, however, succeed in getting small increases in appropriations for the federal Children's Bureau, which one historian describes as the first federal social welfare agency.[85]

Education, on the other hand, was a difficult issue for the administration to approach, not because they thought it unimportant, but because they shared the conviction of most Americans that education should be under local control. Hoover declared that he was not opposed to "federal aid to [education in] backward areas where there was genuine need," and in 1930 he specifically endorsed the establishment of a cabinet-level department of education, but he backed down in the face of Secretary Wilbur's strong opposition to the idea. The fact that a National Advisory Committee on Education appointed by Secretary Wilbur in 1929 took two years to study the situation before recommending federal funding for education and a federal department of education strengthened Wilbur's hand. With the depression deepening, no expensive new federal programs were likely to win the president's support.[86]

Voluntary efforts were a different matter. In November 1929 Hoover set up an Advisory Committee on Illiteracy, funded by Julius Rosenwald and John D. Rockefeller Jr. Working through branches in forty-four states, the committee arranged with state and local governments, and churches, fraternal, and civic organizations to conduct adult literacy classes. The president also gladly embraced a congressional initiative to create a National Institute of Health.[87] He saw the promotion of health, like education, as an important aspect of the conservation of human resources.

More difficult to fit into any reasonable definition of conservation were the obligations of the Interior Department to administer the American territories of the Virgin Islands, Hawaii, and Alaska. In a book published in 1932, Secretary Wilbur and William Atherton Du Puy tried to force their territorial policies under the definition of conservation by saying that "in each case problems of conservation and the development of natural and human resources" had "presented themselves," but the reality was that policy toward the territories was shaped more by development than conservation.[88]

The Virgin Islands, administered by the navy from 1917 until President Hoover's executive order put them under the Interior Department in February 1931, were dreadfully poor even before the beginning of the depression. Hoover and Wilbur visited the islands at the end of March of that year and were appalled at the poverty they saw. Their plans to stimulate the islands' economy through the construction of water and irrigation systems, by the promotion of new crops salable on the American mainland, and by the construction of a tourist hotel were, however, largely stymied when Congress imposed a 35 percent budget cut.[89]

In Hawaii, on the other hand, economic development was progressing rapidly and more traditional conservation concerns were dominant. A campaign to control the rats that damaged the sugar and pineapple crops echoed predator control programs in the western United States, while reforestation to protect watersheds and the National Park Service's administration of the Hawaiian National Park involved activities and policies very similar to those of the Interior Department on the mainland. Secretary Wilbur, whose Stanford connections had acquainted him with many of the islands' leaders, soon concluded that Hawaii had "every quality required for statehood."[90]

Alaska seemed to fall somewhere between the Virgin Islands and Hawaii in its prospects for development. Although it was potentially rich in fish, minerals, and timber, relatively little had been done to exploit these resources, except for fish, which had been overexploited. The territory, Wilbur believed, deserved "the fullest possible development" to attract new settlers who would enable it to "handle its own affairs on a basis of more local responsibility."[91]

During the Hoover years, the department's principal effort to promote Alaskan self-sufficiency was the promotion of reindeer herding. First brought to Alaska from Asia in 1892, reindeer had flourished and multiplied rapidly. By 1931 estimates of their numbers varied between six hundred thousand and eight hundred thousand.[92] Although the largest herds were owned by whites, ownership of at least small herds had become widespread throughout the native population, and the total number of animals had become so great that a commercial market for hides and meat was developing. Determination of who owned young animals and who should control various ranges, as well as the development of slaughterhouses, packing plants, and shipping facilities all required some regulation of the industry. Soon after the inauguration of the new administration, Secretary Wilbur asked Ernest Walker Sawyer, an executive assistant, who later became head of the Alaskan railroad, to study the matter closely. Sawyer's extensive report was turned over in January 1931 to a special Reindeer Committee that had been appointed by Wilbur. On the basis of the committee's recommendations, in March 1931 the secretary established a permanent Reindeer Council under the Alaskan governor to supervise the industry, adopted new rules for the apportionment of ranges, and promised that regulations on the marketing of reindeer products would be implemented as soon as Congress provided an increased appropriation for the Alaska Reindeer Service.[93] The secretary reported proudly that here was "a great natural resource which the people of Alaska could develop into a newborn industry."[94] In this instance, development and preservation were united under the rubric of conservation.

The Hoover administration's conservation policy is difficult to categorize because it blurred the Progressive Era's clear dichotomy between utilitarian and esthetic preservation, and because it experimented with methods for achieving conservation that were largely unprecedented. Although administration leaders still talked in traditional terms about "endeavoring to stimulate the development of resources," they also demonstrated a new awareness that some resources were "irreplaceable" or had value "which we are not yet able to grasp," and they even alluded to an undefinable need of urban people to experience the outdoors.[95] In each of these cases nature's value was still measured in terms of human interests and needs, and even wilderness was assigned a commodity value, but Hoover and Wilbur vastly extended the timescale for the measurement of worth. More important, they were willing to admit that there was an enormous amount they did not know.[96] In addition to these important changes in the definition of conservation, the Hoover administration also proposed novel methods for implementing their policies. These included shifting responsibility for some programs to states, local governments, or private groups; the recruitment of volunteers both to finance programs and to implement them; and, paradoxically, the expansion and tightening of federal control over other programs. This eclectic mix of methods, like the administration's growing complexity of purposes, marks in some ways a maturing of conservation within the federal government, but it also raised new questions about both purposes and methods that would not be answered for many years.

8 | "Wrong Side Up": The Commission on the Public Domain

The first federal director of grazing sometimes told a story, probably apocryphal, of an Indian who rode up one day to watch a new homesteader plowing the virgin sod. After a few minutes, he rode away, saying "Ugh, wrong side up."[2]

The Indian's comment seems an apt observation on federal administration of grazing on the public domain in the West from the late nineteenth century through the first third of the twentieth century. Virtually every aspect of it was "wrong side up," and Herbert Hoover saw in the situation a perfect opportunity for a vast experiment with decentralized conservation that he believed would work better than federal authority. Ironically, however, in his attempt to transfer control over grazing lands from federal to state authority, the weakness of the case for state control was revealed and the way cleared for the passage of the Taylor Grazing Act of 1934, which gave the federal government more sweeping control over this particular resource than it had ever had before.

By the end of the nineteenth century virtually all of the immediately usable land in the western United States had been sold or given away—to homesteaders, miners, ranchers, timber interests, or railroads. Beginning in 1891, millions of acres of the remainder had been set aside in national forests. What remained, about 200 million acres, was generally too dry for farming, too barren for timbering, too devoid of minerals to attract miners. The only people interested in most of it were stockmen, who regarded it as free pasture.[3]

When the first national forests were established in 1891, they were closed to grazing. Ranchers usually ignored this prohibition, and in 1898 the government tried to make the best of a bad situation by instituting a permit system for the forests. In 1906 the Forest Service began charging monthly fees for each head of livestock pastured in the forests, and by 1929 they estimated

---

In his announcement of the appointment of the body on 18 Oct. 1929, Hoover described it as the "Commission on Conservation and Administration of the Public Domain," but the group's letterhead substituted "Committee" for "Commission." I have chosen to follow Hoover's original usage.[1]

they were collecting an average of twelve cents per head of cattle and four cents per head of sheep for each month in the forests.[4] The principle governing the fee system in the national forests, explained Forester William B. Greeley in 1925, was that the government should receive "compensation for a commodity that is commercial in character and utilized for a commercial purpose."[5]

Greeley to the contrary notwithstanding, the government did not receive anything like full market value for grazing on the public domain. Forest Service fees were set well below those charged by private landholders, and cattle and sheep grazed on the millions of acres outside the national forests without either permits or fees. Since no one was responsible for these public grazing lands, everyone exploited them ruthlessly. As one critic wrote in 1924, "the range has been treated as booty rather than as property."[6] A decade later, when the Forest Service conducted the first scientific study of the grazing situation, they found that land that had once been able to support almost 23 million animals per season could by then sustain less than 11 million.[7]

Conservationists and stockmen recognized the range problem as early as the turn of the century, but interagency rivalries and the determination of those who benefitted from the existing system not to lose any of their privileges prevented any action from being taken. Bill after bill was introduced in Congress only to disappear before the opposition of special interests. By the mid-1920s advocates of reform were in despair.[8]

In the same period westerners grew increasingly unhappy about what they saw as unwarranted intrusions of federal authority into their lives. Until the late nineteenth century, federal policy had been to transfer natural resources from public to private ownership as rapidly as possible. That policy began to change with the rise of the conservation movement, which led to the withdrawal of millions of acres from the public domain for parks and national forests, to the reservation of other lands for future development of mineral and water resources, and to the adoption of increasing numbers of regulations governing what people could do on all public lands. Presidents Taft and Wilson somewhat muted western complaints by appointing officials sympathetic to development, but westerners remained suspicious of the federal government, and overgrazing of western ranges during the severe drought of 1916–19 and the Teapot Dome scandal of the early 1920s showed what could happen if federal supervision was loosened without being replaced by other authority.[9]

With all initiatives stalled by the mid-1920s, an old idea that had never previously received much serious attention began to be reexamined. Since the federal government appeared to be incapable of designing and adopting a viable range policy, why not privatize the ranges or at least turn them over to the states to administer? State or private owners, it seemed, might have an incentive to restore and maintain the ranges—an incentive that stockmen lacked when everyone pastured on the commons.[10]

The issue came to a head in 1926–27 when western mining and stock raising interests began to push aggressively for the transfer of federal lands in the West to state control.[11] Although Secretary of the Interior Hubert Work counseled caution and full study of the issue before decisions were made, by late 1926 western political leaders were increasingly insistent on the transfer.[12] In the spring of 1927 the case for transfer was strengthened when Charles L. Gilmore, a California attorney, published a five-part series of articles in the *Mining Congress Journal*, to which Hoover was a subscriber. Gilmore's argument, which stressed the importance of strengthening local government and curbing excessive federal interference with private initiatives, was one that would later be emphasized by Hoover and Ray Lyman Wilbur. Apparently, it was also sufficiently effective so that William B. Greeley, chief of the Forest Service, felt called upon to write a vigorous rejoinder to Gilmore's arguments. Greeley overstated the case when he declared that the United States was "in a period of almost hysterical reaction against government," but many Republicans, including Hoover, were eager to find ways to reinvigorate local government and diminish Washington's power. They found the idea of turning over the public domain to the states very attractive.[13]

When the Hoover administration took office early in 1929, however, Secretary of the Interior Ray Lyman Wilbur seems to have given the range question little thought. The central problem, as he then saw it, was the conservation of watersheds, and he drew the conventional conclusion that "the control of the unreserved and undisposed of public lands should remain in the federal Government and be administered in a uniform manner rather than under such varying plans as the several states might adopt."[14] Two months later, in a speech to a conference of western governors, Wilbur reiterated his belief that "we must replace homestead thinking with water shed thinking since water sheds are primary to Western homes," but he then went on to propose a novel means of reaching that goal:

> It seems to me that it is time for a new public land policy which will include transferring to those states willing to accept the responsibility the control of the surface rights of all public lands not included in national parks or monuments or in the national forests. With sound state policies based on factual thinking it may

eventually develop that it is wiser for the states to control even the present national forests. . . .

The states of the West are water conscious and they can more readily build up wise conservation measures upon which their very life depends than can the distant Washington Government.[15]

In addition to the advantages to be expected in conservation from the transfer of public lands to the states, Wilbur explained in a news release a few days later, it would produce "the stimulation to greater vigor of local government through placing more responsibility on it." Westerners, he suggested, had come "to lean too heavily on the national government," and "local government should be allowed to assert itself."[16]

Wilbur's speech reflected the administration's belief that the methods of controlling public lands must change, but not an adoption of privatization. It was an accommodation to Hoover's desire to decentralize power from Washington to the states. In the draft of a letter of his own to the governors' conference, the president wrote that he had been thinking for some years about how "to strengthen the state governments in our Western states and at the same time decrease the centralization and bureaucratic tendencies in the Federal Government."[17] From his point of view, the western land proposal was an ideal test case for his belief that conservation could be transferred from federal to local control.

If Wilbur's speech was a trial balloon for Hoover's idea, initial reactions to it in the press were few in number and muted in tone.[18] No one at this point knew exactly what the administration was proposing—how much land might be turned over to the states, and under what conditions, and how much the federal government might continue to control in national parks and forests, military oil reserves, Indian reservations, and wildlife preserves, or how much it might wish to reserve for future homestead claims and reclamation projects. Not for another two weeks would Wilbur be able to supply figures on those matters or to recommend the next steps to be taken.[19]

On 2 August Wilbur presented the president with a specific seven-point plan:

1. Create a special commission with congressional funding to study the issue and develop legislation.
2. Emphasize the importance of water conservation as the principal benefit to be gained.
3. Stress the value to the states of controlling and taxing their own lands.

4. Reserve additional areas for oil conservation.
5. Consider turning over minerals along with surface rights if the states develop adequate conservation legislation.
6. Keep national forests under federal control until the states have their own strong protection plans.
7. Perhaps put Indian reservations on a tax-paying basis to encourage the development of a sense of responsibility among Indians.[20]

The seventh point of this plan, which Wilbur recognized was controversial, was quietly dropped; the other six points would guide the development of the administration's policy. A letter by Hoover, which Assistant Secretary of the Interior Joseph M. Dixon read to the governors' conference on 26 August, outlined the proposal in very much the same way as Wilbur had.[21]

The governors' conference quickly adopted a unanimous declaration of appreciation for Hoover's "constructive proposals," and from several governors and prominent westerners came messages of support for the idea.[22] But uncritical enthusiasm was fleeting. In the West, a handful of newspapers endorsed the plan wholeheartedly; and in the East, a similarly small number denounced the idea of giving lands owned by all Americans to a few states. The great majority of papers, in both East and West, applauded Hoover's effort to find a policy that would advance both "the principle of conservation and the principle of State autonomy," as the New York *World* put it, but almost all warned that the idea must be studied carefully and implemented cautiously. Cassandras included those who argued that without mineral rights, the public domain lands were "poor skimmed milk," as Montana's Great Falls *Tribune* put it, as well as those who predicted that the states would adopt inadequate and clashing laws for the administration of the lands. Governor George Dern of Utah spoke for many when he warned that the proposal "may turn out, on closer inspection, to be a white elephant."[23] When the editors of the *Mining Congress Journal* polled a representative group of businessmen, economists, editors, and producers of raw materials, they found opinion very evenly divided, with 37 percent of the respondents favoring transfer to private control; 34 percent opposed; and 29 percent unable to reach a conclusion.[24]

Equally serious, from the president's point of view, were rumblings of criticism from within the powerful and well-connected ranks of the Forest Service.[25] To mute this potential opposition, Hoover and Wilbur dropped the argument that the primary purpose of their proposal was to transfer power to the states and played up its conservation benefits. They contended that it would secure "a positive conservation program" for the "neglected" and "overgrazed" public rangelands, would promote reclamation, and would contribute to the development of conservation measures for oil, coal, and other minerals. At a news conference on 18 October 1929 Hoover announced the creation of a Commission on the Conservation and Administration of the Public Domain charged "to study the whole of the problems of the public domain," which he now defined as "altogether a problem in water conservation" resulting from overgrazing. Three states, Hoover admitted, had already expressed reservations about taking over the public lands, but he was certain that all shared his concern about water conservation and overgrazing and would participate in the work of the commission on that basis.[26] By broadening the charge to the commission and saying little about the novelty of his proposal to transfer a major federal responsibility to the states, Hoover deflected public scrutiny from the most controversial and vulnerable aspect of his proposal. He did not, however, intend to retreat from the idea of transferring the lands to the states. He and Wilbur believed that if conservation of watersheds was the commission's first priority, the members would soon recognize that "there should be a great western strategy for the protection of watersheds and that the Western States, being water conscious, are ready to develop it."[27]

The national members of the new commission were mostly Republican, and many were committed to transferring public lands to the states even before the commission began work. The chairman was James R. Garfield, who had been secretary of the interior under Theodore Roosevelt.[28] Other at-large members were publishers George Horace Lorimer and Gardner Cowles, Republican ex-governors James P. Goodrich of Indiana and Huntley Spaulding of New Hampshire, former head of the Forest Service W. B. Greeley, writer (and the only female member) Mary Roberts Rinehart, former Republican senator from New Mexico H. O. Bursum, and former Republican congressman from Arkansas Wallace Townsend. Goodrich, Spaulding, Rinehart, Bursum, and Townsend proved to be relatively unimportant in the commission's work, taking part only occasionally. Except for Greeley, who continued to defend the federal government's role in conservation (and especially that of the Forest Service) aggressively, the commission included no conservationist of national stature.

In addition to these presidentially appointed members, the commission also included representatives chosen by the governors of each of the public land states. Not surprisingly, they all favored turning over public lands to the states. Among the most important were Elwood Mead, federal Reclamation Commissioner and California irrigation consultant; New Mexico lawyer

Francis Wilson; and eccentric Wyoming cattleman Perry Jenkins. Mead had enormous prestige as Reclamation Commissioner and was a widely recognized expert on the subject. Wilson knew both Garfield and Hoover well and had kept up a close relationship with Hoover since they were colleagues on the Colorado River Commission. Jenkins had a long-running feud with the Forest Service over how many cattle he could pasture in the national forest and was one of the most radical advocates of transferring the lands to the states. Hugh A. Brown, the director of reclamation economics in the Bureau of Reclamation, served as the commission's executive secretary and played a considerable role in shaping its investigation and report.[29]

A draft agenda probably prepared by Garfield or Brown prior to the commission's first meeting in November 1929 made it clear that the group's objective was not a broad review of conservation policy but a focused consideration of the public land issue. The agenda did indeed list a wide variety of conservation issues, including policy for the national forests and parks; regulations governing the development of oil, coal, and other minerals; reclamation and flood control programs; and even the futures of the Geological and Coast and Geodetic Surveys and the Indian office. But the first and last items on the agenda, as well as parts of other items, stressed a single question: "Should the remaining public lands . . . be granted to the several States within which they are located, and if so under what, if any, conditions?" That same question was also the keynote of brief welcoming remarks by Secretary Wilbur at one of the commission's first meetings on 23 November 1929.[30]

The commissioners quickly grasped their assignment. In a series of resolutions adopted at an early meeting, they declared that their objective was to recommend the disposition of the unreserved federal lands, the minerals under those lands, and future reclamation policy. Stockmen, mining interests, and other users of the public lands would, they assumed, shape the commission's proposals. "Each member of the Commission from the Public Land States," the resolutions declared, should "confer with the Governor and the officials charged with the administration of land affairs, the livestock associations, and the representatives of other associations whose interests would be affected by the programs under discussion . . . and obtain from those representatives their opinions regarding the problems."[31]

By the time the commission first met on 23 November 1929, the stock market had collapsed and the nation was sliding rapidly into depression. Although the minutes of the first meetings do not mention the disaster, it is difficult to believe that the economic crisis did not encourage commission members to proceed cautiously. At any rate, that is certainly what they did. Of the six state members who responded to a request from Huntley Spaulding for a thumbnail sketch of their states' positions, the representatives of Colorado, Montana, California, and New Mexico declared that their states would not take the lands without mineral rights; Arizonan Rudolph Kuchler said that his state was ready to take over the public lands but made it clear the state wanted to be assured of continued federal support for reclamation and highway construction; and George Malone declared that Nevada was not willing at present to take over the federal lands, whether or not subsurface mineral rights were included.[32]

Among the most zealous supporters of the idea of transferring the lands to the states were western conservatives who applauded President Hoover's determination to "decrease the centralization and bureaucratic tendencies in the Federal Government." As Perry Jenkins of Wyoming put it, "I firmly believe that if some decisive action is not taken by our President to simplify our government and turn back to the states the functions that belong to the states, we will find that the National Government will continue to drift further and further away from the fundamental principles laid down by the founders as those essential for the preservation of a Republican form of Government."[33] To conservatives, the appeal of Hoover's proposal was political as much as economic.

A second argument frequently advanced by proponents of transferring lands to the states was that except in the eleven western states, the federal government had already surrendered public lands to state control. In the West, they argued, the federal government had served as a trustee over the lands, administering them until the states adopted "proper laws and regulations." That trusteeship was now amply fulfilled, in their opinion, and it was time for the federal government to do for the West what it had done for the East.[34]

Theoretical debate did not long occupy the commissioners, however. They saw their mission as a very practical one—to find out what westerners wanted. Dispersing to their states in late 1929 and early 1930, they began to gather opinions. When they did, they found surprisingly little support for Hoover's proposal.

States that had benefitted from the federal reclamation program did not want to lose Washington's support for new projects, and many stockmen, when asked, turned out to prefer federal to state administration of grazing lands. Above all, the idea that the surface of the public domain might be transferred to the states without the mineral rights aroused western opposition.[35] Even those who thought that both mineral and surface rights might be transferred began to have second thoughts as they realized that the federal government could not continue to fund reclamation and road-building projects without revenues from mineral leases and royalties.[36] At the commission's second meeting, in early June 1930, the only thing upon which there was unanimous agreement was that the federal reclamation program must continue.[37]

In the depression spring of 1930 the commissioners began to hear a lot about roads as well as reclamation. The federal government, it turned out, had been paying at least half of the cost of new roads in every one of the eleven public land states, as well as providing free rights-of-way over public lands and free sand, gravel, and rock from other public lands to assist construction. But road construction money, like the funding for reclamation, came from mineral leases and reclamation repayments. If mineral resources were transferred to the states along with the surface rights, federal funding for road construction as well as reclamation would be severely reduced. All told, federal road construction payments to the states between 1916 and 1927 totaled more than $670 million, with nearly $83 million expended in 1927 alone. As the economy grew worse, those figures began to loom very large. No wonder that in June 1930 the commission found itself sharply divided "as to even the general principles concerning the problem."[38]

It also became clear, as the states responded to a request from the commission for information about their public land policies, that if one assumed, as virtually everyone did, that some measure of governmental regulation of public lands was necessary to prevent abuses, the states were hardly in a position to take responsibility for federal lands. Although several states claimed to have grazing, mineral, and forest policies, their policies were so weak that they were obviously incapable of managing public lands even as well as the federal government. Nevada, New Mexico, and Oregon had no system in place for classifying state lands, and of the others, only Colorado distinguished clearly among lands suitable for timber, grazing, agriculture, or mining.[39] Given that situation, the prospects for the adoption of a coherent and consistent state regulatory system for the public lands seemed uncertain at best. Stockgrowers faced the probability of a bewildering tangle of regulations from state to state, and there was no assurance that state control would mean any improvement at all in the condition of the ranges. Full privatization, a possibility favored by later free market environmentalists, came up from time to time but was never seriously considered by either the administration or the commission.[40]

A staggering variety of western reactions to the president's proposal poured into the commission. Mining and oil interests generally seemed to prefer dealing with a single set of federal regulations than with a plethora of state requirements.[41] Small farmers and ranchers warned that transfer to the states would "shut out the little fellows completely" or benefit only "a Few Big Cattle Companys."[42] Groups as varied as the Los Angeles County Conservation Association, the Los Angeles and Spokane Chambers of Commerce, the National Grange, livestock raisers' associations in California, Oregon, and Utah, the Columbia Basin Irrigation League, the American Library Association and the Carnegie Library of Pittsburgh, and an American Legion post in Nogales, Arizona, all went on record as opposed to the transfer.[43] Idaho, with its lands mostly forested, was happy with Forest Service administration; Nevada, with huge amounts of barren public land and a small population, was unwilling to take on the costs of administering the lands.[44] Cattle and wool growers' associations in Arizona, Colorado, Montana, New Mexico, Oregon, Washington, and Wyoming, as well as the National Wool Growers' Association, endorsed Hoover's proposal. So did the Wyoming Bankers' Association and the Mining Association of California (provided mineral rights went with the lands).[45] A small number of individuals proposed an even more radical idea—that lands should be given or sold cheaply to small homesteaders or individual ranchers.[46] If there was any consensus, even in the West, it was difficult to discern.

Adding to the confusion was a report from Commissioner of Indian Affairs Charles J. Rhoads. Rhoads estimated that about 32 million acres remained in Indian reservations, and that about 39 million acres had been transferred to individual Indian owners. Of this land, approximately 37 million acres were grazing land, and about two-thirds were tribal lands under federal control. Neither tribal ranges nor Indian-owned lands were well managed, Rhoads admitted, although the federal government had long had the authority to regulate tribal ranges. In many cases Indian agents had leased tribal lands to white stock owners or had permitted unregulated overgrazing. Where former tribal lands had been allotted to individual Indians, "a generation of Indians [had] come to the age of productive effort with little practical knowledge of the technique of the livestock industry and under conditions that seem[ed] to have destroyed incentive."[47] Neither the agency's experience with federal range management nor its large-scale experiment with privatization was encouraging.

In fact, as George Otis Smith, the director of the Geological Survey, pointed out, a simple solution to the range problem had been at hand for many years, if anyone chose to take it. Virtually all of the rangelands were for sale, at a price that Smith estimated would average 5.1 cents per acre. Yet ranchers had not found it worthwhile to buy the lands even at this bargain price. The plain implication of Smith's report was that despite their talk of local control, stockmen really cared only about free rangelands. Smith expressed no preference for putting grazing under federal or state control, but he argued urgently that *someone* needed to undertake it.[48]

From a purely practical point of view, there were immense difficulties in the way of transferring federal lands to the states, even if everyone agreed that it was a good idea. C. C. Moore, the commissioner of the General Land Office, reported to the commission in June 1930 that of approximately 190 million acres of unappropriated federal lands outside of Alaska, about 50 million had never been surveyed, so that no one knew what should be released and what reserved in these areas. More than 21 million more acres had pending private claims against them that were guaranteed by various federal laws for periods up to five years, while an unspecified amount of other land was set aside by various federal laws for indemnities to railroads and Indians, for veterans' benefits, and for federal agencies to use as locations for such things as air mail beacons and stock drive ways. In short, Moore indicated, it would be incredibly difficult to define exactly which lands and how much land would be affected by the "radical changes" contemplated by the commission, and it was likely that attempting to carry out a wholesale transfer of the public domain to the states would create a nightmare of title challenges and litigation that would occupy the Land Office and the courts for years. Instead of any transfer, Moore endorsed a proposal put before the commission in May 1930 to create a federal grazing program under the authority of the General Land Office.[49]

During the summer of 1930, members of the commission went west, examining local conditions, familiarizing themselves with general problems, and talking with citizens' groups. Traveling mostly by automobile, they first made a swing through Montana, Idaho, Washington, and Oregon, and then, in September, a three-thousand-mile trip through Utah, Nevada, California, Arizona, New Mexico, Colorado, and Wyoming.[50]

When the commission reconvened in Washington on 10 November 1930, two possible drafts of a report were submitted. One, favoring federal control of the public lands, was offered by William B. Greeley; the other, proposing transfer of the lands to the states, came from Francis Wilson. Chairman Garfield attempted to pour oil on the troubled waters with a rambling speech that harked back to his own days as secretary of the interior and urged the commissioners to find a plan that would assure "that those resources be used in such fashion that the good of the entire Nation be considered as well as the need and to the advantage [sic] of the separate States." For the next sixteen days, the two sides labored to reconcile their differences. Not surprisingly, agreement proved elusive. The commission's official minutes state that "a consolidated draft was presented to the Committee on November 26," but although a version based on Francis Wilson's proposal was roughed out, there was no real agreement. Instead of voting on the draft, the commissioners voted to endorse the continuation of the activities of the Bureau of Reclamation and the National Park Service, and the opening of Indian lands to settlement "in the same manner as other public domain land."[51]

In the aftermath of the November meeting, some members apparently suggested as a compromise transferring all mineral rights to the states *except* known oil deposits. This proposal immediately drew a sharp denunciation from Solicitor E. C. Finney of the Interior Department, who reiterated and emphasized points previously made by George Otis Smith of the Geological Survey. It was absurd, they argued, to think that all oil deposits under the public lands had already been located, and there were large deposits of other valuable minerals, most notably coal, that needed to be safeguarded in the interest of the public as a whole. Even where mineral claims had been filed and then canceled, Finney wrote, there was no proof that valuable minerals were not present. He concluded, therefore, "that the public good would be best obtained by not making the grant to the States proposed."[52]

By the end of 1930, as the commission appeared despite all disagreements to be moving toward a report recommending the transfer of the public lands to the states, opposition grew in the federal conservation agencies. The Biological Survey and National Park Service, fearing that once lands were transferred to the states, opportunities for expansion of their activities would be curtailed, urged rapid and substantial expansions of wildlife refuges and parks before any transfer was completed. Henry Graves, former head of the Forest Service, publicly proposed an extension of the service's grazing system to all public lands.

Most important of all, Agriculture Secretary Arthur Hyde broke with Secretary Wilbur and the president. Saying that he believed the issue needed "further study," Hyde pointed out that the proposal made no provision for interstate conservation problems such as flood control and watershed protection, and suggested that it might create a situation under which some states would accept public lands and others refuse, thus making the whole problem worse rather than better. What was more, Hyde thought that there was danger that administrative boards proposed for each state might actually remove lands from national forests, parks, wildlife refuges, or reclamation sites. Although

Hyde denied that his observations were "offered in any spirit of criticism," his mild comment that the whole matter needed more study "from a national rather than a state point of view" was an attack on the assumptions that lay behind the appointment of the commission in the first place.[53]

Equally serious was the opposition of William B. Greeley. The former forester, now secretary-manager of the West Coast Lumbermen's Association, was bitterly unhappy at the adoption of Francis Wilson's draft as the basis of the commission's report. In a long letter to Garfield on 3 January 1931, Greeley took strong exception to the idea of reducing the National Forests only to timber-growing areas and instead proposed that forest boundaries be extended to include neighboring grazing areas essential to protection of watersheds. He argued that transfer of rangelands to the states would give insufficient protection to watersheds in general and urged that watershed protection instead of grazing be made the first priority of the report.[54] Inasmuch as President Hoover's original charge to the commission had stressed water conservation as its principal objective, Greeley's objections were potentially very damaging.[55]

Nevertheless, by the time the commission met for the last time in Washington in January 1931, a majority had agreed on the main points of the report. Prior to the meeting, Francis Wilson saw President Hoover on Saturday, 13 December, and showed him a draft that called for transferring surface lands but reserving mineral rights.[56] Despite conservationists' criticisms of the proposal, and complaints from the West that withholding mineral rights would vitiate the value of the gift, the president's approval made the transfer administration policy.[57] Perhaps Hoover and Wilbur had convinced themselves that criticism from both sides proved that they had found a genuine middle course.

On 12 January 1931, when the commission met in Washington, the agreement threatened to break down. Greeley, pleading unbreakable commitments, did not attend, but even in his absence, the meeting was characterized by marked disagreement. The main issue was the old and still unresolved problem of mineral rights. Now at last there was no avoiding it, and finally, at the request of Colorado's Charles J. Moynihan, it was put to a direct vote. The result, a 10 to 3 vote against including mineral rights in the proposed transfer, showed that even the most zealous advocates of state sovereignty had come to realize that their only hope of securing a majority for the report was by giving up their claim to mineral rights. Included among those voting to exclude mineral rights when lands were transferred were such ardent states' righters as Francis Wilson and Perry Jenkins.[58]

The reason that a majority of the members of the commission were willing to vote against the transfer of mineral rights to the states became obvious in the draft of the commission's report. As Hoover had wanted, the report recommended that the public domain, with the exception of areas reserved for defense, reclamation, National Forests, National Parks and Monuments, and wildlife refuges, should be transferred to the states willing to accept the lands within their borders. If a state were unwilling to accept such lands, the report recommended the creation of a National Range for the lands within that state (which agency would administer it was not specified). Mineral resources lying under the rangelands were to be kept by the federal government only until the states adopted conservation policies congruent with federal policies, at which time the states were to acquire mineral as well as surface rights. Decisions about areas that might be added to or excised from National Forests were to be made by five-member state boards; three members would be chosen by the federal government and two by the state.[59]

In several ways the report attempted to avoid or bridge intractable disagreements within the commission. Although most members wanted to transfer the ranges to the states, Nevada in particular was unable and unwilling to take over the task. The National Range proposal was an attempt to provide better administration for the ranges in states unwilling to take over the federal lands. On the even more controversial issue of subsoil resources, the report attempted a compromise between those who demanded immediate transfer to the states and those who believed that a transfer made before states had practical conservation policies in place would be unwise. A third issue, the question of what lands should be included or excluded from National Forests, could not be resolved and gave rise to the proposal for the creation of state boards. In a letter to the members of the commission, Garfield explained these compromises and the reasons for them, and expressed his hope that everyone would see the necessity for them. "Unanimity of action," wrote the chairman, "is of utmost importance if we are to give the President the aid that he needs in submitting to Congress the recommendations of the Committee and obtaining the much-needed legislation to settle the many controversial problems connected with the public domain."[60]

Garfield's plea seemed to fall on deaf ears. James Goodrich, one of the at-large commissioners, joined representatives of Montana and Arizona in drafting a minority report calling for the immediate cession of mineral rights to the states and opposing the creation of federally administered ranges in states that refused to take over public lands.[61] Others also expressed varying degrees of discomfort with the report, but all except William B. Greeley eventually dropped their objections. Greeley declared flatly that he could not agree to a proposal "under which the Federal oil, coal, and other mineral reservations, Federal water power withdrawals, National Parks and Forests, Migratory Bird Refuges, and other natural resources subject to present National policies of conservation and development, should ultimately be transferred to the States." In addition, he argued vigorously for expansion of the National Forests to include all "areas of evident importance for the conservation of stream flow or control of destructive erosion," and contended that "National Forest range management is an established, going method of practical administration" that ought to be expanded rather than curtailed.[62]

Despite two weeks of telegrams, letters, and telephone calls, Garfield was unable to budge Greeley. The most he could win was Greeley's agreement that the report would go to the president without Greeley's signature, but without a dissenting minority report either.[63] That concession seems to have been of little importance, because Greeley's disagreement with the majority was quickly picked up by the press, and he was delighted to explain to anyone who wanted to listen exactly what he thought was wrong with the report.[64]

Aside from Greeley's dissenting views, the timing of the release of the commission's report, in early March 1931, was terrible. The worsening depression undermined confidence in anything Hoover supported, and the administration's conservation policies were particularly under attack. Ralph S. Kelley, former head of the Denver bureau of the General Land Office, had charged in a series of sensational articles in the New York *World* that the Interior Department had virtually given away vast tracts of oil shale lands in the West to the large oil companies. Although Secretary Wilbur was able to show that Kelley had been paid $12,000 for the articles while still a government employee, and that his motives were entirely political, the fact that the Senate Committee on Public Lands was investigating Kelley's corruption charges at exactly the same time as the Garfield Commission delivered its report created a very unfavorable atmosphere.[65] The suspicion that the Interior Department had been overly generous to the big oil companies in the oil shale case was further reinforced by the apparent failure of the administration's attempts to control the national oil surplus—again, a situation that seemed to hurt small producers more than the large companies. Under the circumstances, many Americans were inclined to assume that the recommendations of the Garfield Commission were another sellout to big interests, in this case the large cattle companies.[66]

Nor had the compromises written into the final report really solved the conflicts that had plagued the commission's consideration of the problem of the public lands. Members of the commission who returned to the West reported local reactions ranging from disinterest to unhappiness with the report's failure to recommend immediate transfer of mineral rights to the states.[67] Equally serious was the continuing opposition of important parts of the federal conservation bureaucracy, especially the Forest Service, to the commission's plan. Rumors circulated that Greeley, a former forester, would attack the proposal as anticonservationist, and others suspected dark plots against the proposals. Perry Jenkins, one of the most outspoken advocates of transferring the lands to the states, implied that a Forest Service reduction in the number of cattle he was permitted to graze in the National Forest was part of a conspiracy aimed at the commission.[68]

Why Hoover and Wilbur were so blind to the evidence of huge obstacles facing any attempt to transfer the public domain to the states is hard to understand. Even if one ignored the tepid or conflicting public responses to the idea in the West and the opposition from within the federal bureaucracy, the practical problems in the way of the transfer that had been outlined by the Geological Survey, the General Land Office, and the Forest Service appeared virtually insurmountable. If the commission's investigations had demonstrated anything, they had proved that federal land policy was hostage to previous decisions and policies that had created vested interests in the status quo. Given the administration's already perilous political situation, its decision to recommend the transfer to Congress seems explicable only as a triumph of ideological commitment over rationality and even self-interest.

Perhaps understandably, the administration was in no rush to put a specific bill before Congress. Garfield and Francis Wilson, the leaders of the implementation phase, agreed to meet during the summer of 1931 to begin drafting legislation, but they seem to have done little serious work before late October or early November.[69]

In the meantime, public opposition to the transfer of lands to the states was growing. Although the Western Governors' Conference adopted a resolution expressing its appreciation for the work of the Garfield Commission and applauding its recommendations as "in many respects meeting the requirements of justice in the arid regions," this somewhat equivocal endorsement was overshadowed by more negative responses.[70] Most notable among these were the actions of the National Land Utilization Planning Commission, a body appointed by Agriculture Secretary Hyde, which met in Chicago from 19 to 21 November. Among the approximately three hundred delegates, professors from the land grant colleges predominated in numbers, but the National Park Service, the National Forest Service, and the U.S. Timber Conservation

Board were able to control the meeting's direction. Park Service Director Horace Albright reported to Secretary Wilbur that the conference's recommendations "varied considerably from the recommendations of the President's Land Commission." That was an understatement. In fact, although the conference did not refer to the Garfield Commission directly, it rejected all of the commission's major recommendations, instead endorsing federal control of grazing, the establishment of public ranges, federal control of watersheds, and the retention of most federally owned lands in public ownership.[71]

What Hoover, Wilbur, and Garfield thought of this open challenge to their policy from within the federal bureaucracy is unknown, but an article by Ward Shepard published in *Harper's* in October caused a considerable furor within the administration. Entitled "The Handout Magnificent," the article lauded the Forest Service's grazing policies, lambasted the Interior Department as "often . . . strongly anti-conservation," charged that the administration's policy would favor "the big outfits with money or credit," and concluded that the commission's recommendation was "a reactionary proposal that ignores decades of conservation experience." Hoover, charged Shepard, "seeks to solve an engineering problem [water conservation] by political maxims which do not fit the case." The plan amounted to nothing more than "a good old-fashioned land-grab."[72]

Stung by Shepard's charges, Hugh Brown, secretary of the commission, lamented privately that Shepard, a former Forest Service employee and associate of Gifford Pinchot, was "a man of rather radical and somewhat undigested views." Publicly, the administration responded by having Francis Wilson write a rejoinder to Shepard's article that was published in George Lorimer's *Saturday Evening Post* in January 1932 and provided free of charge to 150 senators and congressmen. Wilson denied that the proposed plan would benefit large stock owners, argued that it would affect only about one-third of federal lands in the West, asserted that it would promote conservation, and blasted "the zealots who speak unofficially for the Forest Service."[73]

Brown praised Wilson for his article, but in the same letter he included a long extract from the *Congressional Record,* in which Senator William Borah of Idaho read into the record a sharp denunciation of the commission's plan that had been adopted by the Idaho Wool Growers' Association, whose members did not want to lose their access to virtually free federal rangelands.[74] With the opposition of the Forest Service to the commission's plan now out in the open, and with criticism of the proposal coming from such powerful western leaders as Borah, the administration's plan was in serious trouble.

Undeterred, Garfield, Francis Wilson, and Interior Department lawyer

Northcutt Ely worked on a series of bills to implement the commission's reports.[75] The principal bill, which provided for the transfer of public lands to those states that wanted them and for the creations of national ranges elsewhere, with mineral rights reserved to the federal government, was introduced in the House by Frank Evans of Montana as HR 5840 on 15 December, and by Gerald Nye of North Dakota in the Senate as S 2272 on 18 December.[76] Hearings in both houses were scheduled for mid–March, and Garfield was confident that the administration bills would be reported positively.[77]

When the hearings began in both houses on 15 March, things seemed at first to go exactly as the administration hoped. Early witnesses, including Secretary Wilbur, Garfield, Francis Wilson, and Northcutt Ely, endorsed the transfer of lands to the states, with the reservation of mineral rights to the federal government. Then things began to slip away, with a series of western witnesses who demanded that the mineral rights go with the surface, and with the testimony of William Greeley and Gifford Pinchot, who urged delaying any cession until all lands could be surveyed and classified and all public interests protected.[78] A bizarre note was added by the unpredictable Perry Jenkins, who appeared before the House committee not as a member of the Garfield Commission but as a representative of Wyoming, in which guise he rejected the report that he had signed and demanded that all mineral resources be surrendered to the states along with the surface.[79] As the days passed and criticisms of the bills piled up on various sides, Hugh Brown became increasingly pessimistic. By the beginning of April he was doubtful that any bill would even be reported from committee, let alone passed, during the current session of Congress.[80]

Whipsawed between westerners who demanded the federal government give the states mineral as well as surface rights, and those who believed that only the federal government would pursue active conservation, the administration's bill was dead by the beginning of May. On 5 May Representative Don B. Colton of Utah introduced, with the support of both the Agriculture and the Interior Departments, a possible substitute. Colton's bill, HR 11816, authorized the secretary of the interior to establish grazing districts on all public lands outside of Alaska and not included in National Forests, parks, monuments, or Indian reservations. The administration's support of the Colton bill was a tacit admission that the Garfield Commission's plan had no chance of adoption. The bill's surprising support in the House pointed to a growing western consensus that in the absence of agreement on alternatives, an effective federal program of regulation would be better than continuation of the existing situation. With astonishing unanimity, the House Public

Lands Committee agreed to set aside all other business until work on the bill was completed and reported it favorably to the full House in June. It was only the second grazing bill ever to reach the floor of Congress and became the first to receive a favorable vote in either chamber when the House passed it. Unfortunately, however, it died in the Senate, although the Committee on Public Lands and Surveys held hearings on it. Revived the following year, the bill again failed, this time at least in part because an amendment provided that it would not go into effect until each state approved it and until each state created a state board that would administer the grazing districts cooperatively with the Interior Department.[81]

Garfield and Francis Wilson, the principal authors of the commission's bill, disagreed about whether the Colton bill was a setback for their approach. Garfield believed that adoption of the Colton bill "would not interfere with the ultimate consideration of the general [commission] bill," but Wilson was convinced that its passage would "destroy forever . . . any hope that any State may ever own the present, unreserved, unappropriated public domain within its boundaries."[82] The failure of the Colton bill in the Senate made their debate moot, but it is obvious in retrospect that momentum had shifted toward federal control of grazing. With the election of Franklin Roosevelt—and more important, a Democratic majority in both houses of Congress—in November 1932, any chance for passage of legislation transferring the public domain to the states disappeared. In 1933 Representative Edward T. Taylor of Colorado, a longtime opponent of federal grazing leases on the public lands who had recently undergone a remarkable conversion, reintroduced the Colton bill. Supported fully by the Roosevelt administration, the Taylor Act became law in 1934.[83] Thus ended Hoover's attempt to divest the federal government of authority over grazing on the public domain and to reinvigorate the states.

As is commonly the case with American political debates, it is difficult to say with certainty what the lessons of the Garfield Commission are. Tentatively, it might be suggested that the fundamental question of whether grazing could be better regulated at the federal or the local level was never evaluated on its merits. Federal conservation agencies came to regard the whole issue as a referendum on their stewardship and reacted with vigorous if indirect defenses of their bureaucratic turf. In some ways, the defeat of the administration bill can be seen as an example of bureaucratic politics at work. On the other hand, westerners frequently demonstrated an intransigence about states' rights over minerals and grazing that was difficult to defend, given their own poor records on protecting resources. Even Ray Lyman Wilbur could only claim weakly that "in many instances" state administration of ranges had been "effective and salutary."[84] Although westerners were correct that they were being treated differently than the citizens of longer-settled regions, times had changed, and the dependence of a populous, industrial, urban nation on natural resources explained, if it did not logically justify, a different national policy. The fundamental argument of the Garfield Commission was that western states, if given an opportunity, would behave differently than they had in the past; it was a difficult position to sell.

Ironically, a model of what the Hoover administration wanted to achieve for the public domain was in operation, but the Garfield Commission did not examine it. The model was the Mizpah–Pumpkin Creek Grazing District, created by act of Congress in 1928. In that area of southeastern Montana, stock owners had set up a grazing district encompassing both public and private lands, and in 1928 Congress authorized them to administer the district under the supervision of the Department of the Interior. The experiment was a great success. By 1933 Secretary of the Interior Harold Ickes reported that the amount of grass in the district had doubled and the carrying capacity of the range greatly increased, but Ickes nevertheless concluded that "rather than deal with the matter piecemeal, it would be wiser to deal at one swoop with the whole public domain by giving this department authority to regulate grazing on it."[85] Had the Garfield Commission recognized the potential of the Mizpah–Pumpkin Creek District, the future of the public domain in the American West might have been very different.

Whatever the possibilities suggested by the limited privatization exemplified in the Mizpah–Pumpkin Creek District, the Garfield Commission never seriously considered full privatization as an option; its charge was to study the desirability of substituting one form of governmental management of the public lands (state) for another (federal). Like many such bodies, the commission was not set up to conduct a full and impartial investigation of its subject. Except for William Greeley, its members were nearly all determined to recommend turning the lands over to the states even before the commission studied its first document or talked to its first expert. Knowing where they would end up before they started, the commissioners ignored the tangle of land laws and claims governing the public domain that made a simple transfer to the states virtually impossible and failed to see that there was no consensus among westerners on the subject. Instead of making a case for state control, the commission's narrow approach highlighted problems in its proposals, energized its opponents, and strengthened the case for retention of the public domain under federal control and the adoption of a national grazing policy. Blinded by ideology, the Garfield Commission thus inadvertently prepared the way for the passage of the Taylor Grazing Act.

Many years later, Hoover commented bitterly on the reluctance of the states to take what he described as a "gorgeous gift." "They refused," he declared, "because they wanted Federal money for the improvement and administration of these lands," and they had no one but themselves to blame for the fact that the Interior Department had subsequently built up "a new bureaucracy directed from Washington . . . to convey guidance to the cattlemen and the sheepmen toward the paths of sweetness and light."[86]

9 | "The Balm of Words"

The beginning of the Great Depression after the stock market crash in October 1929 faced the conservation movement with novel problems. Although conservationists had often predicted that economic collapse could follow the prodigal consumption of resources, they were confident that properly managed natural resources were essentially limitless.[1] Alarms about the exhaustion of forests in the 1920s were countered by waste management, standardization, and reforestation programs; even a short-lived panic about the exhaustion of petroleum reserves vanished in the oil glut of the late 1920s. Pervading the movement was an assumption that, as Hoover said in 1926, the planned use of resources and the elimination of waste would lead to "the building up of an economic structure infinitely more stable than the world has ever seen before and a standard of living infinitely higher."[2] And Hoover further assumed, as did many of his contemporaries, that high living standards would be accompanied by increased leisure whose "constructive" use required the improvement and enlargement of parks, the elimination of water pollution, and the adoption of other environmental policies that would attract affluent Americans to natural rather than commercial entertainments.[3] The collapse of the economy thus cast into doubt both the justification for the conservation movement and the rationale for a nascent environmentalism.[4]

The crash also had a particular personal meaning for Hoover. It undermined his confidence in rising living standards based on growth and development and forced him back upon his fundamental moral values, which were grounded in a religious and geographical context that emphasized individual responsibility and self-reliant production. As he told the people of West Branch during a 1928 visit to his birthplace, his memory of childhood was of a time when "only a small part of the family living came by purchases from the outside." There were hardships in that world, he recalled, but it provided a "comfort and freedom from anxiety" that contrasted with the "debts and discouragements" of the market economy.[5] If some of this was a romanticized view of the past inspired by the circumstances, the reality is that Hoover's background conditioned him to be suspicious of affluence and consumption. When times were hard, his instinct was to work harder, pare expenses, and depend on himself, and these were the lessons he applied to the national crisis. Conservation and environmentalism, policies he saw as intended to perpetuate and extend the benefits of prosperity, seemed to him irrelevant or less important in straitened times. When the collapse came, he and other Americans readily concluded that more production, not conservation, was needed.

Yet if the depression threatened the philosophical basis of the conservation movement, there was at least a tenuous link between Hoover's ideas about macroeconomic management in the 1920s and the maintenance and even extension of conservation programs after the beginning of the depression. Essentially, his waste elimination program and his policy of using the Commerce Department to provide economic statistics to business were attempts to use the government to reduce fluctuations in business production, investment, and employment.[6] The Unemployment Conference of 1921 was an early demonstration of Hoover's belief that the government, in cooperation with businesses and private charities, could ameliorate economic downturns and promote recovery. In opening the conference, Hoover emphasized his belief that "it is not consonant with the spirit of [sic] institutions of the American people that a demand should be made upon the public treasury for the solution of every difficulty," and urged "the mobilization of co-operative action of our manufacturers and employers," but he also proposed that "Federal, state, and municipal governments . . . increase public works."[7] The conference report reversed his priorities, placing public actions first by recommending the immediate adoption of "plans for advancing and increasing public works," but it was clear even in 1921 that Hoover believed the government should play a regular role in stabilizing and managing the national economy.[8]

By the time the Unemployment Conference delivered its report in October 1921, the economy was already improving, and its recommendations were not much needed. The authors of the report paid little attention to conservation programs in the conference's proposals for government actions, although there was evidence to suggest that there was considerable potential in that area. Only the Reclamation Bureau was queried about beginning or accelerating projects that might relieve unemployment, and that did not happen until the final days of the conference. The service responded with an enthusiastic assessment of its ability "to furnish employment to men now out of work, and to do this in a way which will produce the largest ultimate results in permanently reducing unemployment," but its recommendations depended on Congress approving a $20 million loan to the reclamation fund, and no one expected that to happen.[9]

The Unemployment Conference, with its focus on curing an immediate problem, was of less interest to Hoover than the idea of long-term counter-cyclical planning that might "stabilize" (one of Hoover's favorite words) the business cycle. Following the conference, he turned that problem over to the Committee on Unemployment and Business Cycles, for which he secured a $50,000 grant from the Carnegie Corporation. The committee's report, published in 1923, recommended careful management of monetary policy by the Federal Reserve, the use of public works to counter economic downturns, and the provision of government statistics to enable private business to regularize its capital expenditures and employment. As early as 1924, Hoover had begun warning that prosperity based largely on speculation and credit could not last, and he continued searching throughout the decade for ways to head off a major crash. During a 1927 recession, he commissioned another group, the Committee on Recent Economic Changes, to study the economy further. Its 1929 report echoed the conclusions of the earlier committee: "the outstanding fact which is illuminated by this survey is that we can not maintain our economic advantage, or hope fully to realize on our economic future, unless we consciously accept the principle of equilibrium and apply it skillfully in every economic relation."[10]

The fact that during the 1920s Hoover commissioned economic studies that suggested that the government could do much to counter downturns in the economic cycle (although none of the committees seriously considered deficit spending) does not mean that he was prepared to implement their recommendations wholeheartedly. His recognition of the value of government spending on public works both to stimulate the economy and to employ workers was at odds with his conviction that big government was pernicious, and that solutions to problems could be found through associational activities and organized voluntarism. His understanding of the arguments of the economists was in conflict with the ingrained lessons of a Quaker childhood in the West and a business career on the world's frontiers where self-sufficiency and individual enterprise were cardinal virtues.[11]

Hoover's initial reaction to the crash, like almost everyone else's, was shock followed by an attempt to assert that the gyrations of the stock market had no implications for the overall health of the economy. As he realized the seriousness of the actual situation, he began a flurry of activity, urging the Federal Reserve to lower interest rates and Congress to reduce taxes, and summoning leaders of major industries to Washington to encourage them to maintain employment and plan capital expenditures. He also promised increases in federal public works expenditures and urged the nation's governors and mayors to cooperate by doing the same.[12]

In November 1929 Hoover asked Interior Secretary Ray Lyman Wilbur to consider, in regard to his department in particular,

> the following possibilities for expansion of activities as a contribution to allayment of unemployment that may occur this winter:
>
> (a) Earlier initiation of authorized construction and repair work under present appropriations.
>
> (b) Earlier orders for supplies in general.
>
> (c) What construction could be initiated which is authorized but for which appropriations are not now available.
>
> (d) What construction might be advantageously authorized and appropriated for.[13]

There were three major problems with the sort of countercyclical campaign that Hoover implemented in late 1929 and early 1930. First, it largely failed to reach the nearly half of all Americans who lived on farms or in small towns, and who had been the victims of a rural depression for almost a decade before the administration began to contemplate a recovery program. Second, Hoover envisioned his program as a corrective to a short-term and relatively moderate downturn of the economy, not as a solution for a major depression. And third, Hoover emphasized the voluntary aspect of his program and never accepted the necessity of a major, sustained government role. Seeing the costs of government as an impediment to private recovery, he was torn between wanting government to assist and believing that the private sector must be freed of the burden of taxation.

In 1921 the Reclamation Bureau had touted the potential of dam building and irrigation as public works programs. When the depression began in 1929, however, the service had no capital available for new construction. Because American farmers never recovered from the postwar depression, irrigators had difficulty throughout the 1920s in paying fully for the water they used and in amortizing their dams and ditches. In May 1929 the bureau hired private consultants to review current and planned projects, and to reexamine the whole basis of the program. Whether the administration would have followed up on their suggestion that Congress adopt some new scheme for paying for reclamation is impossible to determine. By the time they delivered their report in March 1930, the Reclamation Bureau was in economic crisis. Instead of being a force for recovery, it became just one more problem for the administration.[14]

In the summer of 1929 Commissioner Elwood Mead reported that "the financial condition of reclamation today is satisfactory," with most projects making payments on time.[15] Six months later, the situation had so deteriorated that western members of Congress introduced legislation to reduce or suspend payments for several reclamation districts. The administration opposed the proposals to cut users' payments and rejected the construction of new projects, including a Columbia River development that Hoover had long favored.[16] In late 1931, under pressure from Congress to declare a moratorium on all payments by farmers on reclaimed lands, the administration argued that if a moratorium were adopted, the Reclamation Bureau would have no funds for new construction. Nevertheless, on 1 April 1932 Hoover signed a bill providing for the reduction of interest rates to be paid by water users of reclamation projects.[17]

Such legislation benefitted farmers on existing reclamation projects but eliminated new projects because the service had always operated on the conservative principle of using only income to finance construction. When Mead and others in the government suggested that the depression warranted federal loans to reclamation districts to provide relief, conservation, and beneficial public works, Hoover showed no interest in the idea.[18] In March 1933, as the Republicans left office, the only major reclamation project under construction was Hoover Dam, where construction began in September 1930, and even appropriations for that had been curtailed in 1932. Otherwise, Mead reported sadly, "lack of funds . . . precluded progress" on several partially completed and planned projects.[19] Far from becoming an instrument of relief and recovery, the Reclamation Bureau itself barely avoided becoming a casualty of the depression. Apparently abandoned was the president's frequently voiced conviction that every drop of water must provide a full measure of service before it escaped to the sea.

By contrast, the administration made at least some use of public works spending to provide relief for rural areas through road and trail construction programs in the Interior and Agriculture Departments. In fiscal year 1930, beginning on 1 July 1929, the government spent just over $13 million on the construction of National Forest and Park Service roads and trails (as compared to just over $11 million in FY 1929, the last pre-depression year). In FY 1931 the figure dropped to just over $11 million, but in FY 1932 it jumped to over $17 million; it increased again in FY 1933 to over $23 million; and there were plans to increase it to almost $24 million for FY 1934.[20] Members of the federal conservation bureaucracies quickly grasped the advantages that such policies might have for them. Forester R. Y. Stuart alerted his agency to "take advantage of any opportunity open to us under the President's plan for an enlarged construction program," and others urged that "construction of roads, trails, fire lines, and similar capital improvements . . . should be classed among the public works which are now being pushed to the front."[21]

A famous and dramatic example of conservation policies directly related to relief was the construction of the Skyline Drive in Shenandoah National Park in Virginia. The proposed park bordered on Hoover's Camp Rapidan, and one day in the summer of 1930, the Hoovers, along with National Park Director Horace Albright, rode on horseback up to the ridge that runs through the area. As they rode, the president turned to Albright and said, "You know, this mountain is just made by God Almighty for a highway. . . . There's nothing like it in the country really, where you can see such vistas first one side and then the other, and sometimes both ways. . . . I think we should have a survey made here." When they returned to Washington, Albright passed the president's idea on to William E. Carson, chairman of the Virginia Conservation and Development Commission, who eagerly embraced the opportunity to open up an area of the state that had long been isolated and to provide work for local farmers who were suffering from a severe drought. Carson lobbied the Virginia congressional delegation aggressively, and early in 1931, they succeeded in earmarking one-third of a $1.5 million federal emergency road-construction fund to start the proposed Skyline Drive. Hoover insisted that construction should be done by local people, using horse-drawn plows and graders rather than "a lot of heavy equipment," so that the project would provide the maximum amount of relief. By the summer of 1931, grading of the first section of the road was well under way, and the Hoovers were able to drive over a section of it before they left office. The highway was completed under the New Deal.[22]

Another popular proposal for the alleviation of unemployment through conservation was the Forest Service's reforestation program. From 1929 through 1932 the service's tree nurseries increased their annual output of seedlings from 14 million to 26 million. In 1929 just over 18 million acres were planted; by 1931 the number was up to nearly 27 million, although it dropped back the next year to 23 million.[23] Yet the administration never showed much enthusiasm for reforestation as a relief measure. Initially, the Agriculture Department insisted that relief bills passed by Congress did not provide money for reforestation, that all planting had to be thoroughly planned to maximize its value for the control of floods and erosion, and that there were not enough available seedling trees to permit a major expansion of reforestation. Secretary Hyde suggested that farmers living on marginal lands plant trees to supplement their incomes in the future, and he proposed a vague program to employ some of them in "rehabilitating" neglected national forest lands, but his ideas lacked specificity and were of little immediate help to hungry farmers.[24]

Not until the summer of 1932, when Franklin Roosevelt suggested the possibility of putting a million men to work in the forests, and Charles Lathrop Pack, president of the American Tree Association, strongly urged reforestation as a way of fighting unemployment, did the administration take the matter seriously. Belatedly recognizing the political appeal of Roosevelt's proposals, the Republicans scrambled to publicize and place their own accomplishments in the most favorable light. But even then, administration leaders could not quite accept the idea of reforestation as relief. Such a program, wrote Secretary Hyde, would not be "self sustaining nor is it adequate security for a bond issue"; its only "returns would lie in social values, recreational values, in conservational values." There was "little or nothing *additional* 'that we can do (directly) along this line' until additional legislation and funds are available," declared acting Forester Leon F. Kneipp.[25] When the administration began slashing expenses in 1932, money available for the Forest Service's planting program dropped from $250,000 to $154,000.[26]

The administration claimed to have given 70,000 men work through reforestation and to have created several thousand more jobs on the Skyline Drive, but carefully planned projects on this relatively small scale were not a solution for the depression. They neither pumped enough money into the economy nor employed enough people to have a major effect. Moreover, there was always uneasiness within the administration about spending money for public works when federal revenues were falling. In October 1930, for example, Secretary of Agriculture Hyde wrote the president about "the possibility of deferring [$10 million in] payments on Federal aid road projects, flood relief payments and forest roads and trails" until after the beginning of the 1932 fiscal year in July 1931. Hoover replied that he did not want "to reduce any public works at any point where that would reduce employment," but he agreed that there might be "sections of the country where there is no unemployment of any consequence" and where cutbacks could be made.[27] Public works programs, wrote the president in May 1932 in a long letter to Herbert S. Crocker, president of the American Society of Civil Engineers, should be continued only if they did not "place a strain on the taxpayer and [did] not necessitate government borrowing." Projects that were "income-producing," he continued, were entirely desirable; "non-productive" projects begun simply to provide employment would require "immediate increased taxation or the issuance of government bonds," either of which would be "inescapably a burden upon the taxpayer." What was needed, Hoover proclaimed, was not a massive public works program financed by borrowed money, such as a committee of civil engineers had suggested, but "the return of confidence and a capital market through which credit will flow in the thousand rills with its result of employment and increased prices." Only a balanced federal budget and unimpaired national credit could achieve that end.[28]

Hoover's letter to Crocker, with its promise that prosperity would trickle down through the thousand rills of business confidence, was written in the midst of a major battle over the budget for fiscal year 1933. Initially, Hoover had been willing to use federal credit and at least limited deficit spending to finance recovery programs. In December 1929, for example, he proposed an actual increase in spending for conservation of natural resources for FY 1931, and a similar increase was discussed in June 1930 for FY 1932.[29] But by July 1930, declining federal revenues and rising expenditures had begun to alarm the president, who instructed all members of the cabinet to seek ways to economize. Their efforts produced substantial cutbacks in most areas of planned spending, but in the autumn of 1930 conservation agencies remained optimistic that many proposed projects would be authorized as relief measures.[30]

By the end of the fiscal year on 30 June 1931, it was obvious that the situation was worsening. The Budget Office reported a $1 billion deficit for the year just ended, and conservation agencies anticipated suffering pretty heavy cuts in the coming year. Forester Stuart predicted the loss of funding for new roads and trails and, far from expecting to hire more workers, was uncertain whether there would be enough money "to carry our permanent personnel."[31] In November the Bureau of the Budget was pessimistically predicting a $2 billion deficit in overall expenditures during 1932.[32]

Hoover labored mightily to put a cheerful face on this dismal situation in his annual message on 8 December 1931. Difficult times, he declared, had produced "a remarkable development of the sense of cooperation in the community," and there had been "an enlargement of social and spiritual responsibility among the people," but he could not claim that the depression would soon end. Instead, he offered a long list of new proposals to deal with its effects and to cure its causes. Spending on public works, including such conservation measures as flood control and waterway development, would, he predicted, be almost three times as great in 1932 as in 1928.[33]

The members of Congress, already thinking ahead to the 1932 election, did not seem very impressed by Hoover's ideas. The Democrats had a small majority in the House, but even in the Republican-controlled Senate there was much criticism of the president's policies. One member of the House Appropriations Committee reportedly suggested closing the national parks as unnecessary luxuries.[34] Fearing that there would be an overwhelming demand in the legislature for expensive relief programs of various sorts, the administration launched an aggressive campaign in December 1931 to persuade Congress that what was needed was more taxes and less spending in order to bring the budget back toward balance. Leading the chorus was Ogden L. Mills, who would become secretary of the treasury in February 1932 when Andrew Mellon was confirmed as the new ambassador to Great Britain. Mills and Hoover were mutual admirers, and the president listened to Mills as he had never listened to Mellon. Mills argued strongly that the growing national debt was undermining business confidence and preventing recovery. He also contended that the rich were bearing too large a share of the country's tax burden and that shifting some of the tax load to lower-income people would free capital for recovery and growth.[35] Under Mills's influence, the administration took an even more conservative course.

In a message to Congress on 9 December 1931, Hoover announced a budget for FY 1933 that anticipated, through a combination of tax increases and spending cuts, halving the annual deficit and achieving a balanced budget in FY 1934. Such a course was essential, he argued, to maintain "the financial integrity of the Federal Government" and to provide for "the rebuilding of a sound national prosperity."[36] Among the more substantial cuts he proposed were a 28 percent reduction in spending on "conservation of natural resources," a 66 percent cut in "aids to agriculture" (mostly drought relief), and a 26 percent cut in "public buildings and public works" (for which the administration contended that spending was still nearly 70 percent greater than in 1927). In terms of dollars, these three categories of expenditures, which included most relief projects related to conservation, would be reduced by about $294 million over FY 1932, thus accounting for almost 20 percent of the total savings the administration proposed to realize. Among specific conservation cuts were $1.4 million from the Agriculture Department's road and trail budget, $1 million from the Boulder Canyon project, $2 million from the Reclamation Bureau, and $1.5 million from the National Park Service.[37] Here was tangible evidence of the low priority that Hoover gave to conservation issues in a time of economic crisis.[38]

In conferences with House leaders during the spring of 1932, the administration agreed to increase public works appropriations enough to trim the cuts in the three major conservation areas from $294 million to $204 million. But the Revenue Act Hoover signed into law in June 1932 was pretty close to what he had recommended back in December 1931 in terms of real conservation spending, and it included an additional 10 percent cut in the Interior

Department's budget imposed by Congress.[39] Many Americans, facing a national unemployment rate approaching 23 percent in the spring of 1932, would undoubtedly have liked to see the Boulder Canyon project (cut by 20 percent) and the Reclamation Service (a 23 percent cut) fully funded.[40] On the eve of the 1932 presidential election, the Interior Department was gloomily calculating where still deeper cuts might be made for FY 1934.[41]

As part of Hoover's campaign to reduce spending, he revived his earlier proposals to reorganize the executive branch, arguing that reorganization, including but not limited to conservation, would save a significant amount of money. "A patchwork organization compels inefficiency, waste, and extravagance," he declared in a special message to Congress on 17 February 1932, and he predicted that "a proper reorganization of our departments, commissions, and bureaus will result, not only in much greater efficiency and public convenience, but in the saving of many millions of dollars now extracted annually from our overburdened taxpayers." To implement these changes, he asked Congress for authority to issue executive orders redistributing and consolidating agencies that would take effect after sixty days if Congress did not countermand them.[42]

A week later, the House's Select Committee on the Economy chaired by Democratic Representative Joseph W. Byrns of Tennessee took up the president's request along with his proposals for tax increases and budget cuts. In an all-day meeting with the committee on 9 April, Hoover pressed the issue, but the committee apparently did not share his confidence that reorganization would save large amounts of money. The proposal was deferred for future consideration.[43] The president expressed public optimism about congressional action, but the reality was that the approach of the presidential election and the continuing opposition of the agencies concerned made it unlikely he would get what he wanted. Although Hoover "bombarded Congress with messages urging general reorganization," the "Economy Act" passed at the end of June turned the president's proposal inside out. Instead of having executive orders on reorganization take effect after sixty days unless Congress rescinded them, the bill provided that such orders would be implemented only if Congress specifically affirmed them. In a press statement Hoover said that he signed the bill "with but limited satisfaction," which was a considerable understatement. Congress's action, he observed in his memoirs, "made the orders amount to no more than a message recommending something," and he could not even do that much unless Congress were in session.[44]

Nevertheless, Hoover did not abandon his long-standing dream, and when Congress convened again in December 1932, he sent to the Hill a series of

executive orders proposing the consolidation of fifty executive and adminis-
trative agencies. Shrewdly, the president this time dropped the idea of bringing all conservation and public works agencies into the Department of Inte-
rior. Instead, he proposed to establish a Division of Public Works in the
Interior Department into which would be put the Bureau of Reclamation, the
Geological Survey, the rivers and harbors and flood control activities of the
Army Corps of Engineers, Alaskan public works functions, the Bureau of
Public Roads, and other small agencies having to do with the planning and
maintenance of public properties. He also proposed to create a Division of
Education, Health, and Recreation in the Interior Department that would include the National Park Service and the national monuments, cemeteries, and
battlefield parks previously under the War Department. The Agriculture Department would have a new Division of Land Utilization that would include
the Forest Service, the Biological Survey, the General Land Office (from Interior), and the previously independent Commission on the Conservation and
Administration of the Public Domain.[45]

As Hoover had feared, his proposals ran into overwhelming opposition in
the Democratically controlled Congress. Publicly, congressional Democrats
argued that incoming President Roosevelt ought to have a free hand in something so important as reorganization, but many observers believed that spite
against Hoover and private pettiness were the real motives. One member of
the Forest Service reported, for example, that Senator Patrick McCarran of
Nevada opposed reorganization for no better reason than that his nephew, who
worked in the General Land Office, did not want to be transferred to the
Agriculture Department from Interior.[46]

In late January 1933 the House rejected Hoover's reorganization proposals, but to his pleased surprise, on 7 February Congress passed a bill giving
the new president a two-year grant of emergency power to reorganize executive agencies of the government.[47] Embittered by the defeat of a decade-old
dream, however, Hoover omitted all mention of this bill from his memoirs. A
footnote alludes only to his efforts to revive reorganization proposals in the
postwar Hoover Commission.[48]

Although Hoover blamed the depression mainly on worldwide conditions,
he and his followers always believed that the measures he proposed, including
reorganization, would have led to recovery if they had not been blocked by
political opposition. Adding to his gloomy sense of being the victim of events
beyond anyone's control were the great drought that began in 1930, and the
continuing oil glut that drastically depressed that industry.[49]

Indeed, the drought that began in the summer of 1930 seemed almost malevolently intended to undermine Hoover's recovery efforts. Earlier that year, the stock market had rebounded significantly from the previous autumn's crash, and the administration was confident that things were getting better. Then came July, the hottest month across the country in Weather Bureau records, and August was hardly better. In Arkansas, the temperature stayed above the 100 degree mark for forty-two of forty-three days. And in most of the twenty-seven-state area extending on the East Coast from Maryland to Florida, and west to the Rockies through the whole Midwest, there was little or no rain either. Crops never came up or withered in the fields; rivers were reduced to stagnant pools; farmers had no feed for their animals and no food for their families. Day after day the sun blazed down, and millions of farmers were baked into near-starvation.[50]

The drought was an environmental as well as a human disaster. Wildfires burned thousands of acres in Virginia, West Virginia, North Carolina, and Arkansas. Fish died in huge numbers, and their rotting corpses polluted the remaining water of lakes and rivers. Farmers used guns to defend their shrinking ponds and dwindling wells from parched wildlife. Dust clouds began to fill the skies as dry winds swept across the empty fields. Human diseases resulting from pollution and malnutrition, such as typhoid and pellagra, became common.[51]

There was not much the federal government could do about the environmental aspects of the drought disaster, but Hoover seemed exactly the right man to take charge of relieving human suffering. This, after all, was the sort of challenge that had made him famous during and after World War I when he organized international aid programs for Belgium and Russia, the domestic Food Administration during the war, and relief for victims of the 1927 Mississippi floods. The president turned to this familiar sort of crisis with enthusiasm, and in August 1930 he summoned governors of the drought-stricken states to the White House and met with John Barton Payne, the chairman of the Red Cross. When the governors arrived in Washington, the president promised relief for people through the private charity of the Red Cross and federal loans to farmers to enable them to buy seed and fertilizer. Railroads, he announced, would transport feed for farm animals at reduced rates, and he urged local banks and businesses to extend credit to farmers. The situation, he insisted, was not serious enough to justify large-scale federal relief spending to assist individuals.[52]

As the governors left the White House, rain began to fall in the Midwest, and in September the heat wave broke in the South. News of rural problems was soon pushed off the front pages by growing unemployment in the cities, but the problems did not go away. Rain had come too late to save most crops, and on top of a decade's agricultural depression, this was the last straw. Nor had Hoover's efforts inspired the private relief for which he had hoped. Bankers and businessmen, already overextended, did not offer new credit; road-building projects hired too few men; the Red Cross provided a little aid, but in the face of the national depression, "national officials did not want to publicize that it had the money or that the national organization would come into the relief." During the summer of 1930, the Red Cross gave drought sufferers little direct relief; usually it offered only garden seeds and homilies on self-help. With starvation a growing possibility, Red Cross and congressional leaders met at the Agriculture Department late in November 1930 to discuss the situation. They agreed to support a $60 million bill to provide loans for seed, fertilizer, tractor fuel, animal feed, and—despite doubts—food relief.[53]

Hoover was unconvinced. In his annual message on 2 December, he argued that the Red Cross had thus far used only a half million dollars of its $5 million relief fund within the drought area and expressed his confidence that "the Red Cross can relieve the cases of individual distress." A week later, at a press conference, he insisted that new appropriations for relief would require tax increases that would worsen the depression. Those advocating a relief program for farmers, he charged, were merely "playing politics at the expense of human misery"—an unfortunate phrase if ever there was one.[54] When the drought-aid bill passed in February 1931, it did so without the $15 million originally intended for relief. Even the normally staid *Literary Digest* was appalled. "The farmer asked for bread," it reported, "and they gave him a $45,000,000 loan for mule-feed, fertilizer, and seed." Senator Joseph T. Robinson of Arkansas was even more blunt: "It is all right to put a mule on the dole, but it is condemned, I see, to put a man on a parity with a mule."[55]

On 3 January 1931 H. C. Coney, a tenant farmer in Lonoke County, Arkansas, was visited by a neighbor, who told him that her children had not eaten in two days. Coney and his wife got into their truck and drove to where the Red Cross was supposed to be handing out relief. There they found a crowd of men begging for help, but the Red Cross worker would not hand out anything without properly signed forms—and his supply of forms had run out. Coney shouted to the crowd to jump on his truck, saying that they would get food in the town of England, if they had to take it by force. About forty of them joined him, and they drove into town, where other hungry people also gathered. When the Red Cross again refused aid unless signed forms were presented, local merchants grew alarmed and agreed to distribute free food. Within a few hours, the whole incident was over; several hundred people had been given food, and no one was hurt.[56]

News reports commonly described the events in Lonoke County as a "riot," although there is no credible evidence of any violence, nor any indication that the demonstrators were armed. The president sent his military aide, Col. Campbell Hodges, to investigate the incident and concluded that the "alleged riot by 'starving people' . . . was a fake." The whole incident, Hoover believed, was planted in the press by his political enemies.[57] Others took the matter more seriously, and the Senate voted to add $15 million for food loans to the drought bill. When the House rejected the amendment, Senator Robinson proposed to appropriate $25 million to subsidize Red Cross relief work. That, too, was defeated in the House after Hoover issued a statement lauding the Red Cross's relief work and hinting that he might veto a bill that included food loans.[58] Passionately convinced that, given time, the country would voluntarily rally to the aid of drought victims, Hoover perhaps underestimated how badly the depression had undermined the foundations of private charity. Although he promised that if charities and local governments proved unable to feed the hungry, he would use the full resources of the federal government, he could not accept that the moment of crisis had arrived. Many Americans would never forgive him for his ideological rigidity.[59]

In the spring of 1931 rains returned to much (although not all) of the drought region, and the crisis receded from public view. The Red Cross later claimed that it had fed 2 million people during the emergency, but their relief normally amounted to no more than forty to fifty cents worth of food per person per week. That was less than most states of the region allotted to feed prisoners, and as even Hoover admitted, African Americans facing relief committees dominated by planters received less than whites.[60]

For much of the East, the summer of 1931 brought the end of the drought. But in the Midwest drought continued, and in some places, it actually worsened as the Great Plains entered a dry cycle. By the winter of 1931–32, the skies darkened with the first of a series of great dust storms.

California Senator Hiram Johnson, one of Hoover's harshest critics on the relief issue, said that the president's inflexible position in regard to relief for drought sufferers, drove "another nail in his [political] coffin."[61] The administration ultimately authorized almost $250 million in federal works projects, but the slowness with which such projects got started, and the paucity of jobs in them for unskilled farmers, gave Hoover a reputation for callous insensitivity to human suffering. What was more, the administration's preference for capital improvements rather than labor-intensive projects such as reforestation slowed the delivery of money to people in need and reduced the number of aid recipients.[62] The longer the depression dragged on, the less Hoover seemed in touch with the situation in the country, and the more inflexible he seemed in his responses to the crisis. Even ideas that might in the past have appealed to him, such as the bittersweet suggestion by Representative U.S. Stone of Oklahoma that he speed up construction of flood control works along the Mississippi in order to help people suffering from the drought, brought no response from the White House.[63] With Roosevelt's call in the summer of 1932 to put a million men to work in the forests, he both appealed to the desire for conservation that Hoover seemed to have forgotten and exploited the administration's vulnerability on the relief issue.

The Hoover administration did not regard the drought as a conservation issue, but they did recognize that traditional agricultural land use patterns contributed to soil erosion and watershed degradation, which in turn worsened the effects of the drought.[64] In November 1931 Secretary of Agriculture Arthur Hyde called a national land use conference to discuss what Hyde described as the problem of "submarginal land" upon which "no farmer, however skillful, can support a decent standard of living." The solution to this problem, Hyde argued, was "purchase and reforestation by the Government." Interior's Geological Survey attempted to facilitate this process by classifying public lands into categories that would, in Secretary Wilbur's words, advance "the policy of utilizing [devoting?] land to the use by which the greatest benefit may be derived by the greatest number." At Hyde's urging, the 1932 Republican platform also included a plank calling for "the acquisition of submarginal lands for water shed protection, grazing, forestry, public parks, and game reserves."[65] It seems unlikely, however, that anything would have come of this idea if Hoover had been reelected. Aside from the problems of funding a large-scale land purchase program during the depression, Hoover's philosophical commitment to local initiatives and voluntary cooperation rather than federal action to implement conservation goals made adoption of Hyde's proposal improbable. As the report of the Commission on the Public Domain demonstrated, Hoover believed in transferring federal lands to the states, not in acquiring more federal property needing management.

Whether Hoover was right or wrong from the standpoint of economic theory, his ideological rigidity prevented his administration from developing policies to ameliorate the human suffering that accompanied the drought of 1930–31 and from attacking the broader conservation and environmental issues that were revealed during it. An unwillingness to mobilize the full resources of the federal government helped to turn a natural disaster into a political one. The same mind-set also affected the administration's approach to the continuing crisis in the oil fields.

The onset of the depression following the October 1929 stock market crash substantially worsened the problems of the oil industry. Desperate to bring overproduction under control but unwilling to consider federal production restrictions, the Federal Oil Conservation Board (FOCB) suggested in March 1930 that oil producers cut back from a seven- to a six-day week as a means of cutting production. In addition, the administration chose to look the other way when producers on the Pacific Coast conspired illegally to set the price of gasoline and when other oil companies agreed informally not to cut prices.[66]

For a time voluntary approaches seemed to be successful, but by the end of the year American production was up 10 percent over 1929 and imports were undiminished. Early in 1931, crude oil prices stood at seventy-five cents a barrel. Not surprisingly, desperate oil producers demanded a tariff on foreign oil, and a bill placing a dollar-a-barrel levy nearly passed Congress in the spring of 1930, despite the administration's opposition.[67]

In the midst of all of this the administration's troubles were increased when Ralph S. Kelley, a disgruntled field investigator for the Denver branch of the U.S. Land Office, charged that leases of oil-shale lands worth billions of dollars were being given away by the Interior Department to oil companies. Secretary Wilbur snorted that the editors of the New York *World*, which published Kelley's charges in October 1930, should have reached "for a nutcracker instead of the checkbook when Kelley showed up," but the attacks were embarrassing. Several months would pass before a Justice Department investigation demonstrated that there was no merit in Kelley's accusations.[68]

In January 1931 the opening of a vast new field in East Texas dramatically worsened the situation, dropping the price of crude oil in the next several months as low as ten to twenty-five cents a barrel. Major producers demanded the government act to control domestic production, and Wirt Franklin, the president of the Independent Petroleum Association, declared that "the only quick and practical method of restoring prosperity to the people of this nation is through the adoption by Congress of a tariff upon cheap foreign oil."[69] When Secretary Wilbur responded to the situation only with a call for vague conservation measures, and the FOCB reiterated its conviction that a tariff or embargo on imported oil was undesirable, an outcry arose from the producers and the governors of the oil states.[70]

Recognizing that the administration's efforts had thus far failed, Hoover sent Secretary of Commerce Robert P. Lamont to negotiate with importers and the large oil companies about imposing voluntary restrictions on imports. No one was sure that such an agreement was legal under the antitrust laws, but the situation was so desperate that agreement was quickly reached on a 25 percent cutback on imports and production for at least sixty days. That agreement was in effect from April through June 1931.[71]

Although Wilbur tried to be optimistic that the cutback would raise petroleum prices "above distress levels within a month," he had to admit that there was "still strong feeling for a tariff in Oklahoma" and Texas oil was selling for eight and three-quarter cents a barrel.[72] Adding considerably to his difficulties was the fact that although everyone concerned professed to favor an interstate compact as the best means of reducing the oil surplus, small producers wanted only to curtail production from existing wells, while large companies sought to restrict new drilling. The impasse prevented any action, and upon the expiration of the voluntary restrictions negotiated by Secretary Lamont, the East Texas companies began dumping enormous quantities of oil on the market. In August, Texas Governor Ross Shaw Sterling placed East Texas under martial law and ordered the state militia to shut down all wells in the area. As the issue then moved into the courts, everyone concerned at last recognized that some government had to regulate production.[73]

In September 1931, Oklahoma, Kansas, and Texas signed an agreement to control production, but Congress, focused on the oil tariff bill, failed to approve the compact.[74] Indeed, even if the compact had been approved, there was little hope it would have reversed the slide in prices because public demand for petroleum products was falling faster than production could be cut. Wilbur urged producers to enter into unit-operation agreements, but he had to admit that overdrilling, waste, and overproduction continued despite all he had been able to do.[75] By December Mark Requa was saying bluntly—if privately—that the administration had failed to deal adequately with the oil crisis. "Much, I am sure, could have been accomplished," he wrote, "but it would have required a much more vigorous action on the part of the administration" than it had been willing to take.[76]

Early in 1932 the administration at last began to take some of the actions Requa believed necessary. In February Secretary Wilbur issued a statement supporting a bill pending in the Senate that imposed a tariff on oil, while Northcutt Ely worked on the final details of another bill authorizing interstate compacts to regulate production. The administration, wrote Secretary Wilbur, had "no desire to concentrate the forces of government in Washington," but it was eager to "lend such aid as it can" to "the industry and . . . the governments of the States."[77] In April the Interior Department yielded to pressure from western states with large amounts of public lands and authorized the reopening of those lands to oil prospecting, provided new fields were run under unit agreements.[78] Leaders of the states that had been most affected by the closure were pleased, but the decision was hard to justify in the face of the continuing oil glut.

Limited measures had little effect on the oil crisis, and although the FOCB warned that oil "reserves are exhaustible and should not be exploited heedlessly," oil continued to gush out of the Southwest at ruinous rates during the final months of the Hoover administration.[79] Oilmen voiced public praise for the administration and the FOCB because they feared the Roosevelt administration might do even less, not because Hoover's efforts had been a success. In the presidential election oil state voters clearly registered their opinion of the failure of the Hoover administration to solve the overproduction dilemma.[80]

The oil glut was a difficult and intractable problem, which two philosophical limitations made even more difficult for the Hoover administration. One problem was that Hoover consistently rejected the possibility that the oil crisis was a national one warranting federal action; instead, he insisted on attacking it only through voluntary private actions and state legislation, neither of which proved adequate. A second problem was that Hoover's whole approach to conservation, which had been posited on an assumption that prudent use of resources would assure prosperity, was undermined by the beginning of the depression. It seemed to him that increased production was necessary to relieve unemployment, yet overproduction was obviously the problem in the oil fields. Conservation that would reduce production seemed to make economic sense under the circumstances, but how did one rationalize reducing production in a depressed economy?

Although Hoover's belief that conservation was primarily something with which to increase and enhance prosperity led him to propose a reduction in spending for the Interior Department from $311 million in 1930 to $58 million for FY 1934, and for the Agriculture Department from $155.7 million in 1930 to $118.8 million in FY 1934, officials within the administration still found it possible to pursue a surprisingly active and innovative conservation program. Thus the Bureau of Fisheries negotiated restrictions with the Canadians on halibut fishing in the Northwest, and Commissioner Henry O'Malley set off a controversy in the middle of the 1932 campaign by suggesting a ban on salmon fishing in most northwestern rivers.[81] The Interior Department continued to reserve federal lands for migratory bird refuges and wildlife sanctuaries, and to expend funds (almost a million dollars between 1929 and 1933) to study and purchase wetlands suitable as refuges for migratory wildfowl.[82] At the same time, the Forest Service purchased 1.5 million acres of eastern lands that were added to the national forests under the 1911 Weeks Law at a cost of a little over $5 million, noting proudly that declining values of forestlands had enabled it to spend less per acre than in the past.[83] The Interior Department also set aside thousands of acres of public lands for watershed protection and other conservation uses. In addition, the Forest Service pioneered a novel concept, the establishment of wilderness or primitive areas in which human intrusion would be minimized; almost 8 million acres of national forestland in eight western states were set aside for this purpose by 1933, and another 1.2 million acres were reserved in Minnesota.[84] With the aid of private contributions and transfers from other public lands, the Park Service contrived to increase the area of national parks and monuments by 40 percent.[85]

The onset of the depression revealed curious and contradictory things about the Hoover administration's conservation policies. Policy initiatives that relied on voluntarism and decentralization broke down, but the federal conservation bureaucracy, established by now for nearly thirty years in some cases, continued to function and even to expand its activities despite the efforts of the administration to reduce federal responsibility for conservation. In some cases, bureaucratic inertia saved federal conservation policies, while in others, attempts to turn toward local initiatives and voluntarism, as with oil regulation or interstate water compacts, actually ended up enhancing federal power. On the whole, Hoover's attempts to set conservation policy on an entirely new course did not succeed. The most lasting conservation legacies of his administration were the products of established federal agencies working in traditional ways. It was almost as if there were two governments in the field of conservation—one, led by Hoover, trying to divest Washington of responsibility and preaching voluntarism and localism; and another, led by established federal agencies, quietly carrying on and even expanding traditional programs.[86]

Hoover was simply the wrong person to deal with the depression. His pragmatic, flexible engineering approach might have served him well had it not been, in the opinion of Craig Lloyd, "undercut by his dogmatic faith in 'American Individualism' and by the 'American system,' which constituted for him . . . a kind of ultimate truth."[87] In comparable situations in the past—the Belgian relief program or the World War I Food Administration, for example—Hoover had been able to combine the rhetoric of voluntarism with strong, centralized administration, but the depression hurricane demolished the structure of voluntarism. The president tried manfully to arouse the volunteer spirit, and seemed at first to succeed, but as the depression deepened, public confidence in voluntarism vanished. "It is worse than it was during the war," Hoover complained to a friend one day. "Then we had a militant cooperation. That we cannot get now."[88] Ultimately, repeated invocations of voluntarism actually undermined public confidence in Hoover's ability to deal with the crisis. "The administration's continued insistence on local voluntarism and its optimistic evaluations of the situation," concludes Craig Lloyd, "opened up a wide credibility gap between observable reality and official assessment."[89]

The depression also demolished Hoover's philosophical justification for conservation. His conviction that conservation was a component of permanent prosperity and that environmental improvements were amenities of the consumer society left him with no particular reason for continuing these policies when prosperity collapsed. Conservation programs continued to run because the bureaucrats were committed to them, but at the policy level the administration never developed a conservation philosophy for an era of scarcity and economic collapse. The idea of linking conservation to the reduction of production in industry, mineral extraction, and agriculture was contrary to what Hoover felt instinctively was needed in the crisis. Raising prices by reducing production would be left to the New Deal.

Even before Hoover was elected, the *New Republic* had predicted that his romantic conception of America, under which prosperity was supposed to be assured through "a system of self-government founded on 'decentralized local responsibility,'" would fail in a crisis. People thought of him as an engineer, wrote the editors, but in fact his political philosophy came "out of books," and it was only "the balm of the words he uses" that enabled him to believe that in some magic way businessmen would take care of the nation.[90] The judgment was too harsh. Hoover proved more flexible and creative in the economic crisis than the editors imagined. But it was also true that his political philosophy limited what he was willing to do and cocooned him in the comforting belief that doing more would make the situation worse. Beliefs that had seemed to work brilliantly in good times neither prevented nor cured the catastrophe of the 1930s, and it was left to Roosevelt to call upon the pragmatic methods of the engineer while Hoover sought the balm of theoretical rectitude.

10 | The Conservative and Conservation

During the 1932 election and the New Deal, an old argument about the closing of the American frontier reemerged. The Democrats asserted that the closing of the frontier meant that resources had become finite, that prosperity could only be restored through rational government planning that would reduce waste and overproduction and assure the general welfare. Hoover rejected this "counsel of despair." The last frontier had not been reached, he wrote in 1934. "There are vast continents awaiting us of thought, of research, of industry, of human relations, potentially more prolific of human comfort than even the Boundless West."[1]

In rejecting the New Deal's theory of a closed frontier that required government management of remaining resources, Hoover was, although perhaps not consciously, finally turning away from a traditional justification for conservation with which he had never been entirely comfortable. Implicit in his 1934 argument was the conviction that human ingenuity, if not restricted by government, would always find replacements for dwindling resources. As later free market environmentalists put it, Hoover had become convinced that government management was a flawed system, and that if left alone, the free market would "react to problems of scarcity by reducing consumption, finding substitutes, and improving production."[2] In this view, conservation would become an automatic byproduct of a free market economy, not a policy to be consciously implemented by government.

Repudiated in the 1932 presidential election, Hoover left the White House an embittered man. Convinced that the New Dealers were wrong about the causes of the depression and wrong about how to cure it, he spent much of the next thirty years actively seeking ways to strip away the new powers assumed by the federal government during the emergency. Whatever limited role in conservation he had previously been willing to assign to the federal government was now further curtailed. As chair of two postwar commissions on federal reorganization, he reiterated old ideas about consolidating federal conservation agencies but focused the commissions' environmental recommendations on attacking public power projects. So long as conservation remained mainly a federal responsibility, it was included in Hoover's general antipathy to everything in Washington. Although he occasionally took an interest in conservation projects after 1933 and certainly enjoyed fishing trips on the West Coast, in the Rockies, and in Florida, environmental issues were no longer near the center of his economic and political philosophy.

The depression had brought out the worst in President Hoover. Dour and uncommunicative, he appeared to care more about troubled corporations than suffering individuals. Working from early in the morning until late into the night, he was reluctant even to take time out to campaign for reelection, and his staff was no help. His jovial, hard-drinking press secretary, George Akerson, was succeeded in 1931 by Theodore Joslin, a loyalist to be sure, but so sour and defensive that even Hoover found him trying. Joslin, declared a frustrated reporter, was "the first known instance of a rat joining a sinking ship." Lawrence Richey, the president's appointments secretary, contributed to his isolation by cutting him off from the public in the name of preserving his strength.[3] In the time of greatest need, the network of friends and admirers who had so skillfully presented Hoover to the public during his earlier years seemed to collapse.

When Hoover first became a national figure during and just after World War I, his admirers depicted him to the public as a brilliant engineer and administrator who scorned personal celebrity. This image fitted both the public needs of the time and Hoover's own shyness and passionate desire to conceal personal matters from public view.[4] In the White House, however, and particularly after the depression began, Hoover's style became a liability. Terrified and suffering, Americans needed reassurance and human warmth. Hoover offered long-range plans and impersonal, technical analysis.

The president's relations with the press exemplified his problem. Although he regularly held what were called press conferences, he used them mostly to present prepared statements. He almost never answered questions from reporters, even written ones submitted in advance. Convinced that the press would misquote him or deliberately distort his ideas, he became more and more hostile to reporters as the depression deepened. In August 1932 he told Ted Joslin that if he was reelected, he was "going to clean that bunch out whatever the consequences may be. I have stood for all from them that I can."[5] The result of this attitude was that the administration's relations with the press spiraled steadily downward. Hoover demanded that reporters treat official handouts as hard news or talked privately to a favored few. The rest of the press corps reacted predictably, digging for negative stories and depicting the president and his aides as unsympathetic reactionaries.[6]

By the time the 1932 presidential campaign began, Hoover was unable to use the press to calm public anxiety about the economic collapse.[7] Convinced that journalists and the Democrats had been waging "a continuous campaign of misrepresentation" against him personally and against his administration's efforts to counter the depression, Hoover's campaign speeches quickly moved from presenting his policies positively to bitter and defensive attacks on Roosevelt and the Democrats. Compounding the impression the country received of the president's negativity and pessimism was the fact that he gave only nine major speeches during the campaign. The pressure of work prevented him from making more appearances, Hoover later claimed, and he was proud that he had written every word of his speeches himself.[8] He would have been far better advised to have spoken more frequently and allowed others to draft the sort of optimistic, reassuring speeches he could not write.

Under the circumstances, Hoover's substantial achievements in many areas, including conservation, received little attention in the campaign. The president's best effort to present his administration in a positive light came at the outset of the campaign, in his 11 August speech accepting the Republican nomination. Here he reiterated his long-standing support for conservation, urged the development of river systems (particularly the St. Lawrence waterway and the project to control the Mississippi), and called on Congress to endorse his proposals for reorganization of government agencies, including those having to do with conservation. Yet even at this early stage of the campaign, he could not resist a jab at people who proposed to turn the administration's public works program into "pork-barrel nonproductive works which impoverish the Nation." The Democrats, he charged, were promising to "squander [the country] to prosperity on the ruins of its taxpayers."[9]

Throughout the remainder of the campaign, Hoover scarcely mentioned conservation again, except to react defensively to the Democrats. He denounced at length Senator George Norris's plan to have the federal government develop Muscle Shoals, and failed to grasp the opportunity to argue that the Hoover Dam project showed the administration's flexibility on the public power issue.[10] He claimed that the implementation of Democratic promises would "transfer vast responsibilities to the Federal Government from the States, the local governments, and the individuals," and would, in effect, "crack the timbers of our Constitution," but he passed by the chance to explain that his own proposals in conservation and other areas had been designed to strengthen local governments and decentralize authority.[11]

No issue offered Hoover a greater opportunity during the campaign to set forth his conservation philosophy in a positive light than a published letter from Franklin Roosevelt to Lowe Shearon of New York City—and no issue showed more clearly how ineffectively Hoover defended his programs when challenged. The letter, which Hoover claimed had been widely distributed among the unemployed, declared Roosevelt's belief in "the inherent right of every citizen to employment at a living wage" and promised his support for "self-liquidating public works, such as utilization of our water resources, flood control and land reclamation, to provide employment for all surplus labor at all times."[12] With most of this—the concepts of self-liquidating public works, development of water resources, flood control, and reclamation— Hoover had no quarrel. The letter offered him an opportunity to demonstrate how much his administration had done in those areas and to promise further progress. But instead, the president chose to emphasize only the last phrase of the letter, which promised employment for all surplus labor at all times. Of course he was correct that this was "a promise that no government on Earth can fulfill," but he entirely missed the broader point: that conservation projects that Hoover favored every bit as enthusiastically as Roosevelt had provided and could continue to provide badly needed relief jobs.[13]

Typical of the way the administration fumbled conservation issues was its handling of a suggestion made by Roosevelt in his acceptance speech that reforestation offered an immediate means of putting a million men to work. Secretary of Agriculture Hyde, speaking for the administration, ridiculed the idea. A million men, declared Hyde, "could plant 1,000,000,000 trees in a day. But all the nurseries in America do not possess 1,000,000,000 seedlings." To acquire enough land to plant a billion trees, Hyde scoffed, would cost $2 billion and force thousands of farmers into unemployment, while the planting would provide work for no more than 27,900 men and would destroy the market for forest products.[14]

Roosevelt "smilingly refused to answer Secretary Hyde," but the Democratic chairman of the House Agriculture Committee and a representative of the American Forestry Association derided "'Farmer' Hyde" for not understanding that reforestation required labor-intensive soil preparation and erosion and flood control, not just sticking seedlings in the ground.[15] Recognizing that Hyde had blundered, Hoover-supporter Charles Lathrop Pack of the American Tree Association tried to salvage the situation. Agreeing with Hyde that immediately employing a million common laborers in planting trees was a mere politician's dream, Pack nevertheless urged that federal *and state* spending be increased from about $100,000 to about $2 million a year for thinning and improving existing forests as well as replanting trees. In addition, Pack argued, it would actually be possible to put millions of men to work on flood control, in building modern sewage treatment systems, and in working with industries to reduce pollution.[16]

Pack's proposal ought to have appealed to Hoover. It combined conservation and pollution control, both long-standing interests of the president, and it promised that the whole could be undertaken through self-liquidating public works, which Hoover constantly asserted were the only justifiable forms of public spending. What was more, friends of the administration warned that "Roosevelt has made a considerable dent in the forces of conservationists in advocating tree planting by the federal government as a means for relieving unemployment."[17] Whether or not all of Pack's suggestions were practical, the administration needed to reclaim conservation as a Republican issue.[18]

Yet Secretary Hyde and the Forest Service showed no interest in Pack's proposal. Even if it were "desirable . . . to do additional planting for the relief of unemployment and to restore denuded lands to productivity" (he had argued in 1930 for just such a program), declared Hyde, existing laws did not authorize spending money on such projects.[19] A modest suggestion from Pack that Hoover at least include an endorsement of planned forestry in a forthcoming speech was brushed off by the president with the remark that "at the present moment the public mind is concentrated on more emotional things."[20] Not until Pack went public in late October with his proposal in the American Tree Association's newspaper, the *Forestry News Digest,* and other papers picked up the idea, did the White House finally react. In a panicky telegram to Hyde, Hoover's secretary Walter Newton ordered the Agriculture Department to publicize the $5 million that the Forest Service was already spending on similar projects on public lands and recommended that Hyde urge the states to apply to the Reconstruction Finance Corporation for loans to finance conservation activities on state lands.[21] Coming on the eve of the election, it was too little, too late. Having defined conservation as a handmaiden of prosperity, Hoover had missed the relief and recovery potential in the tree planting proposal.

In the bitter months after the election, Hoover's suspicions of Roosevelt's conservation proposals grew even deeper. He declared to Ted Joslin in July 1933 that the new administration was achieving only short-term, false economies by firing technical experts from the "Scientific and Economic Bureaus," while the new Civilian Conservation Corps was a "fabulous waste," bringing "little of results today" and "little of consequence for the future." The sinister, hidden purpose of the program, he speculated, was not to assist the "helpless unemployed," but to create "a new military arm of the Government," a view that he moderated only slightly in succeeding years.[22]

The reforestation debate, such as it was, demonstrated the degree to which Hoover had lost his creativity and retreated into ideological rigidity. Convinced that economic recovery depended on freeing individual creativity by reducing government expenditures and raising taxes in order to bring the budget into balance, the president found it difficult to consider any idea that involved expanding federal authority or spending money, even if the projects proposed could be seen as investments rather than simply doling out money in the form of relief.

Yet Hoover also showed in regard to the St. Lawrence waterway project in 1932 that where a proposal did not appear likely to cost the government money immediately, he was still capable of energy and creativity. Hoover's interest in a ship channel that would connect the Great Lakes to the Atlantic went back at least to 1920, when he testified in favor of such a project during a hearing conducted by the International Joint Commission set up by the American and Canadian governments to study and report on the idea. Following the commission's positive report in 1921, Hoover became the Harding and Coolidge administrations' most enthusiastic advocate of a waterway, urging the State Department to press it on the Canadian and British governments. In 1924 President Coolidge named him chairman of an American St. Lawrence Commission instructed to cooperate with its Canadian counterpart in evaluating the technical and political feasibility of a waterway. The American commission's 1926 report estimated that a waterway making use of the St. Lawrence and canals on the Canadian side of the border would be three to four times less expensive than any all-American route, suggested that the project had huge hydroelectric potential, and strongly recommended immediate negotiations for a "joint undertaking with the Dominion of Canada."[23]

There was much less enthusiasm about the project in Canada than in the United States, for it seemed to many Canadians that the waterway would be enormously costly and would bring few benefits to them. Although the American government continued to favor the project, and Hoover promised during the 1928 campaign that he would push it, little progress was made until the summer of 1931, when changing conditions in Canada at last removed political objections to the proposal. In November 1931 serious Canadian-American negotiations began, amid predictions that a treaty would soon be signed, but progress proved slow. Quebec Premier L. A. Taschereau insisted that no agreement could be reached without Quebec's approval, while in New York the legislature demanded that the Power Authority of the State of New York must be an equal partner with the federal and Canadian governments in the distribution of power generated as a byproduct of the seaway development. Hoover consistently took the position that the construction of the seaway was the only matter in negotiation between the United States and Canada, and that distribution of incidental power was a domestic question to be settled later, but New York Governor Franklin Roosevelt, now a presidential candidate, saw an opportunity to gain political points while defending New York's interests. Early in July, he sent a telegram to Hoover offering to come to Washington to negotiate an agreement about power distribution. The president rejected Roosevelt's offer, pointing out that "the domestic questions which may arise [under a ratified treaty] must be settled in accordance with federal and state law and in accord with the interest of all the states of the Union." He would "be glad to consult with you and other governors" after the treaty was ratified.[24] Hoover may have been correct in his statement of the situation, but Roosevelt emerged from the contretemps sounding like an advocate of inexpensive public power, while the president appeared to be opposed to it.

Unfortunately for Hoover's dreams, the treaty was not signed until 18 July 1932. With Congress in recess, there was no hope of action on it until after the presidential election. By the time Hoover presented it to the Senate in December, he had lost the election and enthusiasm for the treaty was waning. President Roosevelt subsequently gave it only tepid support, and in March 1934 it was rejected by the Senate, 46 to 42, far short of the two-thirds vote needed for approval.[25]

Hoover's long fight for the St. Lawrence Seaway rested firmly on his conviction that the principles of conservation required the full and efficient use of every river system. Yet in the end, his inept handling of the power issue, and his failure to present the project as an immense public works and relief measure, which of course it could have become, prevented it from winning popular support. Not for another quarter-century would the seaway be built, the triumph of a Republican administration shrewder than Hoover's about popularizing its goals.[26]

Hoover blamed the defeat of the seaway treaty in 1934 on Democratic partisanship, although a study of the distribution of negative votes suggests that regional interests had more to do with it than party affiliation.[27] In these first years after his electoral defeat, the former president found it difficult to say anything good about the New Deal, including its conservation policies. Thus he denounced mineral conservation policies of the National Recovery Administration as "Fascist regimentation," enthusiastically circulated to fellow Republicans a copy of a memorandum from Secretary of the Interior Harold Ickes to the director of the National Park Service ordering him to consider political loyalty when hiring, and fumed privately at what he considered "a public defamation" of his record when Ickes renamed Hoover Dam Boulder Dam.[28] Only with the passage of considerable time did he begin to recover some perspective, going so far as to say publicly in 1936 that "certain groups must be appropriately regulated to prevent waste of natural resources," but that was nearly his only public statement on conservation policy during the 1930s. The absence of responses to letters from old friends touching on the topic, and a reluctance to publicly endorse the work of the Save the Redwoods League and the Izaak Walton League, suggest that the onset of the depression had turned Hoover's attention to issues that seemed to him more important than conservation.[29]

From time to time friends persuaded the former president to take a small part in some conservation project. One such case was his involvement in the effort during the 1930s and 1940s to expand Grand Teton National Park to include Jackson Hole. Hoover had been president when Grand Teton Park was created in 1929 and was a friend of John D. Rockefeller Jr., but the administration was careful to keep hands off during succeeding years as Rockefeller attempted secretly to buy the land around Jackson Hole in order to add the valley to the park. At one point in the late 1930s, Park Service Director Horace Albright feared that Hoover might come under the influence of opponents of the Rockefeller scheme, but there was never any danger of that. In 1944 Hoover urged Congressman Christian A. Herter, an old friend, to support the incorporation of the Jackson Hole National Monument, created in 1942, into Grand Teton Park. Park expansion would make a fine memorial to Ray Lyman Wilbur, who had recently suffered a serious stroke and might soon die, wrote the former president.[30]

But Wilbur did not die, the park was not expanded, and after a 1946 fishing trip to the area as Rockefeller's guest, in 1947 Hoover again took a behind-the-scenes role in an effort to protect Jackson Hole. This time the threat came in the form of a bill sponsored by Wyoming Representative Frank A. Barrett to abolish the Jackson Hole National Monument. At the request of Albright, Hoover did some quiet lobbying against the bill, which was ultimately defeated. In 1950 the national monument was finally added to the park, which must have pleased Hoover, although there is no evidence that he had any part in the final resolution of a twenty-year struggle.[31]

The key to Hoover's role in the Jackson Hole controversy was less his interest in conservation than his personal ties to Ray Lyman Wilbur, Horace Albright, and John D. Rockefeller Jr. Nevertheless, he was a jealous defender of the Republicans' record in conservation. In 1948 he urged party leaders to claim credit for conservation achievements and berated them when they did not do so, and in 1952 he used an opportunity to make a nationally broadcast radio and television speech to claim that Republicans, not Democrats, were the party of conservation.[32]

Yet politics aside, Hoover continued to believe that the government should leave resource management to the free market. As had always been the case, he had a marked preference for private rather than public power development, but in one odd twist of events, his conservative philosophy contributed to the preservation of a wild area, the upper Colorado River valley, in the 1950s. In this instance, Hoover's opposition to public power made him an ally of conservationists fighting a proposal that the federal government build several dams.

When Dwight Eisenhower was elected president in 1952, Hoover did not acquire as much influence as he hoped.[33] He urged the new president to appoint a conservative as secretary of the interior and suggested J. Bracken Lee of Utah and Robert Moses of New York as suitable candidates, but Eisenhower instead chose Governor Douglas McKay of Oregon, a former Chevrolet dealer with little knowledge of environmental issues.[34] Nevertheless, the new administration understood the value of maintaining Hoover's goodwill, and early in 1953 Attorney General Herbert Brownell sought his advice about apportionment of Colorado River water between the upper and lower basins. Hoover replied that he did not have complete copies of the minutes of the Colorado River Commission meetings in 1922, but he noted that the commission had overestimated the flow of the river and recommended that "the real cure for all this [an inadequate supply for the upper basin states] is the construction of another large dam somewhere about Lee's Ferry."[35]

Hoover's recommendation to Brownell was in keeping with his belief that conservation required the full development of all river systems. But that conviction was soon to be challenged for Hoover and many other Americans by a major controversy over the construction of dams on the upper Colorado at Echo Park and Split Mountain within the Dinosaur National Monument. Only a few days after he wrote to Brownell, Hoover received a letter from Leslie A. Miller, a former governor of Wyoming who was currently serving on the Hoover Commission's Task Force on Water Resources and Power, urging him to oppose the construction of the proposed upper Colorado project, which included a major dam at Glen Canyon and smaller dams at Echo Park and Split Mountain. The dams, wrote Miller, would generate more power than was needed in the area and would compete directly with private utilities, an argument that exerted a powerful appeal to Hoover.[36]

Miller's warning about the threat of public power projects was reinforced the following year as the task force looked more closely at the upper Colorado proposal. In April 1954 Hoover wrote to Eisenhower urging delaying authorization of the project until the task force completed its study, and in a personal meeting with the president in early May he argued vigorously that the project was "another TVA" that would irrigate unneeded farmlands at prohibitive cost and would produce power that could not be sold at a profit sufficient to defray construction costs. Hoover hoped that his personal intervention plus the opposition of the Water Resources Task Force would be sufficient to stop the project, but on 26 May Eisenhower announced the appointment of a Cabinet Committee on Water Resources Policy headed by Secretary McKay and made up of representatives from Interior, Agriculture, Commerce, Health, Education and Welfare, Labor, the Department of the Army, and the Federal Power Commission to "assist in the Executive Branch consideration and review of the Hoover Commission Recommendations." Privately, Hoover referred to the appointment of this review board as a "double cross," fearing that it meant the Colorado project would be authorized after all.[37]

Hoover's objections to the upper Colorado project were partly practical, having to do with its likely cost, and partly ideological, having to do with his opposition to public power development, and those arguments did not outweigh practical politics in the administration's thinking. Pressed hard by supporters of development from the upper basin states, Eisenhower gave in, to Hoover's intense disgust. In his budget message in January 1955 the president requested authorization for the entire upper Colorado project, including the Echo Park dam in Dinosaur National Monument.[38]

In the meantime, the American conservation community had been waging a battle against the dams proposed for Dinosaur National Monument on entirely different grounds. This was a campaign in which Hoover had taken no part, and of which he had seemed entirely oblivious, but he now embraced the conservationists as allies.[39] Uniting groups ranging from the Sierra Club, the Izaak Walton League, and the National Wildlife Federation to the General Federation of Women's Clubs, the conservationists mobilized more than 3 million people and generated a flood of letters to members of Congress that ran 80 to 1 in opposition to the proposed dams. The conservationists succeeded where Hoover had failed, and the upper Colorado bill that passed in April 1956 eliminated the Echo Park dam and prohibited any dam in a national park. Largely overlooked by most conservationists was authorization for the construction of a large dam at Glen Canyon near Lee's Ferry, just as Hoover had recommended several years earlier.[40]

In some ways both Hoover and the conservationists who fought the Echo

Park dam were pioneering new approaches to conservation. Hoover had ignored objections to building dams in a national monument and had focused his argument on the probable costs of providing irrigation and public power to such a remote area. His arguments anticipated those of later free market environmentalists, although they were not fully worked out. The conservationists, on the other hand, demonstrated the enormous power of organized single-issue lobbying on federal policy. Although all of the arguments raised by the contenders in this case would recur in future environmental battles, the Echo Park controversy marked a turning point in American environmental history from a period when struggles were waged primarily in terms that would have been familiar to the pioneers of the movement to a new era of interest-group politics and conservative environmentalism.[41] Just as the conservationists' success in mobilizing a mass following anticipated the environmentalism of the 1960s and 1970s, so Hoover's conservative ideological approach fitted well with an evolving free market environmentalism.

If the Echo Park controversy showed the influence of a conservative economic philosophy on Hoover's conservation ideas, his work on the two Hoover commissions on government reorganization also demonstrated the consistency of his belief that conservation had a limited but significant place in federal policy. The Commission on Organization of the Executive Branch of the Government (Hoover I) was authorized by Congress in July 1947 to propose ways to integrate and rationalize federal agencies following the war and demobilization. A second commission with the same name (Hoover II) was created by Congress in 1953 to seek ways to reduce government expenditures and to eliminate competition with private enterprise.[42] In both commissions Hoover closely supervised every phase of investigation and strongly influenced the final recommendations, although by the time the second commission made its report in 1955, he was over eighty. He also worked seven days a week, with business meetings beginning at breakfast and continuing after dinner, presided over every conference of the commissioners, and attended many of the meetings of the task forces whose members he had chosen personally to study specific problems. "His accomplishments in analyzing data and drafting reports were greater than those of any other one person," declared a resolution adopted unanimously by the commissioners of Hoover II at their last meeting in 1955, and the texts of the final reports, terse and unadorned, are typical of his personal writing style.[43] There can be little doubt that the recommendations of both commissions reflected his philosophy and many of his specific ideas.

Yet despite the identity of the names of the two Hoover commissions, and the chairman's domination of their work, neither the goals nor the results of the two commissions were the same. Hoover I, created in 1947 in the midst of a Democratic administration, emphasized the necessity of rationalizing the governmental structure left over from the New Deal and the war. Had Dewey rather than Truman won in 1948, its recommendations might have been quite different, but under the circumstances, its report concentrated on the consolidation and reorganization of agencies in order to increase the president's control over the administration and thus his accountability to the voters.[44] Hoover II, set up under the Eisenhower administration, reflected a general Republican desire to reduce the size and cost of government, and to curtail cases in which governmental agencies seemed to compete with private businesses, as well as Hoover's personal belief that this was an opportunity to "lessen this invasion of State and local governments by a Federal bureaucracy from Washington." The resulting report concentrated more on governmental policy and function than on organization of the executive branch.[45]

In regard to conservation, there was strong continuity between the two commissions, and both bore the imprint of Hoover's long-standing opinions. Particularly striking in the 1949 report was the forceful reaffirmation of Hoover's belief in regrouping agencies related to conservation. Specifically, the report recommended that "all major soil, range, and forest conservation agencies," including the Bureau of Land Management, then in Interior, be put into an Agricultural Resources Conservation Service in the Department of Agriculture. This change, the report argued, would encourage the development of consistent forest and range management policies administered by the same personnel and would eliminate "conflicting, confusing, and duplicating activities" by different agencies.[46] At the same time, the report recommended that all agencies related to water development and use, such as reclamation, river and harbor improvement, flood control, and various organizations dealing with electric power, be transferred to the Department of the Interior (although Agriculture was to have an opportunity to "comment" on all reclamation projects before they were undertaken). In this way, the report concluded, water development projects could be used to relieve unemployment, and irrigation, power, and transportation uses of water could be coordinated.[47] Agencies or units of agencies having to do with mineral resources should not be transferred to the Agriculture Department, the report concluded, but consolidated in a new agency of the Interior Department to be called Mineral Resources Services. The Bureau of Fish and Wildlife should stay in the Interior Department, but a new Commercial Fisheries bureau should be created in the Commerce Department.[48]

Aside from the functional argument advanced in the report for these changes, the main justification for them was the same one that Hoover had proposed while president—that consolidation would save large amounts of money. It would be impossible to estimate how much might be saved annually in the Interior Department through consolidations, the report concluded, but "in preventing unwise projects and disastrous conflicts and by securing consolidated policies, they should [save] large sums"; in the Agriculture Department, the authors estimated, probable savings if all the commission's recommendations were adopted would amount to over $44 million.[49]

The report did not address ways to secure better planning in the development of resources. This was hardly surprising, given Hoover's own outlook, and the general business and commercial-agriculture orientation of most members of the task forces that undertook the specific studies that were the basis of the report.[50] Hoover I reflected the opinion of its chairman and most members that the market should be fettered as little as possible.

Assessing the results of Hoover I in regard to conservation is difficult. Hoover organized the Citizens Committee for the Hoover Report in 1949 to publicize and lobby for the adoption of the report's reforms. With both national and local branches, the committee was a powerful publicity agency, and through the donated services of the J. Walter Thompson advertising agency, it bombarded the country with propaganda. By some measures, the approach was effective. In 1952 the Citizens Committee estimated that more than half of the report's recommendations had been enacted, and Hoover himself believed that the figure was 55 percent. But what was adopted had to do primarily with national security and general governmental housekeeping. Virtually none of the major conservation proposals was implemented.[51] A plan for the administrative reorganization of the Department of the Interior submitted to Congress by President Truman was approved in 1950, but it did not include the major transfers of agencies proposed by the report. A second presidential plan, for the reorganization of the Department of Agriculture, also proposed in 1950, was defeated by Congress.[52]

In 1953 Hoover got a chance to revisit conservation issues during the work of the second Hoover Commission. He found the terrain somewhat altered. A Republican administration was now in office, and the Ferguson-Brown bill that set up the new commission reflected conservative values, particularly in its stress on the elimination of "non-essential services, functions, and activities which are competitive with private enterprise." The new commission was not required to be nonpartisan, and it was given power to subpoena witnesses and to recommend specific legislation or constitutional amendments. Hoover declared enthusiastically that the commission could recommend measures to "give release of the States from Federal dictation and remove taints of Socialism," in particular by eliminating public competition with private power companies. Two months later, he told friends at the Bohemian Grove in California that the task of the commission would be "to lessen this invasion of State and local governments by a Federal bureaucracy from Washington."[53]

Such comments, which were fairly widely known, must have strengthened a fear already prevalent among Democrats that the real agenda of the new commission was the wholesale repeal of the New Deal. Hoover's election as chairman at the commission's first meeting in September 1953 did little to allay these concerns, although he complained that he was "not in any inner circle of influence" in the new administration.[54] Eisenhower and Hoover met at various official occasions, but not until the summer of 1954 did the president really offer Hoover any sort of intimacy. In August of that year Ike invited the former president to join him for a fishing holiday in the Rockies during which Eisenhower promised to do the cooking.[55] It was a typically gracious—and politically adroit—gesture, but Hoover could not fail to notice that it came more than a year after the new administration was well under way, with appointments and policy pretty well set.

The fact was that Eisenhower did not share Hoover's passion for slashing the federal government, and may have consented to giving Hoover II a broad mandate to study "the vast terrain of policy" in hopes of bogging it down in issues so "swampy" that there was little chance it would produce specific recommendations.[56] If that was the case, Hoover fell into the morass. He declared that although the new commission would urge the adoption of the remaining recommendations of the first Hoover Commission, it would concentrate on seeking methods to reduce spending for everything but defense to "the very minimum."[57] As one expert on administration later observed, Hoover II was "predominantly concerned with what the government should not do rather than how it should be organized and managed" to assure "effective administration accompanied by political accountability."[58] That emphasis on policy rather than on administrative specifics seems to have been exactly what Eisenhower wanted.

The members of Hoover II generally exemplified its antigovernment bias. The twelve members of the commission included seven conservative Republicans and four conservative Democrats, with only one liberal Democrat, Representative Chet Holifield of California, who was usually the lone dissenter from the antigovernmental outlook of the group.[59] Of nearly 150 staff members and members of various task forces who prepared the reports upon which the overall report of the commission was based, the great majority came from business and the professions, not from government. The task force on Water Resources and Power, which was the only one concerned with conservation, was filled with businessmen, lawyers, accountants, and engineers associated with private utilities. It was so hostile to public power that the commissioners, in preparing their final report, softened the task force's conclusions.[60]

Having largely handpicked the members, Hoover dominated Hoover II even more than he had the first commission.[61] He even asked the members to sign a statement automatically assigning him their proxies in case they had to be absent from a meeting. The administration, however, ignored his demand that they promise not to take any action on a broad range of matters that might come before the commission until it completed its report.[62]

The largest, most expensive, and most politically sensitive of the commission's task forces was the one on Water Resources and Power. Chaired by the ultraconservative Admiral Ben Moreell, chairman of the board of Jones and Laughlin Steel Company, the task force was instructed by Hoover to attack the whole concept of public power. In a memorandum he sent to Moreell a month before the task force's first meeting, Hoover simply took for granted that "state governments could do a better job of administration than the remote control from Washington" and instructed the task force to seek out examples of "coercion or bureaucratic tyranny over competitive private enterprise."[63] Frankly avowing their opposition to TVA and other public power projects, Hoover and Moreell clearly intended to strike at this major New Deal legacy.

By the time the Hoover II report was submitted in June 1955, the administration's support of the upper Colorado project had already demonstrated a substantial difference of opinion between the task force and the White House. The report made that difference explicit. The administration was inclined to continue the federal development of water resources that had been the heart of New Deal policy; the commission recommended that the federal role be confined to supporting projects that were essential to furthering the national interest or accomplishing broad national objectives, and whose "size, complexity, or potential multiple purposes or benefits put the project beyond the means or needs of local or private enterprise." Aside from proposing that Congress draft a national water policy to define when the federal government should and should not undertake a specific project, and urging close scrutiny of existing water projects to assure they were being run efficiently, the main commission recommendation was "to minimize competition with private enterprise in future development of Government power."[64]

Hoover was well aware of the potential conflict between the commission's ideas about water policy and the administration's wishes. After talking with presidential assistant Sherman Adams, in the final report Hoover softened the task force's assertion that federal water projects were practically never justified and backed away from the task force's recommendation that TVA be stripped of most of its functions, and he also dropped his personal opposition to the upper Colorado project.[65] He believed that in return for these concessions, the president would support the commission's report on water and power. When the administration responded coolly, Hoover threatened to take his case to the Republican Party and the people through the Citizens Committee for the Hoover Report, an organization of businessmen that he had set up to publicize the work of Hoover I and now reorganized to create public support for Hoover II. In addition, in 1956 he created a Committee of Task Force Members to lobby the administration and Congress directly.[66]

Despite the strenuous efforts of Hoover and other advocates of the report, the White House by no means embraced all of the commission's recommendations. The administration moved fairly expeditiously to implement uncontroversial recommendations involving personnel, paperwork, public property, and various administrative functions. In 1958 they announced that 77.1 percent of the commission's recommendations had been accepted and 76 percent of them put into effect. That was misleading. With regard to the water resources report, the administration accepted just 19 percent of commission recommendations and ended up implementing only 15 percent.[67] Since Hoover and the commissioners regarded the water resources and power recommendations as the most important work of Hoover II, Eisenhower's reluctance to embrace them was particularly galling.

Hoover's threats had little effect in securing support for the commission's water and power recommendations. In addition to the fact that after 1954 Congress was controlled by Democrats who certainly did not share the Hoover commission's hostility to public power, federal water and power projects enjoyed bipartisan support among legislators. No Congressman, Republican or Democrat, was eager to vote against federal programs that brought millions of dollars into states and districts. Even if the administration had pushed Hoover II's more radical water policy recommendations, which they did not, Congress would have killed them. By the end of the 1950s the commission's water and power proposals had largely vanished from public awareness.

Obscured by the political battles over Hoover II's water and power recommendations was an unresolved contradiction built into the report. The problem was that while the report recommended that "water resources be developed to assure their optimum use and maximum contribution to the national economic growth, strength, and general welfare," and that "water resources development generally be undertaken by drainage areas—locally and regionally," it also argued that the federal government should "assume responsibility only when participation or initiative is necessary to further—or safeguard—the national interest or to accomplish broad national objectives. . . . Otherwise responsibility should be discharged by State and local governments, local organizations, or private enterprise."[68] Nowhere in the report was there any explanation of how it would be possible to safeguard the national interest, assure the maximum development of resources, and guarantee development according to drainage basins that often crossed political jurisdictions, and to have all of that done by state, local, or private authorities. The experience of negotiating interstate water and oil agreements, undertaken during the years while Hoover was secretary of commerce and president, suggested that such arrangements could only be achieved with immense pain, toil, and delay, when they could be achieved at all. Some—perhaps most—members of the task force would have been glad to commit absolutely to private control without mentioning the national interest. The unresolved contradiction built into Hoover II was that in an era when water use, especially in the West, was increasing, and even the doctrinaires on the task force recognized that water planning needed to be national or at least regional, neither they nor Hoover could explain how to combine national planning with local and private control. As Congressman Holifield, the most important dissenter from Hoover II, later said, it was possible to believe that the commission's proposals were "carelessly thrown together" in an apparent effort "to stop federal power development for the sake of private utilities" rather than as a serious attempt to resolve the basic question of how to decentralize and privatize conservation activities.[69]

Hoover's chairmanship of the second Commission on Organization of the Executive Branch of the Government was his last major attempt to come to terms with a problem that had occupied much of his public life. Put simply, the problem was whether it was possible to achieve a national conservation program that would secure the efficient use of resources, minimize waste in production, preserve wild areas and wildlife, and secure environmental quality and recreational opportunities for ordinary Americans, all with a minimum of federal planning and control and a maximum of local and private initiative. This was a problem that Hoover had addressed with energy and creativity while secretary of commerce but had found more problematic during and after his presidency when the depression evoked public demands for national policies to control and apportion scarce resources. Convinced that a return to national prosperity depended on liberating individual initiative, Hoover found himself deeply hostile to New Deal environmental planning and management programs, yet he was not, except perhaps briefly in the 1930s, entirely sympathetic to the arguments of conservatives who wanted to eliminate all government guidance and control over the market. Taken together, the depression and political ostracism made it difficult for him to think constructively about how to achieve a national conservation program with local instruments.

Was it possible to implement a national environmental policy through decentralized methods? This is a question much debated by economists and free market environmentalists in recent years.[70] Hoover, with his emphasis on American individualism and his search for ways to decentralize control over conservation moved in that direction while secretary of commerce and president, and after 1932 his aversion to the New Deal sometimes led him to express extreme free market/antigovernmental sentiments. But in the end he always believed that a positive role for government was necessary to protect the public interest and prevent abuses by selfish individuals. Moreover, although he attempted to minimize the role of the federal government in conservation, he fully expected that its supervisory role would be taken over by state and local governments. He did not share the confidence of free market environmentalists that market mechanisms alone could be expected to assure the conservation of resources and the quality of the environment.

Hoover was aware that conditions of the early 1920s were not necessarily permanent, and his efforts to develop countercyclical planning and conservation programs were attempts to perpetuate and deepen prosperity. What he did not fully come to terms with, however, was the tendency toward increasing centralization in the modern corporation and in the national economy. When he spoke of his desire to "centralize ideas and decentralize execution," he was proposing an approach that was not only contrary to the great economic tendency of the times, but that was self-contradictory as well. It was an approach that could work only in some idealized world in which all men were rational, where the great majority was willing to subordinate their judgment to that of leaders even on matters affecting their personal welfare, and where everyone would pass up immediate gratification in return for a promise that even more wonderful benefits would be available in the future. In a time of prosperity and optimism, Americans accepted some—though never all—policies based on this sort of thinking, but they could not accept it after the crash.

Hoover, too, found his faith shaken by the depression. The very qualities of hard work, determined rationalism, and long-range thinking that had seemed to explain both his personal success and national success prior to 1929 now seemed discredited. Methods of decentralization, voluntarism, and individual initiative that had seemed to work well a few years earlier were no longer effective. Expanding prosperity could not be taken as inevitable, and Hoover responded to the crisis in a very human fashion. Rather than reexamine his basic philosophy, he reaffirmed it more vigorously than ever, rejected all criticisms of it, and blamed the New Dealers for the nation's failure to enter the new era the Republicans had promised in the 1920s.

Although Hoover's failures were partly the result of personal limitations that crippled his political leadership after the beginning of the depression, his career should not be seen as a tragedy. The same qualities of devotion to work, determined rationalism, long-range thinking, and inability to reveal emotion in public that contributed to his failure as president also explain his success prior to 1929. His ideas about decentralization, voluntarism, and individual initiative that seemed politically anachronistic in the 1950s and 1960s prefigured the envirocapitalist movement but also, ironically, embodied the same values that Samuel P. Hays has described as defining the popular environmental movement of the 1960s and 1970s.[71] Just as Hoover constantly sought a middle route between governmental activism and passivity and a balance between federal and local initiatives in conservation during the 1920s, at the end of his life he was exploring a path between those who believed that environmental protection could be left entirely to market mechanisms and those who sought to mobilize mass demands for ever more extensive governmental management. Progressive and conservative, Hoover died as he had lived, resisting all efforts to pigeonhole him ideologically.

Notes

Abbreviations Used in Citing Manuscript Collections

Herbert Hoover Papers, Hoover Presidential Library, West Branch, Iowa:

GENERAL CITATION	HP
Pre-Commerce Period, 1874–1921	Pre-Com
Commerce Period, 1921–28	Com
Campaign & Transition Period, 1928–29	C&T
Presidential Period, Cabinet Offices, 1929–33	PC
Individual File, 1929–33	PI
Personal File, 1929–33	PP
Secretary's File, 1929–33	PSec
States File, 1929–33	PSt
Subject File, 1929–33	PS
Post-Presidential Period, Subject File, 1933–64	PPS
Individual File, 1933–64	PPI
General File, 1933–64	PPG

Other Collections at the Hoover Library to which abbreviated references are made:

Colorado River Commission, 1921–33	CRC
Commission on the Conservation and Administration of the Public Domain (Garfield Commission), 1929–33	GC
Ray Lyman Wilbur Papers	RLW

Collections at the Hoover Institution on War, Revolution and Peace at Stanford University:

Herbert Hoover Papers	HPS
Ray Lyman Wilbur Papers	RLWS

Collections at the National Archives, Washington, D.C.:

Agriculture Department

Office of the Secretary, General Correspondence, 1906–70 (RG 16)	AGC
Office of the Secretary, Letters Sent, 1893–1929 (RG 16)	AL
Office of the Secretary, Press Copies of Personal Letters Sent, 1921–25 (RG 16)	APL

Office of the Secretary, Letters Sent, Forest Service, 1906–29 (RG 16)	AFS
Forest Service Records (RG 95)	FS

Commerce Department

Office of the Secretary, General Records (RG 40)	CGF
Bureau of Fisheries, Central File (RG 22)	BFC
Fish & Wildlife Service, General Classified Files (RG 22)	FWS
Fish & Wildlife Service, Concerning Oil Pollution of Waters, 1920–33 (RG 22)	FWSP

Interior Department

Office of the Secretary, General Files, 1907–36 (RG 48)	IGF
Office of the Secretary, Hubert Work, 1923–28 (RG 48)	IHW
Bureau of Reclamation (RG 115)	BR
Geological Survey, Office of the Director, 1912–49 (RG 57)	GSD
National Park Service (RG 79)	NPS
Federal Oil Conservation Board (RG 48)	FOCB

Miscellaneous

National Conference on Outdoor Recreation, 1924–33 (RG 220)	NCOR

Introduction

1. *The New Day: Campaign Speeches of Herbert Hoover, 1928* (Stanford, Calif.: Stanford University Press, 1928), p. 16.

2. Quoted in Olivier Zunz, *Why the American Century?* (Chicago: University of Chicago Press, 1998), p. 85.

3. The first of these questions has been little studied. For a meditation on the second, see Daniel Horowitz, *The Morality of Spending: Attitudes toward the Consumer Society in America, 1875–1940* (Baltimore: Johns Hopkins University Press, 1985).

4. Robert H. Wiebe, *Self-Rule: A Cultural History of American Democracy* (Chicago: University of Chicago Press, 1995), pp. 141–43.

5. I am indebted to George Nash for pointing out that this tension helps to make sense of Hoover's approach to conservation. Samuel Hays notes a similar tension as characteristic of early-twentieth-century thought as well. See his *Conservation and the Gospel of Efficiency: The Progressive Conservation Movement, 1890–1920* (Cambridge, Mass.: Harvard University Press, 1959). Nowhere was Hoover's desire to make the expertise of the national class available for the voluntary guidance of local leaders more obvious than in the report of the President's Research Committee on Social Trends, which published in 1933 fifteen hundred pages of text, charts, and tables

surveying its subject. But the compilers were careful not to translate their findings into recommendations for federal programs. Their volumes contained, they wrote, "such substantial stuff as may serve as a basis for social action, rather than recommendations as to the form which action should take." Quoted in Barry Karl, "Presidential Planning and Social Science Research: Mr. Hoover's Experts," *Perspectives in American History* 3 (1969): 379.

6. Arthur S. Link, "What Happened to the Progressive Movement in the 1920s?" *American Historical Review* 44 (July 1959): 833–51.

7. Daniel O. Buehler, "Permanence and Change in Theodore Roosevelt's Conservation Jeremiad," *Western Journal of Communication* 62 (Fall 1998): 439–40.

8. Ibid., 454.

9. Although these assumptions are drawn from a modern work on conservative environmentalism, I believe they accurately depict Hoover's outlook. See James R. Dunn and John E. Kinney, *Conservative Environmentalism: Reassessing the Means, Redefining the Ends* (Westport, Conn.: Quorum, 1996), p. xii.

10. Herbert Hoover, *The Challenge to Liberty* (New York: Scribner's, 1934), pp. 2–3.

11. Quoted in Craig Lloyd, *Aggressive Introvert: A Study of Herbert Hoover and Public Relations Management, 1912–1932* (Columbus: Ohio State University Press, 1972), p. 56 n. 33.

12. Among the many valuable works that might be cited are J. Leonard Bates, *The Origins of Teapot Dome: Progressives, Politics, and Petroleum, 1909–1921* (Urbana: University of Illinois Press, 1963); Norris Hundley, *Water and the West: The Colorado River Compact and the Politics of Water in the American West* (Berkeley: University of California Press, 1975); Gerald D. Nash, *United States Oil Policy, 1890–1964: Business and Government in Twentieth Century America* (Pittsburgh: University of Pittsburgh Press, 1968); Burl Noggle, *Teapot Dome: Oil and Politics in the 1920s* (Baton Rouge: Louisiana State University Press, 1962); William G. Robbins, *Lumberjacks and Legislators: Political Economy of the U.S. Lumber Industry, 1890–1941* (College Station: Texas A&M University Press, 1982); Donald C. Swain, *Federal Conservation Policy, 1921–1933* (Berkeley: University of California Press, 1963).

13. "Recent scholarship," writes one historian, "suggests that environmental integrity cannot be achieved if the autonomy of the market economy is maintained." William G. Robbins, "Prospects for Environmental History: A Review Essay," *Journal of Forest History* 22 (Apr. 1978): 104. For a discussion of conservatives and conservation in the 1980s that concludes that their policies fostered development and exploitation of resources, see Patrick Allitt, "Conservatives and Conservation in the Reagan-Bush Era," paper delivered at the meeting of the Organization of American Historians, 1996.

14. Ellis Hawley, who has contributed so notably to the modern rediscovery of Hoover, makes a similar point in his work on Hoover's attempt to create a self-regulating economic system through a partnership between government and business

associations. See, for example, Ellis Hawley, "Herbert Hoover, the Commerce Secretariat, and the Vision of an 'Associative State,' 1921–1928," *Journal of American History* 61 (June 1974): 116–40.

15. William J. Barber, *From New Era to New Deal: Herbert Hoover, the Economists, and American Economic Policy, 1921–1933* (Cambridge, England: Cambridge University Press, 1985), and William Leach, *Land of Desire: Merchants, Power, and the Rise of a New American Culture* (New York: Pantheon, 1993), are among the few historians of consumerism in this period who pay serious attention to Hoover.

1. Through a Child's Eyes

1. There is no firsthand account of the evening described here, but there is evidence that something of the sort did happen. For Herbert Hoover's recollections of sledding, see *The Memoirs of Herbert Hoover: Years of Adventure, 1874–1920* (New York: Macmillan, 1951), pp. 1–2 [hereafter cited as *Memoirs* 1], and Herbert Hoover, *On Growing Up: Letters to American Boys and Girls* (New York: Morrow, 1962), p. 21. For Tad Hoover's rather different recollections of Bert's disappointments, see his unpublished memoir, "Memoranda, Being a Statement by an Engineer," pp. 14–15, 20, in the Theodore Hoover Memoranda, Box 1, Folder "HOOVER, Theodore J.," Herbert Hoover Presidential Library, West Branch, Iowa [hereafter HHPL].

2. Quoted in Will Irwin, *Herbert Hoover: A Reminiscent Biography* (New York: Grosset & Dunlap, 1928), p. 7.

3. George H. Nash, *The Life of Herbert Hoover: The Engineer, 1874–1914* (New York: W. W. Norton, 1983), pp. 2–5 [hereafter cited as Nash, *Hoover* 1].

4. Hulda Hoover to her mother and Agnes [Minthorn Miles], 15 Mar. 1883, in Hulda H. McLean Papers, Box 1, "Letters of Hulda Randall Minthorn Hoover," Hoover Institution on War, Revolution and Peace, Stanford University [hereafter Hoover Institution]; Nash, *Hoover* 1:8–9.

5. Hoover, *Memoirs* 1:4. Major Miles was Indian agent from 24 June 1878 until 30 June 1885, and again from 20 May 1889 to 16 June 1893. Hoover's residence with him took place some time between the death of his father on 13 Dec. 1880, and that of his mother on 24 Feb. 1884, but the exact dates and the length of the visit are uncertain.

6. Ibid., 5.

7. "Tribute to Dr. Henry John Minthorn and Laura Ellen, His Wife," by Mary Minthorn Strench, ca. 16 Jan. 1955, General Acquisitions, Box 1, "Barker, Burt Brown, Unitled Folder," HHPL.

8. Levi D. Johnson to HH, 6 Apr. 1926, Herbert Hoover Papers, HHPL, Commerce Period [hereafter Com], Personal File, Box 268; Theodore Hoover Memoranda, p. 15, HHPL. There are good accounts of this event in David Burner, *Herbert Hoover: A Public Life* (New York: Knopf, 1979), p. 6, and Nash, *Hoover* 1:4. Nash quotes

Grandmother Minthorn as saying at the time almost exactly the same thing as Johnson later wrote.

9. Hoover, *Memoirs* 1:5. Buried between the two quoted phrases is the bleak sentence: "My own parents were among their [contagious diseases] victims." See also "Information for Biographers," HHPL, Pre-Com, Subject, "Articles about or by HH, 1916—Information for Biographers by HH," Box 28; Irwin, *Herbert Hoover,* passim.

10. Hoover, *Memoirs* 1:2–3; Theodore Hoover Memoranda, p. 24, HHPL.

11. Hoover, *Memoirs* 1:7. An evangelist named David Updegraff visited West Branch in 1879 and preached a revivalism foreign to old-line Quakers. Jesse and Hulda seem to have been influenced by him and stayed with their meeting when conservatives left it. In 1883 the Springdale Monthly Meeting formally entered Hulda's name as a minister. See Nash, *Hoover* 1:9–10.

12. Nash, *Hoover* 1:8–9.

13. Hoover, *Memoirs* 1:4–5; Nash, *Hoover* 1:10. Psychoanalyst Heinz Kohut argued that the child deprived of an empathetic response and an appropriate model of maturity by the absence of parents or by their distancing behavior never really develops a mature, integrated personality. See, for example, Heinz Kohut, *The Restoration of the Self* (Madison, Wis.: International Universities Press, 1977), pp. 233–37, 274. Kohut's theories and their implications are explained very clearly by Michael St. Clair, *Object Relations and Self Psychology: An Introduction,* 2nd ed. (Pacific Grove, Calif.: Brooks/ Cole, 1996), pp. 151–74. St. Clair paraphrases Kohut's interpretation of the sense of loss felt by children who had experiences comparable to those of the Hoover children this way: "To be separated from the perfect object [the parent] is to be powerless and empty" (p. 163). Kohut's theories built on the work of D. W. Winnicott, W. R. D. Fairbairn, and Harry Stack Sullivan, among others. See Jay R. Greenberg and Stephen A. Mitchell, *Object Relations in Psychoanalytic Theory* (Cambridge, Mass.: Harvard University Press, 1983), pp. 366–70.

14. Theodore Hoover Memoranda, pp. 33, 24. The second quotation was in reference to the death of Jesse Hoover, but it applies equally forcefully to the mother's death as well.

15. Hoover, *Memoirs* 1:1 n. 1.

16. "Information for Biographers," HHPL, Pre-Com Subject, Box 28, "Articles about or by HH, 1916–."

17. Hoover, *Memoirs* 1:5–6; Hoover, "Information for Biographers," p. 1, HHPL. The uncle in Oregon who took Bert in was Dr. Henry John Minthorn, who had earlier saved Bert's life during his croup attack, an event that is also unmentioned in the *Memoirs.* For the spelling of Uncle Allen's name, see Nash, *Hoover* 1:11; Hoover's son's name was spelled Allan.

18. Hoover, *Memoirs* 1:3, 6.

19. Rose Wilder Lane, *The Making of Herbert Hoover* (New York: Century, 1920), p. 62.

20. Levi T. Pennington oral history, p. 14, HHPL.

21. Hoover, *Memoirs* 1:10-11.

22. Ibid., 11-12.

23. Charles A. and Hulda Hoover McLean oral history, p. 27, HHPL.

24. M. Leona Nichols, "Pioneer Woman Tells of Hungry, Hard-Working Boy, Now President," from the Portland *Oregonian*, 15 July 1931, in President's Personal File, Box 149, "Hoover, Herbert Bio. Info. 1931-33," HHPL; Elmer Edson Washburn, "Westward across Four Frontiers," p. 3, in Pre-Com File, Box 29, "Subj-Articles about HH," HHPL; Burt Brown Barker oral history, p. 83, Hoover Institution.

25. Quoted in Burner, *Hoover*, p. 14.

26. Loren Chandler oral history, p. 4, HHPL.

27. Hoover, *Memoirs* 1:11.

28. Theodore Hoover Memoranda, p. 57, HHPL.

29. Ibid., p. 58.

30. Nash, *Hoover* 1:14-16.

31. Ibid.

32. Copy of Henry John Minthorn to William F. Smith, ca. (?) August 1917, Ray Lyman Wilbur Papers, Hoover Institution, Box 120, "HH-RLW (2)."

33. Nash, *Hoover* 1:23-25. Many years later Hoover recalled that the books Miss Gray introduced him to "opened a new world" for him. He wrote "Thank You, Miss Gray!" for the July 1959 issue of *Reader's Digest* and often sent copies of it to children who wrote to him. See Hoover, *Growing Up*, p. 150.

34. Hoover, *Memoirs* 1:15.

35. Nash, *Hoover* 1:19-23.

36. Hoover, *Memoirs* 1:3, 13.

37. Hoover, "In Praise of Izaak Walton," *Atlantic* 139 (June 1927): 819. The order of the sentences has been reversed.

38. For example, Hoover, *Memoirs* 1:14. For more detailed discussion of Hoover's concerns with water pollution and fisheries, see pages 65-72 of this volume.

39. Hoover, *Memoirs* 1:3; Hoover to Will H. Dilg, 2 Dec. 1924, Box 130, Com, 1921-28, HHPL. For further speculation on the meaning of fishing to Hoover, see Kendrick A. Clements, "Herbert Hoover and the Fish," *The Journal of Psychohistory* 10 (Winter 1983): 333-48. A number of people who knew Hoover in the Oregon period believed that he was frequently hungry, but the Minthorns were not impoverished, and they certainly did not mistreat the boy. If Bert was hungry, it was probably because he was a growing teenager. Not for Hoover, however, was the relaxed attitude exemplified by the wonderful first line of Norman Maclean's *A River Runs Through It* (Chicago: University of Chicago Press, 1983), "In our family, there was no clear line between religion and fly fishing" (p. 3).

40. Hoover, *Memoirs* 1:8, 7; Martin L. Fausold, *The Presidency of Herbert Hoover* (Lawrence: University Press of Kansas, 1985), pp. 1-3.

41. Fausold, *Presidency of Herbert Hoover*, p. 4.

42. Hoover, *Memoirs* 1:7–8. See also David Burner, "The Quaker Faith of Herbert Hoover," in *Understanding Herbert Hoover: Ten Perspectives*, ed. Lee Nash (Stanford, Calif.: Hoover Institution Press, 1987), pp. 55–64.

43. Burt Brown Barker oral history, p. 17. See also Craig Lloyd, *Aggressive Introvert: A Study of Herbert Hoover and Public Relations Management, 1912–1932* (Columbus: Ohio State University Press, 1972), pp. 3–6.

44. Clipping, "Herbert Hoover through the Eyes of His Puget Sound Cousin," Seattle *Daily Times*, 12 Feb. 1928, in HHPL, Com Papers, Box 37, "Articles & Speeches Referring to HH, 1928 February–March."

45. George H. Nash, *Herbert Hoover: The Humanitarian, 1914–1917* (New York: W. W. Norton, 1988), p. 255 [hereafter Nash, *Hoover* 2]. It is worth noting, however, that in 1939 Hoover sought and received reinstatement as a member of the Society of Friends meeting in Newberg, Oregon. See Hoover to Newberg Monthly Meeting of Friends, 27 June 1939, and Mary C. Sutton, Recording Clerk of the Newberg Meeting, to Hoover, 10 July 1939, HP:PPS, Box 182, Folder "Hoover Church Affiliation, 1939–40."

46. Byron Price oral history, p. 9; Russel V. Lee, M.D., oral history, p. 8; Mildred Hall Campbell oral history, p. 18, all at Hoover Institution; George Akerson to Ray Lyman Wilbur, 12 Aug. 1930, Herbert Hoover Papers, Box 43, "Interior, 1930 (A,B,C)," Hoover Institution.

47. Felix Morley oral history, p. 80, HHPL; Calvin Albury oral history, pp. 23–24, Hoover Institution. Hoover's successor in the White House well understood the value to the country in a time of economic crisis of seeing the president relaxed, laughing, and confident; in the presidency, style can be substance.

48. See, for example, Robert W. Wall oral history, pp. 12–13, and Charles A. and Hulda Hoover McLean oral history, p. 27, both in HHPL; Eugene Lyons oral history, p. 18, Hoover Institution. This is not to suggest that Hoover was constantly trying throughout his life to recreate through others a relationship with his dead parents. The need for others is constant throughout life, but the quality of the need changes. See Arnold Goldberg, ed., *Advances in Self-Psychology* (New York: International Universities Press, 1980), p. 130.

49. Eugene Lyons oral history, p. 6, and William C. Mullendore oral history, Pt. I, pp. 3–4, both at Hoover Institution; Felix Morley oral history, p. 16, HHPL.

50. Quoted from a 1928 article by Henry F. Pringle by Lloyd, *Aggressive Introvert*, p. 4. Hoover's excessive sensitivity to slights is suggestive of a "narcissistic self disorder" resulting from his sense of being abandoned by his parents and the absence of empathetic understanding from those who raised him. See St. Clair, *Object Relations and Self Psychology*, p. 164. To put the matter another way, "disorders of the self in general are understood as environmental deficiency diseases; the caretakers have failed to allow the child to establish and slowly dissolve the [relationships which] generate

healthy structures within the self," and "disorders of the self reflect desperate and necessarily futile attempts to shore up the defective self." Greenberg and Mitchell, *Object Relations in Psychoanalytical Theory*, p. 356.

51. Nash, *Hoover* 2:371–72. If, as seems likely, Hoover's drive to achievement was in part a compensation for "defects in the structure of the self . . . due to deficits in childhood," who would wish that he had had a perfectly balanced personality? See St. Clair, *Object Relations and Self Psychology*, p. 164; Greenberg and Mitchell, *Object Relations in Psychoanalytic Theory*, p. 369.

52. James H. Rowe oral history, p. 10, Hoover Institution.

2. The Engineer and the Gentleman

1. Herbert Hoover, *The Memoirs of Herbert Hoover. Volume 1: Years of Adventure, 1874–1920* (New York: Macmillan, 1951), pp. 131–32 [hereafter cited as *Memoirs* 1]; George H. Nash, "The Social Philosophy of Herbert Hoover," in *Herbert Hoover Reassessed: Essays Commemorating the Fiftieth Anniversary of the Inauguration of Our Thirty-First President*, ed. Mark O. Hatfield (Washington: Government Printing Office, 1981), pp. 92–93.

2. George H. Nash, *The Life of Herbert Hoover: The Engineer, 1874–1914* (New York: W. W. Norton, 1983), pp. 22–24 [hereafter cited as Nash, *Hoover* 1]; Hoover, *Memoirs* 1:14. At a time when most "engineers" were more skilled workmen than trained professionals, Hoover's shrewd decision to seek university-level technical training would help him become a leader of a new technical elite that increasingly dominated many fields of American life in the early twentieth century.

3. Hoover, *Memoirs* 1:15.

4. Copy of Joseph Swain to Hoover, 6 Mar. 1899, HP:Pre-Com, Box 17, Folder "General Accession—Swain, Joseph, 1899–1920."

5. Nash, *Hoover* 1:24–25.

6. Ibid., 19–39, 573.

7. For Lou Henry's early years, see Rosemary F. Carroll, "Lou Henry Hoover: The Emergence of a Leader, 1874–1916," in *Lou Henry Hoover: Essays on a Busy Life*, ed. Dale C. Mayer (Worland, Wyo.: High Plains Publishing, 1994), pp. 13–34.

8. Nash, *Hoover* 1:30.

9. Ibid., 30–44; Hoover, *Memoirs* 1:17.

10. Hoover, *Memoirs* 1:24. With a Stanford engineering degree and valuable contacts in the field, Hoover was hardly a helpless youth.

11. Nash, *Hoover* 1:44–47; Hoover, *Memoirs* 1:25–27. The quotation is found on p. 27. Interestingly, Hoover's account of this period downplays the importance of his special knowledge and skills in securing a permanent position with the Janin firm and seems instead to stress chance and luck.

12. Hoover, *Memoirs* 1:17–18; copies of Hoover to Nell May Hill, 19 July 1894, 9

Nov. 1894, 9 July 1895, 7 Sept. 1895, HP:Pre-Com, Box 8, Folder "Hill, Nell May, 1894–1895."

13. Hoover to Dr. J. C. Branner, 2 Sept. 1894, John Caspar Branner Papers, Box 25, Folder 98, Stanford University Archives [hereafter Stanford Archives]; copy of Hoover to Nell May Hill, 19 July 1894, HP:Pre-Com, Box 8, Folder "Hill, Nell May, 1894–1895."

14. Copy of HH to May Hoover, 4 Aug. 1895, HP:Pre-Com, Box 8, Folder "Hoover, May, 8-4-95."

15. Ibid.; Hoover to J. C. Branner, 2 Sept. 1894, Branner Papers, Box 25, Folder 98, Stanford Archives.

16. Edwin T. Layton Jr., *The Revolt of the Engineers: Social Responsibility and the American Engineering Profession* (Baltimore: The Johns Hopkins University Press, 1986), p. viii.

17. Nash, *Hoover* 1:50–222.

18. Hoover, *Memoirs* 1:28, 74.

19. Nash, *Hoover* 1:60–61, 71–73, 80–81, 101–102. By 1909 Hoover had changed his mind about unions and had even come to believe that the compulsory arbitration systems of Australia and New Zealand were a good idea. See Herbert Hoover, *Principles of Mining: Valuation, Organization and Administration: Copper, Gold, Lead, Silver, Tin and Zinc* (New York: McGraw-Hill, 1909), pp. 167–68.

20. Quoted in Nash, *Hoover* 1:384; ibid., 225.

21. *Memoirs* 1:89.

22. Hoover, *Principles of Mining*, pp. 154–60.

23. George Nash has traced Hoover's part in the complex web of international financial transactions of this period as fully and clearly as anyone is ever likely to be able to do. See *Hoover* 1:223–513.

24. Will Irwin, *Herbert Hoover: A Reminiscent Biography* (New York: Grosset & Dunlap, 1928), p. 107.

25. Ibid., pp. 101, 108.

26. Ibid., p. 123. Hoover began talking about getting out of business as early as 1904 but could not disentangle himself completely until the beginning of the war a decade later. See Nash, *Hoover* 1:379–81, 512–13. The exact amount of Hoover's fortune is difficult to assess, but Nash estimates that by his fortieth birthday in 1914, he was worth at least $1 million. Ibid., 570.

27. George H. Nash, *The Life of Herbert Hoover: The Humanitarian, 1914–1917* (New York: W. W. Norton, 1988), p. 250 [hereafter cited as Nash, *Hoover* 2].

28. Ibid., pp. 3–14; Martin Fausold, *The Presidency of Herbert Hoover* (Lawrence: University Press of Kansas, 1985), pp. 8–9.

29. Nash, *Hoover* 2:17–30. Nash's full and meticulously honest account of the Belgian relief program, which is the main topic of this volume, makes it clear that Hoover's role was both larger and more important than he remembered, and in some ways more petty and self-serving. A reputation for successfully organizing large

enterprises made Hoover a logical candidate to run the Belgian relief program, but as James P. Johnson points out, his passionate commitment to the CRB was probably related to the psychic stresses of his childhood. See "Herbert Hoover: The Orphan as Children's Friend," *Prologue* 12 (Winter 1980): 193–206.

30. Nash, *Hoover* 2:362–65, sums up the achievements of the CRB. My summary greatly understates the magnitude of the achievement.

31. David Burner, *Herbert Hoover: A Public Life* (New York: Knopf, 1979), pp. 79–81.

32. From a speech by Hoover, 18 Dec. 1914, quoted in Nash, *Hoover* 2:95.

33. Burner, *Hoover*, pp. 80–81. Burner calculates that 78 percent of CRB funds came from governmental sources. See also Nash, *Hoover* 2:27, 34–35.

34. Hoover to [Spanish minister to Great Britain and co-chair of the CRB] Don Alfonso Merry del Val, 25 Oct. 1914, quoted in Nash, *Hoover* 2:34.

35. Irwin did not identify Hoover by name in the March 1917 article but did so in another article in June. Quoted in ibid., 349–50.

36. Ibid., 345–51.

37. Burner, *Hoover*, pp. 96–100; *Herbert Hoover: The Great War and Its Aftermath, 1914–23*, ed. Lawrence E. Gelfand (Iowa City: University of Iowa Press, 1979). See especially the editor's introduction to the essay by Witold S. Sworakowski, "Herbert Hoover, Launching the American Food Administration, 1917," pp. 40–41.

38. The fullest account of this period is George H. Nash, *The Life of Herbert Hoover: Master of Emergencies, 1917–1918* (New York: W. W. Norton, 1996) [hereafter cited as Nash, *Hoover* 3]; Burner, *Hoover*, pp. 97–98.

39. Quoted in Nash, *Hoover* 2:349. Hoover added that if they could "set the people to saving," it would be "good not only for the conduct of the war but for our souls"— an echo of his Quaker youth that suggests he may have hoped for some lasting effect from his efforts after all.

40. Nash, *Hoover* 3:345–46, summarizes Hoover's indirect methods of coercion; Burner, *Hoover*, pp. 101–106. One of the volunteers serving in the Food Administration was Gifford Pinchot. Pinchot believed that hog prices should be set in the same way as wheat prices, but Hoover contended that he lacked the legal authority to do so. After bitterly denouncing Hoover to anyone who would listen, Pinchot resigned. Their dispute became an issue in the 1920 California presidential primary, in which Hoover was a candidate, and forty years later Hoover was still steaming about it. See, for example, Ray Lyman Wilbur to Hoover, 17 Apr. 1920, HP:Pre-Com, Box 19, Folder "Wilbur, Ray Lyman 1920—January–June"; Henry C. Wallace to Hoover, 11 Feb. 1918, Henry Cantwell Wallace Papers, Box 1, Folder 6, University of Iowa Library; undated, handwritten memorandum by Herbert Hoover, given to the Hoover Library by Allan Hoover on 14 Nov. 1966, HP:Pre-Com, Box 14, Folder "Pinchot, Gifford, 1917–18." In later years Pinchot urged upon Hoover federal regulation of resources in the West, even if those resources were privately owned. This was an unpalatable idea to most westerners, but one wonders if Hoover's recollection of the Food Administration dispute did not harden his objections to any such policy. See

Pinchot to Hoover, 10 Dec. 1928, HP:C&T, General Correspondence, Folder "Pinchot, Gifford"; Gerald D. Nash, *United States Oil Policy, 1890–1964: Business and Government in Twentieth Century America* (Pittsburgh: University of Pittsburgh Press, 1968), pp. 75–76.

41. Burner, *Hoover,* pp. 101–2.

42. Hoover, *Memoirs* 1:267–71. That wartime production increases contributed to a postwar farm depression and led to cultivation of some lands that might better have been left for other uses was one of those unintended consequences that often attend human actions.

43. Burner, *Hoover,* p. 130; Hoover, *Memoirs* 1:425–27.

44. For a more general account of the gentrification of the engineering profession, and especially the role of MIT in the process, see Bruce Sinclair, "Inventing a Genteel Tradition: MIT Crosses the River," in *New Perspectives on Technology and American Culture,* ed. Bruce Sinclair (Philadelphia: American Philosophical Society, 1986), pp. 1–18. Those who came into conflict with Hoover in business or in his relief activities might have disagreed with the characterization of him as a gentleman; they found him often blunt and tactless. When in pursuit of something he thought important, he had little patience for courtesies, but at moments of relaxation, or when he thought it would serve his purposes, he could indeed be the gentleman.

45. Burner, *Hoover,* pp. 131–32; Hoover, *Principles of Mining,* p. 186.

46. Hoover, *Principles of Mining,* p. 185.

47. Samuel Haber, *Efficiency and Uplift: Scientific Management in the Progressive Era, 1890–1920* (Chicago: University of Chicago Press, 1964), pp. 103–5. The idea of giving technically trained administrators power to control much of government attracted the attention at various times of such notable intellectuals as Frank Goodnow, John Dewey, Lester Frank Ward, John R. Commons, and Thorstein Veblen. See ibid., 140–47. For a striking example of the way in which early administrative theorists proposed to enlarge the powers of administrators, see Woodrow Wilson, *The State: Elements of Historical and Practical Politics* (Boston: Heath, 1889), p. 638. Wilson later drew back from this position.

48. John F. McClymer, *War and Welfare: Social Engineering in America, 1890–1925* (Westport, Conn.: Greenwood, 1980), p. 3.

49. Hoover, *Memoirs* 1:132.

50. Burner, *Hoover,* 62, 71.

51. Martin Fausold points out that there is little evidence that Hoover read Veblen, but he concludes that Hoover would have been led by experience to the same conclusions anyway. See his *Presidency of Hoover,* pp. 7–8. For Hoover's belief that the engineer could make a unique social contribution by showing labor and capital their common interest in a smoothly functioning economy, see his presidential address to the Federated American Engineering Societies, "The Engineer's Relation to Our Industrial Problems," 19 Nov. 1920, in *Engineering News-Record,* 25 Nov. 1920, p. 1053.

52. It is perhaps worth noting, however, that Hoover was considered in the autumn

of 1914 for the presidency of the American Institute of Mining Engineers—the organization leading the professionalization of his field. Nash, *Hoover* 2:15. He was a member of this organization from 1896 onward. See the undated memorandum in HP:Pre-Com, Box 24, Folder "American Institute of Mining and Metallurgical Engineers, 1896-1919."

53. Robert H. Wiebe, *The Search for Order, 1877-1920* (New York: Hill and Wang, 1967), pp. 113, 129-31.

54. Robert D. Cuff, "Herbert Hoover, the Ideology of Voluntarism and War Organization during the Great War," in *Herbert Hoover: The Great War and Its Aftermath, 1914-1923*, ed. Lawrence E. Gelfand (Iowa City: University of Iowa Press, 1979), p. 24.

55. Cecelia Tichi, *Shifting Gears: Technology, Literature, Culture in Modernist America* (Chapel Hill: University of North Carolina Press, 1987), p. 169.

56. Hoover, *Memoirs* 1:133.

57. Nash, *Hoover* 1:572-73.

58. Layton, *Revolt of the Engineers*, pp. viii-xi. The quotation is found on p. x.

59. Robert Wiebe, *Self-Rule: A Cultural History of American Democracy* (Chicago: University of Chicago Press, 1995), pp. 141-49.

60. Mark Sullivan Diary, 22[?] April 1922, Sullivan Papers, Box 1, Hoover Institution on War, Revolution and Peace, Stanford University [hereafter Hoover Institution].

61. From Hoover's presidential address to the Federated American Engineering Societies, 19 Nov. 1920, published in *Engineering News-Record*, 25 Nov. 1920, p. 1053. The order of phrases has been altered slightly.

62. Hoover to Richard L. Humphrey, 1 Feb. 1923, HP:Com, Box 200, Folder "Federated American Engineering Societies, 1923-1924 & undated."

63. Quoted in Craig Lloyd, *Aggressive Introvert: A Study of Herbert Hoover and Public Relations Management, 1912-1932* (Columbus: Ohio State University Press, 1972), p. 56 n. 33.

64. Ibid., p. xi.

65. Lloyd contends that Hoover really did not want to draw attention to himself. Perhaps so, but a closer examination of Hoover's childhood suggests that he felt deprived and unloved. Such feelings leave unfulfilled needs that do not disappear with the end of childhood. See ibid., pp. 76-86.

66. David E. Green, *Shaping Political Consciousness: The Language of Politics in America from McKinley to Reagan* (Ithaca, N.Y.: Cornell University Press, 1987), p. 96.

67. Hugh Gibson to his mother, 11 and 26 Nov. 1917, Hugh S. Gibson Papers, Box 35, Folder "November 1917"; George Barr Baker to Hugh Gibson, 3 June 1921, George Barr Baker Papers, Box 3, Folder "Gibson, Hugh"; Sydney Sullivan Parker oral history, pp. 2, 28; Philippi Harding Butler oral history, p. 15; Marguerite Rickard Hoyt oral history, p. 7; Mrs. Ben S. Allen oral history, pp. 23-24; statement given out by Hulda H. McLean on the death of Hoover, 20 Oct. 1964, Hulda H. McLean Pa-

pers, Box 1, untitled, all at Hoover Institution; Charles A. and Hulda Hoover McLean oral history, p. 9, HHPL.; Hoover, *Memoirs* 1:273. It is striking that dam building is virtually the only activity mentioned in these accounts. Hoover's longtime friend, Ray Lyman Wilbur, remembered that President Hoover pressed his male guests at Camp Rapidan into building ponds along the stream. Wilbur observed drily that "Herbert Hoover has always liked to play with water and build dams." *The Memoirs of Ray Lyman Wilbur, 1875–1949*, eds. Edgar Eugene Robinson and Paul Carroll Edwards (Stanford: Stanford University Press, 1960), p. 547.

68. Nash, *Hoover* 1:507.

69. Samuel P. Hays, *Conservation and the Gospel of Efficiency: The Progressive Conservation Movement, 1890–1920* (New York: Atheneum ed., 1969), p. 2.

70. Ibid., from the Preface to the 1969 ed., unnumbered third page.

71. Hays characterizes this tension between centralization and decentralization as being between modernization and traditionalism, between the urban and the rural. To some extent it was, but it was also a conflict within individuals such as Hoover, who believed deeply in the value of science, technology, and modern organization, but who also believed that the whole structure depended at bottom on individual initiative. See ibid., unnumbered pp. 6–8.

3. Consumption and Conservation

1. *The New Day: Campaign Speeches of Herbert Hoover, 1928* (Stanford, Calif.: Stanford University Press, 1928), pp. 50–52. As noted in chapter 1, Hoover's memories of his childhood were not reliable. His father was a blacksmith and farm equipment dealer, not a subsistence farmer. Although elements of a subsistence economy lingered in West Branch at the time Hoover was a child, the region was already deeply affected by the market revolution that began to transform agrarian America earlier in the nineteenth century. See Charles Sellers, *The Market Revolution: Jacksonian America, 1815–1846* (New York: Oxford University Press, 1991). Richard Hofstadter points out, in *The Age of Reform: From Bryan to F.D.R.* (New York: Vintage, 1960 [1955]), pp. 23–59, that Hoover was not alone in feeling nostalgia for his rural past and in evoking a somewhat mythological version of it.

2. My attention was drawn to this speech by William Leach, who analyzes its contradictions at some length in *Land of Desire: Merchants, Power, and the Rise of a New American Culture* (New York: Pantheon, 1993), pp. 375–77. Leach concludes that in the end Hoover comes down firmly on the side of progress; I think the resolution is less definite. For an introduction to recent British work on how the industrial revolution changed leisure, see Stephen G. Jones, *Workers at Play: A Social and Economic History of Leisure, 1918–1939* (London: Routledge & Kegan Paul, 1986), pp. 1–3; John Clarke and Chas Critcher, *The Devil Makes Work: Leisure in Capitalist Britain* (Urbana: University of Illinois Press, 1985). It is also possible to interpret this speech,

and to some extent Hoover's environmental approach as well, as an example of the longtime American tension between city and country in which, James L. Machor contends, reformers sought to bridge the hostility between the two regions by proposing ways to combine the amenities of urban life with the values and virtues of the country. I think Hoover was not primarily concerned with maintaining "his elemental connection to his spontaneous, natural self" (p. 14) in the development of his environmental policies and that he saw outdoor recreation and environmentalism primarily as consumable amenities of urban life. The 1928 speech suggests, however, that to some extent he did believe in what Machor describes as a myth of the "organic city" that enabled Americans to reconcile apparently incompatible values of nostalgia for the country and constant struggle for urban progress. See *Pastoral Cities: Urban Ideals and the Symbolic Landscape of America* (Madison: University of Wisconsin Press, 1987).

3. Herbert Hoover, *The Memoirs of Herbert Hoover: The Cabinet and the Presidency, 1920–1933* (New York: Macmillan, 1952), p. 2 [hereafter Hoover, *Memoirs* 2]; Will Irwin, *Herbert Hoover: A Reminiscent Biography* (New York: Grosset & Dunlap, 1928), pp. 251–52. The quotations come from Hoover's letter to his sister, 4 Aug. 1895. For the full letter, see chapter 2.

4. Guy Alchon, *The Invisible Hand of Planning: Capitalism, Social Science, and the State in the 1920s* (Princeton, N.J.: Princeton University Press, 1985), p. 37. For an account of the 1920 campaign in California by one of Hoover's supporters, see Ralph Arnold, "Laying Foundation Stones," Historical Society of Southern California *Quarterly* 37 (June 1955): 99–124.

5. Quoted in Robert F. Himmelberg, "Hoover's Public Image, 1919–20: The Emergence of a Public Figure and a Sign of the Times," in *Herbert Hoover: The Great War and Its Aftermath, 1914–23,* ed. Lawrence E. Gelfand (Iowa City: University of Iowa Press, 1979), pp. 209–32. The quotation is on p. 222.

6. Ibid., p. 212. One historian who has studied Hoover's 1920 campaign suggests that had he run as a Democrat, he would still have lost but might have forced the Republicans to nominate a Progressive. See Gary Dean Best, "The Hoover-For-President Boom of 1920," *Mid-America* 53 (Oct. 1971): 227–44.

7. Kurt Wimer, "Woodrow Wilson and a Third Nomination," *Pennsylvania History* 29 (April 1962): 192–211.

8. Himmelberg, "Hoover's Public Image," pp. 211–12.

9. David Burner, *Herbert Hoover: A Public Life* (New York: Knopf, 1978), pp. 150–51; Himmelberg, "Hoover's Public Image," pp. 226–27.

10. In 1917, on the eve of becoming Food Administrator, Hoover told Will Irwin that the war offered an opportunity to "check extravagance in living, dress, travel and amusement, and set the people to saving. It will be good not only for the conduct of the war but for our souls." From an article published in the *Saturday Evening Post* as quoted in George H. Nash, *The Life of Herbert Hoover: The Humanitarian, 1914–1917* (New York: W. W. Norton, 1988), p. 349 [hereafter Nash, *Hoover* 2]. Given his prewar views, Hoover might have been expected to call for meeting the postwar crisis

with frugality and retrenchment. Daniel Horowitz points out, however, that Hoover was not alone in taking an ambivalent attitude toward saving and spending during and just after the war; many Americans talked economy but assumed that expenses that before the war would have been labeled luxuries had become necessities. See *The Morality of Spending: Attitudes toward the Consumer Society in America, 1875-1940* (Baltimore: Johns Hopkins University Press, 1985), pp. 109-18.

11. Gary Dean Best, "President Wilson's Second Industrial Conference, 1919-1920," *Labor History* 16 (Fall 1975): 507-9, and Best, *The Politics of American Individualism: Herbert Hoover in Transition, 1918-1921* (Westport, Conn.: Greenwood, 1975), pp. 38-54; Burner, *Hoover,* pp. 143-45; Kendrick A. Clements, *The Presidency of Woodrow Wilson* (Lawrence: University Press of Kansas, 1992), pp. 215-16; *Report of Industrial Conference Called by the President* (n.p. [Dept. of Labor], 6 Mar. 1920). The call for an "organic" relationship between labor and capital came from Hoover's speech to the Boston Chamber of Commerce in March 1920; see Burner, *Hoover,* p. 145. Hoover's estimate about the gains in production to be realized by reducing strikes and lockouts may be found in Hoover to Samuel Gompers, 23 Oct. 1920, HP:Pre-Com, Box 6, Folder "Gompers, Samuel, 1917-22." For a negative evaluation of Hoover's labor ideas, see Robert H. Zieger, "Labor, Progressivism, and Herbert Hoover in the 1920s," *Wisconsin Magazine of History* 58 (Spring 1975): 196-208; and Zieger, "Herbert Hoover, the Wage-earner, and the 'New Economic System,' 1919-1929," *Business History Review* 52 (Summer 1977): 161-89.

12. Olivier Zunz, *Why the American Century?* (Chicago: University of Chicago Press, 1998), pp. 80-83.

13. The FAES was never as important as Hoover hoped. Because of conflicts over the organization's goals, more than half of the engineering societies that participated in the organizing conference never actually became members. Nevertheless, the FAES came closer than any other engineering organization to speaking for the profession. See Edwin T. Layton Jr., *The Revolt of the Engineers: Social Responsibility and the American Engineering Profession* (Baltimore: Johns Hopkins University Press, 1986), pp. 187-89, 195.

14. "The Engineer's Relation to Our Industrial Problems," 19 Nov. 1920, in *Engineering News-Record,* 25 Nov. 1920, pp. 1053, 1055. Guy Alchon contends that Hoover's enormous reputation made him the natural leader of those engineers, economists, and social workers who shared a "managerial consensus" that increased production would solve all social problems. See *The Invisible Hand of Planning,* pp. 45-47. Hoover's address to the FAES was reprinted in other engineering publications—for example, *Mining and Metallurgy* 168 (Dec. 1920): 3-7.

15. Paul A. C. Koistinen, *Mobilizing for Modern War: The Political Economy of American Warfare, 1865-1919* (Lawrence: University Press of Kansas, 1997), p. 148.

16. "Abstract of Minutes First Meeting of Executive Board American Engineering Council Nov. 20, 1920," HP:Pre-Com, Box 38, Folder "FAES Office Files—Executive Board Nov. 1920-Feb. 1921"; Hoover, *Memoirs* 2:31; Best, *Politics of American*

Individualism, pp. 159–61. A helpful overview of Hoover's antiwaste campaign is William R. Tanner, "Secretary of Commerce Hoover's War on Waste, 1921–1928," in *Herbert Hoover and the Republican Era: A Reconsideration,* eds. Carl E. Krog and William R. Tanner (Lanham, Md.: University Press of America, 1984), pp. 1–35.

17. The Committee on Elimination of Waste in Industry of the Federated American Engineering Societies, *Waste in Industry* (New York: McGraw-Hill, 1921), p. ix. Alchon, *The Invisible Hand of Planning,* pp. 63–67, provides a brief account of the committee and the report.

18. Hoover's speech to the American Institute of Mining and Metallurgical Engineers, 16 Sept. 1919, HP:Pre-Com, Box 26, Folder "AIMME Speeches, Sept. 16, 1919."

19. Hoover, *Memoirs* 2:29.

20. Quoted in David Green, *Shaping Political Consciousness: The Language of Politics in America from McKinley to Reagan* (Ithaca, N.Y.: Cornell University Press, 1987), p. 100.

21. Robert H. Wiebe, *Self-Rule: A Cultural History of American Democracy* (Chicago: University of Chicago Press, 1995), pp. 142–43.

22. Herbert Hoover, *The Challenge to Liberty* (New York: Scribner's, 1934), pp. 200–201.

23. From a circular fund-raising letter sent out by the Committee on Elimination of Waste in Industry of the FAES, March 1921, HP:Pre-Com, Box 41, Folder "FAES Industrial Waste Comm.—Cir. Ltr., 1921."

24. Leach, *Land of Desire,* p. xiii; Donald R. Stabile, "Research Note: Herbert Hoover, the FAES, and the AF of L," *Technology and Culture* 27 (Oct. 1986): 819–27.

25. Telegram: Franklin K. Lane to Hoover, 19 Dec. 1916; telegram: Hoover to Lane, 4 Jan. 1917, HP:Pre-Com, Box 10, Folder "Lane, Franklin K., 1916–21"; Nash, *Hoover* 2:302–3.

26. Samuel P. Hays, *Conservation and the Gospel of Efficiency: The Progressive Conservation Movement, 1890–1920* (Cambridge, Mass.: Harvard University Press, 1959), pp. 2–3.

27. J. Leonard Bates, "Fulfilling American Democracy: The Conservation Movement, 1907 to 1921," *Mississippi Valley Historical Review* 44 (June 1957): 29–57; James Penick Jr., "The Progressives and the Environment: Three Themes from the First Conservation Movement," in *The Progressive Era,* ed. Lewis L. Gould (Syracuse, N.Y.: Syracuse University Press, 1974), pp. 122–23; Clayton R. Koppes, "Efficiency/Equity/Esthetics: Towards a Reinterpretation of American Conservation," *Environmental Review* 11 (Summer 1987): 127–46.

28. Hays, *Conservation and the Gospel of Efficiency,* p. 1, emphasizes—and perhaps overstates—the pro-business origins of the conservation movement. Its sources, and the motives of leading conservationists, were diverse and sometimes contradictory. Likewise, Clayton Koppes's characterization of the conservation movement in the

1920s as "more obviously pro-business" conveys only a part of a complex whole. See Koppes, "Efficiency/Equity/Esthetics," 133.

29. Elmo Richardson, *The Politics of Conservation: Crusades and Controversies, 1897-1913* (Berkeley: University of California Press, 1962), pp. 86-120. The quotation from Governor Bowerman is on p. 107.

30. Keith W. Olson, *Biography of a Progressive: Franklin K. Lane, 1864-1921* (Westport, Conn.: Greenwood, 1979), pp. 52-58; Richardson, *Politics of Conservation,* pp. 145-59.

31. Olson, *Biography of a Progressive,* pp. 76-119.

32. Donald C. Swain, *Federal Conservation Policy, 1921-1933* (Berkeley: University of California Press, 1963), p. 1; William G. Carleton, "Government's Historical Role in Conservation," *Current History* 58 (June 1970): 324-25.

33. Swain, *Federal Conservation Policy,* 1-2; Craig R. Humphrey and Frederick R. Buttel, *Environment, Energy, and Society* (Belmont, Calif.: Wadsworth, 1982), p. 119.

34. Humphrey and Buttel, *Environment, Energy, and Society,* pp. 9-12, 30-33, 53-57, 73-81, 126-30.

35. See, for example, Donald Worster, *The Wealth of Nature: Environmental History and the Ecological Imagination* (New York: Oxford University Press, 1993), pp. 72-73, 108-9; Roderick Nash, *Wilderness and the American Mind,* 3rd ed. (New Haven, Conn.: Yale University Press, 1982), pp. 187-99.

36. Stephen Fox, *John Muir and His Legacy: The American Conservation Movement* (Boston: Little, Brown, 1981), p. 159. Fox describes the other organizations elsewhere in the book; membership estimates are on p. 162. In addition to their large membership, the Waltonians were also important as the first conservation organization to organize state and local chapters as well as the national organization. See also, Humphrey and Buttel, *Environment, Energy, and Society,* pp. 127-28; John F. Reiger, *American Sportsmen and the Origins of Conservation* (New York: Winchester, 1975). The large membership of the Walton League suggests that Samuel P. Hays was in error when he declared that there was "little in the way of broad popular support for the substantive objectives of conservation" before the 1970s. See "From Conservation to Environment: Environmental Politics in the United States since World War Two," *Environmental Review* 6 (Fall 1982): 17.

37. Fox, *John Muir and His Legacy,* pp. 160-63.

38. Will H. Dilg to Hoover, 14 Mar. 1922; Henry O'Malley (Commissioner of the Bureau of Fisheries) to Hoover, 1 July 1922; draft of Hoover's article, July 1922, all in HP:Com, Box 346, Folder "Izaak Walton League of America, 1922-23." Hoover to Izaak Walton League convention, 15 Jan. 1923; Hoover to Izaak Walton League, 20 Apr. 1923; Hoover to Will H. Dilg, 16 Sept. 1925 (quotation from this letter), all in HP:Com, Box 182, Folder "Dilg, Will H., 1922-1928 and undated." For Hoover's honorary presidency of the Waltonians, see HP:Com, Box 270, Folder "Hoover, Herbert, Memberships It-Jun." Henry Baldwin Ward to Hoover, 21 Apr. 1929;

George E. Scott to Hoover, 26 Apr. 1930; Hoover to M. D'Arcy Magee, 28 Jan. 1931; Hoover to George E. Vincent, 22 Apr. 1931; Fred N. Peet to Hoover, 2 May 1932, HP:PP, Box 165, Folder "Izaak Walton League, 1929-1932."

39. William J. Barber, *From New Era to New Deal: Herbert Hoover, the Economists, and American Economic Policy, 1921-1933* (Cambridge, England: Cambridge University Press, 1985), pp. 1–2; Ellis W. Hawley, *The Great War and the Search for a Modern Order: A History of the American People and Their Institutions, 1917-1933* (New York: St. Martin's, 1979), p. 81; W. Elliot Brownlee, *Dynamics of Ascent: A History of the American Economy* (New York: Knopf, 1974), pp. 264–73. Agriculture, bituminous coal, cotton textiles, and railroads did not share in the boom of the 1920s, and in these industries low wages, labor conflict, and declining profits raised serious questions about the boosters' vision of universal prosperity. In addition, prosperity led to degradation in things like air and water quality that affected the lives of workers. See Hawley, *Great War,* pp. 87–90.

The movement for paid vacations, which became a goal of labor agitation in Europe in the 1920s, did not have a counterpart in the United States. Americans predicting greater leisure for workers expected it to result from a reduced workweek. See Gary S. Cross, *A Social History of Leisure since 1600* (State College, Pa.: Venture, 1990), pp. 165–67.

40. Mark Sullivan diary, 2 Dec. 1923, Mark Sullivan Papers, Box 1, Hoover Institution on War, Revolution and Peace, Stanford University. Sullivan's bemusement makes it clear that the economy was not only a political and economic issue in the 1920s, but a moral and cultural one as well. Contemporaries were well aware that traditional values were under attack and were consciously trying, as was Hoover, to shape standards appropriate to the new situation.

41. Hoover is quoted in Stabile, "Research Note," 822; Hoover, *Memoirs* 1:133. The historiography of consumerism is growing rapidly, but there is little consensus on the subject. The conventional view has been that the consumer society began with mass production in the late nineteenth and early twentieth centuries, but recent work is pushing its origins back into the nineteenth, the eighteenth, or even earlier centuries. Some recent work suggests that the commercialization of leisure that Hoover saw as the result of affluence was in fact a byproduct of the industrial revolution from the outset as preindustrial people were forced into new patterns of behavior by the demands of the factory. See Jean-Christophe Agnew, "Coming Up for Air: Consumer Culture in Historical Perspective," in *Consumption and the World of Goods,* eds. John Brewer and Roy Porter (London: Routledge, 1993); Stephen G. Jones, *Workers at Play,* pp. 1–8; Daniel J. Boorstin, *The Americans: The Democratic Experience* (New York: Random House, 1973), pp. 91–164. Another heated debate is about the degree to which people create their culture or are shaped and constrained by the corporations and mass markets that dominate commercialized leisure. In addition to Agnew's article cited above, see the essays in *The Culture of Consumption: Critical Essays in American History, 1880-1980,* eds. Richard Wightman Fox and T. J. Jackson Lears

(New York: Pantheon, 1983), and Richard Butsch, "Introduction: Leisure and Hegemony in America," in *For Fun and Profit: The Transformation of Leisure into Consumption*, ed. Richard Butsch (Philadelphia: Temple University Press, 1990), pp. 3–27. For a discussion of the consumer in a monopolistic economy as a passive figure who "is neither an originator nor really a consentor," see R. Jeffrey Lustig, *Corporate Liberalism: The Origins of Modern American Political Theory, 1890–1920* (Berkeley: University of California Press, 1982), p. 238.

Although some thinkers realized the possibilities of an affluent society and began to theorize about its implications in the eighteenth or nineteenth century, the concept entered popular consciousness only at the end of the nineteenth and the beginning of the twentieth century, along with shorter working hours, the growth of advertising, and the rise of institutions such as amusement parks devoted to commercialized leisure activities. But old moral strictures against consumption died hard, and it was not until after World War I that attitudes changed widely enough to justify general acceptance of the consumer society. See Horowitz, *Morality of Spending*, pp. 30, 130–33. It is important to note that Hoover saw the management of leisure as an issue only of the *affluent* society, not as a problem of capitalism in general.

42. Leach, *Land of Desire*, p. 234.

43. Daniel M. Fox, *The Discovery of Abundance: Simon N. Patten and the Transformation of Social Theory* (Ithaca, N.Y.: Cornell University Press, 1967), p. 144.

44. Leach, *Land of Desire*, p. 244. Leach overstates the case, but the basic point that behavior was determined by living conditions was widely accepted by social scientists of the Progressive Era. It followed from this assumption that rising standards of living would improve behavior and solve social problems. See Horowitz, *Morality of Spending*, pp. 50–66.

45. All quotations from Patten's works except "country . . . picnics" come from Leach, *Land of Desire*, pp. 238–40. The other quotation is in Horowitz, *Morality of Spending*, p. 35. See also Fox, *Discovery of Abundance*, pp. 52–55. From the beginning of the twentieth century, advertisers have commonly attempted to associate their products with "nature," apparently on the assumption that consumers view nature, the outdoors, and "natural" products in a favorable light. Only since the 1970s have advertisers portrayed themselves aggressively as "nature's caretakers: environmentally friendly, responsible, and caring." See Michael Howlett and Rebecca Raglon, "Constructing the Environmental Spectacle: Green Advertisements and the Greening of the Corporate Image, 1910–1990," *Environmental History Review* 16 (Winter 1992): 53–68.

46. Fox, *Discovery of Abundance*, pp. 143–44.

47. Jesse Frederick Steiner, *Americans at Play: Recent Trends in Recreation and Leisure Time Activities* (New York: McGraw-Hill, 1933), p. 9. This book is one of a series of reports on "recent trends" in American society commissioned by the president's committee appointed by Hoover and chaired by Wesley C. Mitchell. See also Horowitz, *Morality of Spending*, pp. 109–18; Hawley, *Great War*, pp. 82–85. "Leisure"

is not a self-evident or value-free word. The commonsense definition of the term as "activity (or inactivity) freely chosen and enjoyed" runs head-on into "functionalist," "Gramscian," and "Althusserian" contentions that all activities, including leisure, are culturally or economically controlled and defined. A third approach, with a heritage going back to Aristotle, holds that mere rest or relaxation cannot be defined as leisure; true leisure must entail "the disinterested cultivation of personality." See Sue Glyptis, "Perspectives on Leisure and the Environment" in *Leisure and the Environment: Essays in Honour of Professor J. A. Patmore,* ed. Sue Glyptis (London: Belhaven, 1993), pp. 3–4; Cross, *Social History of Leisure,* p. 1; Chris Rojek, *Ways of Escape: Modern Transformations in Leisure and Travel* (Lanham, Md.: Rowman and Littlefield, 1993), pp. 3–5; Grant Jarvie and Joseph Maguire, *Sport and Leisure in Social Thought* (London: Routledge, 1994), pp. 1–23; David Harris, *From Class Struggle to the Politics of Pleasure: The Effects of Gramscianism on Cultural Studies* (London: Routledge, 1992), pp. 147–73. Hoover recognized intuitively that acceptable leisure pursuits could be culturally defined. Leisure as an aspect of industrial society appears to have received little scholarly attention before the 1960s. See David Riesman (with Warner Bloomberg Jr.), "Work and Leisure: Fusion or Polarity? (1957)," in David Riesman, *Abundance for What?* (New Brunswick, N.J.: Transaction ed., 1993), pp. 147–61.

48. Alchon, *Invisible Hand of Planning,* p. 77; on Gay, see Herbert Heaton, *A Scholar in Action: Edwin F. Gay* (Cambridge, Mass.: Harvard University Press, 1952); on Klein, see Leach, *Land of Desire,* pp. 361–68. For Wolman, see Joseph Dorfman, *The Economic Mind in American Civilization,* 5 vols. (New York: Viking, 1959), 5:521–24; on Mitchell, see ibid., 4:360–77; on Barnett, see ibid., 5:516–18; on Young, see ibid., 4:222–33. Further information on these and other important economists whose opinions Hoover sought may be found in Barber, *From New Era to New Deal,* passim. Hoover relied heavily on professional economists for advice. In addition to those named in the text, he also consulted John B. Andrews, Carroll W. Doten, Irving Fisher, Samuel A. Lewisohn, Otto Mallery, Samuel McCune Lindsay, William S. Rossiter, Edwin R. A. Seligman, and Walter F. Willcox, among others.

49. Another economist of the period, Harvard professor Thomas Nixon Carver, two of whose books were in Hoover's collection, and with whom Hoover carried on a substantial correspondence after 1933, argued in the 1920s that voluntary cooperation between capital and labor had become a permanent feature of the American economy and would lead to prosperity for all. "The time has come," he wrote, "when it is no longer necessary to rely upon theoretical analysis to show that wealth can be diffused under the system of voluntary agreement." See *The Present Economic Revolution in the United States* (Boston: Little, Brown, 1925), p. 6. Also in Hoover's library was Carver's *The Distribution of Wealth* (New York: Macmillan, 1904). For the correspondence between Hoover and Carver, see HP:PPI, Box 31, Folder "Carver, T. N. (Prof.), Correspondence 1933–1955." Joseph Dorfman offers a brief analysis of Carver's work in *The Economic Mind of American Civilization* 4:247–50.

50. *Recent Economic Changes in the United States: Report of the Committee on Recent Economic Changes of the President's Conference on Unemployment, Herbert Hoover, Chairman*, 2 vols. (New York: McGraw-Hill, 1929), 1:xv–xvi. The order of phrases has been altered. On the high wage doctrine, see Barber, *From New Era to New Deal*, pp. 27–30. Although Hoover formally chaired the committee, its actual director was Wesley C. Mitchell. The same conclusions about the reduction of work hours resulting from technological progress and the commodification of leisure are reiterated in the 1933 "recent social trends" volume by Steiner, *Americans at Play*, pp. 9–12.

51. Steiner, *Americans at Play*, pp. 10–13.

52. Gary Cross argues that at the beginning of the 1920s most people did not imagine a huge increase in consumption. They believed that "free time, not the endless increase of consumption, was the inevitable consequence of growth," and that with most workers' wants limited, the problem would be to find things for them to do with their leisure—not to find constructive activities that would compete with commercial entertainments. See Gary Cross, *Time and Money: The Making of Consumer Culture* (London: Routledge, 1993), pp. 7–10. Hoover's statements do not make clear what he thought about this issue, but whether he sought to fill workers' empty leisure hours with constructive amusements or hoped to substitute desirable leisure activities for undesirable consumerism, the result was the same.

In sharp contrast to the views of Hoover and others who worried about leisure were those of Luther H. Gulick and G. Stanley Hall, who regarded play, not work, as the natural state of man. Gulick believed that play was structured by society's norms, but he did not see a need to provide formalized recreational activities. See Donald J. Mrozek, "The Natural Limits of Unstructured Play, 1880–1914," in *Hard at Play: Leisure in America, 1840–1940*, ed. Kathryn Grover (Amherst: University of Massachusetts Press, 1992), pp. 210–26.

53. Christopher Lasch, *The True and Only Heaven: Progress and Its Critics* (New York: W. W. Norton, 1991), pp. 342–44. As noted in subsequent chapters, there was no shortage of people with ideas about organizing leisure for Americans. For a brief discussion of some of these, see Cross, *Social History of Leisure*, pp. 172–73.

54. In addition to his fundamental conviction that production was more important than consumption, Hoover also had a pessimistic doubt that people would use their new affluence to support constructive and socially valuable leisure activities. In this outlook he seems closer to Thorstein Veblen than to Patten. On Veblen, see Horowitz, *Morality of Spending*, pp. 38–39. Gary Cross points out that this was a concern shared by Sigmund Freud, Sandor Ferenczi, and a number of European economists and sociologists. See Cross, *Social History of Leisure*, pp. 168–69.

55. Fox, *Discovery of Abundance*, p. 164. John Kenneth Galbraith argues that Hoover and other liberals of the 1920s believed that the total output of the economy was a relatively fixed sum that could not be increased dramatically, and that they therefore concerned themselves primarily with redistributing existing income, enhancing

economic security, and protecting weaker groups and individuals from being crushed. To that list he might have added reducing waste. See Galbraith, *The Affluent Society*, 3rd ed., rev. (Boston: Houghton Mifflin, 1976), pp. 138–39.

56. Steiner, *Americans at Play*, p. 12; Horowitz, *Morality of Spending*, pp. 134–37, 148–53. The quotation is on p. 160. Businessmen, economists, psychologists, and social theorists of the period, both in the United States and Europe, expressed deep doubts about whether more leisure was desirable, and about whether workers would not be degraded by tawdry commercial entertainments. See Cross, *Social History of Leisure*, pp. 167–69.

Historians looking at the period have also been ambivalent about the consumer society. Pessimists tend to emphasize the rise of a "mass culture" and the "commodification of leisure" under the "hegemony" of monopoly capitalism, while optimists (or "populists") discuss "popular culture" and emphasize the role that ordinary people have in defining the meaning of their world. For an interesting discussion of this issue, see John Clarke, "Pessimism versus Populism: The Problematic Politics of Popular Culture," in Butsch, *For Fun and Profit*, pp. 28–44.

57. Herbert L. May and Dorothy Petgen, *Leisure and Its Use: Some International Observations* (New York: A. S. Barnes, 1928), p. 6. See also George Barton Cutten, *The Threat of Leisure* (New Haven, Conn.: Yale University Press, 1926), pp. 66–101, and passim.

58. Burner, *Hoover*, p. 46. All quotations from *American Individualism* are from an edition published by the Herbert Hoover Presidential Library Association, West Branch, Iowa, n.d.

59. Hoover, *American Individualism*, p. 4.

60. Ibid., pp. 8–9, 13. The order of phrases has been changed. As David Green points out, Hoover's argument here assumes that government will not be passive but will have both promotional and regulatory functions, although he believed it would be safer for individual freedom to assign such functions to private voluntary organizations under the stimulus and leadership of government rather than directly to the government itself. See Green, *Shaping Political Consciousness*, pp. 99–101.

61. Hoover, *American Individualism*, pp. 15, 20, 24–25, 21. For the seminal study of Hoover's outlook in the 1920s, see Ellis W. Hawley, "Herbert Hoover, the Commerce Secretariat, and the Vision of an 'Associative State,' 1921–1928," *Journal of American History* 61 (June 1974): 116–40.

62. Hoover, "In Praise of Izaak Walton," *Atlantic* 139 (June 1927), 819; Hoover, *Addresses Upon the American Road, 1933–1938* (New York: Scribner's, 1938), p. 238. Hoover's desire to promote constructive leisure activities can be explained in two quite different ways. It can be seen as an attempt to assert hegemonic control over workers liberated by affluence, or it can be seen as Hoover's attempt to resolve his own inner conflict between the ingrained lesson of his childhood that life is earnest and must be centered on constructive work, and his realization that so much work was no longer necessary for survival or for the welfare of the community. The two explana-

tions are not incompatible, and both may have played a role in determining Hoover's outlook, but I think the weight of evidence is on the side of the second rather than the first interpretation. If Daniel Horowitz is correct in his contention, in *The Morality of Spending*, that anxiety about the morality of consumer society was widespread in early-twentieth-century America, then Hoover was not alone in his concern. On the other hand, Hoover's definition of what should be considered constructive was clearly an attempt to impose class- and culture-based standards on mass leisure activities. On the problems of defining leisure and its purposes, see Chris Rojek, *Decentring Leisure: Rethinking Leisure Theory* (Thousand Oaks, Calif.: Sage, 1995).

63. For a recent discussion of the same problem, see Worster, *The Wealth of Nature*, pp. 210–11. Perhaps because of his background, Hoover retained what Daniel Bell describes as the Weberian belief in asceticism as an essential component of capitalism. Bell argues that for most businessmen, by the 1960s, "the ascetic element, and with it one kind of moral legitimation of capitalist behavior, has virtually disappeared." See Bell, *The Cultural Contradictions of Capitalism* (New York: Basic Books, 1978 [1958]), pp. xx, 65–80.

64. Andrew Ross, *The Chicago Gangster Theory of Life: Nature's Debt to Society* (London: Verso, 1994), p. 8.

4. Conservation in Commerce

1. Harding to Hoover, 5 Nov. 1920, HP:Pre-Com, Box 7, Folder "Harding, Correspondence Feb. 1920–1922"; Christian Herter to Hoover, 7 Dec. 1920, ibid., Box 7, Folder "Harding, Corres. (Letter Book) July 1, 1920–Feb. 23, 1921"; H. M. Daugherty to Hoover, 27 Nov. 1920, ibid., Box 4, Folder D; Robert K. Murray, "Herbert Hoover and the Harding Cabinet," in *Herbert Hoover as Secretary of Commerce: Studies in New Era Thought and Practice*, ed. Ellis W. Hawley (Iowa City: University of Iowa Press, 1981), p. 19; Murray, "President Harding and His Cabinet," *Ohio History* 75 (Spring–Summer 1966): 113–14.

2. Hoover to Harding, 22 Dec. 1920, HP:Pre-Com, Box 7, Folder "Harding, Corres. (Letter Book) July 1, 1920–Feb. 23, 1921." Senator Hiram Johnson of California was a particularly bitter opponent of Hoover's nomination to the cabinet. See, for example, Hiram Johnson to Carlos McClatchy, 9 Nov. 1920, Johnson to Hiram Johnson Jr., 7 Dec. 1920, and Johnson to Meyer Lissner, 7 Jan. 1921, all in Hiram Johnson Papers, Pt. VI, Box 2, Folders "1920 Nov.–Dec." and "1921 Jan.–Feb.," Bancroft Library, University of California at Berkeley.

3. Murray, "Hoover and the Harding Cabinet," 19–21; Gary Dean Best, *The Politics of American Individualism: Herbert Hoover in Transition, 1918–1921* (Westport, Conn.: Greenwood, 1975), pp. 146–72.

4. Hoover to Harding, 23 Feb. 1921, HP:Pre-Com, Box 7, Folder "Harding Corres. (Letter Book) July 1, 1920 to Feb. 23, 1921." Hoover also asked for permission

to continue and complete his work in European relief. See *The Memoirs of Herbert Hoover: The Cabinet and the Presidency, 1920–1933* (New York: Macmillan, 1952), p. 36 [hereafter Hoover, *Memoirs* 2].

5. A good, brief introduction to Hoover's economic thought is Ellis W. Hawley, "Herbert Hoover and Economic Stabilization, 1921–22," in *Herbert Hoover as Secretary of Commerce: Studies in New Era Thought and Practice*, ed. Ellis Hawley, pp. 44–77; William Leach, *Land of Desire: Merchants, Power, and the Rise of a New American Culture* (New York: Pantheon, 1993), pp. 352–58. For fuller evaluations of New Era economic thought, see William J. Barber, *From New Era to New Deal: Herbert Hoover, the Economists, and American Economic Policy, 1921–1933* (Cambridge, England: Cambridge University Press, 1985), and Guy Alchon, *The Invisible Hand of Planning: Capitalism, Social Science, and the State in the 1920s* (Princeton, N.J.: Princeton University Press, 1985).

6. For a fuller discussion of the report, see chapter 3.

7. William R. Tanner, "Secretary of Commerce Hoover's War on Waste, 1921–1928," in *Herbert Hoover and the Republican Era: A Reconsideration*, eds. Carl E. Krog and William R. Tanner (Lanham, Md.: University Press of America, 1984), pp. 1–35, describes the standardization and simplification program and links it to Hoover's belief in industrial self-regulation.

8. Unsigned typescript, "Hoover as Secretary of Commerce," ca. 1923, HP:Com, Box 120, Folder "Commerce Dept. Achievements, 1921–23."

9. Ibid.; [Edward Eyre Hunt], "The National Bureau of Standards under Hoover," (typescript), ca. 1928, HPS, Box 14, Folder "National Bureau of Standards." The difference between simplification and standardization was never very clear and was often blurred in practice. In general, simplification meant the reduction in numbers, sizes, colors, etc. of individual products, while standardization meant that such things as screw threads and dimensions of lumber would be the same for all producers.

10. Memorandum from Hoover to [William A.] Durgin, 4 Jan. 1922, HP:Com, Box 145, Folder "Simplified Coml. Practice, 1921–22 June"; see also memorandum by William A. Durgin, "Simplified Practice: What It Is and What It Does," ca. July 1922, ibid., Folder "Simplified Coml. Practice, 1922, July–Aug."

11. A typed extract from a speech by Hoover given to a representative of *World's Work*, Dec. 1922, HP:Com, Box 145, Folder "Simplified Coml. Practice, 1921–22 June."

12. Memorandum, "Division of Simplified Practice," 1928, HP:Com, Box 1, Folder "Accomplishments of the Department, 1921–28." Estimates of the program's success, all of which came from within the Commerce Department, must be viewed with some skepticism.

13. Memorandum enclosed in Paul S. Clapp to George H. Bailey, 18 Mar. 1924, HP:Com, Box 101, Folder "Coal: Elimination of Waste, 1924."

14. Press release on Department of Commerce annual report, 27 Nov. 1924, HP:Com, Box 190, Folder "Elimination of Waste in Industry, 1923–24."

15. Quoted in William G. Robbins, "Voluntary Cooperation vs. Regulatory Paternalism: The Lumber Trade in the 1920s," *Business History Review* 56 (Autumn 1982): 360. See also Robbins's chapter on the 1920s, "Voluntary Cooperation and the Search for Stability," in *Lumberjacks and Legislators: Political Economy of the U.S. Lumber Industry, 1890–1941* (College Station: Texas A&M University Press, 1982), pp. 112–32.

16. Clipping, "Court Decision Disturbs Co-Operation with Hoover," no source, 6 Jan. 1922, HP:Com, Box 253, Folder "Hardwood Case, 1922"; Hawley, "Herbert Hoover and Economic Stabilization, 1921–22," p. 61.

17. See David T. Mason to Hoover, 25 Nov. 1927, HP:Com, Box 228, Folder "Foreman, Evan H.—Forests 1922–1927 & undated"; David T. Mason oral history, transcript of tape 186, 1 Dec. 1966, Forest History Society Archives, Durham, N.C.

18. "Previous Standardization Activities of Lumber Industry, under the Auspices of the National Lumber Manufacturers Association," n.d., National Forest Products Association Records, Box 50, Folder "Standardization, 1913–22 (Basement)," Forest History Society Archives.

19. Hoover to Wallace, 8 Feb. 1922, HP:Com, Box 11, Folder "Agriculture Dept.—Secy. of Agriculture Wallace, Henry C., 1922"; Wallace to Hoover, 7 Mar. 1922, ibid., Box 145, Folder "Simplified Coml. Practice, 1921–22, June." Wallace refers to a letter from Hoover dated 16 rather than 8 Feb., which I have not found. It appears from Wallace's reply, however, that the 16 Feb. letter must have said very much the same things as that of 8 Feb. A telegram from W. C. Mullendore to Hoover, 23 Mar. 1922, in ibid., Box 11, Folder "Agriculture Dept.—Secy. of Agriculture Wallace, Henry C., 1922," quotes a letter just arrived from Wallace to Hoover in which Wallace seems to claim that the Forest Service *did* have authorization to study lumber grading and asserts, and furthermore, that he had maintained this point in a letter to Hoover on 16 Feb., which has not been found either. This is all very confusing, but the important point is that in the end the Forest Service left the field to Commerce. Conflict between Hoover and Wallace dated back to the Food Administration during the war, but in the 1920s it was exacerbated by sharp differences over agricultural policy. See Edward L. Schapsmeier and Frederick H. Schapsmeier, "Disharmony in the Harding Cabinet: Hoover-Wallace Conflict," *Ohio History* 75 (Spring–Summer 1966): 126–36, 188–90; James H. Shideler, "Herbert Hoover and the Federal Farm Board Project, 1921–1925," *Mississippi Valley Historical Review* 42 (Mar. 1956): 710–29; Joan Hoff Wilson, "Hoover's Agricultural Policies, 1921–1928," *Agricultural History* 51 (Apr. 1977): 335–61. Wallace's successor, William M. Jardine, was much more in harmony with Hoover. See C. Fred Williams, "William M. Jardine and the Foundations for Republican Farm Policy, 1925–1929," *Agricultural History* 70 (Spring 1996): 216–32.

20. Press release, "Secretary Hoover's Remarks to Lumbermen," 22 May 1922, HP:Com, Box 434, Folder "Natl. Lumber Manufacturers Assn., 1921–27 & undated."

Hoover believed that standardization would help small companies compete on an equal footing with larger ones. That may have been true, but equal competition tended to freeze companies in relation to each other. What small firms wanted was growth, which in the extractive industries was mainly the result of increasing production, not standardization.

21. Message to Southern Forestry Congress, 28 Jan. 1924, HPS, Box 11, Folder "Forest (wood util., etc.)."

22. Wallace to Hoover, 8 Oct. 1924; Hoover to Wallace, 11 Oct. 1924, HP:Com, Box 163, Folder "Conferences—Wood (Forest) Utilization, 1924–25"; Harold Phelps Stokes to Ward Shepard, 9 Dec. 1924, ibid., Box 6, Folder "Agriculture, Forest Service 1913–1925," seems to indicate that Hoover did address the conference. Wallace and Hoover did not get along well, and it is possible that Wallace's death on 25 October 1924 and his replacement by Howard M. Gore led Hoover to change his mind about attending the meeting. For examples of the way in which conservation became a generally accepted objective of the standardization policy, see President Calvin Coolidge to John W. Blodgett, 1 Dec. 1924, and Hoover to Coolidge, 12 Mar. 1925, ibid., Box 163, Folder "Conferences—Wood (Forest) Utilization, 1924–25." For Hoover's heavy stress on conservation while he chaired the National Committee on Wood Utilization, see the Department of Commerce press releases dated 30 Apr. 1925, 2 May 1925, in HP:Com, Box 130, Folder "Commerce Dept. Fisheries, Bureau of, 1925," and Box 163, Folder "Conferences—Wood (Forest) Utilization, 1924–25," and a series of releases of various dates in Box 163, Folder "Conferences, Wood (Forest) Utilization 1926."

23. Extract from remarks by Hoover at a meeting of the National Committee on Wood Utilization, 28 Apr. 1926, National Forest Products Association Papers, Box 74, Folder "Dept. of Commerce, National Comm. on Wood Utiliz.," Forest History Society Archives. The National Committee on Wood Utilization promoted a number of measures intended to conserve wood, including the use of saws that could handle small logs more efficiently, the adoption of joining methods to permit utilization of short or odd-length lumber, the utilization of sawdust, and the reuse of wooden boxes and crates instead of burning them. See undated memorandum, "National Committee on Wood Utilization," HP:Com, Box 1, Folder "Accomplishments of the Department, 1921–28."

24. Ward Nicke and Lucille DeMert, "De Woods of Pine," ca. 1925–26, HP:Com, Box 470, Folder "Pine Institute of America, 1925–26."

25. Press release by National Lumber Manufacturers Association, ca. 10 May 1927, HP:Com, Box 376, Folder "Lumber, 1926–28 & undated."

26. Hoover to Edwin F. Gay, 12 Feb. 1922; Gov. Scott Bone (Alaska) to HH, 17 Feb. 1922; Ray Lyman Wilbur to Hoover, 27 Mar. 1922, all in HP:Com, Box 204, Folder "Fisheries, Bureau of Miscellaneous 1922." O'Malley was appointed in May 1922.

27. The characterization of O'Malley as a warm-hearted Irishman is quoted in Donald C. Swain, *Federal Conservation Policy, 1921–1933* (Berkeley: University of California Press, 1963), pp. 48, 45. Hoover's remark about the importance of the chief's commitment to commercial fishing is quoted in Joseph E. Taylor III, "Rationalizing the Western Fisheries: Secretary Hoover and the Bureau of Fisheries," unpublished paper delivered at a symposium on "Conservation and Consumption in the American West," George Fox University, Newberg, Oreg., 4 Oct. 1997. Horace Albright, superintendent of Yellowstone Park and later director of the Park Service, thought O'Malley "a very fine man." See Horace Albright oral history, HHPL, p. 16.

28. Hoover's speech before the sixth annual convention of the U.S. Fisheries Association at Atlantic City, 5 Sept. 1924, HP:Com, Box 130, Folder "Commerce Department, Fisheries, Bureau of, 1924"; press release, "Statement of Secretary Hoover: Progress in National Fisheries Conservation and Development," ibid., Box 166, Folder "Conservation, 1923–28 & undated"; Taylor, "Rationalizing the Western Fisheries."

29. Donald J. Pisani, "Fish Culture and the Dawn of Concern over Water Pollution in the United States," *Environmental Review* 8 (Summer 1984): 117–31; Adam W. Rome, "Coming to Terms with Pollution: The Language of Environmental Reform, 1865–1915," *Environmental History* 1 (July 1996): 8–14.

30. Address by Hoover to the Izaak Walton League at its Chicago meeting, 12 Apr. 1924, p. 7, HP:Com, Box 14, Folder "Alaska—Alaskan Fisheries, Reservations, etc., 1924 Apr.–May." For the concerns of scientists see, for example, C. Alsberg (Chief of the Department of Agriculture's Bureau of Chemistry) to [?] Harrison, 9 May 1917, AGC, Drawer 483, "Oil, 1917," National Archives. Alsberg argued that oil on the surface of water could kill the microscopic plant and animal life below. Dr. E. W. Nelson, chief of the Biological Service, had described in 1916 the damaging effects of oil on waterfowl plumage. See Douglas C. Drake, "Herbert Hoover, Ecologist: The Politics of Oil Pollution Control, 1921–1926," *Mid-America: An Historical Review* 55 (July 1973): 208.

31. Transcript of the minutes of fish industry conference, p. 31, HP:Com, Box 203, Folder "Fish Industry Conf. of State Fish Commissioners, Anglers and Producers, 1921 June 16–Nov. 25."

32. Drake, "Herbert Hoover, Ecologist," 209–10. At Hoover's instructions, representatives of the Bureau of Navigation and the Bureau of Fisheries worked with members of Congress in drafting oil pollution legislation. See Hoover's memorandum for Mr. Lamb, 23 June 1921, HP:Com, Box 472, Folder "Pollution of Waters, 1921."

33. For examples of these various arguments, see George Shiras III to Hoover, 13 June 1921; Joseph P. Howe to P. L. Smithers, 17 June 1921; Smithers to Hoover, 28 June 1921, HP:Com, Box 203, Folder "Fish Industry, Migratory Fish Conservation Committee, 1921–1922"; R. L. Welch (Gen. Sec., American Petroleum Institute) to Hoover, 1 Feb. 1922; Hoover to Rep. Wallace Dempsey, 17 June 1922, and Hoover to Secretary of War John W. Weeks, 24 June 1922, ibid., Box 472, Folder "Pollution of

Waters, 1922"; Hoover to Rep. Frank W. Mondell, 1 Mar. 1923, ibid., Box 280, Folder "House of Representatives, Mondell, Frank W., 1921–1923"; Drake, "Herbert Hoover, Ecologist," 210–14.

34. Hoover to President Harding, 23 June 1922; Hoover to Secretary of State Charles Evans Hughes, 12 July 1922; Hoover to Hughes, 27 July 1922; Rep. T. Frank Appleby to Hoover, 11 Jan. 1923, HP:Com, Box 472, Folder "Pollution of Waters, 1922"; Report of Inter-Departmental Committee on Conference on Pollution of Navigable Waters, 31 Mar. 1923, ibid., Box 472, Folder "Pollution of Waters, 1923 January–March"; Drake, "Herbert Hoover, Ecologist," 217–18. An Anglo-American convention to regulate pollution in Canadian-American boundary waters was negotiated by the State Department in August 1922. See Hoover to Secretary of State Hughes, 12 Oct. 1922, enclosing a memorandum by Department of Commerce Acting Solicitor Stephen B. Davis, 10 Oct. 1922, HP:Com, Box 472, Folder "Pollution of Waters, Proposed Convention, U.S. & Gt. Britain, 1922."

35. See Hoover's testimony on 23 Jan. 1924 before the Hearings on the Subject of the Pollution of Navigable Waters by the House Committee on Rivers and Harbors of the 68th Cong., 1st Sess. (Washington: GPO, 1924), pp. 9–16. See Frelinghuysen to Hoover, 30 Jan. 1924; Hoover to Frelinghuysen, 30 Jan. 1924; Frelinghuysen to Hoover, 31 Jan. 1924; Hoover to Frelinghuysen, 6 Feb. 1924, all in HP:Com, Box 472, Folder "Pollution of Waters, 1924—Jan.–Mar." The sentences quoted come, respectively from Hoover's telegrams of 6 Feb. and 30 Jan.

36. Hugh Gorman, "The Gospel of Efficiency and Measures of Environmental Quality: Congressional Debates and the Oil Pollution Act of 1924," unpublished paper delivered at the American Society of Environmental History conference, 17 April 1999. See also Gorman's dissertation, "From Conservation to Environment: The Engineering Response to Pollution Concerns in the U.S. Petroleum Industry, 1921–1981" (Carnegie Mellon University, 1996).

37. W. R. Snyder to Hoover, 9 June 1924, HP:Com, Box 472, Folder "Pollution of Waters, 1924 Mar.–Dec."; Drake, "Herbert Hoover, Ecologist," 220–23. Hoover had reason for pride. Under the 1924 act, the only defense for liability was an emergency or an unavoidable accident. That this was a significant deterrent is suggested by the fact that in 1966 Congress amended the act to provide that in order for pollution to be illegal, it must be "willful" or "grossly negligent." Under the amended statute, there have been few successful prosecutions. See Max N. Edwards, "The Role of the Federal Government in Controlling Oil Pollution at Sea," in *Oil on the Sea*, ed. David P. Hoult (New York: Plenum, 1969), pp. 109–10.

38. Drake, "Herbert Hoover, Ecologist," 223–27. I have found no evidence that Hoover took any interest in the 1953 conference.

39. Report to the secretary of state by the Interdepartmental Committee on Oil Pollution of Navigable Waters, 13 Mar. 1926, HP:Com, Box 472, Folder "Pollution of Waters, 1925–1926."

40. Hoover to Henry O'Malley, 2 Dec. 1925; Lewis Radcliffe to Hoover, 2 Dec.

1925; unsigned memo about conference with Gen. Edgar Jadwin of the Army Engineers, 16 Dec. 1925; Paul S. Clapp to W. H. Hunt, 20 Feb. 1926; W. H. Hunt to Hoover, 17 June 1926; Lewis Radcliffe to Paul S. Clapp, 29 June 1926; Hoover to W. H. Hunt, 30 June 1926, all in HP:Com, Box 472, Folders "Pollution of Waters, 1925–1926," and "Pollution of Waters, Mississippi River, 1925–1926 & undated"; Hoover, "Comments on Pollution," *Outdoor America* 6 (Oct. 1927), 29.

41. Hoover, *Memoirs* 2:149. Horace Albright recalled that Hoover "loved the Bureau of Fisheries" and pointed out that when Hoover had a new Commerce Department building erected, "he had a nice aquarium built in it." Albright oral history, p. 16, HHPL.

42. From Bureau of Fisheries Annual Report, 19 Nov. 1924, HP:Com, Box 130, Folder "Commerce Department, Fisheries, Bureau of, 1924."

43. Hoover to President Coolidge, 2 Apr. 1925, HP:Com, Box 477, Folder "President Coolidge, 1925 March." The order of phrases has been altered. In some cases the Bureau of Fisheries actively promoted new uses of fish products—the use of fish meal for cattle feed or fertilizer, for example—that ran counter to state conservation efforts. See Arthur F. McEvoy, *The Fisherman's Problem: Ecology and the Law in the California Fisheries, 1850–1980* (Cambridge, England: Cambridge University Press, 1986), pp. 156–70. A list of Bureau of Fisheries achievements prepared for the 1928 campaign stressed its conservation activities and did not mention the promotion of fish products. See undated memorandum, "Bureau of Fisheries," HP:Com, Box 1, Folder "Accomplishments of the Department, 1921–28."

44. Hoover to Secretary of Agriculture Henry C. Wallace, 29 Dec. 1921; undated draft of executive order, both in HP:Com, Box 14, Folder "Alaska—Aleutian Islands, 1921." Wallace Martin to Hoover, 19 Jan. 1922; H. C. Strong to Hoover, 1 Feb. 1922; Wm. B. Dillon to Hoover, 21 Mar. 1921; J. R. McCarl to Hoover, 27 Mar. 1922, all in ibid., Box 13, Folder "Alaska, 1922 January–April"; Hoover to Secretary of the Treasury Andrew Mellon, 18 May 1925, ibid., Box 13, Folder "Alaska, 1924–1928 & undated"; Statement Covering Fishery and Fur-Seal Industry of Alaska for Use in the Governor's Annual Report, 21 June 1922, ibid., Box 13, Folder "Alaska, 1922, May–Dec."; Hoover to Asst. Sec. of Interior Edward C. Finney, 27 Oct. 1922, ibid., Box 294, Folder "Interior Dept., Miscellaneous, 1921–28 & undated"; Hoover to President Harding, 2 Nov. 1922, ibid., Box 480, Folder "President Harding, 1922 Oct.–Dec."; press release on Presidential Proclamation Creating Fisheries Reservation in Alaska, 5 Nov. 1922, ibid., Box 13, Folder "Alaska—Alaskan Fisheries, Reservations, etc., 1921–22"; Swain, *Federal Conservation Policy*, p. 47. In 1934 O'Malley wrote to Hoover that "the largest pack of salmon in the history of the industry" that year proved that Hoover's policy had been correct. See O'Malley to Hoover, 3 Oct. 1934, HP:PPI, Box 172, Folder "O'Malley, Henry, Correspondence 1933–1936." For analysis of commercial fishing on both east and west coasts that graphically illustrate the temporary impact of Hoover's policies, see *A Century of Fisheries in North America*, ed. Norman G. Benson (Washington, D.C.: American Fisheries Society, 1970).

45. Quoted in Taylor, "Rationalizing the Western Fisheries." Taylor points out that the draft of the announcement went further to identify the supporters of the policy as "the more responsible canners," and to claim unanimous support for it. "Responsible" was changed to "representative" in the official announcement, and the unsupportable claim of unanimity was dropped. As with standardization and simplification in the timber industry, the fishing reserves tended to freeze the relative positions of existing businesses, preventing smaller canneries and fishing companies from growing.

46. The quotations come from Hoover to Rep. Arthur M. Free, 7 Feb. 1924, HP:Com, Box 277, Folder "House of Rep.—Free, Arthur N., 1921–26." The principal complainant was Dan Sutherland, Alaska's delegate to the House of Representatives. See, for example, Hoover to Harding, 18 Dec. 1922, ibid., Box 480, Folder "President Harding, 1922 Oct.–Dec."; Hoover to Rep. Dan S. Greene, 21 Dec. 1922, ibid., Box 13, Folder "Alaska—Alaskan Fisheries, Reservations, etc., 1921–22"; Dan Sutherland to Hoover, 26 Dec. 1922, and Hoover to Sutherland, 30 Dec. 1922, ibid., Box 282, Folder "House of Reps—Sutherland, Dan, 1921–23"; Hoover to Gov. Scott Bone (Ark.), 14 Feb. 1923, ibid., Box 13, Folder "Alaska—Alaskan Fisheries, Reservations, etc., 1923, Jan.–Mar."; Hoover to Sen. Wesley L. Jones, 16 Mar. 1923, and Jones to Hoover, 22 Oct. 1923, ibid., Box 548, Folder "Senate, Jones, Wesley L., 1923"; Henry O'Malley to [Richard S.] Emmet, 25 Apr. 1923, ibid., Box 549, Folder "Senate—Nelson, Knute, 1921–23." Hoover's six-page briefing paper for Harding, dated 10 May 1923, is in ibid., Box 481, Folder "President Harding, 1923 Mar.–May."

47. The hearings were announced in a message sent to Alaskan newspapers from the USS *Henderson*, upon which the official party was traveling. See message to various Alaskan newspapers, 11 July 1923, HP:Com, Box 13, Folder "Alaska—Alaskan Fisheries, Restrictions, etc., 1923 July." For the patronage attack, see Richard S. Emmet to Editor, Baltimore *Evening Sun*, 24 Aug. 1923, ibid., Box 13, Folder "Alaska—Adv. Bd. Fish Commission, 1923."

48. Hoover to Sen. William H. King, 20 Nov. 1923, HP:Com, Box 14, Folder "Alaska—Alaskan Fisheries, Reservations, etc., 1923 Oct.–Dec."; Hoover to Rep. William S. Greene (Chair, Committee on Merchant Marine and Fisheries), 7 Feb. 1924, ibid., Box 278, Folder "House of Rep.—Green, Wm. S., 1921–25"; Hoover to Henry O'Malley, 28 Feb. 1924, ibid., Box 14, Folder "Alaska—Alaskan Fisheries, Reservations, etc., 1924 Jan.–Feb." President Harding strongly endorsed restrictions on salmon fishing after his trip to Alaska in the summer of 1923. See press release, "President's Address at Seattle on the Territory of Alaska," 27 July 1923, ibid., Box 13, Folder "Alaska, 1923 July–Aug."

49. Hoover to Sen. Wesley L. Jones, 29 Apr. 1924, HP:Com, Box 548, Folder "Senate, Jones, Wesley L., 1924"; Hoover to C. Bascom Slemp, 30 Apr. 1924, enclosing draft of Coolidge to Sen. Jones, and Slemp to Hoover, 1 May 1924, ibid., Box 477, Folder "President Coolidge, 1924 April"; Hoover to Sen. Simeon D. Fess, 6 May 1924 and 15 May 1924, ibid., Box 546, Folder "Senate—Fess, Simeon D., 1922–26"; Mark

Sullivan Diary, 9 May 1924, Sullivan Papers, Box 2, Hoover Institution, Stanford University; Hoover to Senator Peter Norbeck, 12 May 1924, HP:Com, Box 549, Folder "Senate—Norbeck, Peter, 1921-28"; The Department of Commerce press release on "Alaskan Salmon," 28 May 1924, contains the quoted words, ibid., Box 14, Folder "Alaska—Alaskan Fisheries, Reservations, etc., 1924 Apr.-May"; Hoover to President Coolidge, 6 June 1924, ibid., Box 471, Folder "President Coolidge, 1924 May-July"; Hoover to President Coolidge, ibid., Box 14, Folder "Alaska—Alaskan Fisheries, Reservations, etc., 1924 June-Dec."; press release on "New Alaska Fisheries Regulations," 25 June 1924, ibid., Box 11, Folder "Fishing (also Wildlife)"; Henry O'Malley to Senator William H. King, ibid., Box 548, Folder "Senate—King, William H., 1921-24"; Hoover to Henry B. Ward, 28 Dec. 1927, ibid., Box 346, Folder "Izaak Walton League, 1927."

50. Quoted in Taylor, "Rationalizing the Western Fisheries." The Bureau of Fisheries continued to enforce the North Pacific Sealing Convention signed by the United States, Great Britain, Japan, and Russia in 1911. Although the treaty permitted regulated killing of fur seals, its ban on pelagic sealing led to a steady growth (about 5 percent per year, according to Hoover) of the fur seal herd. See Department of Commerce press release, "Alaska Investigation by Department of Commerce," 15 Mar. 1922, HP:Com, Box 13, Folder "Alaska, 1922 Jan.-Apr."; Hoover to Sen. W. L. Jones, 25 June 1926, ibid., Box 13, Folder "Alaska, 1924-28 & undated."

51. Taylor, "Rationalizing the Western Fisheries."

52. Commerce Department press release, "Statement of Secretary Hoover: Progress in National Fisheries Conservation and Development," 30 June 1924, HP:Com, Box 166, Folder "Conservation, 1923-28 & undated."

53. Hoover to President Coolidge, 2 Apr. 1925, HP:Com, Box 477, Folder "President Coolidge, 1925 March"; Department of Commerce press release, "Secretary Hoover Calls Fish Conservation Conference," 29 Apr. 1925; Department of Commerce press release, "Appointment of Fish Rehabilitation Commission to Represent Atlantic and Gulf States Requested by Fish Conference," 22 May 1925, both in ibid., Box 130, Folder "Commerce Dept.—Fisheries, Bureau of, 1925"; Hoover to Gov. Henry L. Fuqua (La.), 28 May 1925, ibid., Box 154, Folder "Conferences-Fisheries-Atlantic Coast & Gulf States, 1925." A letter from the president of the United States Fisheries Association to President Coolidge expressed the gratitude of the industry for the support it had received during the Hoover years. See Dana F. Ward to President Coolidge, ibid., Box 130, Folder "Commerce Dept.—Fisheries, Bureau of, 1926-28."

54. Department of Commerce press release, "Address of Secretary of Commerce Hoover at the Izaak Walton League, Chicago, Ill., Saturday Evening, April 12, 1924," HP:Com, Box 14, Folder "Alaska—Alaskan Fisheries, Reservations, etc., 1924 Apr.-May"; Hoover to Will H. Dilg, 2 Dec. 1924, ibid., Box 130, Folder "Commerce Dept.—Fisheries, Bureau of, 1924." Hoover took considerable care with this letter setting out his proposal for involving the Waltonians in raising fish; the draft includes

numerous handwritten corrections and changes. See also Herbert Hoover, "In Praise of Izaak Walton," *Atlantic* 139 (June 1927), 813–19. Hoover joined with the Walton League in lobbying on behalf of a bill to create the Upper Mississippi Wildlife and Game Reserve and gave the organization major credit for its passage. See Will H. Dilg to Hoover, 3 and 28 Mar. 1924, Dilg to Henry O'Malley, 28 Mar. 1924, and Hoover to Dilg, 13 June 1924, HP:Com, Box 346, Folder "Izaak Walton League, 1924."

55. Hoover's coup in securing the transfer of the Bureau of Mines from the Interior Department in 1925 gave him legal authority to act in the general field of mineral conservation and management, both in regard to oil and coal. Fall's successor, Hubert Work, was not jealous of his prerogatives and often allowed Hoover to poach on matters really under the jurisdiction of the Interior Department. See Ellis Hawley, "Herbert Hoover, the Commerce Secretariat, and the Vision of an 'Associative State,' 1921–1928," *Journal of American History* 61 (June 1974): 128–29; Hawley, "Secretary Hoover and the Bituminous Coal Problem, 1921–1928," *Business History Review* 42 (Autumn 1968): 254–64; Frank E. Smith, *The Politics of Conservation* (New York: Pantheon, 1966), 166–67.

56. Gerald D. Nash, *United States Oil Policy, 1890–1964: Business and Government in Twentieth Century America* (Pittsburgh: University of Pittsburgh Press, 1968), pp. 1–30; J. Leonard Bates, *The Origins of Teapot Dome: Progressives, Politics, and Petroleum, 1909–1921* (Urbana: University of Illinois Press, 1963).

57. M. L. Requa, *Petroleum Resources of the United States: An Article on the Exhaustion of the Petroleum Resources of the United States, Showing the Present and Future Supply and Demand, also the Production of the Principal Oil Fields of the United States,* Sen. Doc. 363, 64th Cong., 1st Sess. (Washington, D.C.: GPO, 1916).

58. Nash, *United States Oil Policy,* pp. 30–48; M. L. Requa, "Some Fundamentals of the Petroleum Problem," *Saturday Evening Post* 193 (28 Aug. 1920): 29, 57–58. See also Requa's follow-up articles in the 4 Sept. and 30 Oct. issues of the same magazine.

59. Hoover to Harding, 13 Dec. 1920, HP:Com, Box 7, Folder "Harding, Corres. (Letter Book), July 1, 1920–Feb. 23, 1921"; Hoover to Harding, 2 Apr. 1921, ibid., Box 480, Folder "President Harding, 1921 Oct.–Nov."; draft of statement on oil by Hoover, 2 May 1921, ibid., Box 452, Folder "Oil 1921, May–December." For material on possible foreign sources of oil gathered by Hoover's Commerce Department, see HPS, Boxes 14 and 15.

60. Nash, *United States Oil Policy,* pp. 49–71. The seriousness of the situation as it was seen by experts was suggested by the fact that in 1923 Mark Requa, long a leading advocate of voluntary cooperation among producers, came out in favor of government regulation of domestic oil production. See Requa's "(Confidential) Memorandum Dealing with the Possibility of Government Regulation of the Petroleum Industry," 17 Sept. 1923, Mark Requa Papers, Division of Rare Books and Special Collections, University of Wyoming [hereafter Requa Papers]. See also Rep. John E. Raker to Hoover, 15 Jan. 1924, and Hoover to Raker, 21 Jan. 1924, HP:Com, Box 281, Folder "House of Representatives—Raker, John E., 1921–25."

61. The specific impetus for the creation of the board seems to have been a letter to the president from Cities Service president Henry L. Doherty, which, when circulated through the Interior Department, aroused a chorus of assent. See Doherty to Coolidge, 11 Aug. 1924; C. B. Slemp (Coolidge's secretary) to Secretary Work, 12 Aug. 1924; H. Foster Bain (director of Bureau of Mines) to Work, 19 Aug. 1924; George Otis Smith (director of Geologic Survey) to Work, 20 Aug. 1924; Work to Coolidge, 20 Aug. 1924, all in HP:Com, Box 477, Folder "President Coolidge, 1924 August"; Coolidge to the members of the board, 18 Dec. 1924, ibid., Box 198, Folder "Federal Oil Conservation Board, 1924 & undated." The records of the Federal Oil Conservation Board may be found in RG 48, Department of the Interior Central Classified File, 1907-1936, Box 424, 1-242, National Archives.

62. For the California situation, see Ralph Arnold (president of the American Petroleum Institute) to Hoover, 1 July 1922; Arnold to A. W. Ambrose (Bureau of Mines), 1 July 1922; [?] Huston to Hoover, 26 Sept. 1923, HP:Com, Box 452, Folder "Oil 1922-1923." The situation at the outset of the board's investigation is set out in Mark Requa to Hoover, 6 Jan. 1925, ibid., Box 517, Folder "Requa, Mark L., 1925 Jan.-Feb."; J. Edgar Pew (president of the API) to Hubert Work, 16 Jan. 1925, ibid. Box 453, Folder "Oil, Federal Oil Conservation Board, 1925"; speech by H. G. James (secretary, American Oilmen's Assoc.), 12 Feb. 1925, ibid., Box 452, Folder "Oil, 1925."

63. Mark Requa to Hoover, 6 Jan. 1925, HP:Com, Box 517, Folder "Requa, Mark L., 1925 Jan.-Feb."; John G. Clark, *Energy and the Federal Government: Fossil Fuel Policies, 1900-1946* (Urbana: University of Illinois Press, 1987), pp. 146-58.

64. For the Teapot Dome scandal and its implications, see J. Leonard Bates, "The Teapot Dome Scandal and the Election of 1924," *American Historical Review* 60 (Jan. 1955): 303-22; Burl Noggle, *Teapot Dome: Oil and Politics in the 1920s* (Baton Rouge: Louisiana State University Press, 1962). Hoover had no connection to the Teapot Dome scandal, except that he liked Fall and was slow to believe him culpable.

65. M. L. Requa, "American Petroleum Supply and Demand" [a critique of the American Petroleum Institute's hostile response to the first FOCB report], undated (but summer 1925), and "Memorandum" by Requa, 18 Dec. 1925, Requa Papers; Hoover to Requa, 28 Aug. 1925, HP:Com, Box 466, Folder "Petroleum, 1921-26 & undated"; Nash, *United States Oil Policy*, pp. 72-85.

66. For a careful analysis of the work of the FOCB, see Clark, *Energy and the Federal Government*, pp. 156-65. The Bureau of Mines, transferred from the Interior to the Commerce Department by an executive order of 4 June 1925, was constructing a pilot plant at Rifle, Colorado, to test the feasibility of using oil shales. See D. A. Lyon (acting director of the bureau) to Hoover, 17 Dec. 1925, HP:Com, Box 550, Folder "Senate—Phipps, Lawrence C., 1921-27"; Memorandum, "Bureau of Mines," undated, ibid., Box 1, Folder "Accomplishments of the Department, 1921-28."

67. Norman E. Nordhauser, *The Quest for Stability: Domestic Oil Regulation, 1917-1935* (New York: Garland, 1979), p. 31. Hoover's support for modification of the

antitrust laws in this instance is atypical. Normally, both as secretary of commerce and as president, he believed that the laws needed to be maintained and enforced.

68. A committee chaired by Senator Robert LaFollette in 1923 had held hearings on the oil situation and concluded that monopoly by Standard Oil remained the foremost threat to the public's interest in the oil business. Coolidge was unwilling to challenge public sentiment on this matter. See Clark, *Energy and the Federal Government*, pp. 188–90.

69. Requa also favored the creation of a Federal Minerals Conservation Board comparable to the Federal Oil Conservation Board to propose conservation policies for other minerals. See Requa's untitled memorandum, filed 18 Jan. 1927, HP:Com, Box 395, Folder "Minerals—Mineral Resources Investigation, 1924–27 & undated"; untitled memorandum by Requa, 6 June 1927, Requa Papers; Ray Lyman Wilbur to Requa, 9 Oct. 1925, Ray Lyman Wilbur Papers, Box 62, Folder "Requa, Mark L.," Stanford University Archives.

70. Nash, *United States Oil Policy*, pp. 86–97.

71. "The Department of Commerce by Herbert Hoover," 30 June 1926, HP:Com, Box 121, Folder "Commerce Department, Achievements 1924 August–December & undated."

72. Ibid.; "Hoover as Secretary of Commerce," undated, ibid., Box 120, Folder "Commerce Dept. Achievements, 1921–23." The figures cited for the expansion of Commerce expenditures include the activities of a few agencies not in Commerce, such as the Food and Drug Administration (Agriculture), the Bureau of Agricultural Economics (Agriculture), and the Copyright Office (Library of Congress), but the major increases in spending took place in Commerce. See Carroll H. Wooddy, *The Growth of the Federal Government, 1915–1932* (New York: McGraw-Hill, 1934), pp. 543, 566.

73. See Julius Klein to Hoover, 23 Mar. 1945, HP:PPI, Box 113, Folder "Klein, Dr. Julius—Correspondence, 1934–1946." Klein, who was head of the Bureau of Foreign and Domestic Commerce under Hoover, reported that Henry A. Wallace had just asked him "what made the Commerce Department do such a good job in the old days."

74. "The Department of Commerce by Herbert Hoover," 30 June 1926, HP:Com, Box 121, Folder "Commerce Department, Achievements 1924 August–December & undated." Hoover claimed explicitly that his attempt to reduce waste at all stages of production was an extension of Progressive Era conservation ideas: "Just as twenty years ago we undertook nation-wide conservation of natural resources, so now we must undertake nation-wide elimination of waste."

75. Hoover's speech to the fourteenth annual meeting of the Chamber of Commerce of the United States, 12 May 1926, HP:Com, Box 191, Folder "Elimination of Waste in Industry, 1926."

76. Ibid.

5. Engineering the Good Life

1. William Hard, "Giant Negotiations for Giant Power: An Interview with Herbert Hoover," copy of article from *Survey Graphic* (March 1924): 577, in HP:Com, Box 162, Folder "Conferences—Superpower, 1924 Jan.-Apr."

2. President Harding asked Hoover to take over Interior in late 1922 when Albert Fall resigned (partly because he felt that Hoover was encroaching on his authority); and following the death of Henry C. Wallace (who had disliked Hoover for the same reason) in 1924, President Coolidge asked Hoover to consider becoming secretary of agriculture. Satisfied where he was, Hoover declined both offers, but he often acted as if he had accepted. Press release, 6 Jan. 1923, HP:Com, Box 295, Folder "Interior Dept.—Secy. Work, Hubert, HH as Secretary of Interior, 1923-24"; press release, "Statement by Secretary Hoover," 15 Jan. 1925, ibid., Box 6, Folder "Agriculture— HH & Secy. of Ag. Dept., 1924-25 & undated."

3. Hoover to Secretary of the Interior Albert Fall, 2 Aug. 1921, HP:Com, Box 294, Folder "Interior Dept. Secy. Fall, Albert, 1921"; Clarence C. Stetson (secretary to Hoover) to Edgar Rickard, 5 Jan. 1922, ibid., Box 228, Folder "Foreman, Evan H.—Forests, 1922-27 & undated"; President Harding to Walter F. Brown, enclosing chart showing proposed reorganizations, 13 Feb. 1923, ibid., Box 514, Folder "Reorg. of Gov't Depts., 1922-23"; Hoover to Pres. Coolidge, 27 Dec. 1924, ibid., Box 514, Folder "Reorg. of Gov't Depts., 1924." For examples of the opposition, see Horace Albright to Stephen T. Mather, 4 Jan. 1922, and Robert Sterling Yard to William B. Greeley, 13 Nov. 1922, both in NPS, Box General 201.12-201.14, Folder "Re-Organization." Hoover liked Fall and generally shared his belief that exploitation of resources was essential to the development of the West. See Mark Sullivan Diary, 10 Jan. 1923, Sullivan Papers, Box 1, Hoover Institution on War, Revolution and Peace, Stanford University [hereafter Hoover Institution].

4. Robert Sterling Yard to William B. Greeley, 13 Nov. 1922, NPS, Box General 201.13-201.14, Folder "Re-Organization." The official history of the National Parks Association (of which Yard was executive secretary) says only that Hoover's proposal was "controversial." John C. Miles, *Guardians of the Parks: A History of the National Parks and Conservation Association* (Washington, D.C.: Taylor & Francis, 1995), pp. 54-55.

5. Stephen T. Mather to Albert Fall, 29 Dec. 1921, NPS, Box General 201.14-201.15, Folder "Reorganization Dec. 17, 1921-Nov. 30, 1932, Pt. I."

6. Hoover to Charles W. Folds, president of Izaak Walton League, 6 Apr. 1927, HP:Com, Box 166, Folder "Conservation, 1923-28 & undated"; Hoover to Rep. William Williamson, 28 Mar. 1928, ibid., Folder "Conservation, Department of, 1928." Legislative proposals to accomplish the consolidation failed partly because they attempted to establish a new cabinet-level Department of Conservation, a proposal that Hoover consistently described as impractical. Even more far-reaching and impractical

was a plan advanced by the American Engineering Council to replace the Department of the Interior with a Department of Public Works and Domain. See New York *Herald Tribune,* 12 Nov. 1926, clipping in ibid., Box 514, Folder "Reorg. of Gov't Depts., 1926–27 & undated."

7. Following Secretary Fall's resignation, the opposition of Secretary of the Interior Hubert Work to consolidation largely doomed Hoover's idea. See, for example, Work to T. Gilbert Pearson, 27 Sept. 1927, IGF, Central Classified File, 1907–36, Sect. I, Administrative, 1–81, Box 202, Folder "Reorganization: General, Pt. 2, May 10, 1925–July 7, 1930."

8. Hoover, *Memoirs: The Cabinet and the Presidency, 1920–1933* (New York: Macmillan, 1952), p. 112 [hereafter Hoover, *Memoirs* 2].

9. From the Annual Report of the Commerce Department, 1926, quoted in ibid., p. 114. See also Hoover's address to the National Rivers and Harbors Congress, 9 Dec. 1925, in the *Proceedings of the National Rivers and Harbors Congress,* pp. 16–23, in HP:Com, Box 157, Folder "Conferences—Natl. Rivers & Harbors Cong., 1923–28 & undated." Some people saw Hoover's outspoken support of the development of water resources as evidence of his desire to encroach on Interior Department prerogatives, but Secretary of the Interior Hubert Work seemed unconcerned. See President Coolidge to Hoover, 25 Oct. 1926, Hoover to Secretary Work, 25 Oct. 1926, and Hoover to Coolidge, 2 Nov. 1926, all in HP:Com, Box 478, Folder "President Coolidge, 1926 Aug.–Nov."

10. Northcutt Ely, "Herbert Hoover and the Colorado River" (1982), pp. 2–3 (manuscript given to the author by Mr. Ely).

11. Colorado Water Investigation Commission, *The Future Operation of Glen Canyon Reservoir as Related to the Colorado River Compact* (np: July 1959), p. 5, Northcutt Ely Papers, Acc. 273, Box 73, Dept. of Special Collections, Cecil H. Green Library, Stanford University; "Memorandum on Interview which Dr. Ray Lyman Wilbur had with Mr. Harry Chandler, in Los Angeles, on October 3, 1938," HP:PPI, Box 555, Folder "Wilbur, R. L., Correspondence, 1933–38." For additional pressures on the federal government on behalf of the Imperial Valley, see Elwood Mead to Secretary of Interior Franklin K. Lane, 9 Aug. 1916, 29 Aug. 1916, and Mead to Reclamation Service Director Arthur P. Davis, 4 Oct. 1916 and 13 Mar. 1917, all in Box 1, Elwood Mead Correspondence and Papers, Water Resources Archive, University of California at Berkeley [hereafter Mead Papers].

12. "Report on Problems of Imperial Valley and Vicinity Required by Act of Congress approved May 18, 1920" (Feb. 1922), HP:Com, Box 290, Folder "Imperial Valley and Vicinity, Problems of, 1922"; Franklin K. Lane to Board of Directors, Imperial Engineering District, 21 Mar. 1917, Mead Papers, Box 1; Joseph E. Stevens, *Hoover Dam: An American Adventure* (Norman: University of Oklahoma Press, 1988), pp. 15–18.

13. Ely, "Herbert Hoover and the Colorado River," p. 3; Undated "Summary of

Decision in *State of Wyoming vs. State of Colorado,*" CRC, Box 24, Folder "*Wyoming vs. Colorado.*"

14. Delph Carpenter of Colorado later claimed that he originated the idea of the interstate compact, but it seems probable that the proposal arose more or less simultaneously in several people's minds as they studied the problem. See the notes on the history of the Colorado River Commission gathered by Charles A. Dobbel, RLW, Box 12, Folder "Hoover Dam—Dobbel Material—History, undated."

15. Albert Fall to Harding, 24 Sept. 1921, Albert B. Fall Collection, Box 47 (10), Folder "Colorado River Project, Sept. 21, 1921–Feb. 9, 1923," Henry Huntington Library, San Marino, Calif. [hereafter Fall Collection]. The order of phrases has been changed slightly.

16. Hoover to Harding, 2 Nov. 1921, HP:Com, Box 480, Folder "President Harding, 1921 Oct.–Nov." Although Hoover was an obvious candidate, it is not clear who first proposed his name; Secretary Fall suggested his name on 17 Nov., more than two weeks after Hoover's letter to Harding indicates that the two men had already settled the appointment. See Fall to Harding, 17 Nov. 1921, Fall Collection, Box 47(10), Folder "Colorado River Project, Sept. 1921–Feb. 9, 1923."

Los Angeles *Times* publisher Harry Chandler later asserted that Hoover, despite his appearance of neutrality, was really a strong supporter of Southern California's interests. See "Memorandum of Interview which Dr. Ray Lyman Wilbur had with Mr. Harry Chandler, in Los Angeles, on October 3, 1938," HP:PPI, Box 555, Folder "Wilbur, R. L., Correspondence, 1933–1938." Inasmuch as this tale, which allots a key role to Chandler, rests only on the publisher's unsupported recollections fifteen years after the events described, the historian must treat it with caution.

17. Hoover's official commission, dated 17 Dec. 1921, is in CRC, Box 10, Folder "Appointment of Mr. Hoover to Serve on Commission, 1921"; Ely, "Herbert Hoover and the Colorado River," pp. 4–5. Opponents of the agreement included some of the power companies of Southern California, who feared the competition of cheap, publicly produced power from the dam at Boulder Canyon. On this point, see an unsigned memorandum by Clarence C. Stetson, Executive Secretary of the commission, 24 Dec. 1921, CRC, Box 22, Folder "Stetson, Clarence C.—September–December 1922." Also complicating the situation were the suspicions of Hoover harbored by California Congressman Phil Swing and Senator Hiram Johnson. Johnson and Hoover in particular had a running feud throughout the 1920s, with each denouncing the other bitterly, but they managed to work together on the Colorado project. For Hoover's concern about these potential problems, see Mark Sullivan Diary, 6 Apr. 1922, Mark Sullivan Papers, Box 1, Hoover Institution.

18. Hoover claimed that the fifty-fifty split idea came to him as a midnight inspiration during the two weeks in November that the commission met at Santa Fe. Hoover, *Memoirs* 2:116. The minutes of the commission's 11 Nov. 1922 meeting lend some support to this recollection, although stripping it of glamour: "Chairman

Hoover asked . . . , inasmuch as we had not been able to arrive at a satisfactory basis for the partition of the water . . . on a basis of land suitable to be irrigated in each state, whether or not it would be possible to partition the water." CRC, Box 35, Folder "Printed Minutes—Meetings 8–14." A letter from California commissioner W. F. McClure to Rep. Phil Swing on 20 Oct. 1922, however, alludes to "Commissioner Carpenter's proposal on a fifty-fifty division upper and lower states," and he says the same thing in two further letters on 28 Oct. Phil D. Swing Papers, Box 135, Folder "Colo. River Commission-Compact-Hoover-1922," Dept. of Special Collections, Library of the University of California at Los Angeles [hereafter Swing Papers]; Beverley Bowen Moeller, *Phil Swing and Boulder Dam* (Berkeley: University of California Press, 1971), pp. viii–x, 32–33. If Carpenter proposed the fifty-fifty division in October, Hoover could hardly have originated it in November. Norris Hundley, in *Water and the West: The Colorado River Compact and the Politics of Water in the American West* (Berkeley: University of California Press, 1975), p. 182, argues that Carpenter had suggested the fifty-fifty division as early as 1920, and that it had been proposed by Arthur Powell Davis at the hearing in Los Angeles five months earlier.

19. A copy of the compact, dated 24 Nov. 1922, is in CRC, Box 4, Folder "Federal Legislation, 1923." See also, Hoover to Albert Fall, 16 Nov. 1922, ibid., Folder "Fall, Albert B., 1922"; press release, 16 Nov. 1922, ibid., Box 18, Folder "Press Releases— November 1922." As it turned out, the most serious inequity in the compact was the result of an overestimation of the river's flow, which exacerbated the conflict between Arizona and California over the lower basin's allotment. Moeller, *Swing*, p. xi.

20. Hoover to Albert Fall, 27 Nov. 1922, CRC, Box 32, Folder "Interior Department 1922–24 and 1926–27"; Clarence C. Stetson to E. W. Libbey (reporting Hoover's 24 Nov. speech at the closing ceremonies of the commission), 25 Nov. 1922, ibid., Box 22, Folder "Stetson, Clarence C., Sept.–Dec. 1922." For Arizona's position, see Malcolm B. Parsons, "Origins of the Colorado River Controversy in Arizona Politics, 1922–1923," *Arizona and the West* 4 (Spring 1962): 27–44.

21. *The New York Times*, 24 Oct. 1926; Parsons, "Origins of the Colorado River Controversy in Arizona," 35–41; Moeller, *Swing*, p. 48.

22. Calif. State Senator William J. Carr to Phil Swing, 2 Dec. 1922, and Swing to Carr, 15 Jan. 1923, Swing Papers, Box 135, Folder "Colo. River Commis.-Compact," demonstrate that this was a long-standing concern in California. For the 1925 opposition led by Carr, see C. A. Dykstra, ed., "Colorado River Development and Related Problems," *Annals of the American Academy of Political and Social Science* 148, Pt. II (Mar. 1930): 14. There was reason for the concern. Clarence Stetson, executive secretary of the Colorado River Commission, suggested a series of small dams, and Hoover's own position was unclear at first. See an unsigned memorandum by Stetson, 8 May 1922, CRC, Box 14, Folder "General Information"; Hoover's testimony before the House Committee on Irrigation of Arid Lands, 21 June 1922, ibid., Box 15, Folder "House of Representatives—Hearings re: H.R. 11449, 1922–23"; Richard S. Emmet to Rep. Philip D. Swing (quoting from telegram from Hoover), 28 Nov. 1922, ibid.,

Box 34, Folder "Project File—Swing, Phil D., 1922–24, 1926–27"; Hoover's address to the Los Angeles Chamber of Commerce, 5 Dec. 1922, ibid., Box 15, Folder "Hoover, Hon. H." Emmet quoted Hoover as saying that he thought Imperial Valley growers were "prepared to reduce present effort to the initial item of flood control dam." In his speech to the Los Angeles Chamber of Commerce Hoover specifically endorsed the construction of "a great dam . . . 700 feet high," but suspicions lingered.

23. Hoover had the president send a message to California stating that he favored "immense water storage . . . to provide for the large reclamation possibilities in both California and Arizona." See Hoover to C. Bascom Slemp, 7 Oct. 1924, enclosing draft of telegram from Coolidge to C. C. Teague, and Slemp to Hoover, 8 Oct. 1924, HP:Com, Box 477, Folder "President Coolidge, 1924 Oct.–Nov." Hoover conducted his campaign in California largely through Mark Requa. See Hoover to Requa, 14 Feb. and 3 Mar. 1925, and Requa to Hoover, 10 Mar. and 21 [or 22] Mar., 1925, ibid., Box 517, Folder "Requa, Mark L., 1925 March"; Hoover to Secretary Hubert Work, 28 Mar. 1925, ibid., Box 295, Folder "Interior Department—Secretary Work, Hubert, 1925"; Ralph Merritt to Hoover, 30 Mar. 1925, ibid., Box 391, Folder "Merritt, Ralph P., 1924–25"; pamphlet by Mark Requa, *The Colorado River Compact: Its Relation to [Calif.] Assembly Resolution No. 15* (np: Mar. 31, 1925), ibid., Box 7, Folder "Ratification of Compact, 1923, 1927, 1929"; Hoover to Requa, 31 Mar., and Requa to Hoover, 3 Apr. (telegram and letter), CRC, Box 34, Folder "Project File—Requa Pamphlet, 1925"; Requa to Hoover, 22 Apr. 1925, enclosing former Gov. George C. Pardee to Requa, 19 Apr. 1925, HP:Com, Box 517, Folder "Requa, Mark L., 1925 Apr.–Aug." For a careful analysis of the ratification battles, see Hundley, *Water and the West*, pp. 254–57.

24. C. A. Dobbel to Hoover, 17 May 1933, HP:PS, Box 105, Folder "Colorado River Commission, Correspondence, 1928–33"; Hundley, *Water and the West*, pp. 257–61. Finding a solution to the impasse was complicated by the friction between Hoover and Senator Hiram Johnson. See Hoover to Chester H. Rowell, 11 Apr. 1925, Rowell Papers, Box 16, Folder "Hoover, Herbert Clark"; Hiram Johnson to Hiram Johnson Jr., 12 Dec. 1925, Johnson Papers, Pt. VI, Box 4, Folder "1925 May–Dec."; both at Bancroft Library, University of California at Berkeley. In testimony to the House Committee on Irrigation and Reclamation on 3 Mar. 1926, Hoover suggested writing into the Swing-Johnson bill a guarantee that "no water rights would accrue to the citizens of any non-compact state from storage of water as the result of this dam." CRC, Box 7, Folder "Statements & Speeches by HH, 1925–29."

25. Hoover to Coolidge, 12 Nov. 1927, HP:Com, Box 479, Folder "President Coolidge, 1927 November–December"; Hundley, *Water and the West*, pp. 263–66.

26. Department of the Interior Memorandum for the Press, 11 Feb. 1926, CRC, Box 32, Folder "Project File—Interior Dept., 1922–24 & 1926–27."

27. Chester H. Rowell to Hoover, 18 Feb. 1926, Rowell Papers, Box 6, Folder "1926 Jan.–Feb."; Andrew Mellon to Rep. Addison T. Smith, 18 Mar. 1926, Johnson Papers, Pt. III, Box 8, Folder "Irrig. & Reclam. Comm., 1924–40, Boulder Dam Project,

Miscell. Papers"; notes and speech drafts in Johnson Papers, Pt. III, Box 8, Folder "Irrig. & Reclam. Comm., 1924–40, Boulder Dam Project, Johnson's Notes (Pt. II)"; Hoover to Swing, 13 Jan. 1927, CRC, Box 32, Folder "Project File—Legislation, 1927"; press release: "Mr. Hoover's statement apropos of the DEBATE ON SWING-JOHNSON BILL," 27 Jan. 1927, HP:C&T, Box 81, Folder "Subject: Boulder Dam"; Hiram Johnson, "The Boulder Canyon Project," in "Great Inland Water-Way Projects in the United States," ed. Clyde H. King, *Annals of the American Academy of Political and Social Science* 135 (Jan. 1928): 155–56; Hundley, *Water and the West*, pp. 266–70.

28. Hundley, *Water and the West*, pp. 270–76. Johnson never believed that Hoover really wanted the bill to pass. See, for example, Johnson to Hiram Johnson Jr. ("Jack"), 11 Mar. 1927, Johnson Papers, Pt. VI, Box 5, Folder "1927 Jan.–July"; Johnson to Hiram Jr. and Archibald J. Johnson, 8 May 1928, ibid., Folder "1928 May–June." Swing, on the other hand, supported Hoover vigorously in the 1928 campaign and maintained cordial relations with him. See the materials in HP:C&T, Box 66, Folder "General Correspondence—Swing, Phil D."

29. Hundley, *Water and the West*, pp. 276–81.

30. Hoover, *Memoirs* 2:117.

31. Hoover to Gov. Friend W. Richardson (Calif.), 17 July 1924, HP:Com, Box 74, Folder "California Water Question, 1923–28 & undated"; Northcutt Ely, *Oil Conservation through Interstate Agreement* (Washington: GPO, 1933), pp. 203–206; Department of the Interior Memorandum for the Press, 20 May 1925, HP:Com, Box 526, Folder "Rio Grande River Compact, 1925"; Secretary of Interior Hubert Work to Gov. H. J. Hagerman, 26 May 1925, RG 48, Interior Department Records, Secretary Work, Box 30, File "Bureau of Reclamation, Jan. 1, 1924 to June 30, 1925," National Archives; Douglas R. Littlefield, "The Rio Grande Compact of 1929: A Truce in an Interstate River War," *Pacific Historical Review* 60 (Nov. 1991): 497–515.

32. Hoover to Work, 17 Nov. 1925, HP:Com, Box 295, Folder "Interior Dept.—Bur. of Reclamation, 1921–27." Hoover recommended that the federal government continue to provide 50 percent of the funding for new projects but proposed that states be given full authority to operate existing projects, including setting rates for users. One half of revenues were still to be earmarked to repay federal construction costs.

33. Hoover to Coolidge, 27 Dec. 1926, HP:Com, Box 478, Folder "President Coolidge, 1926 December." The quoted statements are on pp. 7–8. See also Christian Herter to George Barr Baker, 3 Nov. 1921, HP:Com, Box 538, Folder "St. Ann's-St. Lawrence, 1921–28"; Hoover to Rep. A. P. Nelson, 31 Dec. 1921, ibid., Box 281, Folder "House of Representatives, Nee-Ove, 1921–1927 & undated"; Chas. P. Craig (Great Lakes–St. Lawrence Tidewater Assoc.) to Hoover, 17 Jan. 1922, ibid., Box 689, Folder "Waterways, Great Lakes–St. Lawrence, 1922"; Hoover to J. P. Goodrich, 24 Jan. 1924, ibid., Folder "Waterways, Great Lakes–St. Lawrence, 1924 Jan.–Mar.";

press release announcing the creation of the St. Lawrence Commission of the United States, 14 Mar. 1924, ibid.; press release announcing Canada's National Advisory Committee on the St. Lawrence Waterway Project, 17 Mar. 1924, ibid., Box 75, Folder "Canada, 1923–24"; press release on Statement by Secretary of Commerce Herbert Hoover before House Committee on Rivers and Harbors, 30 Jan. 1926, ibid., Box 687, Folder "Waterways, 1926 Jan.–Feb."; Hoover to Arthur Brisbane, 13 Dec. 1926, ibid., Box 688, Folder "Waterways, 1926 Dec."

34. The quotation comes from William Hard, "Giant Negotiations for Giant Power: An Interview with Herbert Hoover," *Survey Graphic* (Mar. 1924), 577. See Hoover to Secretary of State Frank Kellogg, 10 June 1925, HP:Com, Box 449, Folder "Niagara Alkali–Niagara Power, 1921–27"; press release of the Department of State, "Summary of Interim Report of the Special International Niagara Board," 20 Jan. 1928, ibid., Box 695, Folder "Waterways—Great Lakes–St. Lawrence–Niagara Falls, 1928 & undated"; Members of the Special International Niagara Board to the Secretary of State and the Minister of the Interior (Canada), 3 May 1928, ibid.; clipping from the Buffalo *Evening News*, "Dempsey Lauds Hoover in Plan to Save Falls," 17 May 1928, ibid.

35. Minutes of First Meeting of Advisory Board, 24 Sept. 1920; W. S. Murray to Hoover, 4 Oct. 1920; both in HP:Pre-Com, Box 80, Folder "U.S. Geological Survey, September 24, 1920–November 23, 1920." Albert Fall to Hoover, 20 July 1921, HP:Com, Box 590, Folder "Superpower, Waterpower, etc., 1920–1921." The superpower survey was mandated by an Act of Congress of 5 June 1920. See Department of Interior Memorandum for the Press, 24 Feb. 1921, ibid.

36. Summary of Statement of Secretary Hoover to the Superpower Conference, New York City, Saturday, October 13, 1923, HP:Com, Box 120, Folder "Commerce Dept. Achievements, 1921–23"; George O. Smith to Hoover, 20 Nov. 1920; Minutes of Advisory Board Meeting, 5 June 1921, HP:Pre-Com, Box 80, Folder "U.S. Geological Survey, Sept. 4, 1920–Nov. 23, 1920."

37. W. S. Murray to Hoover, 7 June 1921, HP:Com, Box 295, Folder "Interior Dept.—Adv. Bd.—Superpower Survey, 1921 May–July."

38. Hoover to Wm. D. B. Ainey, 20 Oct. 1923; Hoover to Gov. William S. Flynn (R.I.), 24 Oct. 1923; Hoover to M. H. Aylesworth, 6 Dec. 1923, HP:Com, Box 162, Folder "Conferences—Superpower—1923 June–Oct."

39. Suggestions for President Coolidge's Annual Message, enclosed in Hoover to C. Bascom Slemp, 16 Nov. 1923, HP:Com, Box 476, Folder "President Coolidge, 1923 Nov."; Hard, "Giant Negotiations for Giant Power," p. 578; "Superpower and Economic Statesmanship," *Chemical and Metallurgical Engineering* 29 (1923): 17.

40. Northeastern Superpower Committee Report, 14 Apr. 1924, HP:Com, Box 162, Folder "Conferences—Superpower—1924 Jan.–Apr."; summary of report enclosed in Harold Stokes to Paul Clapp, 10 July 1924, ibid., Box 590, Folder "Superpower, Waterpower, etc.—1924 July–Dec."

41. The quotation comes from Henry L. Stimson to Hoover, 13 Jan. 1925; see also Hoover to Stimson, 17 Jan. 1925, both in HP:Com, Box 590, Folder "Superpower, Waterpower, etc.—1925 Jan." For the public vs. private power controversy, see Morris L. Cooke to Gov. Gifford Pinchot (Pa.), 10 Apr. 1924, ibid., Box 162, Folder "Conferences—Superpower, 1924 Jan.–Apr."; excerpt from a speech by Sen. George Norris (Nebr.) at Grand Island, 23 Sept. 1924, ibid., Box 590, Folder "Superpower, Waterpower, etc., 1924 July–Dec."; speech of Governor Gifford Pinchot before the Commonwealth Club, Palace Hotel, San Francisco, 6 July 1925, ibid., Box 469, Folder "Pinchot, Gifford, 1917–1927 & undated"; unidentified clipping, "Hoover Outlines Opinion on Hydro-Development Control," 30 Nov. 1926, ibid., Box 591, Folder "Superpower, Waterpower, etc., 1926 & 1927."

42. Hoover to Norman Hapgood, 12 Nov. 1927, HP:Com, Box 591, Folder "Superpower, Waterpower, etc., 1926–27."

43. Amos Pinchot, "Hoover and Power," *The Nation* 133 (5 Aug. 1931): 125, 127. Quotations are not in their original order.

44. Jean Christie, *Morris Llewellyn Cooke, Progressive Engineer* (New York: Garland, 1983), pp. 72–86.

45. Hoover to Secretary of War John W. Weeks, 22 June 1924, HP:Com, Box 422, Folder "Muscle Shoals, Miscellaneous 1921–1924"; unsigned memorandum on lease offer by Henry Ford, 13 July 1921, ibid., Box 423, Folder "Muscle Shoals, Henry Ford, 1921"; Hoover to Weeks, 19 Nov. 1921, ibid.; Hoover to Robert R. Moton, 23 Jan. 1925, and draft of paragraph for inclusion in president's annual message, 6 Nov. 1925, both in ibid., Box 422, Folder "Muscle Shoals, Miscellaneous, 1925." On the appointment of the Muscle Shoals Inquiry, see Hoover to Coolidge, 9 and 14 Mar. 1925; Coolidge to Hoover, 21 Mar. 1925, ibid., Folder "Muscle Shoals Commission, 1925–26"; Everett Sanders to Hoover, 26 Mar. 1925, ibid., Box 477, Folder "President Coolidge 1925–Mar." The quoted phrase comes from a pessimistic letter to Hoover from inquiry member Russell F. Bower, 6 Nov. 1925, ibid., Box 422, Folder "Muscle Shoals Commission, 1925–26."

46. Both quotations come from a major speech at Elizabethton, Tennessee, on 6 Oct. 1928, in *The New Day: Campaign Speeches of Herbert Hoover, 1928* (Stanford, Calif.: Stanford University Press, 1928), pp. 107, 106. The next day Hoover told a Scripps-Howard reporter that he intended to include Muscle Shoals in his reference to enterprises that could be run by the government, but as David Burner points out, he did not endorse the massive federal project favored by Senator Norris. See David Burner, *Herbert Hoover: A Public Life* (New York: Knopf, 1979), p. 202.

47. Statement on Muscle Shoals Legislation, 28 Feb. 1931, and Veto of the Muscle Shoals Resolution, 3 Mar. 1931, in *Public Papers of the Presidents of the United States: Herbert Hoover; Containing the Public Messages, Speeches, and Statements of the President, January 1 to December 31, 1931* (Washington, D.C.: GPO, 1976), pp. 116, 126.

48. The fact that Hoover's close friend, Dr. Ray Lyman Wilbur, was active in the

organization may have influenced him to support it also. See William E. Colby to Wilbur, 29 Aug. 1919, Box 66, Folder "Save the Redwoods League (1919–25)," Ray Lyman Wilbur Papers, Stanford University Archives. For Hoover's role, see J. D. Grant to Hoover, 4 June 1921, HP:Com, Box 244, Folder "Grant, Joseph, 1921–27"; Gov. Wm. D. Stephens (Calif.) to Hoover, ibid., Box 576, Folder "Stephens, T.— Stept, 1921–27 & undated"; Hoover to J. D. Grant, 28 Dec. 1923 and 26 Apr. 1924, ibid., Box 512, Folder "Redwoods, Save the Redwoods League, 1923–26 & undated"; John C. Merriam to Hoover, 17 Apr. 1925, and Hoover to Merriam, 23 Apr. 1925, ibid.; J. D. Grant to Hoover, 15 Apr. 1926, and Hoover to Grant, 24 Apr. 1926, ibid., Box 272, Folder "Hoover, Herbert—Memberships, Saf-Sav." Susan Schrepfer says that although Hoover declined to meet with the Save the Redwoods League, he spoke to several lumber company officials about preservation. He shared the league's belief that federal money should not be used to establish redwood parks. See *The Fight to Save the Redwoods: A History of Environmental Reform, 1917–1978* (Madison: University of Wisconsin Press, 1983), pp. 21–22.

49. Senator Coleman duPont (Del.) to Hoover, 4 May 1922; Caspar Hodgson to Hoover, 16 May 1922; Ernest Thompson Seton to Hoover, 18 May 1922; Hoover to Seton, 23 May 1922, all in HP:Com, Box 555, Folder "Seton, M&M Ernest Thompson, 1921–22."

50. Hoover to Charles D. Walcott, 26 Feb. 1924, HP:Com, Box 272, Folder "Hoover, Herbert—Memberships, National, F–P"; copy of clipping from Washington *Star*, 27 Feb. 1924, printed in *National Parks and Conservation Magazine* 53 (Mar. 1979): 29.

51. Kathryn Karsten Rushing, "NPCA: Sixty Years of Idealism and Hard Work," *National Parks and Conservation Magazine* 53 (May 1979): 6–7; Robert Shankland, *Steve Mather of the National Parks* (New York: Knopf, 1951), p. 167.

52. Yard's draft report for the Executive Committee of the NPA, enclosed in Yard to Hoover, 7 Mar. 1924, HP:Com, Box 432, Folder "National Parks Association, 1921–24."

53. "National Parks Association: Minutes of the Trustees Meeting to Consider a Proposition for Federation, January 12, 1925," RG 48, Interior Dept. Records, General, Box 1971, File 12-0 (Pt. 1), Folder "Parks, Reservations and Antiquities: Parks General; National Parks Association, Sept. 19, 1916 to Apr. 5, 1930."

54. William C. Gregg to Hoover, 21 Jan. 1925, HP:Com, Box 432, Folder "National Parks Association, 1925"; Yard to E. K. Burlew, 17 Feb. 1925, RG 48, Interior Dept. Records, Secretary Work, Box 29, File "National Park Service, Mar. 5, 1930 to Oct. 8, 1925."

55. Hoover to Frederick A. Delano, 3 Apr. 1925, enclosing memorandum on the proposed Public Parks Council; Yard to Hoover, 9 Apr. 1925; Hoover to Yard, 10 Apr. 1925; Yard to Hoover, 15 Apr. 1925, Hoover to Yard, 16 Apr. 1925; Charles Walcott to Hoover, 20 Apr. 1925; Yard to Hoover, 21 Apr. 1925; Hoover to Yard, 22 Apr. 1925;

Yard to Hoover, 24 Apr. 1925; Yard to Hoover, 22 May 1925, all in HP:Com, Box 432, Folder "National Parks Association, 1925." Miles, *Guardians of the Parks,* pp. 53–55, greatly understates the tensions during Hoover's NPA presidency.

56. Roosevelt to Hoover, 31 Dec. 1923, HP:Com, Box 529, Folder "Roosevelt, Theodore Jr., 1922–27 & undated." There are interesting echoes of Turner's frontier argument in the statements of Roosevelt and other outdoor recreation advocates.

57. Leon F. Kneipp, "Land Planning and Acquisition, U.S. Forest Service," oral history interview by Amelia R. Fry, Edith Mezirow, and Fern Ingersoll, Bancroft Library, University of California at Berkeley, 1:113. Donald Swain contends, without citing specific evidence, that Coolidge created the new organization as a way of reducing the conflict between the Forest Service and the National Park Service over control of recreation on public lands, which had been going on for several years. See Swain, *Federal Conservation Policy,* p. 135. Arthur Ringland, who became the permanent Executive Secretary of the NCOR after Kneipp returned to his position in the Forest Service, disputes Swain's assertion. See Arthur C. Ringland, "Conserving Human and Natural Resources," oral history interview by Amelia R. Fry, Edith Mezirow, Fern Ingersoll, and Thelma Dreis, Bancroft Library, University of California at Berkeley, 1:149.

58. Contemporary documents give the attendance figure variously as 309 and 312. See, for example, draft of a proposed booklet on the NCOR (1924) in the National Archives, Records of the National Conference on Outdoor Recreation, 1924–29 [hereafter NCOR], Box 1, and "Summary of Resolutions Adopted at President's National Conference on Outdoor Recreation," Ray Lyman Wilbur Papers, Stanford University Archives, Box 54, Folder "National Conference on Outdoor Recreation." Swain, *Federal Conservation Policy,* p. 135, gives the attendance as 309. Lou Henry Hoover was a member of the Executive Committee of the NCOR from its inception until May 1929, although her attendance at meetings was irregular. See NCOR, Box 9, Folder "Mrs. Herbert Hoover."

59. Outline of Subjects for the National Conference on Outdoor Recreation to be held May 22, 23, 24, 1924, at the Auditorium of the New National Museum, Washington, D.C., NCOR, Box 1.

60. Records of the organization's finances indicate that contributions from individuals and organizations averaged about $13,000 a year from 1924 through 1928. See NCOR, Box 10, Folder "Correspondence after Closing." The conference paid Arthur Ringland's salary of $7,500 and its office expenses from these donations but depended on other organizations and donors to fund such projects as a survey of municipal and state lands, a recreational survey of federal lands, and a survey of the country's highway system. See L. F. Kneipp to A. C. Ringland, 17 Dec. 1924, in Ringland, "Conserving Human and Natural Resources," vol. 2, and Carl E. Krog, "'Organizing the Production of Leisure': Herbert Hoover and the Conservation Movement in the 1920s," *Wisconsin Magazine of History* 67 (Spring 1984): 213. Krog's important essay

is the first to begin exploring the links Hoover saw between industrial affluence and outdoor recreation.

61. *National Conference on Outdoor Recreation: Proceedings of the Meeting of the Advisory Council, December 11 and 12, 1924*, Senate Document No. 229, 68 Cong., 2 Sess. (Washington, D.C.: GPO, 1925), p. 5.

62. Ibid.

63. "National Conference on Outdoor Recreation: By-Laws of the National Conference on Outdoor Recreation adopted by its General Council December 12, 1924," NCOR, Box 5, Folder "By-Laws of Conference."

64. Address by Secretary Hoover at Dinner of the National Conference on Outdoor Recreation, Washington, D.C., 21 Jan. 1926, HP:Com, Box 157, Folder "Conferences —Natl. Conf. on O. Recreation, 1926."

65. Quoted in Ray Lyman Wilbur and Arthur Mastick Hyde, *The Hoover Policies* (New York: Scribner's, 1937), p. 253.

66. *A Report Epitomizing the Results of Major Fact-Findng Surveys and Projects which Have Been Undertaken under the Auspices of the National Conference on Outdoor Recreation*, Senate Document 158, 70 Cong., 1 Sess. (Washington, D.C.: GPO, 1928), pp. 1–2.

67. Ibid., p. 2.

68. Krog, "'Organizing the Production of Leisure,'" 216; Steiner, *Americans at Play: Recent Trends in Recreation and Leisure Time Activities* (New York: McGraw-Hill, 1933).

69. Steiner, *Americans at Play*, p. ix.

70. Janet Hutchison, "Building for Babbitt: The State and the Suburban Home Ideal," *Journal of Policy History* 9:2 (1997): 184, 191, 197.

71. Julius H. Barnes, "Herbert Hoover's Priceless Work in Washington," *Industrial Management* 71 (April 1926): 197. See also Arthur C. Carruthers, "Herbert C. Hoover: Leader in Conservation and Waste Elimination," *Safety Engineering* (Dec. 1927): 191–92.

6. "Specialist in Public Calamities"

1. "Will Coolidge Shatter the Third-Term Tradition?" *Literary Digest* 93 (14 May 1927): 5–7; "Current Topics in the World's Cartoons," *The American Review of Reviews* 75 (June 1927): 585–88; "The Progress of the World," *The American Review of Reviews* 76 (July 1927): 12–13.

2. "The Progress of the World," 12–13; John M. Barry, *Rising Tide: The Great Mississippi Flood of 1927 and How It Changed America* (New York: Simon & Schuster, 1997), p. 270.

3. Claude M. Fuess, *Calvin Coolidge: The Man from Vermont* (Hamden, Conn.:

Archon, 1965), pp. 392–93; Hoover quoted in Craig Lloyd, *Aggressive Introvert: A Study of Herbert Hoover and Public Relations Management, 1912–1932* (Columbus: Ohio State University Press, 1972), p. 84.

4. "Hoover—'Specialist in Public Calamities,'" *Literary Digest* 97 (21 Apr. 1928): 40; "First Effects of the Mississippi Flood," *Literary Digest* 93 (18 June 1927): 8; Barry, *Rising Tide*, pp. 288–89; Kent Schofield, "The Public Image of Herbert Hoover in the 1928 Campaign," *Mid-America* 51 (Oct. 1969): 278–88.

5. *The Memoirs of Herbert Hoover, Volume 2: The Cabinet and the Presidency, 1920–1933* (New York: Macmillan, 1952), pp. 124–25, 126, 131 [hereafter *Memoirs* 2]; Bruce Lohof, "Herbert Hoover, Spokesman of Humane Efficiency: The Mississippi Flood of 1927," *American Quarterly* 22 (Fall 1970): 698–99.

6. Barry, *Rising Tide*, pp. 173–79.

7. "A Brief Chronology of What Congress Has Done since 1824 to Control the Floods of the Mississippi," *Congressional Digest* 7 (Feb. 1928): 44–45; W. M. Black, "The Problem of the Mississippi," *North American Review* 224 (Dec. 1927): 630–40.

8. Quoted in Pete Daniel, *Deep'n As It Come: The 1927 Mississippi River Flood* (New York: Oxford University Press, 1977), p. 6.

9. Barry, *Rising Tide*, pp. 181–87.

10. Ibid., pp. 189–92.

11. Ibid., pp. 194–209; J. H. O'Neill, "Relief Measures During and Following the Mississippi River Flood," *American Journal of Public Health* 18 (Feb. 1928): 154; Daniel, *Deep'n As It Come*, p. 10.

12. "Steps Taken by the Federal Government for Mississippi Flood Relief," *Congressional Digest* 7 (Feb. 1928): 41; Lohof, "Herbert Hoover," 691; Barry, *Rising Tide*, p. 270.

13. Quoted in O'Neill, "Relief Measures," 155.

14. American Red Cross, *The Mississippi Valley Flood Disaster of 1927: Official Report of the Relief Operations* (Washington, D.C.: American National Red Cross, [1929]), pp. 26–30; David Burner, *Herbert Hoover: A Public Life* (New York: Knopf, 1979), p. 193.

15. Red Cross, *Mississippi Valley Flood*, pp. 117–19; "The Mississippi Flood of 1927," *Congressional Digest* 7 (Feb. 1928): 41 estimates Red Cross spending at $17.3 million; David Burner, *Herbert Hoover*, p. 194, gives it as $16 million.

16. "The Mississippi Flood of 1927," 41; Burner, *Herbert Hoover*, p. 194; Lohof, "Herbert Hoover," 696.

17. Typescript of "Testimony before Senate Commerce Committee, Feb. 24, 1928," HP:Com, Box 401, Folder "Miss. Valley Flood Relief Work Hearings, 1928."

18. "The Mississippi Flood of 1927," 41; Burner, *Herbert Hoover*, p. 194; Red Cross, *Mississippi Valley Flood*, p. 119.

19. Burner, *Herbert Hoover*, p. 194; Lohof, "Herbert Hoover," 696.

20. Lohof, "Herbert Hoover," 692.

21. Red Cross, *Mississippi Valley Flood*, pp. 39–41 (the quotation is on p. 41).

22. Hoover, *Memoirs* 2:130–31.

23. Red Cross, *Mississippi Valley Flood*, pp. 44–45.

24. Ibid., 42–44; Lohof, "Herbert Hoover," 693.

25. Richard Washburn Child, "The Battle of the Levees," *Saturday Evening Post* 199 (June 1927): 7; Will Irwin, "Havoc Beyond the Levees," *The World's Work* 54 (July 1927): 253, 255. (Irwin would later write a campaign biography for Hoover.)

26. "The Receding Flood's Bequest: A Rich Legendry of Anecdote," *Literary Digest* 94 (16 July 1927): 42.

27. Quoted in Lloyd, *Aggressive Introvert*, p. 75. He did write a short account of the flood for *Editor and Publisher* at the request of P. J. Croghan in the Bureau of Foreign and Domestic Commerce. See Croghan to George Akerson, 15 June 1927, and typescript of article by Hoover, HP:Com, Box 412, Folder "Miss. Valley Flood Relief Work Reports, Statements, Press Releases, Herbert Hoover, 1927 June." Hoover missed few chances at publicity, even granting a long interview to a reporter for the *Bell Telephone Quarterly*, in which he praised the telephone as essential to the relief operation. See *Literary Digest* 94 (20 Aug. 1927): 21.

28. Hoover, *Memoirs* 2:125. At the time, Hoover claimed that no more than "half a dozen" lives were lost after he took over. See Daniel, *Deep'n As It Come*, p. 88; Irwin, "Havoc Beyond the Levees," 254. It is impossible to know why he cut this already absurdly small number in half when he wrote his memoirs.

29. The quotation is from Arthur Dewitt Frank, *The Development of the Federal Program of Flood Control on the Mississippi River* (New York: Columbia University Press, 1930), p. 195. Frank, assuming that the missing people had simply moved elsewhere, lamented the "serious blow" to farm labor. See also Donald J. Lisio, *Hoover, Blacks, & Lily-whites: A Study of Southern Strategies* (Chapel Hill: University of North Carolina Press, 1985), pp. 3–20; Irwin, "Havoc Beyond the Levees," 250, and the stunning account of the Mounds Landing levee collapse in Barry, *Rising Tide*, pp. 197–206. In a speech on 3 Oct. 1927, President Coolidge reported that the river broke through the levees in 226 places. See William MacDonald, "Plans for National Flood Relief and Control," *Current History* 27 (Nov. 1927): 269.

30. Barry, *Rising Tide*, p. 286.

31. At the end of June, Hoover estimated that roughly a third of farmlands in the flooded area could not be planted in 1927, and that whether the rest would be usable depended on weather. See "After the Flood," *New Republic* 51 (20 July 1927): 216–17.

32. Quoted in Barry, *Rising Tide*, p. 365.

33. Red Cross, *Mississippi Valley Flood*, pp. 59–60.

34. Barry, *Rising Tide*, pp. 366–69; Frank, *The Development of the Federal Program of Flood Control*, pp. 200–201.

35. Barry, *Rising Tide*, pp. 369–77. The quotation is on p. 375.

36. Dana Burnet, "Between Hoover and High Water," *Collier's* 80 (16 July 1927): 9. Five former Confederate states voted for Hoover in 1928, but not Mississippi, which had benefitted so much from his relief work. Loyalty to the Democratic Party

won out, despite local concerns about Al Smith's Catholicism and "wet" sentiments; there seems also to have been some local concern that Hoover was too liberal on racial issues. See Donald Brooks Kelley, "Deep South Dilemma: The Mississippi Press in the Presidential Election of 1928," *Journal of Mississippi History* 25 (1963): 63–92.

37. Barry, *Rising Tide*, p. 372; Burner, *Herbert Hoover*, p. 194.

38. Herbert Hoover, "Why Inland Waterways Should Be Developed," *American Review of Reviews* 74 (Dec. 1926): 595–98; Hoover, "The Importance of Developing Our Water Resources," *Congressional Digest* 6 (Jan. 1927): 3–4; Fayette S. Warner, "A Synopsis of the [Jan. 1927] Hoover Report on the St. Lawrence Shipway," *Annals of the American Academy of Political and Social Science* 135 (Jan. 1928): 68–71.

39. "The Fight to Prevent Another Mississippi Flood," *Literary Digest* 93 (21 May 1927): 8.

40. Hoover, *Memoirs* 2:124; "Mr. Hoover's Plans for Flood Control," *Literary Digest* 94 (6 Aug. 1927): 10; Burnet, "Between Hoover and High Water," 42. See also Will Irwin, "Can We Tame the Mississippi?" *World's Work* 54 (Aug. 1927): 405–15.

41. Hoover, *Memoirs* 2:124.

42. J. Bernard Walker, "Curbing the Mississippi," *Scientific American* 138 (Feb. 1928): 146; Black, "The Problem of the Mississippi," 631.

43. Frank, *The Development of the Federal Program of Flood Control*, pp. 222–24.

44. Ibid., pp. 224–26; "The President Transmits to Congress Flood Control Plan of Army Engineers," *Congressional Digest* 7 (Feb. 1928): 47. For the Jadwin Plan, see Edgar Jadwin, "The Plan for Flood Control of the Mississippi River in Its Alluvial Valley," *Annals of the American Academy of Political and Social Science* 135 (Jan. 1928): 35–44.

45. Frank, *The Development of the Federal Program of Flood Control*, p. 229.

46. Ibid., pp. 228–29; "Suspicions of 'Pork' in the Flood-Control Bill," *Literary Digest* 97 (14 Apr. 1928): 10–11.

47. Barry, *Rising Tide*, pp. 400–403; Frank, *The Development of the Federal Program of Flood Control*, p. 238. For an account of Hoover's visit to Hot Springs drawn from contemporary newspaper articles, see clipping, "Hot Springs Citizens Honored Herbert Hoover in 1927 for His Work as Flood Administrator," [Hot Springs] *Sentinel-Record* (9 June 1959), HP:PPS, Box 227, Folder "Mississippi Flood of 1927, 1959–63."

48. Frank, *The Development of the Federal Program of Flood Control*, pp. 240–42; "Floods and the Jones Measure," and "Will Mr. Coolidge Approve?" *American Review of Reviews* 77 (May 1928): 454.

49. Herbert Hoover, "The Improvement of Our Mid-West Waterways," *Annals of the American Academy of Political and Social Science* 135 (Jan. 1928): 16. See also draft of an interview with Hoover by Edwin McIntosh for the New York *Herald-Tribune*, undated but ca. Jan. 1928, HP:Com, Box 37, Folder "Articles and Speeches Referring to Herbert Hoover, 1928 January."

50. "Nothing Done Yet for Flood-Control," *Literary Digest* 96 (10 Mar. 1928): 10. Interestingly, Hoover's remarks about methods of paying for the new flood control do not appear in the typed version of his testimony in the Hoover papers. See typescript, "Testimony before Senate Commerce Committee, Feb. 24, 1928," HP:Com, Box 401, Folder "Miss. Valley Flood Relief Work Hearings, 1928."

51. Barry, *Rising Tide,* p. 406; "The Report of the Committee on Mississippi Flood Control Appointed by the United States Chamber of Commerce," *Annals of the American Academy of Political and Social Science* 135 (Jan. 1928): 32 (emphasis in original).

52. "The President's Victory on Flood Control," *Literary Digest* 97 (19 May 1928): 9. The "victory" in the article's title refers to amendments attached to the bill that, Coolidge believed, reduced the probable expense to the government, particularly by declaring that the government would not pay for floodways or for damages to properties in those floodways.

53. Barry, *Rising Tide,* p. 406.

54. Ibid., pp. 423–26.

55. E. A. Sherman, "What Forests Can Do for the Mississippi River," *Annals of the American Academy of Political and Social Science* 135 (Jan. 1928): 45–49; "The Fight with the Rampageous Father of Waters," *Literary Digest* 99 (3 Nov. 1928): 22; Black, "The Problem of the Mississippi," 637; "The Fight to Prevent Another Mississippi Flood," 8.

56. Sherman, "What Forests Can Do for the Mississippi River," 45–49; Gifford Pinchot, "Some Essential Principles of Water Conservation as Applied to Mississippi Flood Control," *Annals of the American Academy of Political and Social Science* 135:1 (Jan. 1928): 57–59. For samples of some of the various schemes to control siltation that were sent to Hoover, see Daniel, *Deep'n As It Come,* pp. 142–46.

57. Article by Charles Michelson quoted in Schofield, "The Public Image of Herbert Hoover in the 1928 Campaign," 279. An article by Herbert McAneny proclaimed him "Hoover: Engineer to the World," *St. Nicholas* 55 (June 1928): 618.

58. Quoted in Schofield, "Public Image," 281.

59. William Hard, "The New Hoover," *American Review of Reviews* 76 (Nov. 1927): 483, 484.

60. Ray T. Tucker, "Is Hoover Human?," *North American Review* 226 (Nov. 1928): 519.

61. Will Irwin, *Herbert Hoover: A Reminiscent Biography* (New York: Century, 1928), pp. 249, 311.

62. Lohof, "Herbert Hoover," 690.

63. Hoover, *Memoirs* 2:131.

64. Oswald Garrison Villard, "Presidential Possibilities, IV, Herbert C. Hoover," *The Nation* 126 (29 Feb. 1928): 236.

65. Irwin, *Herbert Hoover,* p. 314. The order of phrases has been reversed.

7. "Long Run" Conservation

1. *The New Day: Campaign Speeches of Herbert Hoover, 1928* (Stanford, Calif.: Stanford University Press, 1928).

2. Ibid., pp. 183, 16, 170 (the last quotation is from a speech in New York on 22 Oct.). For the platform statement on conservation, see David Burner, *Herbert Hoover: A Public Life* (New York: Knopf, 1979), p. 200.

3. Leon F. Kneipp, "Land Planning and Acquisition, U.S. Forest Service," oral history interview by Amelia R. Fry, Edith Mezirow, and Fern Ingersoll, Bancroft Library, University of California at Berkeley, 1:195.

4. Joan Hoff Wilson, "Herbert Hoover Reassessed," in *Herbert Hoover Reassessed: Essays Commemorating the Fiftieth Anniversary of the Inauguration of Our Thirty-First President*, ed. Mark O. Hatfield (Washington, D.C.: GPO, 1981), p. 107. See also Joan Hoff Wilson, *Herbert Hoover: Forgotten Progressive* (Prospect Heights, Ill.: Waveland, 1992 [copyright 1975]).

5. For a contemporary analysis of the paradoxes in Hoover's thought, see Walter Lippmann, "The Peculiar Weakness of Mr. Hoover," *Harper's* 161 (June 1930): 1–7; a perceptive modern evaluation is David Burner, "Before the Crash: Hoover's First Eight Months in the Presidency," in *The Hoover Presidency: A Reappraisal*, eds. Martin L. Fausold and George T. Mazuzan (Albany: State University of New York Press, 1974), pp. 50–65. A recent forum in the *American Historical Review*, "The Problem of American Conservatism," suggests that American conservatism is not easily defined or distinguished in its origins from liberalism; see *AHR* 99 (Apr. 1994): 409–52. George Nash argues that the lines were particularly blurred in Hoover's political philosophy. See *Herbert Hoover: Political Orphan* (Stanford, Calif.: Hoover Institution Press, 1989). The quotation (with emphasis in original) is on p. 7.

6. Burner, "Before the Crash," 57.

7. Alan Brinkley, "The Problem of American Conservatism," *American Historical Review* 99 (Apr. 1994): 415. Brinkley goes on to point out that many modern conservatives have come from the West and links their outlook in part to the intrusive presence of the federal government in the region as "the greatest landowner in the West." Ibid., 417–19. This western perspective certainly helped to shape Hoover's outlook.

8. Martin L. Fausold, *The Presidency of Herbert C. Hoover* (Lawrence: University Press of Kansas, 1985), p. 36. Hoover and Wilbur first met at Stanford in 1892 when Wilbur entered as a freshman. Later, when he became a successful engineer in Australia, Hoover sent money to Wilbur to help him through medical school. *The Memoirs of Ray Lyman Wilbur, 1875–1949*, eds. Edgar Eugene Robinson and Paul Carroll Edwards (Stanford: Stanford University Press, 1960), p. 40; George H. Nash, *The Life of Herbert Hoover: The Engineer, 1874–1914* (New York: Norton, 1983), pp. 69–70. As a trustee of Stanford, Hoover was influential in selecting Wilbur to become president of the university in January 1916. Nash, *The Life of Herbert Hoover: The Humanitarian, 1914–1917* (New York: Norton, 1988), pp. 275–80. For a detailed dis-

cussion of Hoover's relationship with Stanford, and with Wilbur, see George H. Nash, *Herbert Hoover and Stanford University* (Stanford, Calif.: Hoover Institution Press, 1988).

9. Cammerer to Director Horace Albright, 21 May and 24 Apr., 1929, National Archives, Interior Dept. RG 79, National Park Service, Box 16, Director's Office Files, Cammerer, 1933–40, Folder "Miscellaneous Letters (Personal and Confidential)"; Laurence Veysey, "Ray Lyman Wilbur," *Dictionary of American Biography*, Supp. 4 (New York: Scribner's, 1974), pp. 891–95.

10. Speech at the University of Arizona, 26 Apr. 1930, RLWS, Box 15, Folder "Geological Survey, March 21, 1929 to ."

11. Wilbur, *Memoirs*, p. 411.

12. Kneipp, "Land Planning," 153.

13. Herbert Hoover, *The Memoirs of Herbert Hoover: The Cabinet and the Presidency, 1920–1933* (New York: Macmillan, 1952), 220 [hereafter cited as Hoover, *Memoirs* 2].

14. Ray Lyman Wilbur and Arthur Mastick Hyde, *The Hoover Policies* (New York: Scribner's, 1937), pp. 569–74; Franklin D. Mitchell, "Arthur Mastick Hyde," *Dictionary of American Biography*, Supp. 4 (New York: Scribner's, 1974), pp. 415–16.

15. Hoover, *Memoirs* 2:327–28. Wilbur and Hyde later collaborated on a semi-official account of the Hoover presidency. According to Assistant Secretary of the Navy Ernest Lee Jahncke, himself a longtime member of the Medicine Ball Cabinet, its members in early 1933 were Harlan F. Stone (Supreme Court justice); William DeWitt Mitchell (attorney general); Patrick J. Hurley (secretary of war); Ray Lyman Wilbur (secretary of the interior); Roy D. Chapin (secretary of commerce); Arthur M. Hyde (secretary of agriculture); Thomas D. Thacher (solicitor general); Arthur A. Ballantine (assistant secretary of the treasury); Walter E. Hope (assistant secretary of the treasury); Ferry K. Heath (assistant secretary of the treasury); Alexander Legge (chairman of the Farm Board, 1929–31); Charles Evans Hughes Jr. (solicitor general before Thacher); and Mark Sullivan (journalist and long-standing Hoover friend). See Ernest Lee Jahncke to Mark Sullivan, 26 Jan. 1933, HHPL, Special Collections, "Sullivan, Mark Ac. 498."

16. Although Hoover did not make conservation an issue in the 1928 campaign, administration officials moved so quickly and decisively in these areas that it seems justifiable to speak of an administration "agenda." See Ray Lyman Wilbur to Hoover, 3 Mar. 1933, HP:PC, Box 17, Folder "Executive Depts., Interior, Accomplishments 1929–33"; Ray Lyman Wilbur and William Atherton Du Puy, *Conservation in the Department of the Interior* (Washington, D.C.: GPO, 1932).

17. Du Puy, "Memorandum for Secretary Wilbur," 9 Mar. 1929, RLW, Box 15, Folder "Interior Department, 1912–29." See also Du Puy, "Secretary Wilbur and the Greatest Welfare Job in the World," *World's Work* 58 (Nov. 1929): 61–64.

18. E. W. Sawyer to Wilbur, 29 Mar. 1929; A. F. Walter to Elwood Mead, 3 Apr. 1929; E. M. Mendenhall, "Memorandum Concerning Duplication of Activities in the

War and Interior Departments," 3 May 1929, enclosed in Wilbur to Secretary of War James W. Good, 3 May 1929, all in IGF, Sect. I, Administrative, 1-81, Box 202, Folder "Reorganization, General, Pt. 2, May 10, 1925–July 7, 1930."

19. "Memorandum for the Joint Committee on Cooperation between the Departments of the Interior and Agriculture," 6 June 1929, IGF, Sec. I, Administrative, 1-81, Box 202, Folder "Reorganization, General."

20. "Minutes of [National Park] Service Comm. on Policies & Procedures," 9 May 1929, Entry 8, Drawer 133; Willard GS. Van Name to Walter H. Newton, 8 July 1929, HP:PS, Box 167, Folder "Government Departments, Reorganization of, 1929 June–July"; Theodore S. Woolsey to Lawrence Richey, 21 Oct. 1929; Richey to Woolsey, 29 Oct. 1929, ibid., Box 168, Folder "Government Departments, Reorganization of, 1929 Aug.–Oct."

21. Annual Message to Congress on the State of the Union, 3 Dec. 1929, *Public Papers of the Presidents of the United States: Herbert Hoover, Containing the Public Messages, Speeches, and Statements of the President, March 4 to December 31, 1929* (Washington, DC: GPO, 1974), p. 432 [hereafter cited as *Public Papers,* with year]. See also Ray Lyman Wilbur to Hoover, enclosing memorandum on reorganization, 10 July 1930, HP:PC, Box 15, Folder "Interior—Corres., 1930 June–July"; Wilbur to Hoover, enclosing memorandum proposing the creation of a separate Department of Conservation, 8 Nov. 1930, ibid., Box 16, Folder "Interior—Corres., 1930 Nov.–Dec."

22. *Public Papers: 1929,* pp. 199–201.

23. Wilbur, *Memoirs,* pp. 446–47; Hoover, *Memoirs* 2:228; Northcutt Ely, "Herbert Hoover and the Colorado River," manuscript provided to the author by Mr. Ely, pp. 12–13; Department of Interior, memorandum for the press, 23 Mar. 1930, HP:PC, Box 21, Folder "Interior—Reclamation Service, 1930." For the details of the power contracts, see Ray Lyman Wilbur and Northcutt Ely, *The Hoover Dam Power and Water Contracts and Related Data* (Washington, D.C.: GPO, 1930).

24. From a speech by Hoover at the site of the dam on 12 Nov. 1932, *Memoirs* 2:229. Hoover's words suggest a symbolic linking of the frontier and consumer society—happy homeowners under the open western sky—that is related to the commodification of wilderness being promoted by the National Park Service during the 1920s. See, for example, Kerwin L. Klein, "Frontier Products: Tourism, Consumerism, and the Southwestern Public Lands, 1890–1990," *Pacific Historical Review* 62 (Feb. 1993): 39–71.

25. In his *Memoirs* (2:229), Hoover professed that he did not care about the name of the dam. The Post-Presidential files at the Hoover Library tell a different story.

26. Ely, "Herbert Hoover and the Colorado River," 13; Fausold, *The Presidency of Herbert Hoover,* pp. 135–36; Report of the Muscle Shoals Commission, 19 Nov. 1931, *Public Papers: 1931* (1976), pp. 560–64. See also the president's veto of the Muscle Shoals Resolution, 3 Mar. 1931, ibid., pp. 120–29.

27. *The New Day,* 106. The order of the phrases has been reversed.

28. Norris Hundley, *Water and the West: The Colorado River Compact and the Politics*

of Water in the American West (Berkeley: University of California Press, 1975), p. 333; Donald Worster, "Hoover Dam: A Study in Domination," in *Under Western Skies: Nature and History in the American West* (New York: Oxford University Press, 1992), pp. 64–78.

29. This outcome was not inevitable. By the late 1920s a proven technology existed that might have permitted the construction of even large dams at a low enough cost so that private interests or local governments could have undertaken it, but the approach was scorned by the engineering establishment, and there is no evidence Hoover was even aware of it. For the fascinating story, see Donald C. Jackson, *Building the Ultimate Dam: John S. Eastwood and the Control of Water in the West* (Lawrence: University Press of Kansas, 1995).

30. For Agriculture Department opposition to new projects and responses to it, see Reclamation Director Elwood Mead to Wilbur, 10 Apr. 1929, enclosing undated and unattributed clipping, "Secretary Opposes Further Reclamation," RLWS, Box 49, Folder "Reclamation, April 5, 1929 to Jan. 13, 1932"; "Reclamation Has Not Aggravated the Farm Surplus," *The Northwest* [published by the Agricultural Development Dept. of the Northern Pacific Railway] 2 (June 1929):1, HP:PS, Box 186, Folder "Irrigation, Correspondence, 1929–30." Wilbur reported to the president that a little less than $3.5 million was added to the reclamation fund in 1928 from all sources, but that $10.6 million was spent. See Wilbur's memorandum on "sources of the Reclamation Fund," 9 Apr. 1929, HP:PC, Box 20, Folder "Interior—Reclamation Service, 1928–29."

31. Hoover to Wilbur, 23 Apr. 1929, RLWS, Box 120, Folder "HH—RLW, 1929–1932 Ltrs."

32. Wilbur and Du Puy, *Conservation*, p. 15.

33. Reclamation Bureau press release, 6 May 1929, HP:RLW, Box 24, Folder "Press Releases—Bureau of Reclamation." For an earlier review of reclamation policy that had recommended changes to put the program on a sounder footing, see Brian Q. Cannon, "'We Are Now Entering a New Era': Federal Reclamation and the Fact Finding Commission of 1923–1924," *Pacific Historical Review* 66 (May 1997): 185–211.

34. Memorandum for the Press, 26 Mar. 1930, HP:RLW, Box 24, Folder "Press Releases—Bureau of Reclamation."

35. Gerald D. Nash, *United States Oil Policy, 1890–1964: Business and Government in Twentieth Century America* (Pittsburgh: University of Pittsburgh Press, 1968), pp. 95–97. During the late 1920s, a number of mergers took place in the oil industry, about which see Paul A. C. Koistinen, *Mobilizing for Modern War: The Political Economy of American Warfare, 1865–1919* (Lawrence: University Press of Kansas, 1997), p. 265. Whether Hoover saw such consolidation as creating conditions that might moderate the overproduction problem or just as a different sort of problem is impossible to know. Either explanation can account for his change of attitude about relaxing the antitrust laws.

36. Northcutt Ely, *Oil Conservation through Interstate Agreement* (Washington, D.C.: GPO, 1930), pp. 1–2. According to R. C. Holmes, president of the Texas Company,

members of the American Petroleum Institute earned only 3.27 percent on their investment during the nine years between 1919 and 1927, and less than 1 percent in 1927. See Holmes to members of the API Board of Directors, 3 June 1929, RLWS, Box 13, Folder "Federal Oil Conservation Board."

37. Wilbur and Du Puy, *Conservation*, p. 52.

38. News conferences of 12 and 15 Mar. 1929, *Public Papers: 1929*, pp. 21, 25; Wilbur to Hoover, 13 Mar. 1929, HP:PS, Box 216, Folder "Oil Matters, Correspondence 1929 March."

39. For reactions pro and con, see RLWS, Box 27, Folders "Compliments on Oil Policy" and "Protests on Oil Policy"; Gov. Frank Emerson (Wyo.) to Hoover, 15 Mar. 1929, HP:PS, Box 216, Folder "Oil Matters, Correspondence 1929 March"; Hoover to Wilbur, 10 Apr. 1929, enclosing undated draft of letter to governors of Wyoming, Colorado, and Utah, ibid., Folder "Oil Matters, Correspondence, 1929 Apr.–May"; Nash, *United States Oil Policy*, p. 101. According to the Geological Survey, in 1928 only about 2.58 percent of all petroleum produced came from public lands if production from Indian and naval reserves was excluded, but in Colorado and Wyoming, 37.44 percent and 72.33 percent, respectively, came from public lands, and in Utah, with a very small total production, almost 100 percent came from public lands. See memorandum of 15 Mar. 1929 enclosed in Wilbur to Hoover, 26 Mar. 1929, HP:PS, Box 216, Folder "Oil Matters, Correspondence, 1929 March."

40. Resolutions passed by American Petroleum Institute Committee at Houston, March 16, [1929], HP:PS, Box 216, Folder "Oil Matters, Correspondence 1929 March"; Wilbur to Mitchell, 20 Mar. 1929, and Mitchell to Wilbur, 29 Mar. 1929, ibid., Box 218, Folder "Oil Matters, Federal Oil Conservation Bd., Corres., 1929"; Hoover to Mitchell, 23 Mar. 1929, ibid., Box 216, Folder "Oil Matters, Correspondence, 1929 March"; Hoover's statement at press conference of 2 Apr. 1929, *Public Papers: 1929*, p. 55. The frustration of the oilmen comes through even the carefully worded minutes of the Oil Conservation Board's meeting with representatives of the API on 3 Apr. 1929. See HP:PS, Box 218, Folder "Oil Matters, Federal Oil Conservation Bd. Corres., 1929." Oilman Henry L. Doherty, who had originally proposed the idea of industry cooperation to regulate production, was infuriated by the administration's attitude, and even Mike Ely muttered mutinously that "eventually some judge will decide that the Federal Government, under the war-making power of the Constitution, has the right to enjoin waste of oil by a private operator on private land." See Doherty to Wilbur, 19 Apr. 1929, and Ely to Wilbur, 27 Apr. 1929, RLWS, Box 27, Folder "Oil, Mar. 4, 1929 to Feb. 5, 1930."

41. Wilbur to Hoover, 1 Apr. 1929, enclosing Smith to Wilbur, 1 Apr. 1929, RLWS, Box 27, Folder "Oil—Misc. Mat.—Oil Conservation (Corr., FOCB,, etc.), 1924–30"; E. S. Rochester (secretary of FOCB) to Hoover, 3 Apr. 1929, HP:PS, Box 216, Folder "Oil Matters, Correspondence, 1929 Apr.–May"; FOCB to R. C. Holmes (chairman of executive committee of API), 8 Apr. 1929, ibid., Box 218, Folder "Oil Matters, Federal Oil Conservation Bd. Corres., 1929"; Wilbur to Requa, 19 Apr. 1929, RLWS,

Box 27, Folder "Oil, Mar. 4, 1929 to Feb. 5, 1930." Wilbur released the FOCB's 8 Apr. letter to the API to the newspapers on 12 Apr. See press release, 12 Apr. 1929, RLW, Box 27, Folder "Oil, Oil Conservation Policy, 1929 Apr.–May & undated."

42. Wilbur to Hoover, 15 Apr. 1929, HP:PS, Box 216, Folder "Oil Matters, Correspondence, 1929 Apr.–May." Gerald Nash argues that Wilbur's suggestions would actually have increased overproduction and further depressed prices, but Mark Requa estimated that small changes in industry practices could save "two or three cents a gallon on gasoline" and net the industry $158 million. Nash, *United States Oil Policy*, p. 103; Requa to Lawrence Richey, 1 Apr. 1929, HP:PS, Box 216, Folder "Oil Matters, Correspondence, 1929 Apr.–May."

43. Ely to Wilbur, 26 Apr. 1929, RLWS, Box 24, Folder "Memos to Wilbur, Mar.–July 1929"; Ely to Wilbur, 1 May 1929, ibid., Box 25, Folder "Memos to Wilbur by N. Ely, Mar.–Aug. 1929." A marginal note by the departmental solicitor on the 26 Apr. memo says flatly that "the law does not authorize nor warrant such a procedure."

44. Requa to Wilbur, 24 (two letters), 25, 30 Apr., 2 May 1929, RLWS, Box 27, Folder "Compacts, April 30, 1929 to "; E. B. Reeser (API president) to Wilbur, 24 Apr. 1929, Wilbur to Hoover, 25 Apr. 1929, both in HP:PS, Box 218, Folder "Oil Matters, Federal Oil Conservation Bd., Corres., 1929"; Hoover to Wilbur, 25 Apr. 1929, RLWS, Box 120, Folder "HH-RLW, 1929–1932, Ltrs."; undated draft of compact, sent to various people on 3 May 1929, ibid., Box 27, "Compacts, April 30, 1929 to "; Requa to Wilbur, 10 May 1929, ibid.; Ely to Wilbur, 14, 21 May 1929, ibid., Box 25, Folder "Memos to Wilbur by N. Ely, Mar.–Aug. 1929."

45. Requa to Lawrence Richey, 15 May 1929; Requa to Wilbur, 15 May 1929; Wilbur to Hoover, 22 May 1929, all in HP:PS, Box 217, Folder "Oil Matters, Colorado Springs Petroleum Conference, 1929"; "Remarks of Ray Lyman Wilbur, Secretary of the Interior, at the opening of the Conference on Oil Conservation at Colorado Springs, Colorado, June 10, 1929," ibid., Box 218, Folder "Oil Matters, Federal Oil Conservation Bd., Corres., 1929"; Nash, *United States Oil Policy*, p. 104.

46. Requa to Lawrence Richey, 12 June 1929, HP:PS, Box 217, Folder "Oil Matters, Colorado Springs Petroleum Conference, 1929."

47. Requa to Lawrence Richey, 14 June 1929, enclosing memorandum by Requa, 13 June 1929, HP:PS, Box 217, Folder "Oil Matters, Colorado Springs Petroleum Conference, 1929"; Minutes of Conference, undated, RLWS, Box 13, Folder "Federal Oil Conservation Board."

48. Wilbur and Hyde, *The Hoover Policies*, p. 238.

49. Ely to Wilbur, 17 June 1929, RLWS, Box 13, Folder "Federal Oil Conservation Board"; Report of Oil States Advisory Board, 9 Apr. 1931, is in ibid., unlabeled folder (report endorses uniform state laws and an interstate compact); Report of Voluntary Committee on Petroleum Economics, 24 Aug. 1931, is in ibid., Folder "Oil—Fed. Oil Conserv. Bd., July 10, 1931 to "; Requa to Wilbur, 23 July 1929 (three letters), ibid., Folder "Federal Oil Conservation Board." Acting on the advice of the Oil States Advisory Committee, the states of Oklahoma, Kansas, and Texas signed an interstate

agreement setting quotas for each state's production on 13 Sept. 1931, but other states were slow to adhere to the agreement. See Ely, *Oil Conservation,* pp. 22–25.

50. Requa to Wilbur, 19 July 1929; Assistant Secretary of War Patrick J. Hurley to Wilbur, 25 July 1929, both in RLWS, Box 27, Folder "Oil Mar. 4, 1929 to Feb. 5, 1930"; Nash, *United States Oil Policy,* p. 105.

51. Wilbur and Du Puy, *Conservation,* pp. 58–71 (quotations on pp. 70, 71); Northcutt Ely to Wilbur, 20 July 1929, Northcutt Ely Papers, Dept. of Special Collections, Cecil H. Green Library, Stanford University, Box 2, Folder 9. For letters and documents bearing on the negotiation of the Kettleman Hills agreement, see ibid., Box 4, Folders 28–29. Wilbur reported to the members of the FOCB on 29 July that the unit operation agreement was "on the verge of success." (Memorandum, 29 July 1929, RLWS, Box 27, Folder "Oil, Mar. 4, 1929 to Feb. 5, 1930".) Little did he know.

52. Wilbur to Hoover, 5 Dec. 1929, enclosing report dated 5 Dec. 1929, HP:PS, Box 218, Folder "Oil Matters, Federal Oil Conservation Bd., Corres., 1929."

53. Axel Oxholm to George Akerson, 14 Mar. 1929; Akerson to Oxholm, 27 Mar. 1929; Oxholm to Roy D. Chapin, 27 Feb. 1933, all in HPS, Box 51, Folder "National Committee on Wood Utilization, A&B."

54. Wilson Compton to Hoover, 2 Apr. 1930; unsigned memorandum (probably by Compton) for Hoover, 5 Apr. 1930; Hoover to Compton, 9 Apr. 1930; Bennington Moore to Lawrence Richey, 25 Apr. 1930; Edward Eyre Hunt to Commerce Secretary Robert P. Lamont, 19 May 1930; Hoover to Secretary Lamont, 15 May 1930, all in HP:PS, Box 212, Folder "National Timber Conservation Board, 1930."

55. Timber Conservation Board press release, ca. 1 Aug. 1932, HP:PC, Box 14, Folder "Commerce—Timber Conser. Bd., 1932."

56. Hoover to Arthur Hyde, 14 May 1931; R. Y. Stuart to Hyde, 16 May 1931; R. W. Dunlap to Hoover, 18 May 1931; Hoover to Dunlap, 19 May 1931; F. E. Weyerhauser to Hoover, 2 July 1931, all in HP:PC, Box 5, Folder "Agriculture—Forest Service, Correspondence 1931 May–July"; Compton's testimony, 11 June 1931, National Forest Products Assoc. Collection, Box 71, Folder "Statements Presented before the Timber Conservation Board, June 10th and 11th, 1931," Forest History Society Archives, Durham, N.C.

57. Ray Lyman Wilbur to Rep. Edgar Howard (chair of the Committee on Indian Affairs), 3 Mar. 1932, enclosing memorandum by Indian Affairs Commissioner C. J. Rhoads, 25 Jan. 1932, HP:PC, Folder "Agriculture—Forest Service, Correspondence 1932"; John H. Wilson to Hoover, 13 May 1930, HP:PS, Box 212, Folder "National Timber Conservation Board, 1930"; U.S. Forest Service, "Report on Possibilities of Cooperative Management of National Forest and Private Lands," 30 Oct. 1931, HP:PC, Box 5, Folder "Agriculture—Forest Service Forest Management, 1931 Aug.–1933"; R. Y. Stuart to Raphael Zon, 27 June 1931, FS, Drawer 194, Folder "F-Supervision-1931"; U.S. Forest Service, "The Forest Situation in the United States: A Special Report to the Timber Conservation Board," 30 Jan. 1932, p. 5, HP:PC, Box 5, Folder "Agriculture—Forest Service, Annual & Misc. Reports, 1929–32."

58. Timber Conservation Board press release, ca. 3 Aug. 1932, HP:PC, Box 14, Folder "Commerce—Timber Conser. Bd., 1932"; Secretary of Commerce Roy Chapin to Hoover, 6 Oct. 1932, HPS, Box 51, Folder "National Timber Conservation Board, A-B"; William G. Robbins, "The Great Experiment in Industrial Self-Government: The Lumber Industry and the National Recovery Administration," *Journal of Forest History* 25 (July 1981): 130–31.

59. For a contemporary analysis by an economist that, while arguing that market forces might achieve the conservation of exhaustible resources, recognized the improbability of that happening in a political context, see Harold Hotelling, "The Economics of Exhaustible Resources," *Journal of Political Economy* 39:2 (April 1931): 137–73.

60. Vernon Kellogg to Arthur Ringland, 18 Dec. 1928 and 9 Jan. 1929; Ringland to George E. Scott, 29 Mar. 1929; Ringland to members of the Executive Committee, 23 Apr. 1929; minutes of the 24th meeting of the Executive Committee, 8 May 1929; Chauncey J. Hamlin to Hoover, 25 May 1929, all in NCOR, Box 7, Folder "Liquidation of Conference"; Arthur Ringland, "Conserving Human and Natural Resources," an oral history by Amelia R. Fry, Edith Mezirow, Fern Ingersoll, and Thelma Dreis, Bancroft Library, University of California at Berkeley, vol. 1:162–63.

61. Arno Cammerer to Horace Albright, 16 Aug. 1929, NPS, Box 16, Folder "Miscellaneous Letters (Personal and Confidential)." This certainly did not mean that the NPS was opposed to the promotion of tourism and recreation. Quite the contrary. The development of tourism—particularly automobile tourism—and of the facilities and roads to support and encourage it, was a major thrust of NPS policy in the 1920s. See Klein, "Frontier Products," 47–53.

62. Hoover to Agnes E. Meyer (Mrs. Eugene Meyer), 15 Oct. 1929, *Public Papers, 1929,* p. 328; Meyer to Hoover, 16 Oct., 6 Dec. 1929; Hoover to Meyer, 18 Oct. 1929, all in HP:PS, Box 72, Folder "Athletics, New Recreation Conference, 1929–30"; Arthur Ringland to French Strother, 27 Nov. 1929, NCOR, Box 7, unlabeled envelope, contains the quoted language about the purpose of the organization.

63. Hoover to Meyers [sic], 10 Dec. 1929, HP:PS, Box 72, Folder "Athletics, New Recreation Conference, 1929–30"; Jesse Frederick Steiner, *Americans at Play: Recent Trends in Recreation and Leisure Time Activities* (New York: McGraw-Hill, 1933), pp. v, 196.

64. Hoover, *Memoirs* 2:313.

65. "Statement on the Report of the President's Research Committee on Social Trends," *Public Papers, 1932–33* (1977), p. 917.

66. Johnson to Hiram Johnson Jr. and Archibald Johnson, 9 Apr. 1933, Hiram Johnson Papers, Bancroft Library, University of California at Berkeley, Pt. VI, Box 6, Folder "1933 Apr.–June."

67. For the cancellation of the western trip, see "Statement on Vacation Plans," 12 Aug. 1930, *Public Papers, 1930* (1976), p. 335. Mildred Hall Campbell oral history, p. 18; Russel V. Lee oral history, p. 8; Byron Price oral history, pp. 2–3, 9; all at Hoover

Institution on War, Revolution and Peace at Stanford University; Horace Albright oral history, pp. 68, 93–94, HHPL; George Akerson to Ray Lyman Wilbur, 12 Aug. 1930, HPS, Box 43, Folder "Interior, 1930 (A,B,C)"; Brent Tarter, "'All Men Are Equal Before Fishes': Herbert Hoover's Camp on the Rapidan," *Virginia Cavalcade* 30 (Spring 1981): 156–61. Tarter notes that Hoover refused a $48,000 congressional appropriation to pay for the land and also turned down an offer of $100,000 from the Virginia State Conservation and Development Commission. Hoover did, however, allow the state of Virginia to build a road into the camp in the spring of 1929 and to stock the Rapidan with fish. See William E. Carson to Lawrence Richey, 24 Apr. 1929, and [?] Leach to Richey, 3 June 1929, HP:PS, Box 161, Folder "Fish 1929, March–April." The president's delight in the place is evident in his memoirs. See *Memoirs* 2:322–23.

68. Wilbur, *Memoirs*, p. 439; Wilbur to Hoover, 3 Mar. 1933, RLW, Box 16, Folder "Interior Department, 1933–38 & undated." Some, but not all, park concessionaires lost money in the early 1930s. For an accounting, see "Statement showing comparatively for 1929, 1930 and 1931 the profit or loss of the principal operators in the National Parks," [9 Mar. 1932], RLW, Box 18, Folder "National Parks, 1932 Jan.–June."

69. Since many parks were authorized by Congress years before the lands to establish them were acquired by the NPS, it is difficult to date the beginning of many of them. See Horace Albright, "Outline of Outstanding Accomplishments of the National Park Service during Past Four Years," [1933], RLW, Box 19, Folder "National Parks, undated"; Wilbur, *Memoirs*, pp. 432–35. For the importance of Rockefeller to this process, see *Worthwhile Places: Correspondence of John D. Rockefeller, Jr., and Horace M. Albright,* ed. Joseph W. Ernst (New York: Fordham University Press, 1991), pp. 93–137. The Park Service estimated that by March 1931 Rockefeller had donated $13.8 million and promised $6 million more for various projects. See unsigned memorandum for Director Albright, 3 Mar. 1931, HP:PC, Box 19, Folder "Executive Depts., Interior—Natl. Park Service, 1931." Edsel Ford was a significant contributor to the Shenandoah project. See Arno Cammerer to Edsel Ford, 8 Sept. 1927, and Ford to Cammerer, 14 Nov. 1927, NPS, Box 3, Folder "Mr. Edsel Ford"; Cammerer to Rockefeller, 12 Aug. and 13 Sept. 1927, Rockefeller to Cammerer, 3 Sept. 1927, NPS, Box 6, Folder "Great Smoky Mountains National Park, John D. Rockefeller, Jr., Aug. 12, 1927 to June 1, 1933"; Rockefeller to W. A. Welch, 26 Sept. 1927, Rockefeller to Cammerer, 23 Jan. 1928, and Cammerer to Rockefeller, 12 Mar. 1928, ibid.; Cammerer to Stephen Mather, 19 Sept. 1927, ibid., Box 15, Folder "Miscellaneous Letters"; Beardsley Ruml to Cammerer, 9 Feb. 1928, ibid., Box 4, Folder "Basic Letters (Smoky Mts.)."

70. Horace Albright, "Outline of Outstanding Accomplishments of the National Park Service during the Past Four Years," [1933], RLW, Box 19, Folder "National Parks, undated." Total expenditure figures for Park and Forest Service road construction may be found in chapter 8.

71. Horace M. Albright oral history, HHPL, pp. 4–5, 13–14; Horace M. Albright, *Origins of National Park Service Administration of Historic Sites* (Philadelphia: Eastern National Park & Monument Association, 1971), pp. 8, 13. Under Albright, the NPS subtly modified its mission, stressing the maintenance of the parks "in essentially their primitive condition" for "inspirational influence and educational value," and making "recreation," which director Mather had made a priority, secondary. If Hoover was aware of this shift, which of course placed esthetic values ahead of economic ones, there is no evidence of it. For Albright's statement of purposes, see his "Memorandum Regarding the National Park Service," 2 Mar. 1929, RLW, Box 19, Folder "National Parks, Albright Report on NPS History & Operations, 1929."

72. Wilbur, *Memoirs*, p. 466.

73. Ibid., p. 481.

74. Wilbur to Hoover, 3 Mar. 1933, RLW, Box 16, Folder "Interior Department, 1933–38 & undated"; Wilbur and Du Puy, *Conservation in the Department of the Interior*, pp. 112, 125. Kenneth R. Philp, in *John Collier's Crusade for Indian Reform, 1920–1954* (Tucson: University of Arizona Press, 1977), p. 96, citing an American Indian Rights publication, gives the increase in funding for the Indian Service as $15 million in 1928 to $28 million in 1931. Philp argues that much of the new money was wasted in a huge expansion of Indian Service bureaucracy.

75. Wilbur, *Memoirs*, p. 484; Wilbur and Du Puy, *Conservation in the Department of the Interior*, pp. 132–35; David Burner, *Herbert Hoover*, p. 225.

76. Lawrence C. Kelly, "Charles James Rhoads, 1929–33," in *The Commissioners of Indian Affairs, 1824–1977*, eds. Robert M. Kvasnicka and Herman J. Viola (Lincoln: University of Nebraska Press, 1979), pp. 263–71.

77. Randolph C. Downes, "A Crusade for Indian Reform, 1922–1934," *Mississippi Valley Historical Review* 32 (Dec. 1945): 331–35. Terry L. Anderson advances the revisionist argument, in *Sovereign Nations or Reservations? An Economic History of American Indians* (San Francisco: Pacific Research Institute for Public Policy, 1995), that although Indians did lose lands as a result of allotment policies, privatized lands worked by Indians were much more productive, and the people living on them more prosperous, than was true on lands that remained under federal or reservation control.

78. Ibid., 335–43; Lawrence C. Kelly, *The Assault on Assimilation: John Collier and the Origins of Indian Policy Reform* (Albuquerque: University of New Mexico Press, 1983); Institute for Government Research, *The Problem of Indian Administration* (Baltimore: Johns Hopkins University Press, 1928), pp. 3, 8, 21 (emphasis added); David Wallace Adams, *Education for Extinction: American Indians and the Boarding School Experience, 1875–1928* (Lawrence: University Press of Kansas, 1995), pp. 331–33.

79. Historians are just beginning to discuss the degree to which the rise of tourism in the West tended to create an "'American' space by obliterating indigenous land uses and converting native cultures into exoticized objects for tourist consumption," as Susan Rhoades Neel notes in "Tourism and the American West: New Departures," *Pacific Historical Review* 65 (Nov. 1996): 517. It is important to remember, however,

that although Hoover administration policies may have fitted into this pattern and even reinforced it, Hoover's Indian policy was shaped less by the interests of the tourist industry than by the arguments of Indian reformers and by Hoover's and Wilbur's personal experiences.

80. Philp, *John Collier's Crusade*, pp. 93–96.

81. John Collier, head of the American Indian Defense Association and New Deal Indian Commissioner, was a frequent critic of the administration, but in later years he gave somewhat grudging credit to it for its limited achievements. See *The Indians of the Americas* (New York: Norton, 1947), pp. 259–60. Randolph Downes, "A Crusade for Indian Reform," 348–51, provides a generally favorable assessment of the Hoover years; Kenneth Philp, "Herbert Hoover's New Era: A False Dawn for the American Indian, 1929–1932," *Rocky Mountain Social Science Journal* 9 (Apr. 1972): 56–59.

82. Hoover, *Memoirs* 2:318; Wilbur to Hoover, 3 Mar. 1933, RLW, Box 16, Folder "Interior Department, 1933–38 & undated." For a more negative view of Hoover administration Indian policy that stresses its assimilationist focus, see William G. Robbins, "Herbert Hoover's Indian Reformers Under Attack: The Failures of Administrative Reform," *Mid-America: An Historical Review* 63 (Oct. 1981): 157–70.

83. Burner, *Herbert Hoover*, pp. 224–26.

84. Wilbur and Du Puy, *Conservation in the Department of the Interior*, p. 136.

85. Burner, *Herbert Hoover*, pp. 221–22.

86. Hoover, *Memoirs* 2:316–17; Wilbur, *Memoirs*, pp. 468–69. Hoover's memoirs never mention his 1930 endorsement of a Department of Education and leave the impression that he always opposed the idea. On this point, see Burner, *Herbert Hoover*, p. 224.

87. Hoover, *Memoirs* 2:317; Burner, *Herbert Hoover*, p. 224.

88. Wilbur and Du Puy, *Conservation in the Department of the Interior*, p. 191.

89. Wilbur, *Memoirs*, pp. 493–96.

90. Ibid., pp. 496–500. The quotation is on p. 500. Thomas R. Dunlap notes that predator control policies were beginning to change in the National Park Service in the late 1920s, but that as late as 1930 official policy still generally favored the "elimination or drastic control" of all predators. In 1931 Director Albright announcing a new policy of "total protection to all animal life," including predators, but promised to continue to use traps and poison to control rodents. See "Wildlife, Science, and the National Parks, 1920–1940," *Pacific Historical Review* 59 (May 1990): 189, 192.

91. Ibid., 501, 503, 506. One of Wilbur's executive assistants, Ernest Walker Sawyer, was the principal advocate of Alaskan development within the Hoover administration. See Terrence M. Cole, "Ernest Walker Sawyer and Alaska: The Dilemma of Northern Economic Development," *Pacific Northwest Quarterly* 82 (Apr. 1991): 42–50.

92. Department of the Interior, *Survey of the Alaskan Reindeer Service, 1931–1933* (Washington: GPO, 1933), pp. 1–2.

93. Interior Department press releases, 20 Nov. 1930, 23 Jan. and 6 Apr. 1931, 4 Apr. 1932, RLW, Box 24, Folder "Press Releases—Alaska"; Ray Lyman Wilbur to

Hoover, 3 May 1932, and Hoover to Wilbur, 10 May 1932, HP:PC, Box 15, Folder "Interior—Corres., 1932 May."

94. Wilbur, *Memoirs*, p. 506.

95. Ibid., p. 503; Wilbur and DuPuy, *Conservation in the Department of the Interior*, pp. 157, 163; "Remarks of President Hoover at the 25th Annual Meeting of the Board of Directors of the National Recreation Association," 13 Apr. 1931, HP:PP, Box 179, Folder "National Recreation Assn., 1931–32."

96. See, for example, an unsigned, undated memorandum in HP:PS, Box 111, Folder "Conservation, 1931–32," which expresses ideas very similar to those in Wilbur and Du Puy, *Conservation in the Department of the Interior*, pp. 157–59.

8. "Wrong Side Up": The Commission on the Public Domain

1. See *Public Papers of the Presidents of the United States: Herbert Hoover, Containing the Public Messages, Speeches, and Statements of the President, March 4 to December 31, 1929* (Washington, DC: GPO, 1974), 333 [hereafter, *Public Papers*, with date].

2. Quoted in Phillip O. Foss, *Politics and Grass: The Administration of Grazing on the Public Domain* (Seattle: University of Washington Press, 1960), p. 35.

3. The General Land Office estimated the unappropriated and unreserved public lands in the West, outside of Alaska, at about 180 million acres; some lands technically reserved for mineral rights would actually have been used for grazing, so exact figures on grazing lands are difficult to estimate. See C. C. Moore to James R. Garfield, 7 Oct. 1930, GC, Box 1083, Folder "Reports–Gen. Land Office, 1930 July." Early advocates of irrigation, convinced that most of the West could be made productive through irrigation, urged as early as 1891 the cession of all except mineral lands to the states. See Lawrence B. Lee, "William Ellsworth Smythe and the Irrigation Movement: A Reconsideration," *Pacific Historical Review* 41 (Aug. 1972): 289–311; and Frank Adams, "Notes on the Life of Elwood Mead for Memorial Service, 1936," p. 2, typescript in Mead Papers, Water Resources Archive, University of California at Berkeley. Graziers' attitudes toward the public ranges were paradoxical—they paid no attention to the public's ownership rights in the land, but they insisted upon their own personal rights to use it. For comments on the prevalence of such attitudes among settlers, see Patricia Nelson Limerick, *The Legacy of Conquest: The Unbroken Past of the American West* (New York: Norton, 1987); John C. Weaver, "Beyond the Fatal Shore: Pastoral Squatting and the Occupation of Australia, 1826 to 1852," *American Historical Review* 101 (Oct. 1996): 981.

4. A table of average grazing fees for the years 1906–1975 may be found in William Voigt Jr., *Public Grazing Lands: Use and Misuse by Industry and Government* (New Brunswick, N.J.: Rutgers University Press, 1976), p. 49.

5. Quoted in ibid., p. 63. Elsewhere, Greeley argued that the Forest Service's control over grazing prevented "the door of opportunity" from being "closed to the small

livestock producer or homesteader in the national forests." W. B. Greeley, "The Stockmen and the National Forests," *Saturday Evening Post* 198 (14 Nov. 1925): 10.

6. Benjamin Horace Hibbard, *A History of the Public Land Policies* (New York: Macmillan, 1924), p. 567.

7. Foss, *Politics and Grass*, p. 33. The 1936 study was the first really thorough one, but its conclusions were hardly new to people working in the field. See, for example, a pamphlet by Will C. Barnes, *The Story of the Range* (Washington, D.C.: GPO, 1926). Barnes was Assistant Forester and Chief of Grazing for the Forest Service.

8. Louise Peffer, *The Closing of the Public Domain: Disposal and Reservation Policies, 1900–1950* (Stanford, Calif.: Stanford University Press, 1951), pp. 178–99; Samuel P. Hays, *Conservation and the Gospel of Efficiency: The Progressive Conservation Movement, 1890–1920* (New York: Atheneum, 1969 [1959]), pp. 60–65; Christopher McGrory Klyza, *Who Controls Public Lands? Mining, Forestry, and Grazing Policies, 1870–1990* (Chapel Hill: University of North Carolina Press, 1996), p. 110; Foss, *Politics and Grass*, pp. 48–49; Voigt, *Public Grazing Lands*, pp. 58–64.

9. Hays, *Conservation and the Gospel of Efficiency*, pp. 49–90; G. Michael McCarthy, *Hour of Trial: The Conservation Conflict in Colorado and the West, 1891–1907* (Norman: University of Oklahoma Press, 1977), pp. 210–35; Elmo R. Richardson, *The Politics of Conservation: Crusades and Controversies, 1897–1913* (Berkeley: University of California Press, 1962), *passim;* Daniel R. Mortenson, "The Deterioration of Forest Grazing Land: A Wider Context for the Effects of World War I," *Journal of Forest History* 22 (Oct. 1978): 224–25; Roy M. Robbins, *Our Landed Heritage: The Public Domain, 1776–1932* (Princeton, N.J.: Princeton University Press, 1942), p. 411.

10. Donald Worster, *Under Western Skies: Nature and History in the American West* (New York: Oxford University Press, 1992), pp. 42–43. This is an argument familiar to modern conservatives. See, for example, Terry L. Anderson and Donald R. Leal, *Free Market Environmentalism* (Boulder, Colo.: Westview, 1991), pp. 3–5.

11. "Uneconomic Conservation," *Mining Congress Journal* 12 (Apr. 1926): 236; "Shackling the Public Domain," ibid. (June 1926): 400; "School Land Grant Legislation Proposed," ibid. (July 1926): 528, 550; "Public Land Legislation," ibid. (Sept. 1926): 619–20; "Locking the Door of Opportunity," ibid. (Oct. 1926): 694.

12. Hubert Work, "Our Public Lands Question," *Mining Congress Journal* 12 (Oct. 1926): 706–8, 762; Charles E. Winter, "Relation of Public Land States to the Federal Government," ibid., 709–13, 762; William Spry, "Leasing of the Public Domain," ibid., 714–16; George H. Dern, "School Land Titles in Public Land States," ibid., 717–20, 763; F. W. Mondell, "Future Disposition and Control of Our Public Lands," ibid. 13 (Feb. 1927): 95–97; W. Halverson Farr, "Who Should Control Our Public Lands which Contain Minerals," ibid., 98–100.

13. Charles L. Gilmore, "Federal Domination vs. State Sovereignty," *Mining Congress Journal* 13 (Jan. 1927): 44–45; ibid. (Feb. 1927): 101–2; ibid. (Mar. 1927): 170–72; ibid. (Apr. 1927): 280–82; ibid. (May 1927): 350–51, 356; William B. Greeley,

"Shall the National Forests Be Abolished," ibid. (Aug. 1927): 594–97. The quotation from Greeley is on p. 595.

14. Wilbur to Governor F. B. Balzar (Nev.), 25 May 1929, IGF, Box 791, Folder "Grazing on Public Lands, Pt. 6"; *The Memoirs of Ray Lyman Wilbur, 1875–1949*, eds. Edgar Eugene Robinson and Paul Carroll Edwards (Stanford, Calif.: Stanford University Press, 1960), pp. 426–27.

15. The Future of the Public Domain: Address of the Secretary of the Interior, Ray Lyman Wilbur, at Boise, Idaho, before the Conference of Governors of Several Western States Called by Governor Baldridge, of Idaho, July 9, 1929, HP:PS, Box 186, Folder "Irrigation, Correspondence 1929–30."

16. Undated [ca. 15 July 1929] Memorandum for the Press, RLW, Box 26, Folder "Public Domain, 1931–46 & undated."

17. Draft letter, 9 Aug. 1929, HP:PS, Box 240, Folder "Public Domain 1929–33." The quoted phrases were omitted or significantly modified in the final letter, dated 21 August. Between 1926 and 1929 the Canadian government turned over federal lands and their subsurface resources to the provinces. See Donald Creighton, *Canada's First Century, 1867–1967* (Toronto: Macmillan of Canada, 1970), p. 193. Hoover may or may not have known about the Canadian policy prior to his initiative, but the commission was certainly aware of it. See H.H. [indecipherable] (Canadian Legation, Washington) to James Garfield, 29 May 1930, GC, Box 1084, Folder "Reports— Library of Congress, 1929–30." Even more intriguing is the possibility that Hoover, a mining engineer, may have been influenced by the articles published in the *Mining Congress Journal*, but I have been unable to determine that.

18. A memorandum, "Secretary Wilbur on Dismembering the Public Domain: Editorial Comment July 16 to 22, inclusive," 19 Aug. 1929, HP:PC, Box 15, Folder "Interior—Corres., 1929 June–July," summarizes only two editorials, one from the St. Paul *Dispatch*, the other from the Portland *Oregonian*. The first expresses doubt that Congress would approve such a transfer; the second approves the idea only if it includes the transfer of national forests and mineral rights.

19. Hoover's handwritten list of questions about the public lands was turned by Wilbur into instructions for the Geological Survey, Reclamation Service, and General Land Office. Both documents, dated 16 July 1929, are in RLW, Box 26, Folder "Public Domain, 1929 July–Aug." The results of those inquiries are in Wilbur to Hoover, 2 Aug. 1929, HP:PS, Box 241, Folder "Public Lands Commission, 1929 Mar.–Sept." An unsigned memorandum, dated 30 Sept. 1930, prepared by someone in the Geological Survey, lists twenty-three categories under which public lands had been withdrawn from sale, including national forests, monuments, parks, oil, reclamation, waterpower, and a huge variety of more specific reasons. See GC, Box 1084, Folder "Reports, Geological Survey, 1930 Sept.–1932."

20. Wilbur to Hoover, 2 Aug. 1929, HP:PS, Box 241, Folder "Public Lands Commission, 1929 Mar.–Sept."

21. Address by First Assistant Secretary of the Interior Jos. M. Dixon, Public-Land

States Governor's Conference, Salt Lake City, 26 and 27 August 1929, HP:PC, Box 15, Folder "Interior—Corres., 1929 Aug.–Sept."

22. Governor H. C. Baldridge (Idaho), chair of conference, to Hoover, 26 Aug. 1929; Hoover to Governor Frank C. Emerson (Wyo.) 28 Aug. 1929; Governor Geo. H. Dern (Utah) to Hoover, 30 Aug. 1929; Rep. Don B. Colton to Hoover, 30 Aug. 1929; Robert D. Carey to Hoover, 30 Aug. 1929, HP:PS, Box 169, Folder "Gov. of the States, 1929."

23. For editorial reaction, see "The Row over Mr. Hoover's 'Gift Horse,'" *Literary Digest* 102 (14 Sept. 1929): 14–15. Private letters also cautioned the president about proceeding with the plan without careful study. See Delph E. Carpenter to Lawrence Richey, 6 Sept. 1929, HP:PS, Box 169, Folder "Gov. of the States, 1929"; Meeting 1286, 12 Sept. 1929, FS, Drawer 133, "Minutes of Service Comm. on Policies & Procedures, 1928–30"; L. Ward Bannister to Hoover, 29 Aug. 1929, HP:PS, Box 225, Folder "Power, 1929"; E. C. Van Patten to Senator Chas. L. McNary, 15 Sept. 1929, HPS, Box 79, Folder "Public Domain/Public Lands, 1929 July–Oct."; L. Ward Bannister to Hoover, 20 Sept. 1929, HP:PS, Box 240, Folder "Public Domain, 1929–33"; Grace McDonald Phillips to Lawrence Richey, 23 Sept. 1929, HP:PC, Box 15, Folder "Interior—Corres., 1929 Aug.–Sept."

24. "A Symposium on National Problems," *Mining Congress Journal* 13 (Aug. 1927): 586–87; "Public Land Ownership," ibid. (Oct. 1927): 705–6, 746.

25. R. Y. Stuart to E. A. Sherman, 17 Sept. 1929, FS, Drawer 194, "Forester's File-F Supervisions General"; Meeting 1287, 19 Sept. 1929, FS, Drawer 133, "Minutes of Service Comm. on Policies & Procedures, 1928–30"; John Carver Edwards, "Herbert Hoover's Public Lands Policy: A Struggle for Control of the Western Domain," *Pacific Historian* 20 (Spring 1976): 36–37. It is also worth noting that Edward C. Finney, solicitor of the Interior Department, indicated his support for a federal range lease program in October 1929. See Finney to Ray Lyman Wilbur, 5 Oct. 1929, IGF, Box 791, Folder "GLO, Grazing on Public Lands, Pt. 7." Leon F. Kneipp later recalled that members of the Forest Service believed that "Any child who had given any thought to the subject [of transferring the lands to the states] would know it was not good." Leon F. Kneipp oral history, "Land Planning and Acquisition, U.S. Forest Service," vol. 1:103, Bancroft Library, University of California at Berkeley. Greeley left the Forest Service in 1928, but his opinion was well known and widely shared in the service.

26. Quotations are from the transcript of Hoover's news conferences of 27 Aug. and 18 Oct. 1929, in *Public Papers, 1929,* pp. 268–69, 330–31. See also Wilbur to Hoover, 2 Oct. 1929, RLWS, Box 30, Folder "Public Lands." The bill to create the commission did not actually pass Congress until 10 April 1930, and the $50,000 appropriation to fund the commission's work did not pass until 14 May 1930, but Hoover received assurances of support from the chairs of the relevant congressional committees and began appointing commission members in October 1929, and the group first met in November. See L[awrence] R[ichey], "Memorandum," 2 Dec. 1929, HP:PS, Box 241,

Folder "Public Lands Commission, 1929 Nov.–Dec."; a copy of the act of Congress authorizing an appropriation of $50,000 for the commission's expenses, signed by Hoover, 10 Apr. 1930, is in GC, Box 1081, Folder "3.0 Legislation, General, 1930 & undated."

27. Ray Lyman Wilbur and William Atherton Du Puy, *Conservation in the Department of the Interior* (Washington, DC: GPO, 1932), p. 38.

28. Garfield was the younger brother of Harry Garfield, who worked closely with Hoover during World War I as Fuel Administrator. It is interesting that he seems not to have been in on the real agenda of the commission at first. Taking the president's public statements at face value, he assumed its subject would be the development of national and international resources. See Garfield to Hoover, 22 Oct. 1929, GC, Box 1082, Folder "Organization—Comm. Personnel, 1929–32 & undated." Gardner Cowles was also in the dark as to the real purpose of the commission, although he quickly deduced it from the loading of the organization with representatives of the states "where self-interests might easily be expected to predominate over general welfare." See J. N. "Ding" Darling to Mark Sullivan, 6 Dec. 1929, HPS, Box 79, Folder "Public Domain, Public Lands, 1929 July–Oct."

29. "Statement on the Commission on Conservation and Administration of the Public Domain," 18 Oct. 1929, *Public Papers, 1929*, pp. 333–34. Other members representing the public land states were: Rudolph Kuchler, a sheep-raiser and president of the State Taxpayers' Association of Arizona; Charles J. Moynihan, an attorney from Colorado; I. H. Nash, State Land Commissioner of Idaho; I. M. Brandjord, Commissioner of State Lands and Investments for Montana, and perhaps the only Democrat on the body; George W. Malone, a former U.S. Senator and since 1927 State Engineer of Nevada; E. C. Van Petten, president of a lumber company in Oregon; William Peterson, director of the experiment station and extension division of Utah State Agricultural College; and R. K. Tiffany, former State Supervisor of Hydraulics for Washington. Several of the state representatives were particularly recommended by Elwood Mead, who, although known as an advocate for federally planned and controlled reclamation projects, had come to favor turning over public lands to the states. Bursum is omitted from the list in *Public Papers* and Kuchler's name is incorrectly spelled as Koechler. Useful comments on the various men considered as state representatives may be found in an undated, unlabeled memorandum sent to the president by Wilbur, 9 Oct. 1929, and in a memorandum sent by Assistant Secretary Joseph Dixon to Wilbur, 10 Oct. 1929, both in RLWS, Box 30, Folder "Public Lands." For a list of the commissioners, with their occupations, see "Committee on the Conservation and Administration of the Public Domain," undated, GC, Box 1082, Folder "Organization—Comm. Personnel, 1929–32 & undated." For Jenkins's opinions and motives, see Jenkins to Hugh A. Brown, 7 Apr. 1931, ibid., Box 1090, Folder "Corres. Comm.—Jenkins Perry W., 1929–31." Horace Albright, director of the National Park Service, sent a six-page letter to Wilbur recommending prominent conservationists for the commission; not one was named. See Albright to Wilbur, 8 Oct. 1929, RLWS,

Box 30, Folder "Public Lands." Texas was the only western state not included on the commission because, when it entered the union, it had retained all public lands and never turned them over to the federal government.

30. "Problems," no date, GC, Box 1085, Folder "Report of Committee, Preliminary Materials (2)"; "Remarks Made by Secretary Wilbur on the Occasion of the First Meeting of the Committee on the Conservation and Administration of the Public Domain, November [23], 1929," ibid., Box 1076, Folder "Minutes of Meetings, 1929–31." Preparation of such agendas prior to a meeting was a technique Hoover frequently used to control the direction of discussion and the shape of conclusions, but there is no evidence of the president's direct influence on this document.

31. "Resolutions," 25 Nov. 1929, GC, Box 1076, Folder "Minutes of Meetings, 1929–31"; unsigned draft [probably by Garfield] of letter to commissioners, 26 Nov. 1929, ibid., Box 1082, Folder "Organization—Comm. Personnel, 1929–32 & undated." The three subcommittees created by the commission reflected the priorities set in its resolutions: study the disposal of the public lands, consider the issue of subsurface minerals, and study reclamation. See memo in L. F. Kneipp's handwriting, 26 Nov. 1929, in vol. 2 of Leon F. Kneipp oral history. The Interior Department promoted the transfer of lands to the states by issuing a press release in December 1929 listing the profits western states had received the prior year from leasing state-owned public lands. "Memorandum for the Press," 26 Dec. 1929, RLW, Box 25, Folder "Press Releases—Land Office (Subject)."

32. Minutes of meeting of 19 Nov. 1929, A.M., GC, Box 1076, "Minutes of Meetings, 1929–31."

33. Jenkins to James R. Garfield, 9 Dec. 1929, GC, Box 1090, Folder, "Corres. Comm.—Jenkins, Perry W., 1929–31." Jenkins consistently spoke out for conservative positions on the commission. See, for example, the rough draft of the minutes of the meeting of 2 June 1930, pp. 4–5, GC, Box 1076, Folder "Minutes of Meetings, 1929–30."

34. See the remarks of Governor Frank C. Emerson of Wyoming at the Governors' Conference Proceedings, Salt Lake City, 30 June 1930, HP:PS, Box 169, Folder "Gov. of the States, 1930." This was a central argument in the editorials published in the *Mining Congress Journal* in 1927. See Greeley's article, "Shall the National Forests Be Abolished," *Mining Congress Journal* 13 (Aug. 1927): 594–97.

35. R. K. Tiffany to Garfield, 7 Mar. 1930, GC, Box 1091, Folder "Corres. Committee—Tiffany, R. K., 1929–32 & undated"; Garfield to Francis C. Wilson, 18 Apr. 1930, GC, Folder "Corres. Committee—Wilson, Francis C., 1929–30 June"; George W. Malone to Garfield, 7 July 1930, ibid., Box 1090, Folder "Corres. Committee—Malone, George W., 1931"; memorandum by Malone, 17 Nov. 1930, Ray Lyman Wilbur Papers, Stanford University Archives, Box 84, Folder "U.S. Conservation (Interior Dept.)."

36. Elwood Mead was an exception to this. See Mead to Gov. C. C. Young (Calif.),

31 Oct. 1930, RLWS, Box 30, Folder "Public Lands." In contrast, see H. O. Bursum to Garfield, 28 Dec. 1930, GC, Box 1090, Folder "Corres. Committee—Bursum, H. O., 1930–31." A table provided by the Bureau of Reclamation showed that in 1928, although more money came to the federal government from sales of public lands, oil leases, etc., than was spent on reclamation overall, significantly more was spent in Colorado, Idaho, Nebraska, Nevada, Texas, and Washington than was generated within those states. See undated table in GC, Box 1085, Folder "Reports—Reclamation Bur., 1928–29." A table for 1929 shows similar but not identical distributions.

37. James R. Garfield, "Statement . . . at conclusion of meeting, June 5, 1930," GC, Box 1076, Folder "Minutes of Meetings, 1929–31."

38. Memorandum on "Conservation and Administration of the Public Domain," read by Commissioner C. C. Moore of the General Land Office to a meeting of the commission in June 1930, GC, Box 1083, Folder "Reports—Gen. Land Office, 1930 Jan.–June." Moore's figures are higher than those provided by his subordinate, Thomas H. MacDonald; I cannot account for the discrepancy. See Hugh Brown to James R. Garfield, 5 May 1930, GC, Box 1090, Folder "Corres. Committee—Garfield, James R., 1929–30 June"; Thomas H. MacDonald (Chief, Bureau of Public Roads) to Hugh Brown, 17 June 1930, GC, Box 1088, Folder "Reports—Data Furnished, Public Roads"; table, 3 May 1930, "Apportionments and Payments of Federal Aid to Public Land States," GC, Box 1084, Folder "Reports—Public Roads Bureau, 1929–31"; Minutes of Meeting 1318, 5 June 1930, FS, Drawer 133, "Minutes of Service Comm. on Policies & Procedures, 1928–30."

39. See the state reports in GC, Box 1087, Folder "5.3, Reports, Data Furnished," and Boxes 1088 and 1089, Folders "5.4, Reports, State Committees"; Sanford A. Mosk, "Land Policy and Stock Raising in the Western United States," in *The Public Lands: Studies in the History of the Public Domain*, ed. Vernon Carstensen (Madison: University of Wisconsin Press, 1968), p. 427.

40. See, for example, Terry L. Anderson and Donald R. Leal, *Free Market Environmentalism* (Boulder, Colo.: Westview Press, 1991).

41. Ray Lyman Wilbur to James R. Garfield, 26 Nov. 1929, GC, Box 1091, Folder "Corres. Comm.—Wilbur, Ray Lyman, 1929–31"; A. J. Hazlett to Garfield, 22 Nov. 1929, ibid., Box 1077, Folder "Corres. General, 1929 & undated."

42. Clyde Luddington to Hoover, 26 Nov. 1929, GC, Box 1077, Folder "Corres. General, 1929 & undated"; John Pruitt to Ray Lyman Wilbur, 12 Jan. 1931, ibid., Box 1078, Folder "Corres. General, 1931 Jan.–Apr."; resolution adopted by the Mining Committee of the House of Representatives of Idaho, 3 Mar. 1930, ibid., Box 1079, Folder "Resolutions, 1927–1930."

43. For various resolutions, see GC, Box 1079, Folders "Resolutions, 1927–30," and "Resolutions, 1931–32 & undated"; Wm. Duby to James R. Garfield, 3 Mar. 1930, ibid., Box 1077, Folder "Corres. General, 1930 Jan.–Apr."; B. H. Kizer to Garfield, ibid., Folder "Corres. General, 1930 May–Sept."; clipping from Redlands (Calif.)

Facts, 12 Dec. 1929, RLWS, Box 30, Folder "Public Lands"; statements from the irrigation league and the library association may be found in GC, Box 1089, Folder "Reports, Sources Outside Government, 1929-1932."

44. James R. Garfield, "Statement . . . at conclusion of meeting, June 5, 1930," p. 6, GC, Box 1076, Folder "Minutes of Meetings, 1929-31."

45. See various resolutions in GC, Box 1079, Folders "Resolutions, 1927-1930" and "Resolutions, 1931-1932."

46. David L. Geyer to James R. Garfield, 29 Nov. 1929, GC, Box 1077, Folder "Corres. General, 1929 & undated"; F. V. H. Collins to Joseph M. Dixon, 5 Mar. 1930, ibid., Folder "Corres. General, 1930 Jan.-Apr."; Edward Lawrence to Garfield, [?] July 1930, ibid., Folder "Corres. General, 1930 May-Sept."; Floyd Martin to Hoover, 21 Aug. 1930, ibid.

47. C. S. Rhoads to James R. Garfield, 23 Jan. 1930, GC, Box 1084, Folder "Reports—Indian Affairs Office, 1928-30 Mar." The General Land Office, on the other hand, estimated that almost 71 million acres remained in Indian reservations, and that only about 27 million acres had been allotted to individual Indians. See C. C. Moore to James R. Garfield, 7 Oct. 1930, GC, Box 1083, Folder "Reports—Gen. Land Office, 1930 July."

48. George Otis Smith to Ray Lyman Wilbur, 22 Mar. 1930, GC, Box 1084, Folder "Reports, Geological Survey, 1930 April." Smith's report frustrated those in the Forest Service who had hoped he would come out strongly for federal control, which they hoped to be in position to undertake. See the minutes of Meeting 1313, 24 Apr. 1930, FS, Drawer 133, "Minutes of Service Comm. on Policies & Procedures, 1928-30."

49. C. C. Moore, "Conservation and Administration of the Public Domain," [?] June 1930, GC, Box 1083, Folder "Reports—Gen. Land Office, 1930 Jan.-June"; Moore to James R. Garfield, 11 November 1930, enclosing pamphlet by Moore, "The Future of the Public Domain" (Washington, D.C.: GPO, 1930), GC, Box 1083, Folder "Reports—Gen. Land Office, 1930 Oct.-Nov." Within a short speech to the commissioners at the conclusion of their meeting on 5 June 1930, Garfield gave the amount of unsurveyed public land as both 53 million and 52 million acres. His million-acre slip suggests some of the problems facing the commissioners, but Garfield was certainly correct when he said that resolving such problems was essential to conveying a clear title to whatever entities ultimately took charge of the land. See James R. Garfield, "Statement," 5 June 1930, pp. 2, 5, GC, Box 1075, Folder "Minutes of Meetings, 1929-31."

50. Press releases, 14 July and 11 Sept. 1930; William Peterson, "Tour of the Southwestern States," ca. 1 Oct. 1930, GC, Box 1076, Folder "Press Releases, 1930-31."

51. The official minutes meetings between 10 and 26 November occupy only two typed pages in GC, Box 1076, Folder "Minutes of Meetings, 1929-31." For Garfield's speech, see typed transcript, 10 Nov. 1930, in ibid. See also George H. Lorimer to James R. Garfield, 25 Nov. 1930, GC, Box 1090, Folder "Corres. Committee—

Lorimer, Geo. H., 1930–32"; and press release, 26 Nov. 1930, GC, Box 1076, Folder "Press Releases, 1930–31."

52. E. C. Finney to James R. Garfield, 16 Dec. 1930, GC, Box 1082, Folder "Reports, Fed. Oil Cons. Board, Office of Solicitor, 1930"; George Otis Smith to Ray Lyman Wilbur, 29 May 1930, GC, Box 1083, Folder "Reports—Forest Service, 1930 Jan.–May."

53. Paul G. Redington to James R. Garfield, 9 Jan. 1931, GC, Box 1082, Folder "Reports, Biological Survey, Migratory Bird Conservation Commission, 1930–31"; Horace M. Albright to Garfield, 10 Jan. 1931, GC, Box 1084, Folder "Reports—National Park Service, 1929–32"; Henry Graves, "The Public Domain," *The Nation* 131 (6 Aug. 1930): 147–49; Arthur M. Hyde to Garfield, 12 Jan. 1931, GC, Box 1090, Folder "Corres. Committee—Hyde, Arthur M., 1929–31." Pro-transfer members of the commission were alarmed by these public defections. See I. M. Brandjord to Hugh A. Brown, 25 Nov. 1931, GC, Box 1090, Folder "Corres. Committee—Brandjord, I. M., 1931–32."

54. W. B. Greeley to James R. Garfield, 3 Jan. 1931, GC, Box 1090, Folder "Corres. Committee—Greeley, W. B., 1929–32."

55. Hoover, "Statement on the Commission on Conservation and Administration of the Public Domain," 18 Oct. 1929, *Public Papers, 1929*, pp. 333–34.

56. Hugh Brown to James R. Garfield, 12 Dec. 1930, GC, Box 1090, Folder "Corres. Committee—Garfield, James R., 1930 July–Dec."

57. For western complaints, see Perry Jenkins to James R. Garfield, 23 Dec. 1930, GC, Box 1090, Folder "Corres. Committee—Jenkins, Perry W., 1929–31."

58. Press release, 10 Jan. 1931, GC, Box 1076, Folder "Press Releases, 1930–31"; I. H. Nash to E. C. Van Petten, 15 Jan. 1931, GC, Box 1091, Folder "Corres. Committee—Van Petten, E. C., 1929–31"; statement by Rudolph Kuchler, undated, GC, Box 1086, Folder "5.2 Reports, Report of the Committee, Preliminary Material (5)"; "Minutes, Meeting of January 12–17, 1931," GC, Box 1076, Folder "Minutes of Meetings, 1929–31." Goodrich, Malone, and Moynihan were the three who voted for the motion. The minutes contain no explanation of their position.

59. "Report of the Committee on the Conservation and Administration of the Public Domain," 16 Jan. 1931, GC, Box 1085, Folder "Report of Committee, Preliminary Materials (2)."

60. Garfield to various members of the commission, 16 Jan. 1931, GC, Box 1086, Folder "Reports—Report of the Comm., Preliminary Material (9)."

61. I. M. Brandjord to Hugh A. Brown, 6 Jan. 1931, GC, Box 1090, Folder "Corres. Committee—Brandjord, I. M."; J. P. Goodrich to James R. Garfield, 12 Jan. 1931, ibid., Folder "Corres. Committee—Goodrich, James P., 1930–31"; I. M. Brandjord and Rudolph Kuchler to James R. Garfield, 16 Jan. 1931, GC, Box 1086, Folder "Reports—Report of the Comm., Preliminary Material (4)."

62. W. B. Greeley to James R. Garfield, 26 Jan. 1931, GC, Box 1086, Folder

"Reports—Report of the Comm., Preliminary Material (9)." For the reluctant agreement of some other members, see Hugh Brown to Garfield, 23 and 29 Jan. 1931, GC, Box 1090, Folder "Corres. Committee—Garfield, James R., 1931"; James P. Goodrich to Garfield, 25 Jan. 1931, GC, Box 1086, Folder "Reports—Report of the Comm., Preliminary Materials (9)."

63. Garfield to Greeley, 2 and 5 Feb., 1931; Greeley to Garfield, 9 Feb. 1931; Garfield to the members of the commission, 11 Feb. 1931, GC, Box 1086, Folder "Reports—Report of the Comm., Preliminary Material (9)."

64. Hugh Brown to James R. Garfield, 11 Mar. 1931, GC, Box 1090, Folder "Corres. Committee—Garfield, James R., 1931"; "Greeley Holds Domain Report Inadequate: Former Chief Forester Sets Forth Reasons for Not Signing Committee's Recommendations," *American Forests* (May 1931): 278–79.

65. For the Kelley case, see Ray Lyman Wilbur to Senator Gerald P. Nye, 27 Feb. 1931, Box 6, Folder 43, Northcutt Ely Papers, Stanford University Library [hereafter Ely Papers]; Interior Dept. Press Release, 27 Feb. 1931, and attached copy of a letter from H. E. C. Bryant to Walter Lippmann (n.d.), a copy of Kelley's contract with the N.Y. *World*, 11 Sept. 1930, a copy of Kelley to Wilbur, 28 Sept. 1930, and a copy of a statement by President Hoover on the matter, 28 Oct. 1930, all in RLW, Box 21, Folder "Oil—Oil Shale Report, 1931." Kelley's charges were thoroughly discredited.

66. Edwards, "Herbert Hoover's Public Lands Policy," 39–40.

67. Hugh Brown to James R. Garfield, 15 Dec. 1930, GC, Box 1090, Folder "Corres. Committee—Garfield, James R., 1930 July–Dec."; William Peterson to Brown, 14 Mar. 1931, GC, Box 1091, Folder "Corres. Committee—Peterson, William, 1930–31"; I. H. Nash to Brown, 31 Mar. 1931, GC, Box 1091, Folder "Corres. Committee—Nash, I. H., 1930–31"; I. M. Brandjord to Garfield, 13 Apr. 1931, GC, Box 1090, Folder "Corres. Committee—Brandjord, I. M., 1931–32." George Malone was the lone exception to the general pattern; he reported full support for the proposal in Nevada. See Malone to Garfield, 6 Apr. 1931, GC, Box 1090, Folder "Corres. Committee—Malone, George W., 1931." About a dozen citizens wrote directly to the commission about the report; their responses ran two to one in favor of it. See GC, Box 1087, Folder "5.23. Reports, Comments Received, 1931 Jan.–May."

68. Hugh Brown to James R. Garfield, 14 Apr. 1931, GC, Box 1090, Folder "Corres. Committee—Garfield, James R., 1931." No evidence has been found to support Jenkins's charges; he seems to have been in conflict with the Forest Service over grazing rights for several years prior to this, and his intemperate manner probably exacerbated the situation.

69. James R. Garfield to Hugh Brown, 23 Mar. 1931, GC, Box 1090, Folder "Corres. Committee, Garfield, James R., 1931"; Francis C. Wilson to Brown, 14 Oct. 1931, GC, Box 1091, Folder "Corres. Committee—Wilson, Francis C., 1930 July–1931."

70. Copy of resolution adopted 29 Oct. 1931, Ely Papers, Box 1, Folder 3.

71. Minutes of Meeting 1373, 12 Nov. 1931, and of Meeting 1375, 27 Nov. 1931,

FS, Drawer 134, "Minutes of Service Comm. on Policies & Procedures, 1931–35";
Horace M. Albright to Ray Lyman Wilbur, 5 Dec. 1931, Wilbur Papers, Stanford
University Archives, Box 22, Folder "Horace Albright"; press release, "Recommendations of Land Utilization Conference," 23 Nov. 1931, and summary of conference by
Franklin Reed, 5 Dec. 1931, both in RLW, Box 26, Folder "Public Domain, 1931–46
& undated." A third meeting of the conference, in October 1932, received strong
statements favoring land use planning from Hoover and Franklin Roosevelt and reiterated its support for retention and administration of rangelands by the federal government. See Minutes of Meeting 1415, 5 Oct. 1932, FS, Drawer 134, "Minutes of
Service Comm. on Policies & Procedures, 1931–35."

72. Ward Shepard, "The Handout Magnificent," *Harper's* 163 (Oct. 1931): 595,
597, 601, 602. An earlier article by Silas Bent, "Mr. Hoover's Sins of Commissions,"
Scribner's Magazine 90 (July 1931): 9–14, had accused the Garfield commissioners of
being apologists for special interests, but the article's factual errors and sloppy argument allowed the administration to ignore it.

73. Hugh Brown to James R. Garfield, 25 Sept., 17 Nov. 1931, GC, Box 1090,
Folder "Corres. Committee—Garfield, James R."; Brown to Francis Wilson, 27 Jan.
1932, GC, Box 1091, Folder "Corres. Committee—Wilson, Francis C., 1932 Jan.–
Mar."; Francis Cushman Wilson, "The Problem of the Public Domain," *Saturday
Evening Post* 204 (23 Jan. 1932): 21, 36, 38, 40; Brown to Adelaide W. Neall (*Saturday
Evening Post*), 3 Feb. 1932, GC, Box 1090, Folder "Corres. Committee—Garfield,
James R., 1932–33."

74. Brown to Wilson, 27 Jan. 1932, GC, Box 1091, Folder "Corres. Committee—
Wilson, Francis C., 1932 Jan.–Mar."

75. Ely to Wilbur, 21 Nov. 1931, Ely Papers, Box 10, Folder 65; I. M. Brandjord to
Wilbur, 1 Dec. 1931, GC, Box 1081, Folder "Legislation, Federal, 1918–32 & undated"; George W. Malone to Francis C. Wilson, 3 Dec. 1931, and Malone to Elwood Mead, 22 Dec. 1931, GC, Box 1090, Folder "7.0, Correspondence, Committee,
Malone, George W., 1931."

76. The bills are in GC, Box 1081, Folder "3.1. Legislation, Federal, 1918–1932 &
undated."

77. Hugh Brown to James R. Garfield, 1 and 29 Feb., and 11 Mar. 1932, and
Garfield to Brown, 23 and 29 Feb. 1932, GC, Box 1090, Folder "Corres. Commit-
tee—Garfield, James R., 1932–33"; Garfield to Ray Lyman Wilbur, 24 Feb. 1932,
RLWS, Box 30, Folder "Reorganization, March 4, 1929 to Feb. 1, 1933."

78. Hugh Brown to James R. Garfield, 21 Mar. and 5 Apr. 1932, GC, Box 1090,
Folder "Corres. Committee—Garfield, James R., 1932–33"; Minutes of Meetings
1387, 1388, and 1390, 17 and 24 Mar., and 7 Apr. 1932, FS, Drawer 134, "Minutes
of Service Comm. on Policies & Procedures, 1931–35."

79. Hugh Brown to James R. Garfield, 22 Mar. 1932, GC, Box 1090, Folder "Corres.
Committee—Garfield, James R., 1932–33."

80. Hugh Brown to George F. Malone, 22 Mar. and 11 Apr. 1932, GC, Box 1090,

Folder "Corres. Committee—Malone, George W., 1932"; Brown to Francis C. Wilson, 29 Mar. 1932, GC, Box 1090, Folder "Corres. Committee—Wilson, Francis C., 1932 Jan.-Mar."; Brown to Wilson, 4 and 14 Apr. 1932, GC, Box 1090, Folder "Corres. Committee—Wilson, Francis C., 1932 Apr.-1933"; Wilson to Brown, 19 Apr. 1932, ibid. Garfield was a little more optimistic. See Garfield to Wilson, 2 Apr. 1932, GC, Box 1090, Folder "Corres. Committee—Wilson, Francis C., 1932 Apr.-1933."

81. Minutes of Meetings 1394, 1395, 1397, 1398, 1401, 1433, 1434, and 1437, on 5, 12, and 26 May, 2 and 23 June 1932, and 9 and 16 Feb., and 9 Mar. 1933, FS, Drawer 134, "Minutes of Service Comm. on Policies & Procedures, 1931-35"; Ray Lyman Wilbur to Rep. John H. Evans, 9 May 1932, HP:PC, Box 16, Folder "Interior—Corres., 1932 May"; Wilbur to Sen. Gerald P. Nye, 16 Feb. 1933, ibid., Folder "Interior—Corres., 1933 Jan.-Mar."; Wilbur to Perry Jenkins, 16 May 1932, RLWS, Box 27, Folder "Oil, May 6, 1931 to "; "Memorandum for file" by Hugh A. Brown, 17 May 1932, GC, Box 1081, Folder "Corres. Senate, 1929-32"; Foss, *Politics and Grass,* pp. 50-52.

82. Garfield to Wilson, 18 May 1932, and Wilson to Garfield, 25 May 1932, GC, Box 1091, Folder "Corres. Committee—Wilson, Francis C., 1932 Apr.-1933."

83. Peffer, *Closing of the Public Domain,* pp. 215-23.

84. Wilbur and Du Puy, *Conservation in the Department of the Interior,* p. 172.

85. Ickes quoted in Foss, *Politics and Grass,* p. 50.

86. Herbert Hoover, *Addresses Upon the American Road, 1948-1950* (Stanford, Calif.: Stanford University Press, 1951), p. 144.

9. "The Balm of Words"

1. Bob Pepperman Taylor, *Our Limits Transgressed: Environmental Political Thought in America* (Lawrence: University Press of Kansas, 1992), p. 27.

2. "Extract from Remarks by Secretary Hoover at meeting [of National Committee on Wood Utilization] of April 28, [1926]," National Forest Products Association Papers, Box 74, Folder "Dept. of Commerce, National Comm. on Wood Utiliz.," Forest History Society Archives, Duke University.

3. Gary S. Cross, *A Social History of Leisure since 1600* (State College, Pa.: Venture, 1990), pp. 167-69.

4. No study of the impact of the depression on conservationist thought seems to exist. There is at least some evidence to suggest that conservationists, like other Americans, assumed the crisis was an aberration and that the march toward affluence and leisure would soon resume. See, for example, Stuart Chase, *The Economy of Abundance* (New York: Macmillan, 1934). Susan Strasser notes that, except for automobiles, sales of many consumer goods increased during the depression, and that the use of gasoline and electricity also increased. Susan Strasser, *Waste and Want: The Other Side of Consumption* (Providence, R.I.: Berg Publishers for the German Histori-

cal Institute, 1992), pp. 19–20. These findings are suggestive of the possibility that the depression did not really undermine the theoretical basis of the consumer society and thus did not jeopardize the idea that conservation would stabilize and expand prosperity.

5. *The New Day: Campaign Speeches of Herbert Hoover, 1928* (Stanford, Calif.: Stanford University Press, 1928), pp. 50–52.

6. Evan B. Metcalf, "Secretary Hoover and the Emergence of Macroeconomic Management," *Business History Review* 49 (Spring 1975): 60–80.

7. *The Memoirs of Herbert Hoover: The Cabinet and the Presidency, 1920–1933* (New York: Macmillan, 1952), pp. 45–46 [hereafter Hoover, *Memoirs* 2]. For an analysis of Hoover's general approach to economic recovery and stabilization in this period, see Ellis W. Hawley, "Herbert Hoover and Economic Stabilization, 1921–22," in *Herbert Hoover as Secretary of Commerce: Studies in New Era Thought and Practice*, ed. Ellis W. Hawley (Iowa City: University of Iowa Press, 1981), pp. 44–77.

8. Quoted in Patrick D. Reagan, "From Depression to Depression: Hooverian National Planning, 1921–1933," *Mid-America* 70 (Jan. 1988): 43. See also Carolyn Grin, "The Unemployment Conference of 1921: An Experiment in National Cooperative Planning," *Mid-America* 55 (Apr. 1973): 83–107.

9. Memorandum for Edward Eyre Hunt by Otto T. Mallery, 3 Oct. 1921; Mallery to John T. Summers, 27 Oct. 1921, enclosing report from Reclamation service; Mallery to B. F. Blaine, 8 Nov. 1921, HP:Com, Box 649, Folder "Unemployment—Interior Dept.—Reclamation, 1921."

10. Report of the Committee on Recent Economic Changes of the President's Conference on Unemployment, *Recent Economic Changes in the United States*, vol. 1 (New York: McGraw-Hill, 1929), p. xx; Metcalf, "Secretary Hoover and the Emergence of Macroeconomic Management," 74–79; David Burner, "Before the Crash: Hoover's First Eight Months in the Presidency," in *The Hoover Presidency: A Reappraisal*, eds. Martin L. Fausold and George T. Mazuzan (Albany: State University of New York Press, 1974), p. 53.

11. Martin L. Fausold, *The Presidency of Herbert C. Hoover* (Lawrence: University Press of Kansas, 1985), p. 72.

12. Ibid., pp. 74–77. For a brief and incisive summary of Hoover's early antidepression activities, see Ellis W. Hawley, "Herbert Hoover and American Corporatism, 1931–1933," in *The Hoover Presidency*, pp. 114–16.

13. Hoover to Ray Lyman Wilbur, 18 Nov. 1929, RLWS, Box 120, Folder "HH & RLW (1)."

14. For the administration's earlier review of the service, see Chapter 7, pages 133–34.

15. Mead to Hoover, 14 Aug. 1929, HPS, Box 45, Folder "Interior, Reclamation Service." Considering farm conditions in the 1920s in general, Mead's statement must be viewed with some caution; presumably, he meant that things were going as well as they had been in recent years.

16. J. Clawson Roop, director of the Bureau of the Budget, to Hoover, 3 Feb. 1930, and Roop to Hyde, undated; Senator C. C. Dill (Wash.) to Hoover, 13 Oct. 1930; W. H. Cowles, Charles R. Lund, Charles Hebberd, Mark E. Reed, Roy R. Gill, and J. A. Swallwell to Hoover, 18 Nov. 1930; Charles Hebberd to Lawrence Richey (secretary to the president), 18 Nov. 1930; Richey to Hebberd, 20 Nov. 1930, all in HP:PS, Box 186, Folder "Irrigation, Correspondence, 1929-30." For Hoover's regret that he had to drop his support for the Columbia River project, see Mabel Walker Willebrandt to Lawrence Richey, 16 Jan. 1932; Richey to Willebrandt, 19 Jan. 1932; Hoover to W. H. Cowles, 3 May 1932, HP:PS, Box 186, Folder "Irrigation, Correspondence, 1932."

17. "Requests for a Moratorium and the Effect of Such Action on Federal Reclamation: Statement Submitted by the Commissioner of Reclamation at a Senate Conference Held December 10, 1931," RLWS, Box 49, Folder "Reclamation—Moratorium and the Effect of Such Action on Federal Reclamation"; Walter H. Newton (secretary to the president) to Representative Bertrand H. Snell, 1 Feb. 1932, HP:PS, Box 186, Folder "Irrigation, Correspondence 1932"; Dept. of Interior Memorandum for the Press, 1 Apr. 1932, HP:PC, Box 21, Folder "Interior—Reclamation Service, 1931-33 & undated."

18. D. W. Davis (Chief National Inspector, Crop Production and Farmers' Seed Loans, Agriculture Dept.) to Hoover, 19 Sept. 1932, HP:PC, Box 21, Folder "Interior—Reclamation Service, 1931-33 & undated"; Hoover to W. H. Cowles, 3 May 1932, HP:PS, Box 186, Folder "Irrigation Correspondence, 1932."

19. Elwood Mead to Wilbur, 13 Jan. 1933, RLWS, Box 25, Folder "Reports on Pending Work, Jan. 1933." Secretary Wilbur confirmed the reduction of expenditures on reclamation in his final report to the president. See Wilbur to Hoover, 3 Mar. 1933, RLW, Box 16, Folder "Interior Department, 1933-38 & undated."

20. Bureau of the Budget, "Statement of Expenditures for Roads, Departments of Agriculture and Interior, for Fiscal Years 1921 to 1933, Inclusive," 6 Aug. 1932, HP:PS, Box 85, Folder "Bureau of the Budget, Corres. 1932 July-Dec." Note, however, that appropriations for road and trail construction in the national parks (included in the figures above) reached a peak of $7.5 million in 1932, but requests were reduced in the proposed budget for FY 1934 to $2.4 million. See Ray Lyman Wilbur to Hoover, 3 Mar. 1933, RLW, Box 16, Folder "Interior Department, 1933-38 & undated."

21. R. Y. Stuart to Raphael Zon, 9 Dec. 1929; Zon to Stuart, 29 Nov. 1929, FS, Drawer 194 "F Supervision General."

22. Horace Albright oral history, pp. 53-56, HHPL; Interior Dept. Press Releases, 4 Feb. 1931, 25 Mar. 1931, HP:PC, Box 9, Folder "Interior—Natl. Park Service, 1931 Jan.-May"; Lou Henry Hoover to Horace Albright, 6 Dec. 1932, RLW, Box 18, Folder "National Parks, 1932 July-Dec."; Dennis Elwood Simmons, "The Creation of Shenandoah National Park and the Skyline Drive, 1924-1936" (Ph.D. diss., University of Virginia, 1978), pp. 70-80.

23. Howard Hopkins, "Memorandum for the Files," 14 Feb. 1933, HP:PC, Box 5, Folder "Agriculture—Forest Service Forest Management, 1931–Aug. 1933."

24. R. Y. Stuart to Hoover, 28 Jan. 1931, HPS, Box 18, Folder "Agriculture—Public Roads"; Lawrence Richey to Frederick H. Cowles, 2 May 1931, HP:PC, Box 5, Folder "Agriculture—Forest Service, Correspondence, 1931 Jan.–May"; E. E. Carter to H. R. Smith, 17 Oct. 1931, ibid., Folder "Agriculture—Forest Service, Correspondence, 1931 June–Dec."; Arthur M. Hyde, "Forestry in Farm Relief," *American Forests and Forest Life* 36 (Oct. 1930): 624–25. I am indebted to Albert Hester for finding this article by Hyde.

25. Charles Lathrop Pack to Walter Newton, 20 July 1932; Arthur Hyde to Newton, undated but enclosed in Ernest E. Hall to Newton, 30 July 1932; Rep. Harold Knutson to Newton, 29 Aug. 1932; Newton to Knutson, 1 Sept. 1932; Hyde to Knutson, 12 Sept. 1932; Leon F. Kneipp to [?] Meador, 26 Oct. 1932 (emphasis in original); Hyde to Newton, 27 Oct. 1932; Newton to Hyde, 27 Oct. 1932; copy of pp. 1–4 of *The Forestry News Digest*, Oct. 1932, all in HP:PS, Box 164, Folder "Forest, Fires, Reforestation, 1932."

26. Howard Hopkins, "Memorandum for the Files," 14 Feb. 1933, HP:PC, Box 5, Folder "Agriculture—Forest Service Forest Management, 1931–Aug. 1933."

27. Hyde to Hoover, 2 Oct. 1930; Hoover to Hyde, 3 Oct. 1930, HP:PS, Box 84, Folder "Bureau of Budget, Correspondence, 1930 Oct.–Dec."

28. Hoover to Crocker, 21 May 1932, HP:PS, Box 336, Folder "Unemployment, Correspondence, 1932."

29. Press Release, "Federal Government Appropriations Grouped upon a Functional Basis," 5 Dec. 1929, HP:PS, Folder "Bureau of the Budget—Fed. Expenditures on a Functional Basis, 1929–32"; "Expenditures Classified on a Functional Basis, Fiscal Years 1932, 1931, 1930," [6 June 1930], ibid. Included in "Conservation of Natural Resources" were the Forest Service (salaries and expenses, forest fire work, acquisition of lands, cooperative tree planting activities, construction and maintenance of forest roads and trails, payments to states and territories from national forest funds); the General Land Office (salaries and expenses, surveying costs, and receipts from mineral leases); the National Park Service; the War Department's national cemeteries and national military parks and monuments; the Bureau of Fisheries; the Geological Survey; the Biological Survey; and one-half of salaries and expenses of the secretary's office of the Department of the Interior. See T. E. J. [?] to Budget Director J. Clawson Roop, 19 Dec. 1929, ibid., Folder "Bureau of the Budget—Correspondence, 1929 June–Dec." It should be noted, however, that the Interior Department, with a long-standing reputation for corruption and ineptitude, was already being pinched by Congress even before the beginning of the depression. See, for example, E. K. Burlew, Memorandum on the Budget, 22 Mar. 1929; Arno Cammerer to Burlew, 27 Mar. 1929; Horace Albright to Burlew, 29 Mar. and 8 July 1929; unsigned memorandum, "Condition of Appropriations in the Department of the Interior for the Fiscal Year 1929," 29 Mar. 1929, RLW, Box 16, Folder "Interior Department, Budget, FY

1929–30, 1929 & undated"; Wilbur to Director of Budget, 17 July 1929; Burlew to Wilbur, 15 and 19 Aug. [1929]; Wilbur to Burlew, 17 Aug. 1929, ibid., Folder "Interior Department, Budget FY 1931."

30. Hoover to Cabinet Secretaries, 29 July 1930; Ray Lyman Wilbur to Hoover, 28 Aug. 1930, HP:PS, Box 84, Folder "Bureau of the Budget—Correspondence 1930 July"; J. Clawson Roop to Hoover, 3 Oct. 1930; "Estimated Receipts, Fiscal Year 1931, as of October 1, 1930"; Ray Lyman Wilbur to Hoover, 22 Oct. 1930, ibid., Folder "Bureau of Budget, Correspondence 1930 Oct.–Dec."; Minutes of Meetings 1335, 1338, and 1342, 2 and 29 Jan. and 26 Feb. 1931, FS, Drawer 134 "Minutes of Service Comm. on Policies & Procedures, 1931–35"; Hoover to Wilbur, 21 Apr. 1931, RLWS, Box 120, Folder "HH-RLW, 1929–1932 Ltrs."

31. "Tenth Annual Report of the Director of the Budget for the Fiscal Year Ended June 30, 1931," 4 Nov. 1931, HP:PS, Box 85, Folder "Bureau of the Budget, Corresp. 1931 Nov."; Minutes of Meeting 1355, 4 June 1931, FS, Drawer 134 "Minutes of Service Comm. on Policies & Procedures, 1931–35"; R. Y. Stuart to E. A. Sherman, 6 Oct. 1931, ibid., Drawer "F-Supervision-1931."

32. T. E. J., "Memorandum for Colonel Roop," 5 Nov. 1931, HP:PS, Box 85, Folder "Bureau of the Budget, Corresp. 1931 Nov."

33. *Public Papers of the Presidents of the United States: Herbert Hoover; Containing the Public Messages, Speeches, and Statements of the President, 1931* (Washington, D.C.: GPO, 1976), pp. 580, 592–93 [hereafter *Public Papers*, with year].

34. Arno Cammerer to Horace Albright, 4 Jan. 1932, NPS, Box General 201–201.001, File "Economic Conditions 1932, Part I." The Park Service evidently took this suggestion seriously. Cammerer suggested warning various western business interests of the threat, and this file contains a number of letters of protest from western railroads and chambers of commerce. Traditionally, the Park Service had touted the spiritual, esthetic, and scientific value of the parks, but in this crisis, it stressed their economic importance—a risky approach if tourism fell off, as it did in the summer of 1932. See Horace Albright to W. C. Gregg, 13 July 1932, ibid., Box General 201.1, Pts. 7–9, 1931–33 (Albright), File "Director, Pt. 8, Jan. 2, 1932 to Sept. 27, 1932."

35. Harris Gaylord Warren, *Herbert Hoover and the Great Depression* (New York: Oxford University Press, 1959), pp. 54, 128–29, 151–54, 158–59.

36. *Public Papers, 1931*, pp. 598–615.

37. "Summary of the Budget on a Functional Basis Together with Statement of the Amount of Expenditures on Construction Work in Aid to Unemployment," 14 Dec. 1931, HP:PS, Box 87, Folder "Bureau of the Budget—Fed. Expenditures on a Functional Basis, 1929–32"; J. Clawson Roop to [Walter H.] Newton, 27 Apr. 1932, HP:PS, Box 85, Folder "Bureau of the Budget, Corresp. 1932 Jan.–Apr."; "Principal Changes in Receipts and Expenditures, General and Special Funds," [1 May 1932], ibid., Folder "Bureau of the Budget, Corresp. 1932 May–June."

38. Among the economy measures advocated by the president was the transfer of federal fish hatcheries to the states. The Izaak Walton League passed a resolution

opposing this at its spring 1932 meeting. See Mr. and Mrs. Frank M. Warren to Walter Newton, 6 May 1932; Newton to the Warrens, 7 May 1932, HP:PC, Box 11, Folder "Commerce—Fisheries, Bureau of, Correspondence, 1929-1933."

39. For the administration's negotiations with the House Economy Committee, see the file in RLWS, Box 11, Folder "Economy Committee—Economic Conference, Joint House—Papers of Secy. Wilbur"; Hoover to Rep. John McDuffie, 12 Apr. 1932; McDuffie to Hoover, 12 Apr. 1932, HP:PS, Box 168, Folder "Governmental Departments, Reorganization of, 1932 Apr. 1-10." For the tabulation of what was actually in the Revenue Bill, see "Federal Expenditures Classified on a Functional Basis," [1 Jan. 1933], ibid., Box 87, Folder "Bureau of the Budget, Fed. Expenditures on a Functional Basis, 1933."

40. Ray Lyman Wilbur to Hoover, 26 Jan. 1932, HP:PC, Box 16, Folder "Interior—Corres., 1932 Jan."; Unsigned memorandum on personnel cuts, 15 Oct. 1932, RLW, Box 16, Folder "Interior Department, Budget FY 1934, 1932 July–Nov. & undated"; clipping from the Washington *Evening Star,* "Interior Officials Feel Budget Cut," 31 Oct. 1932, ibid.; *The Memoirs of Ray Lyman Wilbur, 1875-1949,* eds. Edgar Eugene Robinson and Paul Carroll Edwards (Stanford, Calif.: Stanford University Press, 1960), p. 557; Fausold, *Presidency of Herbert Hoover,* pp. 158-62. Wilbur fought energetically to get some of the cuts restored. See, for example, "Letter of the Secretary of the Interior, Ray Lyman Wilbur, to Senators from Public Land and Other States in which the Department of the Interior Functions, February 17, 1932," RLW, Box 2, Folder "Economy Program, 1932."

41. "Proposed Further Reductions in Interior Department Appropriation Estimates—1934," 18 Nov. 1932; "Department of the Interior Comparative Statement," 19 Nov. 1932, RLW, Box 16, Folder "Interior Department, Budget FY 1934, 1932 July–Nov. & undated." Apparently believing that Roosevelt would do what Hoover had not done, in December 1932, three months before the inauguration of the new administration, the Forest Service began developing plans to employ up to 250,000 men in the National Forests on various construction and conservation programs. See draft of circular letter to district foresters, 9 Dec. 1932, FS, Box 1656, Folder "U-Recreation-General-1932."

42. Special Message to the Congress on the Reorganization of the Executive Branch, 17 Feb. 1932, *Public Papers: 1932-33* (1977), pp. 56-61. Hoover attempted to create public interest in his proposals prior to delivering this message through statements at press conferences on 8 Jan. and 16 Feb. See ibid., pp. 11-12, 55-56. The message itself was the result of consultation among members of the administration. See, for example, Arthur M. Hyde to Hoover, 1 Feb. 1932, and Wilbur to Hoover, 11 Feb. 1932, HP:PS, Box 167, Folder "Govt. Depts., Reorg. of, 1932 Feb. 1-20."

43. See the Folder "Economy Committee—Economic Conference, Joint House—Papers of Secy. Wilbur," RLWS, Box 11.

44. For Hoover's public statements, news conferences, and speeches about the reorganization proposal, see *Public Papers, 1932-33,* pp. 74-75, 99, 100-101, 102-3,

132–35, 137, 140–41, 196–97, 263. For his statement on signing the bill, see ibid., p. 283. Quotations about "bombarding" Congress and his later comments on Congress's reception of the proposal come from Hoover, *Memoirs* 2:283. For the role of politics in the frustration of Hoover's plan, see James R. Garfield to Wilbur, 24 Feb. 1932, RLWS, Box 30, Folder "Reorganization, March 4, 1929 to Feb. 1, 1933." For the opposition of agencies to the proposal, see NPS Director Horace Albright's memorandum for Wilbur, 28 Nov. 1932, NPS, Box General 201.14–201.15, File "Re-Organization Dec. 17, 1921–Nov. 30, 1932, Pt. I." As Hoover commented bitterly in his *Memoirs*, the agencies played the game of "log-rolling" brilliantly. When it came right down to specifics, both Secretaries Hyde and Wilbur also opposed the transfer of agencies out of their jurisdiction. See the Minutes of Service Comm. on Policies & Procedures, 1931–35, 10 Mar. 1932, FS, Entry 8, Drawer 134.

45. Special Message to Congress on Reorganization of the Executive Branch, 9 Dec. 1932, *Public Papers, 1932–33*, pp. 882–91. For Hoover's continued concern with the issue throughout the autumn of 1932, see ibid., pp. 423, 424, 820, 846. Keeping the Park Service in Interior and the Forest Service in Agriculture disarmed some of the most militant opponents of reorganization. See Minutes of Service Comm. on Policies & Procedures, 1931–35, 15 Dec. 1932, FS, Entry 8, Drawer 134; Forester R. Y. Stuart to Evan W. Kelley, 15 Dec. 1932, Leon F. Kneipp oral history, vol. 2; Horace W. Albright to Lorne W. Barclay, 30 Dec. 1932, NPS, Box General 201.14–201.15, File "Reorganization 1932–1933."

46. Leon F. Kneipp oral history, "Land Planning and Acquisition, U.S. Forest Service," 107. For the opposition of Democrats to the reorganization proposals, see Rep. William Williamson (S.D.) to Hoover, 7 Jan. 1932[3], HP:PS, Box 168, Folder "Government Depts, Reorganization of, 1932 Nov.–1933 Jan."; Hoover's Press Conference of 3 Jan. 1933, *Public Papers, 1932–33*, pp. 918–21.

47. *Public Papers, 1932–33*, pp. 952–53, 982–83.

48. Hoover, *Memoirs* 2:284.

49. *Memoirs of Ray Lyman Wilbur*, pp. 552, 559.

50. Robert Cowley, "The Drought and the Dole: Herbert Hoover's Dismal Dilemma," *American Heritage* 23 (Feb. 1972): 16–19.

51. Nan Elizabeth Woodruff, *As Rare as Rain: Federal Relief in the Great Southern Drought of 1930–31* (Urbana: University of Illinois Press, 1985), pp. 6–7.

52. Ibid., pp. 8–13; C. Roger Lambert, "Food from the Public Crib: Agricultural Surpluses and Food Relief under Herbert Hoover," in *Herbert Hoover and the Republican Era: A Reconsideration*, eds. Carl E. Krog and William R. Tanner (Lanham, Md.: University Press of America, 1984), p. 163.

53. Lambert, "Food from the Public Crib," p. 166; Cowley, "Drought and the Dole," 92–93; David E. Hamilton, "Herbert Hoover and the Great Drought of 1930," *Journal of American History* 68 (Mar. 1982): 858, 862.

54. *Public Papers, 1930*, pp. 516, 557.

55. "The Row over Feeding Hungry Farmers," *Literary Digest* 108 (31 Jan. 1931): 8; Robinson quoted in Cowley, "The Drought and the Dole," 93.

56. Woodruff, *As Rare as Rain*, pp. 56–63; Cowley, "The Drought and the Dole," 94–95.

57. *The Memoirs of Herbert Hoover: The Great Depression, 1929–1941* (New York: Macmillan, 1952), pp. 55, 224 [hereafter *Memoirs* 3].

58. "Statement on Public vs. Private Financing of Relief Efforts," 3 Feb. 1931, *Public Papers, 1931*, pp. 54–58.

59. Lambert, "Food from the Public Crib," pp. 166–78.

60. Hoover, *Memoirs* 3:55. Hoover claimed the Red Cross fought this discrimination; historians have not agreed.

61. Johnson to Hiram Johnson Jr., 18 Feb. 1931, Hiram Johnson Papers, Bancroft Library, University of California at Berkeley, Pt. VI, Box 5, Folder "1931 Jan.–Feb."

62. Hamilton, "Herbert Hoover and the Great Drought," 858; Hoover, *Memoirs* 3:42.

63. Stone to Hoover, 5 Aug. 1930, HP:PS, Box 117, Folder "Drought—Correspondence 1930, August 1–5."

64. The first national program of scientific soil erosion research was authorized by Congress on 16 Feb. 1929. It was largely the result of work by Hugh Hammond Bennett of the Bureau of Soils in the Agriculture Department. See Donald C. Swain, *Federal Conservation Policy, 1921–1933* (Berkeley: University of California Press, 1963), pp. 152–59.

65. Ray Lyman Wilbur and Arthur Mastick Hyde, *The Hoover Policies* (New York: Scribner's, 1937), pp. 159–62; Wilbur and Du Puy, *Conservation*, p. 155; Ray Lyman Wilbur to Hoover, 3 Mar. 1933, RLW, Box 16, Folder "Interior Department, 1933–38 & undated."

66. Dept. of Interior press release, 4 Mar. 1930, HP:PS, Box 218, Folder "Oil Matters, Federal Oil Conservation Board, Corres., 1930 Jan.–Apr."; J. Edgar Hoover to Lawrence Richey, 14 Jan. 1930; J. F. Lucey to Richey, 7 Mar. 1930, both in ibid., Box 217, Folder "Oil Matters, Correspondence 1930 Jan.–Sept."

67. Gerald D. Nash, *United States Oil Policy, 1890–1964: Business and Government in Twentieth Century America* (Pittsburgh: University of Pittsburgh Press, 1968), pp. 106–107.

68. Wilbur to Curtis Wilbur, 17 Oct. 1930, RLW, Box 21, Folder "Oil—Oil Shale, 1930–47 & undated." Copies of the New York *World*'s series on the Kelley charges, which ran 6–18 Oct. 1930, are in HP:PS, Box 218, Folder "Oil Matters, Kelley Newspaper Stories, 1930 October." For the Justice Dept. investigation, see Attorney General William D. Mitchell to Wilbur, 24 Oct. 1930, RLW, Box 21, Folder "Oil—Oil Shale, 1930–47 & undated," and Interior Dept. "Memorandum for the press," 27 Feb. 1931, ibid., Folder "Oil—Oil Shale Report, 1931." An undated (but contemporary) memorandum by Northcutt Ely analyzes the charges in detail. See Ely Papers, Box 6, Folder 40, and also, Wilbur to Senator Gerald P. Nye, 27 Feb. 1931, ibid., Folder 43.

69. Avis Carlson, "Drowning in Oil," *Harper's* 163 (Oct. 1931): 608–10; Henry L. Doherty to Hoover, 21 Dec. 1930; Hoover to Doherty, 27 Dec. 1930, both in HP:PS, Box 217, Folder "Oil Matters, Correspondence, 1930 Oct.–Dec." Northcutt Ely wrote to Doherty to express his belief that production could be controlled through state laws coordinated by "a cooperative board." See Ely to Doherty, 24 Nov. 1930, Ely Papers, Box 1, Folder 6. For Franklin's comment, see his press release, 15 Jan. 1931, RLWS, Box 27, Folder "Oil, May 6, 1931 to ." The IPA represented smaller, independent producers. The major companies often had foreign concessions and were understandably less enthusiastic about an oil tariff.

70. Wilbur's address before the Governors' Conference on Oil, Mayflower Hotel, Washington, 16 Jan. 1931, HP:PS, Box 218, Folder "Oil Matters, Federal Oil Conservation Board Corres., 1931"; E. S. Rochester (FOCB secretary) to Wilbur, 28 Jan. 1931, RLW, Box 20, Folder "Oil, Fed. Oil Con. Board, 1929–36 & undated"; E. S. Rochester to Wilbur, 7 Feb. 1931, RLWS, Box 27, Folder "Oil Conservation: Misc. Material, 1929–1931"; Govs. Ross Sterling (Tex.), Wm. H. Murray (Okla.), Harry Woodring (Kans.), Arthur Seligman (N.M.) to Hoover, 1 Mar. 1931; Ross Sterling to Hoover, 5 Mar. 1931, all in HP:PS, Box 217, Folder "Oil Matters, Correspondence, 1931 March–May."

71. Hoover to R. S. Sterling, 10 Mar. 1931; Lawrence Richey's memorandum of a telephone conversation with Secretary Lamont, 5 Mar. 1931; Richey's memorandum of a telephone conversation with Secretary Wilbur, 13 Mar. 1931; Wilbur to Hoover, 30 Mar. 1931, all in HP:PS, Box 217, Folder "Oil Matters, Correspondence, 1931 Mar.–May."

72. Wilbur to Hoover, 30 Apr. 1931, RLWS, Box 53, Folder "Oil Matters, 1929–1931–1932–1933, A–D."

73. E. B. Reeser to Secretary of War Patrick J. Hurley, 2 Apr. 1931, HP:PS, Box 217, Folder "Oil Matters, Correspondence 1931 Mar.–May"; Interior Dept. press release, 10 Apr. 1931, ibid., Box 218, Folder "Oil Matters, Federal Oil Conservation Bd., Corres., 1931"; E. S. Rochester to Wilbur, 21 Apr. 1931, RLWS, Box 13, Folder "Oil—Federal Oil Conservation Board, Jan. 2, 1931 to July 9, 1931"; E. S. Rochester to Wilbur, 18 May 1931, Ely Papers, Box 1, Folder 2; clipping from Tulsa *Daily World*, 24 May 1931, enclosed in Roy M. Johnson to Wilbur, 24 May 1931, RLWS, Box 27, Folder "Oil, May 6, 1931 to "; clipping from Baltimore *Sun*, 16 Aug. 1931, ibid.; Interior Dept. press release, 7 Aug. 1931, HP:PS, Box 217, Folder "Oil Matters, Correspondence 1931 June–Aug."; Nash, *United States Oil Policy*, pp. 117–20.

74. Nash, *United States Oil Policy*, pp. 125–27.

75. "Report of Volunteer Committee on Petroleum Economics," 24 Aug. and 9 Nov. 1931, HP:PS, Box 218, Folder "Oil Matters, Federal Oil Conservation Board Correspondence, 1931"; Walter Newton to Mark Requa, 3 Sept. 1931, ibid., Box 217, Folder "Oil Matters, Correspondence 1931, Sept.–Dec."; Northcutt Ely to Wilbur, 26 Oct. 1931 (2 memos), and E. S. Rochester to Wilbur, 5 Nov. 1931, all in RLWS, Box

13, Folder "Oil—Federal Oil Conservation Board, July 10, 1931 to ." One producer estimated that American production had quadrupled during the 1920s, while imports had tripled. See H. Walker to Wilbur, 9 Feb. 1932, Ely Papers, Box 1, Folder 4.

76. Requa to Walter Newton, 31 Dec. 1931, HP:PS, Box 217, Folder "Oil Matters, Correspondence, 1931 Sept.–Dec."

77. Wilbur and Du Puy, *Conservation,* p. 95. The order of the phrases has been reversed.

78. Interior Dept. press releases, 5 Feb. and 4 Apr. 1932, HP:PS, Box 219, Folder "Oil Matters—Stm. & Press Releases, 1932"; Hoover to Wilbur, enclosing draft of proposed interstate compact bill, 26 Jan. 1932, HP:PC, Box 16, Folder "Interior— Corres., 1932 Jan."; C. B. Ames to Northcutt Ely, 9 Feb. and 9 Mar. 1932, Ely to Ames, 11 Feb. 1932, Ely Papers, Box 3, Folder 20. Hoover's political supporters in the West rejoiced at the decision to reopen public lands to oil exploration. See Perry W. Jenkins to Wilbur, 12 May 1932, RLWS, Box 27, Folder "Oil, May 6, 1931 to ."

79. "Conservation and the Diminishing Reserves of Oil and Gas," p. 41, Appendix V of the "Report of the Federal Oil Conservation Board to the President of the United States, October, 1932," IGF, Box 424, File 1-242, "Oil Situation: Federal Oil Conservation Board."

80. Wilbur to Hoover, 16 Nov. 1932, enclosing resolution adopted by the board of directors of the American Petroleum Institute, HP:PS, Box 218, Folder "Oil Matters, Federal Oil Conservation Board, Corres., 1932–33"; Amos L. Beaty to Wilbur, 8 Dec. 1932; Charles W. Ames to Wilbur, both in RLW, Box 20, Folder "Oil, Fed. Oil Con. Board, 1929–36 & undated." Proposals for an interstate compact to govern oil production continued to come up during the 1930s. See Francis C. Wilson to Hoover, 20 Feb. 1935, HP:PPI, Box 560, Folder "Wilson, Francis, Correspondence, 1935–1953"; Northcutt Ely to Wilbur, 31 Oct. 1938, RLWS, Box 22, Folder "Ely, Northcutt #1"; Nash, *United States Oil Policy,* p. 127. Hoover's *Memoirs* take credit for the Kettleman Hills unit production plan and for the administration's efforts to promote interstate compacts to control production but fail to mention the crisis of 1931–32. See Hoover, *Memoirs* 2:238–39; Wilbur's *Memoirs,* pp. 423–26, say even less on the subject.

81. O'Malley to Hoover, 8 Jan. 1932; E. F. Morgan to Hoover, 27 May 1932, both in HP:PC, Box 11, Folder "Commerce—Fisheries, Bureau of, Correspondence, 1929– 33"; Theodore G. Joslin to Lawrence Richey, ? Nov. 1932, HP:PSec, Box 162, Folder "Fish 1932–1933."

82. James M. Dixon to Hoover, 13 July 1929; Ray Lyman Wilbur to Hoover, 19 Nov. 1929, 28 May 1930, 22 Nov. 1930; R. W. Dunlap to Hoover, 26 Mar. 1930; Arthur M. Hyde to Hoover, 16 July 1930, all in HP:PS, Box 164, Folder "Game Protection, 1929–30"; R. W. Dunlap to Rep. Sam D. McReynolds, ca. 30 Jan. 1930, RLW, Box 1, Folder "Agriculture 1930"; "Statement of Policy for the Conduct of Work under the Migratory Bird Conservation Act," 20 May 1930, IGF, Box 435, File 1-256 (Pt. 1), "Migratory Bird Conservation Commission"; "Migratory Bird Conservation

Commission, Review of Work for the Fiscal Year 1930; "Memorandum Number Three for the Migratory Bird Conservation Commission [meeting of] December 3, 1931," ibid., File 1-256 (Pt. 2), "Migratory Bird Conservation Commission"; "Report of Migratory Bird Conservation Commission, Fiscal Year 1932," "Memorandum Number Three for the Migratory Bird Conservation Commission [meeting on] December 6, 1932," "Memorandum for the Migratory Bird Conservation Commission, May 23, 1933," all in ibid., File 1-256 (Part 3), "Migratory Bird Conservation Commission." The "Report of the Migratory Bird Conservation Commission for the Fiscal Year 1933," in ibid., indicates that the ten-year program planned by the 1929 act had originally contemplated expenditures of almost $8 million to study and acquire migratory bird refuges, but that of that sum, less than $1 million ($993,000) was actually appropriated.

83. National Forest Reservation Commission, "Annual Report for Year Ended June 30, 1931," and "Review of the Work of the National Forest Reservation Commission, 1911–1933," IGF, Box 277, File 1-132 (Pt. 1), "National Forest Reservation Committee."

84. For budget figures, see Hoover's budget messages of 4 Dec. 1929 and 7 Dec. 1932, *Public Papers, 1929,* p. 438, and *1932–33* (1977), p. 856. See the large number of executive orders withdrawing lands for various purposes in HP:PC, Boxes 19–20. The last of these withdrawals, 630,000 acres in Arizona and Nevada to establish the Boulder Canyon Wildlife Refuge, was signed on 3 Mar. 1933. For the Forest Service's wilderness policy, see "Record of Primitive Areas Established by Forest Service," 22 Oct. 1932, HP:PC, Box 5, Folder "Agriculture—Forest Service, Forest Management, 1931–Aug. 1933." Frederick Law Olmsted played a key role in stimulating the Forest Service to begin a program intended to "protect the virgin areas within the National Forests which permanently should be reserved in the interests of science and education, or as museum examples of the forest conditions which existed during the earlier stages of our national development," R. Y. Stuart to Olmsted, 12 Jan. 1929, FS, Entry 75, Box 1, "Div. of Land Acquisition: Corres., 1929–30." At this point, however, the service did not intend to bar all development in primitive areas. As Forester R. Y. Stuart explained, the areas would have "primitive conditions of transportation, subsistence, habitation, and environment," but "it is not contemplated that there shall be a complete withdrawal of timber, forage, or water resources from utilization but that the principle of highest use of the land will prevail." R. Y. Stuart to W. C. McCormick, 7 May 1932, FS, Entry 86, Box 1656, "Div. of Rec. & Land Use: U-Recreation-General-1932."

85. Burner, "Before the Crash," in *The Hoover Presidency,* p. 62.

86. In addition to the beginnings of wilderness preservation in the Forest Service in this period, the National Park Service also pioneered a dramatic change by moving away from predator control programs. See Thomas R. Dunlap, "Wildlife, Science, and the National Parks, 1920–1940," *Pacific Historical Review* 59 (May 1990): 187–202.

87. Craig Lloyd, *Aggressive Introvert: A Study of Herbert Hoover and Public Relations Management, 1912-1932* (Columbus: Ohio State University Press, 1972), p. 162.

88. Byron Price oral history, Hoover Institution on War, Revolution and Peace, Stanford University.

89. Lloyd, *Aggressive Introvert*, p. 161.

90. "Hoover: Conservative," *New Republic* 56 (31 Oct. 1928): 287-89. The order of phrases has been changed.

10. The Conservative and Conservation

1. David M. Wrobel, *The End of American Exceptionalism: Frontier Anxiety from the Old West to the New Deal* (Lawrence: University Press of Kansas, 1993), pp. 136-37. The quotations come from Hoover's October 1932 speech in Madison Square Garden and from his book, *The Challenge to Liberty* (New York: Scribner's, 1934).

2. Terry L. Anderson and Donald R. Leal, *Free Market Environmentalism* (San Francisco: Pacific Research Institute for Public Policy, 1991), p. 2.

3. David Burner, *Herbert Hoover: A Public Life* (New York: Knopf, 1979), p. 256. Burner points out that the reporter's comment about Joslin was borrowed from Winston Churchill. See also George E. Akerson Jr. oral history, Hoover Institution on War, Revolution and Peace at Stanford University [hereafter Hoover Institution].

4. See Craig Lloyd, *Aggressive Introvert: A Study of Herbert Hoover and Public Relations Management, 1912-1932* (Columbus: Ohio State University Press, 1972), for an analysis of the way in which Hoover's passion for revealing only results and not processes became a political asset in the early 1920s. And see Cecelia Tichi, *Shifting Gears: Technology, Literature, Culture in Modernist America* (Chapel Hill: University of North Carolina Press, 1987), pp. 169-70, for a discussion of how the popularization of engineering in early-twentieth-century fiction and movies served to create a ready-made heroic image upon which Hoover's supporters drew.

5. Quoted in Louis W. Liebovich, *Bylines in Despair: Herbert Hoover, the Great Depression, and the U.S. News Media* (Westport, Conn.: Praeger, 1994), p. 146.

6. Lloyd, *Aggressive Introvert*, p. 168.

7. Louis Liebovich contends, after a careful analysis of news coverage of the Bonus March, that Hoover's actions in breaking up the march did not alienate public opinion, as most historians of the period have argued. See Liebovich, *Bylines in Despair*, pp. 155-82. For arguments that the president's hostile response to the bonus marchers was a major cause of his defeat in 1932, see David Burner, *Herbert Hoover*, p. 312; Martin L. Fausold, *The Presidency of Herbert Hoover* (Lawrence: University Press of Kansas, 1985), p. 203.

8. *The Memoirs of Herbert Hoover: The Great Depression, 1929-1941* (New York: Macmillan, 1952), pp. 219, 233 [hereafter Hoover, *Memoirs* 3].

9. *Public Papers of the Presidents of the United States: Herbert Hoover; containing the*

Public Messages, Speeches, and Statements of the President, January 1, 1932 to March 4, 1933 (Washington, D.C.: GPO, 1977), pp. 368, 370, 363, 365 [hereafter cited as *Public Papers*, with year].

10. In a speech at Madison Square Garden in New York City, 31 Oct. 1932, *Public Papers, 1932*, pp. 669–71.

11. Ibid., p. 675.

12. At Detroit, 22 Oct. 1932, and more briefly, at Madison Square Garden in New York, 31, Oct. 1932, *Public Papers, 1932*, pp. 588, 671. For the letter, see "National Affairs: By Name," *Time* (31 Oct. 1932): 10.

13. *Public Papers, 1932*, p. 589.

14. "National Affairs: Hyde and Seedlings," *Time* (18 July 1932): 11. Hyde did not explain how a million men had shrunk to 27,900.

15. Ibid., 11–12.

16. Charles Lathrop Pack to Walter Newton, 20 July 1932, HP:PS, Box 164, Folder "Forest, Fires, Reforestation, 1932."

17. Rep. Harold Knutson to Walter Newton, 29 Aug. 1932, HP:PS, Box 164, Folder "Forest, Fires, Reforestation, 1932."

18. This seems to have been one lesson Hoover learned. Before the 1948 and 1952 elections he urged Republican leaders to stress that conservation had been a Republican issue from the beginning.

19. Hyde to Knutson, 12 Sept. 1932, ibid.; Leon F. Kneipp to [?] Meador, 26 Oct. 1932, ibid.

20. Pack to Hoover, 17 Sept. 1932, and Hoover to Pack, 20 Sept. 1932, ibid.

21. Clipping from the *Forestry News Digest*, Oct. 1932; Pack to Walter H. Newton, 8 Oct. 1932, enclosing undated editorial from the *Florida Times Union* (Jacksonville); Newton to Hyde, 27 Oct. 1932, all in ibid.

22. Hoover to Joslin, 3 July 1933, HP:PPI, Box 103, Folder "Joslin, Theodore Correspondence Mar.–Sept. 1933"; Hoover, *The Challenge to Liberty*, p. 107.

23. Ray Lyman Wilbur and Arthur Mastick Hyde, *The Hoover Policies* (New York: Scribner's, 1937), pp. 270–73; Hoover, *Memoirs* 2:122–23; William R. Willoughby, *The St. Lawrence Waterway: A Study in Politics and Diplomacy* (Madison: University of Wisconsin Press, 1961), pp. 93–111.

24. Hoover to Roosevelt, 10 July 1932 (with note giving the text of Roosevelt's telegram of 9 July), *Public Papers, 1932–33*, pp. 301–3; Willoughby, *The St. Lawrence Waterway*, pp. 137–44.

25. Hoover, *Memoirs* 2:235. A good, brief account of the treaty fight is Richard N. Kottman, "Herbert Hoover and the St. Lawrence Seaway Treaty of 1932," *New York History* 56 (July 1975): 314–46.

26. Although as president Hoover had opposed negotiating power distribution arrangements with the New York Power Authority, in September 1957 he accepted an invitation from the chairman of the authority, Robert Moses, to be the authority's guest for a two-day tour of the nearly completed project. See Robert Moses to

Hoover, 16 Aug. 1957, and Hoover to Moses, 21 Aug. and 4 Sept. 1957, HP:PPS, Box 285, Folder "St. Lawrence Seaway Correspondence 1957-64 & undated."

27. Hoover attributed the defeat to the unwillingness of the Democrats to admit that the seaway project had been originated by Republicans, and to the Democrats' commitment to public power. See Hoover to Charles P. Craig, 31 Jan. and 30 Apr. 1934, HP:PPS, Box 285, "St. Lawrence Seaway Correspondence, 1933-49." A map provided by the Great Lakes–St. Lawrence Tidewater Association suggests that regional interests may have been at least as important. Of the twenty-two senators from the New England and Middle Atlantic states, only two voted for the treaty. The map was enclosed in Charles P. Craig to Hoover, 26 Apr. 1934, in ibid.

28. The comment about the NRA's policies was included in a reply to a press inquiry, 15 May 1935, in Hoover, *Addresses Upon the American Road, 1933-1938* (New York: Scribner's, 1938), p. 46; a copy of Ickes's memorandum, dated 2 Oct. 1933, with a pencilled note indicating that a copy was sent to Ogden Mills, is in HP:PPI, Box 98, Folder "Ickes, Harold L. Correspondence 1933-1936"; the "public defamation" phrase comes from a draft of a reply in Hoover's handwriting on the margins of a letter from Rep. Jack Z. Anderson, 7 Mar. 1947, HP:PPS, Box 182, Folder "Hoover Dam Correspondence 1936-60." Horace Albright believed that the idea of renaming the dam came not from Ickes but from Hiram Johnson. See copy of Albright to Paul Edwards, 6 Feb. 1959, enclosed in Albright to Hoover, 5 Mar. 1959, and Hoover to Albright, 9 Mar. 1959, ibid. For other perspectives on Hoover's political posture in this period, see Gary Dean Best, "Herbert Hoover as Titular Leader of the GOP, 1933-35," *Mid-America* 61 (Apr.–July 1979): 81-97; Brant Short, "The Rhetoric of the Post-Presidency: Herbert Hoover's Campaign Against the New Deal, 1934–1936," *Presidential Studies Quarterly* 21 (Spring 1991): 333-50.

29. A speech to the Young Republican League, Colorado Springs, 7 Mar. 1936, in Hoover, *Addresses . . . , 1933-38*, p. 133. See also his speech at Fort Wayne, Indiana, 4 Apr. 1936, in ibid., p. 164. For letters from friends on conservation issues that seem not to have drawn any response, see Ward Bannister to Hoover, 22 Oct. 1937, HP:PPI, Box 10, Folder "Bannister, L. Ward Correspondence July 1936-1938"; Rep. Frank O. Horton to Hoover, 26 Feb. 1940, ibid., Box 92, Folder "Horton, Frank O. Correspondence 1937-1940." For Hoover's unenthusiastic responses to various private initiatives, see John J. Sabo (State Island Conservation Association) to Hoover, 8 Apr. 1935, and Hoover to Sabo, 19 Apr. 1935, HP:PPS, Box 128, Folder "Conservation 1933-64"; Newton B. Drury (Save the Redwoods League) to Hoover, 1 July 1937, and Hoover to Drury, 6 July 1937, HP:PPI, Box 50, Folder "Drury, Newton B. Correspondence 1937-1946"; Hoover to Kenneth A. Reid (Izaak Walton League), 8 July 1939, HP:PPS, Box 202, Folder "Izaak Walton League of America 1933-55."

30. Horace Albright to Lawrence Richey, 12 Sept. 1939, HP:PPI, Box 3, Folder "Albright, Horace M. Correspondence 1934-1951"; Hoover to Christian A. Herter, 31 May 1944, and Herter to Hoover, 3 June 1944, ibid., Box 85, Folder "Herter, Christian A. Correspondence 1944-1948"; Donald C. Swain, *Wilderness Defender:*

Horace M. Albright and Conservation (Chicago: University of Chicago Press, 1970), p. 184; David J. Saylor, *Jackson Hole, Wyoming: In the Shadow of the Tetons* (Norman: University of Oklahoma Press, 1970), pp. 199–200; Joseph W. Ernst, *Worthwhile Places: Correspondence of John D. Rockefeller, Jr., and Horace M. Albright* (New York: Fordham University Press, 1991), pp. 202–10.

31. Albright to Hoover, 25 Sept. 1946, 12 Mar. 1947 (with marginal note in Hoover's handwriting promising to "see what I can do when I go to Washington again next week"), 21 Mar. 1947, 15 and 29 Apr. 1947, HP:PPI, Box 3, Folder "Albright, Horace M. Correspondence 1934–1951"; Ernst, *Worthwhile Places,* pp. 210–11; Saylor, *Jackson Hole,* pp. 203–4.

32. Hoover to Roy W. Howard, 26 Aug. 1948, HP:PPI, Box 93, Folder "Howard, Roy, Correspondence 1945–51"; Hoover to Harrison E. Spangler, 17 Nov. 1951, ibid., Box 219, Folder "Spangler, Harrison E., Correspondence 1945–1948"; Herbert Hoover, *Addresses Upon the American Road, 1950–1955* (Stanford, Calif.: Stanford University Press, 1955), pp. 131–32.

33. Eisenhower's main difference with Hoover was over foreign policy, but it did not help that Hoover supported Robert Taft and the conservative wing of the party during the preconvention period. See Eisenhower's Diary, 5 Mar. 1951, Eisenhower to Arthur B. Eisenhower, 11 Sept. 1951, in *The Papers of Dwight David Eisenhower,* vol. 12, *NATO and the Campaign of 1952,* ed. Louis Galambos (Baltimore: Johns Hopkins University Press, 1988), pp. 91, 536; Eisenhower to Hoover, 29 July 1952, and Eisenhower to Clifford Roberts, 13 Aug. 1952, in ibid. 13:1287, 1320–21. For a helpful exploration of the Hoover-Eisenhower relationship, see Michael Birkner, "Hoover and Ike: An Uneasy Collaboration," an unpublished address delivered to the Herbert Hoover Presidential Library Association on 7 June 1998, and provided to me through the courtesy of the association.

34. Elmo Richardson, *Dams, Parks & Politics: Resource Development & Preservation in the Truman-Eisenhower Era* (Lexington: University Press of Kentucky, 1973), pp. 82–83; Swain, *Wilderness Defender,* p. 302.

35. Hoover to Brownell, 9 Apr. 1953, HP:PPI, Box 25, Folder "Brownell, Herbert Correspondence re Colorado River Litigation, 1953."

36. Miller to Hoover, 20 Apr. 1953, HP:PPI, Box 150, Folder "Miller, Hon. Leslie A. Correspondence 1948–1963."

37. "A Temporary Water Development and Power Policy," furnished by Hoover and Admiral Ben Moreell (task force chairman) to Director of the Budget Joseph M. Dodge, 24 Nov. 1953; Hoover to Dodge, 4 Apr. 1954; Moreell to Hoover, 19 Apr. 1954; Hoover to Eisenhower, 22 Apr. 1954; Hoover's memorandum of a conversation with Eisenhower and Sherman Adams, 3 May 1954; Hoover to Moreell, 4 May 1954; Hoover memoranda, 13 and 14 May 1954; White House press release, 26 May 1954; Hoover memoranda, 28 May and 17, 18, 19 June 1954, all in CRC, Box 5, Folder "Glen Canyon Project 1954." Hoover reiterated his concerns in a meeting with Eisenhower on 18 June 1954. See Eisenhower's Personal and Confidential Memorandum for

Sherman Adams, 18 June 1954, in *The Papers of Dwight David Eisenhower*, vol. 15, *The Presidency; The Middle Way*, eds. Louis Galambos and Daun Van Ee (Baltimore: Johns Hopkins University Press, 1996), p. 1137.

38. Hoover's memorandum, 20 June 1954, CRC, Box 5, Folder "Glen Canyon Project 1954"; Owen Stratton and Phillip Sirotkin, *The Echo Park Controversy: A Case Study in Resources Administration Supported by a Grant from Resources for the Future, Inc.* (University: University of Alabama Press, [1959]), pp. vii–viii.

39. J. N. "Ding" Darling to Hoover, 2 June 1954, and Hoover to Darling, 6 June 1954, HP:PPI, Box 44, Folder "Darling, Jay N. Correspondence 1941-1962."

40. Mark W. T. Harvey, *A Symbol of Wilderness: Echo Park and the American Conservation Movement* (Albuquerque: University of New Mexico Press, 1994), pp. 270–85. For the impact of the ninety-six dams and other facilities that now control the flow of the Colorado, see Peter Friederici, "Stolen River," *Defenders: The Conservation Magazine of Defenders of Wildlife* 73 (Spring 1998): 10–18, 31–33.

41. Hoover of course had always favored the Glen Canyon dam; few of the conservationists realized until too late that its construction would drown a canyon comparable to the Grand Canyon. See Eliot Porter, *The Place No One Knew: Glen Canyon on the Colorado* (San Francisco: Sierra Club, 1963).

42. Robert Emmerich, *Essays on Federal Reorganization* (University: University of Alabama Press, 1950), p. 91; Emmerich, *Federal Organization and Administrative Management* (University: University of Alabama Press, 1971), p. 101.

43. Emmerich, *Essays*, p. 97; Neil Macneil and Harold W. Metz, *The Hoover Report, 1953-1955: What It Means to You as Citizen and Taxpayer* (New York: Macmillan, 1956), pp. 23–24. The resolution quoted is on p. 24.

44. The commission was created by the Republican-controlled 80th Congress to "prepare for the Republican housecleaning that it anticipated would follow the 1948 election," but when Truman won, the commission's role changed. See William E. Pemberton, "Struggle for the New Deal: Truman and the Hoover Commission," *Presidential Studies Quarterly* 16 (Summer 1986): 511–27; *The Hoover Commission Report on Organization of the Executive Branch of the Government* (New York: McGraw-Hill, [1949]), pp. 3–8; Gary Dean Best, *Herbert Hoover: The Postpresidential Years, 1933-1964* (Stanford, Calif.: Hoover Institution Press, 1983), 2:327-30 [hereafter Best, *Hoover* 2].

45. Emmerich, *Federal Organization*, p. 101; Hoover's 1 Aug. 1953 speech to the members of the Bohemian Club is quoted in Best, *Hoover* 2:373.

46. *Hoover Commission Report*, pp. 242, 251–53, 256. A recommendation to move the Bureau of Land Management from Interior to Agriculture was also considered during Hoover II, but ran into congressional opposition and was dropped before the commission's final report. See Eisenhower to Milton Stover Eisenhower, 8 Oct. 1954, *Eisenhower Papers* 15:1339-40.

47. *Hoover Commission Report*, pp. 249, 268, 271, 274–90. This section on water development and conservation is one of the longest in the report.

48. Ibid., pp. 273, 292–94, 315. The Bureau of Fisheries, located in Commerce during Hoover's tenure, was consolidated with the Biological Survey of the Agriculture Department in 1940 and the combined agency was transferred to the Department of the Interior as the Fish and Wildlife Service.

49. Ibid., pp. 295, 254.

50. For the members of the task forces for Agriculture and for Natural Resources and Public Works within the Interior Department, see ibid., pp. 513–16.

51. U.S. Senate, "Reorganization of the Federal Government: Status of Hoover Commission Reports, with List of Public Laws Enacted, Reorganization Plans Approved or Disapproved, and Bills Presently Pending to Effectuate Remaining Commission Recommendations," Sen. Doc. 91, 82d Cong., 2d sess. (Washington, D.C.: GPO, 1952), pp. 1–2; Peri E. Arnold, *Making the Managerial Presidency: Comprehensive Reorganization Planning, 1905–1980* (Princeton, N.J.: Princeton University Press, 1986), pp. 153–58. Hoover proposed making reorganization a Republican campaign issue in 1948, but his advice was ignored. See Hoover to Roy W. Howard, 26 Aug. 1948, HP:PPI, Box 93, Folder "Howard, Roy Correspondence 1945–1951," and Hoover to Harrison E. Spangler, 17 Nov. 1948, HP:PPI, Box 219, Folder "Spangler, Harrison E. Correspondence 1948–1959."

52. Senate Doc. 91, p. 14. Hoover felt that Truman was reluctant to commit himself to the implementation of a specific program developed by a Republican. See Best, *Hoover* 2:330.

53. Best, *Hoover* 2:371–73; Hoover's Notes on Projects for Navigation, Flood Control, Irrigation and Electric Power submitted in a memorandum to Lewis Strauss at the request of President Eisenhower, 9 June 1953, HP:PPI, Box 53, Folder "Eisenhower, Dwight D. Correspondence, 1953."

54. Best, *Hoover* 2:374–75.

55. Eisenhower to Hoover, 6 Aug. 1954, HP:PPI, Box 53, Folder "Eisenhower, Dwight D. Correspondence, 1954."

56. Arnold, *Making the Managerial Presidency*, pp. 168–69.

57. Hoover's 9 June 1953 memorandum for Strauss, HP:PPI, Box 53, Folder "Eisenhower, Dwight D. Correspondence, 1953."

58. Emmerich, *Federal Organization*, pp. 103, 109.

59. Holifield's broadest attack on the commission was buried in a misleadingly titled pamphlet, Commission on Organization of the Executive Branch of the Government, *Final Report to Congress* (Washington, D.C.: Government Printing Office, 1955), pp. 26–31. In fact, this booklet contains not the final report but little more than a table of contents of the report; Holifield's dissent is the longest item in it.

60. Emmerich, *Federal Organization*, pp. 108–09. For the task force's conclusions, see Commission on Organization of the Executive Branch of the Government, *Task Force Report on Water Resources and Power*, vol. 1 (Washington, D.C.: Government Printing Office, 1955), pp. 51–52. In a 1954 speech Hoover claimed disingenuously that his ideas did not "dominate" the task force on water and power resources, and

that he had chosen "no one connected with private utilities" for its membership, although he had included "one or two who are connected with public power." That was nonsense. See Hoover, *Addresses Upon the American Road, 1950-1955* (Stanford, Calif.: Stanford University Press, 1955), p. 176.

61. Eisenhower declared in his diary on 24 July 1953 that he found Hoover's proposed appointees to the commission "a trifle on the moth-eaten side" and wrote that he named three appointees who he hoped would be "reasonably liberal or what I call middle-of-the-road in their approach to today's problems." See *Eisenhower Papers* 14:418-19.

62. Arnold, *Making the Managerial Presidency*, pp. 170-71.

63. Ibid., pp. 184-85.

64. Citizens Committee for the Hoover Report, *Digests and Analyses of the Nineteen Hoover Commission Reports* (New York: Citizens Comm. for the Hoover Report, 1955), pp. 219-32. For the administration's outlook, see Eisenhower to Joseph Morrell Dodge, 17 Dec. 1953, *Eisenhower Papers* 15:766-67.

65. The task force's report stated flatly that the national interest did not "justify the preemption of the activities involved in the development of water resources and power" by the federal government unless such preemption was "essential to provide for the national defense, to preserve the national domain or to regulate interstate and foreign commerce." See *Task Force Report on Water Resources and Power*, vol. 1 (Washington, D.C.: Government Printing Office, 1955), p. 51 (order of phrases reversed). The task force also recommended that TVA be stripped of all of its navigation, flood control, fertilizer research and development, and forest development activities, and that all power generation for the Atomic Energy Commission be transferred to the AEC; such changes would have turned TVA from a regional development program into a single-purpose power company. Ibid., 96.

66. Arnold, *Making the Managerial Presidency*, pp. 192-95. Hoover also lobbied personally for the report, stressing (somewhat misleadingly) its congruence with administration policy. See, for example, Hoover to Rep. Charles Halleck, 29 June 1955, HP:PPI, Box 75, Folder "Halleck, Charles A. Correspondence, 1938-1964." As well as organizing these pressures, Hoover also arranged to have Neil MacNeil, the commission's chief editor, and Harold Metz, chief of its research staff, write a popular, nontechnical summary of the report, MacNeil and Metz, *The Hoover Report, 1953-1955*.

67. Arnold, *Making the Managerial Presidency*, p. 202.

68. Citizens Committee, *Digests*, pp. 219-20.

69. Quoted in Emmerich, *Federal Organization*, p. 115. In an earlier book, *Essays on Federal Reorganization*, Emmerich had already pointed out that Hoover I (like Hoover II) failed to address the problem of how to achieve comprehensive national planning for conservation and other national interests (p. 130).

70. See, for example, Terry L. Anderson and Peter J. Hill, eds., *Environmental Federalism* (Lanham, Md.: Rowman & Littlefield, 1997); Terry L. Anderson and Donald

R. Leal, *Enviro-Capitalists: Doing Good While Doing Well* (Lanham, Md.: Rowman & Littlefield, 1997); Anderson and Leal, *Free Market Environmentalism;* William J. Baumol and Wallace E. Oates, *The Theory of Environmental Policy: Externalities, Public Outlays, and the Quality of Life* (Englewood Cliffs, N.J.: Prentice-Hall, 1975); Walter E. Block, ed., *Economics and the Environment: A Reconciliation* (Vancouver, B.C.: The Fraser Institute, 1990); Daniel W. Bromley, *Environment and the Economy: Property Rights and Public Policy* (Cambridge, Mass.: Blackwell, 1991); James R. Dunn and John E. Kinney, *Conservative Environmentalism: Reassessing the Means, Redefining the Ends* (Westport, Conn.: Quorum, 1996); Julian Simon, *The Ultimate Resource* (Princeton, N.J.: Princeton University Press, 1981). A brief, early analysis of basic economic issues expressed in nontechnical language is Scott Gordon, "Economics and the Conservation Question," *Journal of Law and Economics* 1:1 (Oct. 1958): 110–21. For vigorous critiques of conservative environmentalism, written from a number of perspectives, see volume 15 (Spring 1992) of the *Harvard Journal of Law and Public Policy.*

71. Samuel P. Hays, *Beauty, Health and Permanence: Environmental Politics in the United States, 1955–1985* (New York: Cambridge University Press, 1987). See, e.g., pp. 529–41.

Bibliography

Unpublished Sources

Herbert Hoover Presidential Library, West Branch, Iowa
  Herbert Hoover Papers
  Ralph Arnold Papers
  Burt Brown Barker Papers
  Delph Carpenter Papers
  Colorado River Commission Records
  Records of the Commission on the Conservation and Administration of the Public
      Domain (Garfield Commission or Committee)
  Hugh Gibson Papers
  James H. MacLafferty Papers
  William C. Mullendore Papers
  Gerald P. Nye Collection
  Mark Sullivan Accession 498
  Ray Lyman Wilbur Papers
  Theodore Hoover Memoranda
  Oral histories: Horace Albright, Loren Chandler, Charles A. and Hulda Hoover
      McLean, Marvin M. Meyers, Hugh A. Moran, Felix Morley, Levi T. Pen-
      nington, Rudolph N. Schullinger, Mary Minthorn Strench, Robert W. Wall
      Jr., and Dwight L. Wilber
Hoover Institution on War, Revolution and Peace at Stanford University
  George Barr Baker Papers
  Hugh Gibson Papers
  Herbert Hoover Papers
  Ray M. Hudson Papers
  William H. Irwin Papers
  Julius Klein Papers
  Hulda H. McLean Papers
  Ray Lyman Wilbur Papers
  Mark Sullivan Diary and Papers
  Hubert Work Papers
  Oral histories: George E. Akerson Jr., Calvin Albury, Mrs. Ben S. Allen, Burt
      Brown Barker, Philippi Harding Butler, Mildred Hall Campbell, Harry H.
      Hicks, Marguerite Rickard Hoyt, Captain Harry Jepson, Paul R. Leach, Mr.

and Mrs. VanNess H. Leavitt, Russel V. Lee, Gould Lincoln, Eugene Lyons, Jeremiah Milbank, John Pearce Mitchell, William C. Mullendore, Sydney Sullivan Parker, Michael J. Petti, Byron Price, Bruce H. Quinion, Mr. and Mrs. Lawrence Requa, Arthur Ringland, Dr. Edgar E. Robinson, James H. Rowe, Admiral Lewis L. Strauss, Mark Sullivan Jr., Hanford Thayer, Scott Turner, Mrs. Leon Thompson, and Ray L. Wilbur Jr.

National Archives, Washington, D.C.

Agriculture Department Records: Office of the Secretary, General Correspondence, 1906-70 (RG 16); Office of the Secretary, Letters Sent, 1893-1929 (RG 16); Office of the Secretary, Press Copies of Personal Letters Sent, 1921-25 (RG 16); Office of the Secretary, Letters Sent, Forest Service, 1906-29 (RG 16); Forest Service Records (RG 95)

Commerce Department Records: Office of the Secretary, General Records (RG 40); Bureau of Fisheries Central File (RG 22); Fish & Wildlife Service, General Classified Files (RG 22); and Fish & Wildlife Service, Concerning Oil Pollution of Waters, 1920-33 (RG 22)

Interior Department Records: Office of the Secretary, General Files, 1907-36 (RG 48); Office of the Secretary, Hubert Work, 1923-28 (RG 48); Bureau of Reclamation (RG 115); Geological Survey, Office of the Director, 1912-49 (RG 57); National Park Service (RG 79); and Federal Oil Conservation Board (RG 48)

National Council on Outdoor Recreation, 1924-33 (RG 220)

Bancroft Library, University of California at Berkeley

Horace M. Albright and Newton B. Drury, "Comments on Conservation, 1900 to 1960"

William E. Colby, "Reminiscences"

Newton Bishop Drury, "Parks and Redwoods, 1919-1971"

Francis Farquhar Correspondence and Papers

Francis B. Farquhar, "On Accountancy, Mountaineering, and the National Parks"

Hiram Johnson Papers

Robert Underwood Johnson Papers

Leon F. Kneipp Oral Interview

Arthur C. Ringland Oral Interview

Chester H. Rowell Papers

Department of Special Collections, Cecil H. Green Library, Stanford University: Northcutt Ely Papers, and Paul Shoup Papers.

Division of Rare Books and Special Collections, University of Wyoming Library: Mark Requa Papers

Forest History Society, Durham, North Carolina: L. F. Kneipp Papers, Scott Leavitt Oral History, David T. Mason Oral History, National Forest Products Association Records, National Forest Service Clipping File, and Society of American Foresters Records

Henry Huntington Library, San Marino, California: Ralph Arnold Papers, and Albert B. Fall Collection
University of California at Los Angeles, Department of Special Collections: Phil D. Swing Papers
University of Iowa Library: Henry Cantwell Wallace Papers
University of Oregon Library, Eugene, Oregon: William B. Greeley Papers
Stanford University Archives: John Caspar Branner Papers, and Ray Lyman Wilbur Papers
Water Resources Archive, University of California at Berkeley: Frank Adams, "Notes on the Life of Elwood Mead for Memorial Service, 1936," and Elwood Mead Correspondence and Papers

Published Documents

American Red Cross. *The Mississippi Valley Flood Disaster of 1927: Official Report of the Relief Operations* (Washington, D.C.: American Red Cross, [1929])
Colorado Water Investigation Commission. *The Future Operation of Glen Canyon Reservoir as Related to the Colorado River Compact* (np: July 1959)
Commission on Organization of the Executive Branch of the Government. *Final Report to Congress* (Washington, D.C.: Government Printing Office, 1955)
Commission on Organization of the Executive Branch of the Government. *Task Force Report on Water Resources and Power,* 3 vols. (Washington, D.C.: Government Printing Office, 1955)
Committee on Elimination of Waste in Industry of the Federated American Engineering Societies. *Waste in Industry* (New York: McGraw-Hill, 1921)
Committee on Recent Economic Changes of the President's Conference on Unemployment. *Recent Economic Changes in the United States,* 2 vols. (New York: McGraw-Hill, 1929)
Department of Interior. *Survey of the Alaskan Reindeer Service, 1931-1933* (Washington, D.C.: Government Printing Office, 1933)
Department of Labor. *Report of Industrial Conference Called by the President* (np: 6 Mar. 1920)
Galambos, Louis, and Dawn Van Ee, eds. *The Papers of Dwight David Eisenhower,* vols. 12, 14, 15 (Baltimore: Johns Hopkins University Press, 1988, 1995, 1996)
Hearings on the Subject of the Pollution of Navigable Waters by the House Committee on Rivers and Harbors, 68th Cong., 1st sess. (Washington, D.C.: Government Printing Office, 1924)
The Hoover Commission Report on Organization of the Executive Branch of the Government (New York: McGraw-Hill, [1949])
Institute for Government Research. *The Problem of Indian Administration* (Baltimore: Johns Hopkins University Press, 1928)

National Conference on Outdoor Recreation: Proceedings of the Meeting of the Advisory Council, December 11 and 12, 1924, Senate Document No. 229, 68th Cong., 2d sess. (Washington, D.C.: Government Printing Office, 1925)

Public Papers of the Presidents of the United States: Herbert Hoover; Containing the Public Messages, Speeches, and Statements of the President, 4 vols. (Washington, D.C.: Government Printing Office, 1974–77)

Requa, M. L. *Petroleum Resources of the United States: An Article on the Exhaustion of the Petroleum Resources of the United States, Showing the Present and Future Supply and Demand, also the Petroleum Production of the Principal Oil Fields of the United States,* Sen. Doc. 363, 64th Cong., 1st sess. (Washington, D.C.: Government Printing Office, 1916)

A Report Epitomizing the Results of Major Fact-Finding Surveys and Projects which Have Been Undertaken under the Auspices of the National Conference on Outdoor Recreation, Senate Document 158, 70th Cong., 1st sess. (Washington, D.C.: Government Printing Office, 1928)

Wilbur, Ray Lyman, and Northcutt Ely. *The Hoover Dam Power and Water Contracts and Related Data* (Washington, D.C.: Government Printing Office, 1930)

Dissertations

Gorman, Hugh. "From Conservation to Environment: The Engineering Response to Pollution Concerns in the U.S. Petroleum Industry, 1921–1981" (Carnegie Mellon University, 1996)

Simmons, Dennis Elwood. "The Creation of Shenandoah National Park and the Skyline Drive, 1924–1936" (University of Virginia, 1978)

Books

Adams, David Wallace. *Education for Extinction: American Indians and the Boarding School Experience, 1875–1928* (Lawrence: University Press of Kansas, 1995)

Albright, Horace M. *Origins of National Park Service Administration of Historic Sites* (Philadelphia: Eastern National Park & Monument Association, 1971)

Alchon, Guy. *The Invisible Hand of Planning: Capitalism, Social Science, and the State in the 1920s* (Princeton, N.J.: Princeton University Press, 1985)

Anderson, Terry L. *Sovereign Nations or Reservations? An Economic History of American Indians* (San Francisco: Pacific Research Institute for Public Policy, 1995)

Anderson, Terry L., and Donald R. Leal. *Enviro-Capitalists: Doing Good While Doing Well* (Lanham, Md.: Rowman & Littlefield, 1997)

———. *Free Market Environmentalism* (Boulder, Colo.: Westview, 1991)

Anderson, Terry L., and Peter J. Hill, eds. *Environmental Federalism* (Lanham, Md.: Rowman & Littlefield, 1997)

Arnold, Peri E. *Making the Managerial Presidency: Comprehensive Reorganization Planning, 1905–1980* (Princeton, N.J.: Princeton University Press, 1986)

Barber, William J. *From New Era to New Deal: Herbert Hoover, the Economists, and American Economic Policy, 1921–1933* (Cambridge, England: Cambridge University Press, 1985)

Barnes, Will C. *The Story of the Range* (Washington, D.C.: Government Printing Office, 1926)

Barry, John M. *Rising Tide: The Great Mississippi Flood of 1927 and How It Changed America* (New York: Simon & Schuster, 1997)

Bates, J. Leonard. *The Origins of Teapot Dome: Progressives, Politics, and Petroleum, 1909–1921* (Urbana: University of Illinois Press, 1963)

Baumol, William J., and Wallace E. Oates. *The Theory of Environmental Policy: Externalities, Public Outlays, and the Quality of Life* (Englewood Cliffs, N.J.: Prentice-Hall, 1975)

Bell, Daniel. *The Cultural Contradictions of Capitalism* (New York: Basic, 1978 [1958])

Benson, Norman G., ed. *A Century of Fisheries in North America* (Washington, D.C.: American Fisheries Society, 1970)

Best, Gary Dean. *Herbert Hoover: The Postpresidential Years, 1933–1964*, 2 vols. (Stanford, Calif.: Hoover Institution Press, 1983)

———. *The Politics of American Individualism: Herbert Hoover in Transition, 1918–1921* (Westport, Conn.: Greenwood, 1975)

Boorstin, Daniel J. *The Americans: The Democratic Experience* (New York: Random House, 1973)

Brewer, John, and Roy Porter, eds. *Consumption and the World of Goods* (London: Routledge, 1993)

Bromley, Daniel W. *Environment and the Economy: Property Rights and Public Policy* (Cambridge, Mass.: Blackwell, 1991)

Brownlee, W. Elliot. *Dynamics of Ascent: A History of the American Economy* (New York: Knopf, 1974)

Burner, David. *Herbert Hoover: A Public Life* (New York: Knopf, 1979)

Butsch, Richard. *For Fun and Profit: The Transformation of Leisure into Consumption* (Philadelphia: Temple University Press, 1990)

Carstensen, Vernon, ed. *The Public Lands: Studies in the History of the Public Domain* (Madison: University of Wisconsin Press, 1968)

Carver, Thomas Nixon. *The Distribution of Wealth* (New York: Macmillan, 1904)

———. *The Present Economic Revolution in the United States* (Boston: Little, Brown, 1925)

Chase, Stuart. *The Economy of Abundance* (New York: Macmillan, 1934)

Christie, Jean. *Morris Llewellyn Cooke, Progressive Engineer* (New York: Garland, 1983)

Citizens Committee for the Hoover Report. *Digests and Analyses of the Nineteen Hoover Commission Reports* (New York: Citizens Committee for the Hoover Report, 1955)

Clark, John G. *Energy and the Federal Government: Fossil Fuel Policies, 1900–1946* (Urbana: University of Illinois Press, 1987)

Clarke, John, and Chas Critcher. *The Devil Makes Work: Leisure in Capitalist Britain* (Urbana: University of Illinois Press, 1985)

Clements, Kendrick A. *The Presidency of Woodrow Wilson* (Lawrence: University Press of Kansas, 1992)

Collier, John. *The Indians of the Americas* (New York: Norton, 1947)

Creighton, Donald. *Canada's First Century, 1867–1967* (Toronto: Macmillan of Canada, 1970)

Cross, Gary S. *A Social History of Leisure since 1600* (State College, Pa.: Venture, 1990)

———. *Time and Money: The Making of Consumer Culture* (London: Routledge, 1993)

Cutten, George Barton. *The Threat of Leisure* (New Haven, Conn.: Yale University Press, 1926)

Daniel, Pete. *Deep'n As It Come: The 1927 Mississippi River Flood* (New York: Oxford University Press, 1977)

Dorfman, Joseph. *The Economic Mind in American Civilization*, 5 vols. (New York: Viking, 1959)

Dunn, James R., and John E. Kinney. *Conservative Environmentalism: Reassessing the Means, Redefining the Ends* (Westport, Conn.: Quorum, 1996)

Ely, Northcutt. "Herbert Hoover and the Colorado River," unpublished manuscript given to the author by Mr. Ely

———. *Oil Conservation through Interstate Agreement* (Washington, D.C.: Government Printing Office, 1933)

Emmerich, Robert. *Essays on Federal Reorganization* (University: University of Alabama Press, 1950)

———. *Federal Organization and Administrative Management* (University: University of Alabama Press, 1971)

Ernst, Joseph W., ed. *Worthwhile Places: Correspondence of John D. Rockefeller, Jr., and Horace M. Albright* (New York: Fordham University Press, 1991)

Fausold, Martin L. *The Presidency of Herbert Hoover* (Lawrence: University Press of Kansas, 1985)

Fausold, Martin L., and George T. Mazuzan, eds. *The Hoover Presidency: A Reappraisal* (Albany: State University of New York Press, 1974)

Foss, Phillip O. *Politics and Grass: The Administration of Grazing on the Public Domain* (Seattle: University of Washington Press, 1960)

Fox, Daniel. *The Discovery of Abundance: Simon N. Patten and the Transformation of Social Theory* (Ithaca, N.Y.: Cornell University Press, 1967)

Fox, Richard Wightman, and T. J. Jackson Lears, eds. *The Culture of Consumption: Critical Essays in American History, 1880–1980* (New York: Pantheon, 1983)

Fox, Stephen. *John Muir and His Legacy: The American Conservation Movement* (Boston: Little, Brown, 1981)

Frank, Arthur Dewitt. *The Development of the Federal Program of Flood Control on the Mississippi River* (New York: Columbia University Press, 1930)

Fuess, Claude M. *Calvin Coolidge: The Man from Vermont* (Hamden, Conn.: Archon, 1965)

Galbraith, John Kenneth. *The Affluent Society*, 3rd ed., rev. (Boston: Houghton Mifflin, 1976)

Gelfand, Lawrence E., ed. *Herbert Hoover: The Great War and Its Aftermath, 1914–23* (Iowa City: University of Iowa Press, 1979)

Glyptis, Sue, ed. *Leisure and the Environment: Essays in Honour of Professor J. A. Patmore* (London: Bellhaven, 1993)

Goldberg, Arnold, ed. *Advances in Self-Psychology* (New York: International Universities Press, 1980)

Gould, Lewis L., ed. *The Progressive Era* (Syracuse, New York: Syracuse University Press, 1974)

Green, David E. *Shaping Political Consciousness: The Language of Politics in America from McKinley to Reagan* (Ithaca, N.Y.: Cornell University Press, 1987)

Greenberg, Jay R., and Stephen A. Mitchell. *Object Relations in Psychoanalytic Theory* (Cambridge, Mass.: Harvard University Press, 1983)

Grover, Kathryn, ed. *Hard at Play: Leisure in America, 1840–1940* (Amherst: University of Massachusetts Press, 1992)

Haber, Samuel. *Efficiency and Uplift: Scientific Management in the Progressive Era, 1890–1920* (Chicago: University of Chicago Press, 1964)

Hamilton, David E. *From New Day to New Deal: American Farm Policy from Hoover to Roosevelt, 1928–1933* (Chapel Hill: University of North Carolina Press, 1991)

Harris, David. *From Class Struggle to the Politics of Pleasure: The Effects of Gramscianism on Cultural Studies* (London: Routledge, 1992)

Harvey, Mark W. T. *A Symbol of Wilderness: Echo Park and the American Conservation Movement* (Albuquerque: University of New Mexico Press, 1994)

Hatfield, Mark, ed. *Herbert Hoover Reassessed: Essays Commemorating the Fiftieth Anniversary of the Inauguration of Our Thirty-First President* (Washington, DC: Government Printing Office, 1981)

Hawley, Ellis W. *The Great War and the Search for a Modern Order: A History of the American People and Their Institutions, 1917–1933* (New York: St. Martin's, 1979)

———, ed. *Herbert Hoover as Secretary of Commerce: Studies in New Era Thought and Practice* (Iowa City: University of Iowa Press, 1981)

Hays, Samuel. *Beauty, Health and Permanence: Environmental Politics in the United States, 1955–1985* (New York: Cambridge University Press, 1987)

——. *Conservation and the Gospel of Efficiency: The Progressive Conservation Movement, 1890–1920* (Cambridge, Mass.: Harvard University Press, 1959)

Heaton, Herbert. *A Scholar in Action: Edwin F. Gay* (Cambridge: Harvard University Press, 1952)

Hibbard, Benjamin Horace. *A History of the Public Land Policies* (New York: Macmillan, 1924)

Hofstadter, Richard. *The Age of Reform: From Bryan to F.D.R.* (New York: Vintage, 1960 [1955])

Hoover, Herbert. *Addresses Upon the American Road, 1933–1938* (New York: Scribner's, 1938)

——. *Addresses Upon the American Road, 1948–1950* (Stanford, Calif.: Stanford University Press, 1951)

——. *Addresses Upon the American Road, 1950–1955* (Stanford, Calif.: Stanford University Press, 1955)

——. *American Individualism* (West Branch, Hoover Presidential Library Association, nd [1922])

——. *The Challenge to Liberty* (New York: Scribner's, 1934)

——. *The Memoirs of Herbert Hoover*, 3 vols. (New York: Macmillan, 1951–52)

——. *On Growing Up: Letters to American Boys and Girls* (New York: Morrow, 1962)

——. *Principles of Mining: Valuation, Organization and Administration: Copper, Lead, Silver, Tin and Zinc* (New York: McGraw-Hill, 1909)

Horowitz, Daniel. *The Morality of Spending: Attitudes toward the Consumer Society in America, 1875–1940* (Baltimore: Johns Hopkins University Press, 1985)

Hoult, David P., ed. *Oil on the Sea* (New York: Plenum, 1969)

Humphrey, Craig R., and Frederick R. Buttel. *Environment, Energy, and Society* (Belmont, Calif.: Wadsworth, 1982)

Hundley, Norris. *Water and the West: The Colorado River Compact and the Politics of Water in the American West* (Berkeley: University of California Press, 1975)

Irwin, Will. *Herbert Hoover: A Reminiscent Biography* (New York: Century, 1928)

Jackson, Donald C. *Building the Ultimate Dam: John S. Eastwood and the Control of Water in the West* (Lawrence: University Press of Kansas, 1995)

Jarvie, Grant, and Joseph Maguire. *Sport and Leisure in Social Thought* (London: Routledge, 1994)

Jones, Stephen G. *Workers at Play: A Social and Economic History of Leisure, 1918–1939* (London: Routledge & Kegan Paul, 1986)

Kelly, Lawrence C. *The Assault on Assimilation: John Collier and the Origins of Indian Policy Reform* (Albuquerque: University of New Mexico Press, 1983)

Klyza, Christopher McGrory. *Who Controls Public Lands? Mining, Forestry, and Grazing Policies, 1870–1990* (Chapel Hill: University of North Carolina Press, 1996)

Kohut, Heinz. *The Restoration of the Self* (Madison, Wis.: International Universities Press, 1977)

Koistinen, Paul A. C. *Mobilizing for Modern War: The Political Economy of American Warfare, 1865-1919* (Lawrence: University Press of Kansas, 1997)

Krog, Carl E., and William R. Tanner, eds. *Herbert Hoover and the Republican Era: A Reconsideration* (Lanham, Md.: University Press of America, 1984)

Kvasnicka, Robert M., and Herman J. Viola, eds. *The Commissioners of Indian Affairs, 1824-1977* (Lincoln: University of Nebraska Press, 1979)

Lane, Rose Wilder. *The Making of Herbert Hoover* (New York: Century, 1920)

Lasch, Christopher. *The True and Only Heaven: Progress and Its Critics* (New York: Norton, 1991)

Layton, Edwin T. Jr. *The Revolt of the Engineers: Social Responsibility and the American Engineering Profession* (Baltimore: Johns Hopkins University Press, 1986)

Leach, William. *Land of Desire: Merchants, Power, and the Rise of a New American Culture* (New York: Pantheon, 1993)

Liebovich, Louis W. *Bylines in Despair: Herbert Hoover, the Great Depression, and the U.S. News Media* (Westport, Conn.: Praeger, 1994)

Limerick, Patricia Nelson. *The Legacy of Conquest: The Unbroken Past of the American West* (New York: Norton, 1987)

Lisio, Donald J. *Hoover, Blacks, & Lily-whites: A Study of Southern Strategies* (Chapel Hill: University of North Carolina Press, 1985)

Lloyd, Craig. *Aggressive Introvert: A Study of Herbert Hoover and Public Relations Management, 1912-1932* (Columbus: Ohio State University Press, 1972)

Lustig, R. Jeffrey. *Corporate Liberalism: The Origins of Modern American Political Theory, 1890-1920* (Berkeley: University of California Press, 1982)

Machor, James L. *Pastoral Cities: Urban Ideals and the Symbolic Landscape of America* (Madison: University of Wisconsin Press, 1987)

Maclean, Norman. *A River Runs Through It* (Chicago: University of Chicago Press, 1983)

MacNeil, Neil, and Harold W. Metz. *The Hoover Report, 1953-1955: What It Means to You as Citizen and Taxpayer* (New York: Macmillan, 1956)

May, Herbert L. and Dorothy Petgen. *Leisure and Its Use: Some International Observations* (New York: A. S. Barnes, 1928)

Mayer, Dale C., ed. *Lou Henry Hoover: Essays on a Busy Life* (Worland, Wyo.: High Plains Publishing, 1994)

McCarthy, G. Michael. *Hour of Trial: The Conservation Conflict in Colorado and the West, 1891-1907* (Norman: University of Oklahoma Press, 1977)

McClymer, John F. *War and Welfare: Social Engineering in America, 1890-1925* (Westport, Conn.: Greenwood, 1980)

McEvoy, Arthur F. *The Fisherman's Problem: Ecology and the Law in the California Fisheries, 1850-1980* (Cambridge, England: Cambridge University Press, 1986)

Miles, John C. *Guardians of the Parks: A History of the National Parks and Conservation Association* (Washington, D.C.: Taylor & Francis, 1995)

Moeller, Beverley Bowen. *Phil Swing and Boulder Dam* (Berkeley: University of California Press, 1971)

Nash, George H. *The Life of Herbert Hoover: The Engineer, 1874–1914* (New York: Norton, 1983)

———. *The Life of Herbert Hoover: The Humanitarian, 1914–1917* (New York: Norton, 1988)

———. *The Life of Herbert Hoover: Master of Emergencies, 1917–1918* (New York: Norton, 1996)

———. *Herbert Hoover and Stanford University* (Stanford, Calif.: Hoover Institution Press, 1988)

———. *Herbert Hoover: Political Orphan* (Stanford, Calif.: Hoover Institution Press, 1989)

Nash, Gerald D. *United States Oil Policy, 1890–1964: Business and Government in Twentieth Century America* (Pittsburgh: University of Pittsburgh Press, 1968)

Nash, Lee, ed. *Understanding Herbert Hoover: Ten Perspectives* (Stanford, Calif.: Hoover Institution Press, 1987)

Nash, Roderick. *Wilderness and the American Mind,* 3rd ed. (New Haven Conn.: Yale University Press, 1982)

The New Day: Campaign Speeches of Herbert Hoover, 1928 (Stanford, Calif.: Stanford University Press, 1928)

Noggle, Burl. *Teapot Dome: Oil and Politics in the 1920s* (Baton Rouge: Louisiana State University Press, 1962)

Nordhauser, Norman E. *The Quest for Stability: Domestic Oil Regulation, 1917–1935* (New York: Garland, 1979)

Olson, Keith W. *Biography of a Progressive: Franklin K. Lane, 1864–1921* (Westport, Conn.: Greenwood, 1979)

Peffer, Louise. *The Closing of the Public Domain: Disposal and Reservation Policies, 1900–1950* (Stanford, Calif.: Stanford University Press, 1951)

Philp, Kenneth R. *John Collier's Crusade for Indian Reform, 1920–1954* (Tucson: University of Arizona Press, 1977)

Porter, Eliot. *The Place No One Knew: Glen Canyon on the Colorado* (San Francisco: Sierra Club, 1963)

Reiger, John F. *American Sportsmen and the Origins of Conservation* (New York: Winchester, 1975)

Richardson, Elmo. *Dams, Parks & Politics: Resource Development & Preservation in the Truman-Eisenhower Era* (Lexington: University Press of Kentucky, 1973)

———. *The Politics of Conservation: Crusades and Controversies, 1897–1913* (Berkeley: University of California Press, 1962)

Riesman, David. *Abundance for What?* (New Brunswick, N.J.: Transaction, 1993)

Robbins, Roy M. *Our Landed Heritage: The Public Domain, 1776–1932* (Princeton, N.J.: Princeton University Press, 1942)

Robbins, William G. *Lumberjacks and Legislators: Political Economy of the U.S. Lumber Industry, 1890–1941* (College Station: Texas A&M University Press, 1982)

Robinson, Edgar Eugene, and Paul Carroll Edwards, eds. *The Memoirs of Ray Lyman Wilbur* (Stanford, Calif.: Stanford University Press, 1960)

Rojek, Chris. *Decentring Leisure: Rethinking Leisure Theory* (Thousand Oaks, Calif.: Sage, 1995)

———. *Ways of Escape: Modern Transformations in Leisure and Travel* (Lanham, Md.: Rowman and Littlefield, 1993)

Ross, Andrew. *The Chicago Gangster Theory of Life: Nature's Debt to Society* (London: Verso, 1994)

St. Clair, Michael. *Object Relations and Self Psychology: An Introduction*, 2nd ed. (Pacific Grove, Calif.: Brooks/Cole, 1996)

Saylor, David J. *Jackson Hole, Wyoming: In the Shadow of the Tetons* (Norman: University of Oklahoma Press, 1970)

Schrepfer, Susan. *The Fight to Save the Redwoods: A History of Environmental Reform, 1917–1978* (Madison: University of Wisconsin Press, 1983)

Sellers, Charles. *The Market Revolution: Jacksonian America, 1815–1846* (New York: Oxford University Press, 1991)

Shankland, Robert. *Steve Mather of the National Parks* (New York: Knopf, 1951)

Simon, Julian. *The Ultimate Resource* (Princeton, N.J.: Princeton University Press, 1981)

Sinclair, Bruce, ed. *New Perspectives on Technology and American Culture* (Philadelphia: American Philosophical Society, 1986)

Smith, Frank E. *The Politics of Conservation* (New York: Pantheon, 1966)

Steiner, Jesse Frederick. *Americans at Play: Recent Trends in Recreation and Leisure Time Activities* (New York: McGraw-Hill, 1933)

Stevens, Joseph E. *Hoover Dam: An American Adventure* (Norman: University of Oklahoma Press, 1988)

Strasser, Susan. *Waste and Want: The Other Side of Consumption* (Providence, R.I.: Berg Publishers for the German Historical Institute, 1992)

Stratton, Owen, and Phillip Sirotkin. *The Echo Park Controversy: A Case Study in Resources Administration Supported by a Grant from Resources for the Future, Inc.* (University: University of Alabama Press, [1959])

Swain, Donald C. *Federal Conservation Policy, 1921–1933* (Berkeley: University of California Press, 1963)

———. *Wilderness Defender: Horace Albright and Conservation* (Chicago: University of Chicago Press, 1970)

Taylor, Bob Pepperman. *Our Limits Transgressed: Environmental Political Thought in America* (Lawrence: University Press of Kansas, 1992)

Tichi, Cecelia. *Shifting Gears: Technology, Literature, Culture in Modernist America* (Chapel Hill: University of North Carolina Press, 1987)

Veblen, Thorstein, *The Instinct of Workmanship and the State of Industrial Arts* (New York: Viking, 1937 [1914])

Voigt, William Jr. *Public Grazing Lands: Use and Misuse by Industry and Government* (New Brunswick, N.J.: Rutgers University Press, 1976)

Warren, Harris Gaylord. *Herbert Hoover and the Great Depression* (New York: Oxford University Press, 1959)

Wiebe, Robert. *The Search for Order, 1877–1920* (New York: Hill and Wang, 1967)

———. *Self-Rule: A Cultural History of American Democracy* (Chicago: University of Chicago Press, 1995)

Wilbur, Ray Lyman, and Arthur Mastick Hyde. *The Hoover Policies* (New York: Scribner's, 1937)

Wilbur, Ray Lyman, and William Atherton Du Puy. *Conservation in the Department of the Interior* (Washington, D.C.: Government Printing Office, 1932)

Willoughby, William R. *The St. Lawrence Waterway: A Study in Politics and Diplomacy* (Madison: University of Wisconsin Press, 1961)

Wilson, Joan Hoff. *Herbert Hoover: Forgotten Progressive* (Prospect Heights, Ill.: Waveland, 1992 [1975])

Wilson, Woodrow. *The State: Elements of Historical and Practical Politics* (Boston: Heath, 1889)

Wooddy, Carroll H. *The Growth of the Federal Government, 1915–1932* (New York: McGraw-Hill, 1934)

Woodruff, Nan Elizabeth. *As Rare as Rain: Federal Relief in the Great Southern Drought of 1930–31* (Urbana: University of Illinois Press, 1985)

Worster, Donald. *Under Western Skies: Nature and History in the American West* (New York: Oxford University Press, 1992)

———. *The Wealth of Nature: Environmental History and the Ecological Imagination* (New York: Oxford University Press, 1993)

Wrobel, David M. *The End of American Exceptionalism: Frontier Anxiety from the Old West to the New Deal* (Lawrence: University Press of Kansas, 1993)

Zunz, Olivier. *Why the American Century?* (Chicago: University of Chicago Press, 1998)

Articles and Chapters in Edited Volumes

"After the Flood," *New Republic* 51 (20 July 1927)

Agnew, Jean-Christophe. "Coming Up for Air: Consumer Culture in Historical Perspective," in *Consumption and the World of Goods*, eds. John Brewer and Roy Porter (London: Routledge, 1993)

"AHR Forum: The Problem of American Conservatism," *American Historical Review* 99 (April 1994)

Allitt, Patrick. "Conservatives and Conservation in the Reagan-Bush era," paper delivered at the 1996 meeting of the Organization of American Historians

Arnold, Ralph. "Laying Foundation Stones," Historical Society of Southern California *Quarterly* 37 (June 1955)

Barnes, Julius H. "Herbert Hoover's Priceless Work in Washington," *Industrial Management* 71 (April 1926)

Bates, J. Leonard. "Fulfilling American Democracy: The Conservation Movement, 1907 to 1921," *Mississippi Valley Historical Review* 44 (June 1957)

———. "The Teapot Dome Scandal and the Election of 1924," *American Historical Review* 60 (Jan. 1955)

Bent, Silas. "Mr. Hoover's Sins of Commissions," *Scribner's Magazine* 90 (July 1931)

Best, Gary Dean. "Herbert Hoover as Titular Head of the GOP, 1933-35," *Mid-America* 61 (Apr.-July 1979)

———. "The Hoover-for-President Boom of 1920," *Mid-America* 53 (Oct. 1971)

———. "President Wilson's Second Industrial Conference, 1919-1920," *Labor History* 16 (Fall 1975)

Birkner, Michael. "Hoover and Ike: An Uneasy Collaboration," unpublished address delivered to the Herbert Hoover Presidential Library Association, 7 June 1998

Black, W. M. "The Problem of the Mississippi," *North American Review* 224 (Dec. 1927)

"A Brief Chronology of What Congress Has Done since 1824 to Control the Floods of the Mississippi," *Congressional Digest* 7 (Feb. 1928)

Brinkley, Alan. "The Problem of American Conservatism," *American Historical Review* 99 (Apr. 1994)

Buehler, Daniel O. "Permanence and Change in Theodore Roosevelt's Conservation Jeremiad," *Western Journal of Communication* 62 (Fall 1998)

Burner, David. "Before the Crash: Hoover's First Eight Months in the Presidency," in *The Hoover Presidency: A Reappraisal*, eds. Martin L. Fausold and George T. Mazuzan (Albany: State University of New York Press, 1974)

———. "The Quaker Faith of Herbert Hoover," in *Understanding Herbert Hoover: Ten Perspectives*, ed. Lee Nash (Stanford, Calif.: Hoover Institution Press, 1987)

Burnet, Dana. "Between Hoover and High Water," *Collier's* 80 (16 July 1927)

Butsch, Richard. "Introduction: Leisure and Hegemony in America," in *For Fun and Profit: The Transformation of Leisure into Consumption*, ed. Richard Butsch (Philadelphia: Temple University Press, 1990)

Cannon, Brian Q. "'We Are Now Entering a New Era': Federal Reclamation and the Fact-Finding Commission of 1923-1924," *Pacific Historical Review* 66 (May 1997)

Carleton, William G. "Government's Historical Role in Conservation," *Current History* 58 (June 1970)

Carlson, Avis. "Drowning in Oil," *Harper's* 163 (Oct. 1931)

Carroll, Rosemary F. "Lou Henry Hoover: The Emergence of a Leader, 1874-1916," in *Lou Henry Hoover: Essays on a Busy Life*, ed. Dale C. Mayer (Worland, Wyo.: High Plains Publishing, 1994)

Carruthers, Arthur C. "Herbert C. Hoover—Leader in Conservation and Waste Elimination," *Safety Engineering* (Dec. 1927)

Child, Richard Washburn. "The Battle of the Levees," *Saturday Evening Post* 199 (June 1927)

Clarke, John. "Pessimism versus Populism: The Problematic Politics of Popular Culture," in Richard Butsch, *For Fun and Profit: The Transformation of Leisure into Consumption* (Philadelphia: Temple University Press, 1990)

Clements, Kendrick A. "Herbert Hoover and Conservation, 1921-1933," *American Historical Review* 89 (Feb. 1984)

———. "Herbert Hoover and the Fish," *Journal of Psychohistory* 10 (Winter 1983)

Cole, Terrence M. "Ernest Walker Sawyer and Alaska: The Dilemma of Northern Economic Development," *Pacific Northwest Quarterly* 82 (Apr. 1991)

Cowley, Robert. "The Drought and the Dole: Herbert Hoover's Dismal Dilemma," *American Heritage* 23 (Feb. 1972)

Cuff, Robert D. "Herbert Hoover, the Ideology of Voluntarism and War Organization during the Great War," in *Herbert Hoover: The Great War and Its Aftermath, 1914-1923*, ed. Lawrence E. Gelfand (Iowa City: University of Iowa Press, 1979)

Dern, George H. "School Land Titles in Public Land States," *Mining Congress Journal* 12 (Oct. 1926)

Downes, Randolph C. "A Crusade for Indian Reform, 1922-1934," *Mississippi Valley Historical Review* 32 (Dec. 1945)

"Current Topics in the World's Cartoons," *The American Review of Reviews* 75 (June 1927)

Drake, Douglas C. "Herbert Hoover, Ecologist: The Politics of Oil Pollution Control, 1921-1926," *Mid-America* 55 (July 1973)

Dunlap, Thomas R. "Wildlife, Science, and the National Parks, 1920-1940," *Pacific Historical Review* 59 (May 1990)

Du Puy, William Atherton. "Secretary Wilbur and the Greatest Welfare Job in the World," *World's Work* 58 (Nov. 1929)

Dykstra, C. A., ed. "Colorado River Development and Related Problems," *Annals of the American Academy of Political and Social Science* 148, Pt. II (Mar. 1930)

Edwards, John Carver. "Herbert Hoover's Public Lands Policy: A Struggle for Control of the Western Domain," *Pacific Historian* 20 (Spring 1976)

Edwards, Max N. "The Role of the Federal Government in Controlling Oil Pollution at Sea," in *Oil and the Sea*, ed. David P. Hoult (New York: Plenum, 1969)

Farr, W. Halverson. "Who Should Control Our Public Lands which Contain Minerals?" *Mining Congress Journal* 13 (Feb. 1927)

"The Fight to Prevent Another Mississippi Flood," *Literary Digest* 93 (21 May 1927)

"The Fight with the Rampageous Father of Waters," *Literary Digest* 99 (3 Nov. 1928)

"First Effects of the Mississippi Flood," *Literary Digest* 93 (18 June 1927)

"Floods and the Jones Measure," *American Review of Reviews* 77 (May 1928)

Friederici, Peter. "Stolen River," *Defenders: The Conservation Magazine of Defenders of Wildlife* 73 (Spring 1998)

Gilmore, Charles L. "Federal Domination vs. State Sovereignty," *Mining Congress Journal* 13 (Jan., Feb., Mar., Apr., May 1927)

Glyptis, Sue. "Perspectives on Leisure and the Environment," in *Leisure and the Environment: Essays in Honour of Professor J. A. Patmore*, ed. Sue Glyptis (London: Bellhaven, 1993)

Gordon, Scott. "Economics and the Conservation Question," *Journal of Law and Economics* 1 (Oct. 1958)

Gorman, Hugh. "The Gospel of Efficiency and Measures of Environmental Quality: Congressional Debates and the Oil Pollution Act of 1924," unpublished paper delivered at the American Society of Environmental History conference, 17 Apr. 1999

Graves, Henry. "The Public Domain," *The Nation* 131 (6 Aug. 1930)

Greeley, William B. "Shall the National Forests Be Abolished?" *Mining Congress Journal* 13 (Aug. 1927)

———. "The Stockmen and the National Forests," *Saturday Evening Post* 198 (14 Nov. 1925)

"Greeley Holds Domain Report Inadequate: Former Chief Forester Sets Forth Reasons for Not Signing Committee's Recommendations," *American Forests* (May 1931)

Grin, Carolyn. "The Unemployment Conference of 1921: An Experiment in National Cooperative Planning," *Mid-America* 55 (Apr. 1973)

Hamilton, David E. "Herbert Hoover and the Great Drought of 1930," *Journal of American History* 68 (Mar. 1982)

Hard, William. "Giant Negotiations for Giant Power: An Interview with Herbert Hoover," *Survey Graphic* (Mar. 1924)

———. "The New Hoover," *American Review of Reviews* 76 (Nov. 1927)

Hawley, Ellis W. "Herbert Hoover and American Corporatism, 1931–1933," in *The Hoover Presidency: A Reappraisal*, eds. Martin L. Fausold and George T. Mazuzan (Albany: State University of New York Press, 1974)

———. "Herbert Hoover, the Commerce Secretariat, and the Vision of an 'Associative State,' 1921–1928," *Journal of American History* 61 (June 1974)

———. "Herbert Hoover and Economic Stabilization, 1921–22," in *Herbert Hoover as Secretary of Commerce: Studies in New Era Thought and Practice*, ed. Ellis W. Hawley (Iowa City: University of Iowa Press, 1981)

———. "Secretary Hoover and the Bituminous Coal Problem, 1921–1928," *Business History Review* 42 (Autumn 1968)

Hays, Samuel P. "From Conservation to Environment: Environmental Politics in the United States since World War Two," *Environmental Review* 6 (Fall 1982)

Himmelberg, Robert F. "Hoover's Public Image, 1919–20: The Emergence of a Public

Figure and a Sign of the Times," in *Herbert Hoover: The Great War and Its Aftermath, 1914–23,* ed. Lawrence E. Gelfand (Iowa City: University of Iowa Press, 1979)

Hoover, Herbert. "Comments on Pollution," *Outdoor America* 6 (Oct. 1927)

——. "The Engineer's Relation to Our Industrial Problems," *Engineering News-Record* (25 Nov. 1920)

——. "The Importance of Developing Our Water Resources," *Congressional Digest* 6 (Jan. 1927)

——. "The Improvement of Our Mid-West Waterways," *Annals of the American Academy of Political and Social Science* 135 (Jan. 1928)

——. "In Praise of Izaak Walton," *Atlantic* 139 (June 1927)

——. "Why Inland Waterways Should Be Developed," *American Review of Reviews* 74 (Dec. 1926)

"Hoover: Conservative," *New Republic* 56 (31 Oct. 1928)

"Hoover—'Specialist in Public Calamities,'" *Literary Digest* 97 (21 Apr. 1928)

Hotelling, Harold. "The Economics of Exhaustible Resources," *Journal of Political Economy* 39 (Apr. 1931)

Howlett, Michael, and Rebecca Raglon. "Constructing the Environmental Spectacle: Green Advertisements and the Greening of the Corporate Image, 1910–1990," *Environmental History Review* 16 (Winter 1992)

Hutchison, Janet. "Building for Babbitt: The State and the Suburban Home Ideal," *Journal of Policy History* 9:2 (1997)

Hyde, Arthur M. "Forestry in Farm Relief," *American Forests and Forest Life* 36 (Oct. 1930)

Irwin, Will. "Can We Tame the Mississippi?" *World's Work* 54 (Aug. 1927)

——. "Havoc Beyond the Levees," *World's Work* 54 (July 1927)

Jadwin, Edgar. "The Plan for Flood Control of the Mississippi River in Its Alluvial Valley," *Annals of the American Academy of Political and Social Science* 135 (Jan. 1928)

Johnson, Hiram. "The Boulder Canyon Project," in "Great Inland Water-Way Projects in the United States," ed. Clyde H. King, *Annals of the American Academy of Political and Social Science* 135 (Jan. 1928)

Johnson, James P. "Herbert Hoover: The Orphan as Children's Friend," *Prologue* 12 (Winter 1980)

Karl, Barry. "Presidential Planning and Social Science Research: Mr. Hoover's Experts," *Perspectives in American History* 3 (1969)

Kelley, Donald Brooks. "Deep South Dilemma: The Mississippi Press in the Presidential Election of 1928," *Journal of Mississippi History* 25:2 (1963)

Kelly, Lawrence C. "Charles James Rhoads, 1929–33," in *The Commissioners of Indian Affairs, 1824–1977,* eds. Robert M. Kvasnicka and Herman J. Viola (Lincoln: University of Nebraska Press, 1979)

Klein, Kerwin L. "Frontier Products: Tourism, Consumerism, and the Southwestern Public Lands, 1890–1990," *Pacific Historical Review* 62 (Feb. 1993)

Koppes, Clayton R. "Efficiency/Equity/Esthetics: Towards a Reinterpretation of American Conservation," *Environmental Review* 11 (Summer 1987)

Kottman, Richard N. "Herbert Hoover and the St. Lawrence Seaway Treaty of 1932," *New York History* 56 (July 1975)

Krog, Carl E. "'Organizing the Production of Leisure': Herbert Hoover and the Conservation Movement in the 1920's," *Wisconsin Magazine of History* 67 (Spring 1984)

Lambert, C. Roger. "Food from the Public Crib: Agricultural Surpluses and Food Relief under Herbert Hoover," in *Herbert Hoover and the Republican Era: A Reconsideration,* eds. Carl E. Krog and William R. Tanner (Lanham, Md.: University Press of America, 1984)

Lee, Lawrence B. "William Ellsworth Smythe and the Irrigation Movement: A Reconsideration," *Pacific Historical Review* 41 (Aug. 1972)

Link, Arthur S. "What Happened to the Progressive Movement in the 1920s?" *American Historical Review* 44 (July 1959)

Lippmann, Walter. "The Peculiar Weakness of Mr. Hoover," *Harper's* 161 (June 1930)

Littlefield, Douglas R. "The Rio Grande Compact of 1929: A Truce in an Interstate River War," *Pacific Historical Review* 60 (Nov. 1991)

"Locking the Door of Opportunity," *Mining Congress Journal* 12 (Oct. 1926)

Lohof, Bruce. "Herbert Hoover, Spokesman of Humane Efficiency: The Mississippi Flood of 1927," *American Quarterly* 22 (Fall 1970)

MacDonald, William. "Plans for National Flood Relief and Control," *Current History* 27 (Nov. 1927)

McAneny, Herbert. "Hoover: Engineer to the World," *St. Nicholas* 55 (June 1928)

Metcalf, Evan B. "Secretary Hoover and the Emergence of Macroeconomic Management," *Business History Review* 49 (Spring 1975)

"The Mississippi Flood of 1927," *Congressional Digest* 7 (Feb. 1928)

"Mr. Hoover's Plans for Flood Control," *Literary Digest* 94 (6 Aug. 1927)

Mitchell, Franklin D. "Arthur Mastick Hyde," *Dictionary of American Biography,* Supp. 4 (New York: Scribner's, 1974)

Mondell, F. W. "Future Disposition and Control of Our Public Lands," *Mining Congress Journal* 13 (Feb. 1927)

Mortenson, Daniel R. "The Deterioration of Forest Grazing Land: A Wider Context for the Effects of World War I," *Journal of Forest History* 22 (Oct. 1978)

Mosk, Sanford A. "Land Policy and Stock Raising in the Western United States," in *The Public Lands: Studies in the History of the Public Domain,* ed. Vernon Carstensen (Madison: University of Wisconsin Press, 1968)

Mrozek, Donald J. "The Natural Limits of Unstructured Play, 1890–1914," in *Hard at Play: Leisure in America, 1840–1940,* ed. Kathryn Grover (Amherst: University of Massachusetts Press, 1992)

Murray, Robert K. "Herbert Hoover and the Harding Cabinet," in *Herbert Hoover as Secretary of Commerce: Studies in New Era Thought and Practice,* ed. Ellis W. Hawley (Iowa City: University of Iowa Press, 1981)

———. "President Harding and His Cabinet," *Ohio History* 75 (Spring–Summer 1966)

Nash, George H. "The Social Philosophy of Herbert Hoover," in *Herbert Hoover Reassessed: Essays Commemorating the Fiftieth Anniversary of the Inauguration of Our Thirty-First President,* ed. Mark O. Hatfield (Washington, D.C.: Government Printing Office, 1981)

"National Affairs: Hyde & Seedlings," *Time* (18 July 1932)

"National Affairs: By Name," *Time* (31 Oct. 1932)

Neel, Susan Rhoades. "Tourism and the American West: New Departures," *Pacific Historical Review* 65 (Nov. 1996)

"Nothing Done Yet for Flood-Control," *Literary Digest* 96 (10 Mar. 1928)

O'Neill, J. H. "Relief Measures During and Following the Mississippi River Flood," *American Journal of Public Health* 18 (Feb. 1928)

Parsons, Malcolm B. "Origins of the Colorado River Controversy in Arizona Politics, 1922–1923," *Arizona and the West* 4 (Spring 1962)

Pemberton, William E. "Struggle for the New Deal: Truman and the Hoover Commission," *Presidential Studies Quarterly* 16 (Summer 1986)

Penick, James Jr. "The Progressives and the Environment: Three Themes from the First Conservation Movement," in *The Progressive Era,* ed. Lewis L. Gould (Syracuse, N.Y.: Syracuse University Press, 1974)

Philp, Kenneth. "Herbert Hoover's New Era: A False Dawn for the American Indian, 1929–1932," *Rocky Mountain Social Science Journal* 9 (Apr. 1972)

Pinchot, Amos. "Hoover and Power," *The Nation* 133 (5 Aug. 1931)

Pinchot, Gifford. "Some Essential Principles of Water Conservation as Applied to Mississippi Flood Control," *Annals of the American Academy of Political and Social Sciences* 135 (Jan. 1928)

Pisani, Donald J. "Fish Culture and the Dawn of Concern over Water Pollution in the United States," *Environmental Review* 8 (Summer 1984)

"The President's Victory on Flood Control," *Literary Digest* 97 (19 May 1928)

"The President Transmits to Congress Flood Control Plan of Army Engineers," *Congressional Digest* 7 (Feb. 1928)

"The Progress of the World," *American Review of Reviews* 76 (July 1927)

"Public Land Legislation," *Mining Congress Journal* 12 (Sept. 1926)

"Public Land Ownership," *Mining Congress Journal* 13 (Oct. 1927)

Reagan, Patrick D. "From Depression to Depression: Hooverian National Planning, 1921–1933," *Mid-America* 70 (Jan. 1988)

"The Receding Flood's Bequest: A Rich Legendry of Anecdote," *Literary Digest* 94 (16 July 1927)

"The Report of the Committee on Mississippi Flood Control Appointed by the United States Chamber of Commerce," *Annals of the American Academy of Political and Social Sciences* 135 (Jan. 1928)

Requa, M. L. "Some Fundamentals of the Petroleum Problem," *Saturday Evening Post* 193 (28 Aug., 4 Sept., and 30 Oct., 1920)

Riesman, David, and Warner Bloomberg Jr. "Work and Leisure: Fusion or Polarity?" in *Abundance for What?*, ed. David Riesman (New Brunswick, N.J.: Transaction, 1993)

Robbins, William G. "The Great Experiment in Industrial Self-Government: The Lumber Industry and the National Recovery Administration," *Journal of Forest History* 25 (July 1981)

———. "Herbert Hoover's Indian Reformers Under Attack: The Failures of Administrative Reform," *Mid-America* 63 (Oct. 1981)

———. "Prospects for Environmental History: A Review Essay," *Journal of Forest History* 22 (Apr. 1978)

———. "Voluntary Cooperation vs. Regulatory Paternalism: The Lumber Trade in the 1920s," *Business History Review* 56 (Autumn 1982)

Rome, Adam W. "Coming to Terms with Pollution: The Language of Environmental Reform, 1865–1915," *Environmental Review* 1 (July 1996)

"The Row over Feeding Hungry Farmers," *Literary Digest* 108 (31 Jan. 1931)

"The Row over Mr. Hoover's 'Gift Horse,'" *Literary Digest* 102 (14 Sept. 1929)

Rushing, Kathryn Karsten. "NPCA: Sixty Years of Idealism and Hard Work," *National Parks and Conservation Magazine* 53 (May 1979)

Schapsmeier, Edward L., and Frederick H. Schapsmeier. "Disharmony in the Harding Cabinet: Hoover-Wallace Conflict," *Ohio History* 75 (Spring–Summer 1966)

Schofield, Kent. "The Public Image of Herbert Hoover in the 1928 Campaign," *Mid-America* 51 (Oct. 1969)

"School Land Grant Legislation Proposed," *Mining Congress Journal* 12 (July 1926)

"Shackling the Public Domain, *Mining Congress Journal* 12 (June 1926)

Shepard, Ward. "The Handout Magnificent," *Harper's* 163 (Oct. 1931)

Sherman, E. A. "What Forests Can Do for the Mississippi River," *Annals of the American Academy of Political and Social Sciences* 135 (Jan. 1928)

Shideler, James H. "Herbert Hoover and the Federal Farm Board Project, 1921–1925," *Mississippi Valley Historical Review* 42 (Mar. 1956)

Short, Brant. "The Rhetoric of the Post-Presidency: Herbert Hoover's Campaign Against the New Deal, 1934–1936," *Presidential Studies Quarterly* 21 (Spring 1991)

Sinclair, Bruce. "Inventing a Genteel Tradition: MIT Crosses the River," in *New Perspectives on Technology and American Culture*, ed. Bruce Sinclair (Philadelphia: American Philosophical Society, 1986)

Spry, William. "Leasing of Public Domain," *Mining Congress Journal* 12 (Oct. 1926)

Stabile, Donald R. "Research Note: Herbert Hoover, the FAES, and the AF of L," *Technology and Culture* 27 (Oct. 1986)

"Steps Taken by the Federal Government for Mississippi Flood Relief," *Congressional Digest* 7 (Feb. 1928)

"Superpower and Economic Statesmanship," *Chemical and Metallurgical Engineering* 29:17 (1923)

"Suspicions of 'Pork' in the Flood-Control Bill," *Literary Digest* 97 (14 Apr. 1928)

Sworakowski, Witold S. "Herbert Hoover, Launching the American Food Administration, 1917," in *Herbert Hoover: The Great War and Its Aftermath, 1914–23*, ed. Lawrence E. Gelfand (Iowa City: University of Iowa Press, 1979)

"A Symposium on National Problems," *Mining Congress Journal* 13 (Aug. 1927)

Tanner, Willam R. "Secretary of Commerce Hoover's War on Waste, 1921–1928," in *Herbert Hoover and the Republican Era: A Reconsideration*, eds. Carl E. Krog and William R. Tanner (Lanham, Md.: University Press of America, 1984)

Tarter, Brent. "'All Men Are Equal Before Fishes': Herbert Hoover's Camp on the Rapidan," *Virginia Cavalcade* 30 (Spring 1981)

Taylor, Joseph E. III. "Rationalizing the Western Fisheries: Secretary Hoover and the Bureau of Fisheries," unpublished paper delivered at a symposium on "Conservation and Consumption in the American West," George Fox University, Newberg, Ore., 4 Oct. 1997

Tucker, Ray T. "Is Hoover Human?" *North American Review* 226 (Nov. 1928)

"Uneconomic Conservation," *Mining Congress Journal* 12 (Apr. 1926)

Veysey, Laurence. "Ray Lyman Wilbur," *Dictionary of American Biography*, Supp. 4 (New York: Scribner's, 1974)

Villard, Oswald Garrison. "Presidential Possibilities, IV, Herbert C. Hoover," *The Nation* 126 (29 Feb. 1928)

Walker, J. Bernard. "Curbing the Mississippi," *Scientific American* 138 (Feb. 1928)

Warner, Fayette S. "A Synopsis of the [Jan. 1927] Hoover Report on the St. Lawrence Shipway," *Annals of the American Academy of Political and Social Science* 135 (Jan. 1928)

Weaver, John C. "Beyond the Fatal Shore: Pastoral Squatting and the Occupation of Australia, 1826 to 1852," *American Historical Review* 101 (Oct. 1996)

"Will Coolidge Shatter the Third-Term Tradition?" *Literary Digest* 93 (14 May 1927)

"Will Mr. Coolidge Approve?" *American Review of Reviews* 77 (May 1928)

Williams, C. Fred. "William M. Jardine and the Foundations for Republican Farm Policy, 1921–1929," *Agricultural History* 70 (Spring 1996)

Wilson, Francis Cushman. "The Problem of the Public Domain," *Saturday Evening Post* 204 (23 Jan. 1932)

Wilson, Joan Hoff. "Herbert Hoover Reassessed," in *Herbert Hoover Reassessed: Essays Commemorating the Fiftieth Anniversary of the Inauguration of Our Thirty-First President*, ed. Mark O. Hatfield (Washington, D.C.: Government Printing Office, 1981)

——. "Hoover's Agricultural Policies, 1921–1928," *Agricultural History* 51 (Apr. 1977)

Wimer, Kurt. "Woodrow Wilson and a Third Nomination," *Pennsylvania History* 29 (April 1962)

Winter, Charles E. "Relation of Public Land States to the Federal Government," *Mining Congress Journal* 12 (Oct. 1926)

Work, Hubert. "Our Public Lands Question," *Mining Congress Journal* 12 (Oct. 1926)

Worster, Donald. "Hoover Dam: A Study in Domination," in *Under Western Skies: Nature and History in the American West,* ed. Donald Worster (New York: Oxford University Press, 1992)

Zieger, Robert H. "Herbert Hoover, the Wage-earner, and the 'New Economic System,' 1919–1929," *Business History Review* 52 (Summer 1977)

———. "Labor, Progressivism, and Herbert Hoover in the 1920s," *Wisconsin Magazine of History* 58 (Spring 1975)

Index